P9-CAF-427

SHEEHAN, FREDERICK

PANDERER TO POWER: THE UNTOLD STORY OF
HOW ALAN GREENSPAN...

332. _____   GIFT: JAMES E. KRUEGER

NF   4/3/2010

PANDERER
TO
POWER

To The Pacific-Union Club,

[signature]

PANDERER
TO
POWER

THE UNTOLD STORY OF HOW
ALAN GREENSPAN
ENRICHED WALL STREET AND
LEFT A LEGACY OF RECESSION

FREDERICK J. SHEEHAN

New York   Chicago   San Francisco   Lisbon
London   Madrid   Mexico City   Milan   New Delhi
San Juan   Seoul   Singapore   Sydney   Toronto

The *McGraw·Hill* Companies

Copyright © 2010 by Frederick J. Sheehan, Jr. All rights reserved. Printed in the United States of America. Except as permitted under the United States Copyright Act of 1976, no part of this publication may be reproduced or distributed in any form or by any means, or stored in a database or retrieval system, without the prior written permission of the publisher.

1 2 3 4 5 6 7 8 9 0   DOC / DOC   0 1 6 5 4 3 2 1 0 9

ISBN: 978–0–07–161542–6
MHID: 0–07–161542–3

This publication is designed to provide accurate and authoritative information in regard to the subject matter covered. It is sold with the understanding that neither the author nor the publisher is engaged in rendering legal, accounting, futures/securities trading, or other professional service. If legal advice or other expert assistance is required, the services of a competent professional person should be sought.

—From a Declaration of Principles jointly adopted by a Committee of the American Bar Association and a Committee of Publishers

McGraw-Hill books are available at special quantity discounts to use as premiums and sales promotions, or for use in corporate training programs. To contact a representative please e-mail us at bulksales@mcgraw-hill.com.

To my father, who helped and encouraged me to write this book, even when it seemed futile. My confidence and stamina often flagged; his never did.

CONTENTS

AUTHOR'S NOTE

Following are some explanations of how words with broad general meanings are used specifically.

Money is used in its broadest form. The distinctions between "money" and "currency" (e.g., the dollar) are not addressed.

Bank refers to the large banks. There are about 8,300 federally chartered banks in the United States. Maybe 300 of these share responsibility for the current financial debacle. If a different type of bank is discussed, it is identified, such as a savings and loan. This also applies to hedge funds and private-equity funds. Most of them stick to their knitting and act honorably.

Banks, as they existed when they are first discussed (the 1950s), no longer exist. For instance, at that time, the distinction between commercial and investment banks was clear. Now, they cross each other's lines of business. The easiest description of these businesses is "financial institutions." It is comprehensive, but it is vague. Therefore, firms are described according to the topic under discussion. For instance, Goldman Sachs falls under a discussion of "brokerage firms," even though it was (until recently) an investment bank. Likewise, Goldman Sachs stands under the "underwriters" umbrella when underwriters are discussed.

An *economist*—in this book—has received a graduate degree, probably a Ph.D., in economics.

Most of the economists discussed in this book are the public performers from government–academia–Wall Street and appear on CNBC. There are many economists who do very good work, but are not part of this book. The best are generally unknown to the public, since the only means by which the public would learn of them would be through the publicity they would receive if they joined the performers.

Acquisitions, takeovers, buyouts, and leveraged buyouts (LBOs). The vocabulary can be confusing. This book only addresses the peak periods.

In the late 1980s, *acquisitions* (also called *takeovers or buyouts*) of companies were often in the form of what were called *leveraged buyouts.* The buyouts during this manic final phase were marked by much more debt financing (bonds, bank loans) than equity financing (cash, stock). The companies leading the buyouts were commonly (though imprecisely) called *leveraged buyout* or *LBO firms.* This period is discussed in Chapter 6.

The largest of these "LBO firms" were actually *private equity firms* (for example, Kohlberg Kravis Roberts & Co. (KKR). The "private" refers to equity not traded on a public exchange. During the culmination of the (circa) 2004-2007 buyout mania, some private equity firms were, once again, using less equity financing and much more debt financing. For all intents and purposes, these deals were LBOs. The media had a difficult time deciding the correct vocabulary (since the amount of equity was so small compared to the amount of debt) and firms such as KKR were called *private equity firms,* or *LBO firms,* or sometimes *buyout firms.* These terms are used interchangeably in Chapter 25.

This book stops at the peak. Sort of. Greenspan could not stop talking. He continued his open-mouth policy into 2009. The more he reminded the public of his existence, the more his reputation suffered. This belated condemnation of Greenspan was inseparable from current events. Also, Bernanke's Federal Reserve is inseparable from the financial terrain that Alan Greenspan bequeathed to him. I have not attempted to describe this postbust period comprehensively, but only incidentally.

The book concentrates on the United States and mentions events overseas only as they relate to the United States. The change in how Americans thought and behaved over the past half-century has applications in other countries, but that is a very large topic.

Introduction to Part 1
Prelude to Power

1926–1987

[O]peration in securities is not mainly a matter of reasoning at all.... The stock market ... is just a bunch of minds—there is no science, no IBM machine, no anything of that sort, that can tame it.[1]

    —Edward C. Johnson II, 1963, President, Fidelity Investments

Alan Greenspan's success was partly due to good timing. He reached maturity at mid-century. His strengths attracted an America in which the process of thinking was changing. Substance was yielding to superficiality. Matter surrendered to abstraction.

Money was becoming more abstract. In 1900, Americans, and citizens of most western European countries, held a currency that was convertible into gold. Americans who distrusted the dollar's value had the right to trade their paper for gold at a fixed, statutory rate. The value of the dollar fluctuated within a narrow range, and the prices of goods and services were more or less fixed.

Today, a dollar is worth whatever we wish it to be. It is a symbol, no longer fixed to a disinterested, inert metal. Inflation is one result. The successful careers of pandering politicians and clever opportunists are another. An object that cost $1 in 1913 (when the Federal Reserve Act was passed) costs $20 today. Inflation of money was integrated into the

---

[1] First Annual Contrary Opinion Foliage Forum," 1963, from Charles D. Ellis and James R. Vertin (eds.), *Classics: An Investor's Anthology* (Homewood, III.: Dow Jones-Irwin, 1988), p. 392.

1

twentieth-century inflation of words, constant distractions, and media promotion. Thus, there came the worship of celebrities simply because they are celebrities and the success of one pandering politician and clever opportunist: Alan Greenspan.

Alan Greenspan grew up in New York City, a metropolis that illuminates the changing tendencies and aspirations of Americans. Greenspan spent his young adulthood near or on Wall Street. In 1945, New York was the largest manufacturing city in the United States.[2] It was a city that made things. By 2008, it was no longer a working-class town. Nor was it a middle-income town. In Manhattan, 51 percent of neighborhoods were identified as being high-income and 40 percent as being low income.[3] Publicity and finance priced out the factories. The chairman of Lever Brothers, a soap manufacturer, explained why, in the mid-1950s, he moved his headquarters to Manhattan: "The platform from which to sell goods to America is New York."[4]

Lever Brothers sold an image; the image sold soap. Alan Greenspan also sold an image—productivity—but it was debt that boomed until it was too large to be paid back. From the time Greenspan was named Federal Reserve chairman until he left office, the nation's debt rose from $10.8 trillion to $41.0 trillion.[5] Greenspan usually referred to the debt as "wealth." This image matched what he was selling—first stocks, then houses. He expanded money and credit; he oozed praise for derivatives. The larger volume of credit shrunk the consequences of immediate losses. It was easy to overlook the areas of the economy that had shriveled and the instability of finance that had compounded over the past half-century. In early 2007, this massive inflation of paper claims, many of which were claims on abstractions rather than on material assets, tottered, then collapsed. The first to go was the subprime mortgage market.

Credit creation filled the void of falling production. In 1950, 59 percent of U.S. corporate profits were from manufacturing; 9 percent were from

---

[2] Robert A. M. Stern, Thomas Mellins, and David Fishman, *New York 1960: Architecture and Urbanism between the Second World War and the Bicentennial* (New York: Monacell: Press, 1995), p. 19.

[3] Sam Roberts, "Study Shows Dwindling Middle Class," *New York Times*, June 26, 2006.

[4] Stern et al., *New York 1960*, p. 61.

[5] Figures from end of years he entered and left office. "Beginning of office" is December 31, 1987, from Federal Reserve Flow of Funds Account; "end of office" is December 31, 2005.

financial activities. During the past decade (2000–2008), 18 percent of profits were from manufacturing and 34 percent were from finance.[6]

After graduating from New York University in 1948, Greenspan took a job at the Conference Board. He received a master's degree from NYU in 1950; then studied economics under Arthur Burns at Columbia University. The two became lifelong friends. Arthur Burns served as chairman of the Council of Economic Advisers under President Dwight Eisenhower. He would become Federal Reserve chairman under President Richard Nixon. Greenspan headed President Gerald Ford's Council of Economic Advisers (CEA) when Arthur Burns was Federal Reserve chairman.

In 1953, investment advisor William Townsend recruited Greenspan; the pair formed an economic consulting firm, Townsend-Greenspan & Co. When William Townsend died in 1958, Greenspan became the sole owner.

Greenspan is sometimes described as a disciple of Ayn Rand's Objectivist philosophy or as a libertarian. However, he may not even have understood what Rand was talking about. Nathaniel Branden, who was closest to Greenspan's mind during this period, reflected decades later: "I wondered to what extent he was aware of Ayn's opinions."[7] Alan Greenspan's contributions to group discussions were meager. Alan Greenspan was not philosophical; he was practical and, either by nature or by design, vague, remote, and impenetrable.

Greenspan used his Randian acquaintances to climb the political ladder. He joined Martin Anderson's policy research group during Richard Nixon's 1968 campaign for the presidency. Anderson, who traveled in Objectivist circles, later introduced Greenspan to Ronald Reagan.

Greenspan was riding the wave of the growing influence of accredited economists. By the late 1950s, Greenspan's stock market predictions and economic forecasts were quoted in *Fortune* and the *New York Times*. His forecasts were usually wrong, as are those of most economists. Accuracy was less important than publicity.[8]

---

[6] Bureau of Economic Analysis (BEA) National Income and Product Accounts (NIPA) Table 6.16B,C,D. Income by industry has been so erratic over the past decade that the totals for 2000–2008 are averaged as a comparison to 1950.

[7] Nathaniel Branden, *My Years with Ayn Rand*, (San Franciscio: Jossey-Bass, 1999) p. 160.

[8] The pervasiveness of publicity was to smother American life, but it was not new; the old may have been even bolder than today. From the pitch to sell the movie *Alimony* in 1924: "Brilliant men, beautiful jazz babies, champagne baths, midnight revels, petting parties in the purple dawn, all ending in one terrific smashing climax that makes you gasp."

Greenspan observed Federal Reserve Chairman William McChesney Martin Jr. lose the fight against inflation. In 1957, Martin warned the Senate that the current inflation problem that had persisted since World War II had been fostered by "economic imbalances,"[9] of which the heaviest hit were those who could not protect the value of their income or their savings[10]—the "little man"[11]. Martin predicted that those with "savings in their old age would tend to be the slick and clever rather than the hard-working and thrifty."

This was a foresighted summary of the period from 1957 to the present.

Greenspan seemed to understand that permanent, underlying inflation supported asset prices. In 1959, he told *Fortune* that an "artificial liquidity in our financial system" could power "an explosive speculative boom." According to the *Fortune* reporter: "Once the Federal Reserve was set up, Greenspan reasons, the money supply never really got short. With one eye necessarily cocked towards politics, the Fed has always maintained a more than adequate money supply even when speculative booms threaten."[12]

The stock market rose from 1950 to 1966. The rise was validated by the booming economy, but around the time Greenspan spoke to *Fortune*, fancy finance was playing an expanding role. The conglomerate craze, technology stock bubbles, and the huge growth of institutional money management (mutual funds and hedge funds) would end in tears, but fortunes were made. By 1969, Greenspan was a millionaire.[13] Greenspan described his specialty to Martin Mayer as "statistical espionage."[14] Mayer would later discuss Greenspan's technique at greater length: "the book on him in that capacity was that you could order the opinion you needed."[15]

Richard Nixon was introduced to Greenspan during the 1968 campaign. The candidate's evaluation: "That's a very intelligent man."[16]

---

[9] William McChesney Martin, Statement, Before the Committee on Finance, U.S. Senate, August 13, 1957, pp. 9–10.

[10] Ibid., p. 15.

[11] Ibid., p. 23.

[12] Gilbert Burck, "A New Kind of Stock Market," *Fortune*, March 1959, p. 201.

[13] Justin Martin, *Greenspan: The Man behind Money* (Cambridge, Mass.: Perseus, 2000), p. 65.

[14] Martin Mayer, *New Breed on Wall Street: The Young Men Who Make the Money Go* (New York: Macmillan, 1969), p. 82.

[15] Martin Mayer, *The Greatest-Ever Bank Robbery: The Collapse of the Savings and Loan Industry* (New York: Charles Scribner's Sons, 1990), p. 140.

[16] Martin, *Greenspan*, p. 69.

Greenspan was nominated by Nixon as Council of Economic Advisers chairman in 1973. Gerald Ford was president when Greenspan passed his confirmation hearing in 1974.

This was an ideal time for a publicity-minded economist to enter government. It was the same year that Time introduced *People* magazine. Greenspan, who had cultivated the press for years, maneuvered his portrait on to the front cover of *Newsweek*—the first economist to garner such attention.[17] Greenspan set an example that flattery could get one anywhere.

The United States had been buying more than it produced since the 1950s. The dollars piled up overseas, and creditor nations demanded that the United States redeem dollars with its gold reserves. The U.S. government abandoned its promise to buy dollars for gold in 1971, when it dropped the gold standard. The dollar then traded at whatever people believed it to be worth, which wasn't much.

By the late 1970s, doubters prevailed. The period was plagued with higher inflation and a bewildered society. Many kept up by trading jewelry or houses. In 1980, the *New York Times* spoke to the economist: "Alan Greenspan, the economist, has asserted that the translation of home-ownership equity into cash available for consumer spending is perhaps the most significant reason why the economy in 1975–1978 was consistently stronger than expected."[18] When the Nasdaq crashed in 2000, the Federal Reserve chairman remembered this lesson.

After Ford left office, in January 1977, Greenspan was a celebrity back in New York. He ran Townsend-Greenspan, but he seemed to exert his greatest efforts outside the office. He dated Barbara Walters, a television personality. He was a regular in the *Times*'s "Evening Hours" and "Notes on Fashion" columns.

Greenspan is classified as a Republican. In practice, however, his flattery was nonpartisan. When Ted Kennedy ran for the Democratic nomination in 1980, Greenspan hosted a breakfast for the Massachusetts senator in New York with "key Wall Street figures."[19] At the 1980 Republican convention, Greenspan almost corralled Ronald Reagan into offering him the position of treasury secretary.

---

[17] Ibid., p. 127.

[18] John H. Allan, "Thrift Adrift: Why Nobody Saves," *New York Times*, February 17, 1980.

[19] Steven Rattner, "The Candidates' Economists," *New York Times*, November 18, 1979, p. F1.

Greenspan remained in the public eye during the early Reagan years. He was called a "superstar" (*New York Times*) on the speaking circuit, making 80 speeches a year for up to $40,000 a speech.[20] He joined corporate boards. He spent most of his time in Washington. Martin Anderson, who both worked in the Reagan White House and had introduced Greenspan to politics back in the 1960s, remembered: "I don't think I was in the White House once where I didn't see him sitting in the lobby or working the offices. I was astounded by his omnipresence.... He was always huddling in the corner with someone."[21]

His record as an economic forecaster was unimpressive. Senator William Proxmire castigated the nominee at Greenspan's Federal Reserve confirmation hearing in 1987. Proxmire recited Greenspan's economic predictions as CEA chairman. His Treasury bill and inflation forecasts were the worst of any CEA director.[22]

There was little left of Townsend-Greenspan when he became Federal Reserve chairman.[23]

Proxmire had another concern with Greenspan's nomination. The senator thought that the growing concentration of financial power and solvency of the financial system was heading down a dark road, toward "increased concentration of banking."[24] Proxmire's fears proved correct. Two decades later, the highly concentrated financial system is semi-insolvent.

Nobody contributed more to the concentration of finance than Alan Greenspan. As Federal Reserve chairman, Greenspan, who had recently resigned as a director of J. P. Morgan to take the post, permitted Morgan to underwrite debt, then equity—the first time either had been permitted by a commercial bank since 1933.

Luckily for Greenspan, his nomination preceded the public denouement of Lincoln Savings and Loan and of Charles Keating. Greenspan had been hired by Keating to persuade the Federal Home Loan Bank of San Francisco that Lincoln was in good shape. Greenspan succeeded

---

[20] Martin, *Greenspan*, pp. 139, 276.

[21] Jerome Tuccille, *Alan Shrugged: The Life and Times of Alan Greenspan, the World's Most Powerful Banker* (Hoboken, N.J.: Wiley, 2002, pp. 157–158.

[22] Committee on Banking, Housing and Urban Affairs transcript, July 21, 1987, p. 41.

[23] Tuccille, *Alan Shrugged,* p. 154.

[24] Committee on Banking, Housing and Urban Affairs transcript, July 21, 1987, p. 60.

even though Lincoln was one of Michael Milken's top three junk-bond customers among savings and loans (S&Ls).[25]

The rise of Milken—and of Greenspan—was attuned to the hectic financialization of America in the 1980s. "Maximizing shareholder value" turned out to be a veil for loading corporate balance sheets with debt, a much cheaper and faster route to growth than from retained profits. The market would not have accommodated such indiscretions 30 years earlier.

The capital foundations were growing unstable. Greenspan could (and would) salute the economy's flexibility. The economy was, in fact, vulnerable to collapse and needed constant infusions of money and credit to sustain it. Hands trembled at the word "recession," and rightfully so: balance sheets—government, corporate, and personal—were no longer constructed to weather a storm. This was capitalism with little respect for capital.

An error-prone but malleable Federal Reserve chairman was a predictable choice for the most influential financial position in the world.

---

[25] Barrie A. Wigmore, *Securities Markets in the 1980s*, Vol. 1 (New York: Oxford University Press, 1997), p. 286.

I

EARLY YEARS: THE EDUCATION OF ALAN GREENSPAN

1926–1958

Do you think Alan might basically be a social climber?

—*Ayn Rand*[1]

Alan Greenspan was born in 1926. He grew up in New York City. Alan's parents, Herbert and Rose, divorced when he was young. His father had been a stockbroker in the 1920s, but suffered financially after the Crash. Alan and his mother moved to her parents' small apartment at the corner of Broadway and 163rd Street, in Washington Heights. Alan's father remained distant. Described by one of Alan's biographers as "something of a dreamer, given to aloofness and abstraction," his son gravitated toward an occupation that perpetuated such tendencies: economics.[2]

Herbert was rarely seen. A cousin recalled, "I do remember the ecstasy that Alan exhibited on those rare occasions when his father visited."[3] On one of these visits in 1935, Herbert gave his son a copy of a book he had written, *Recovery Ahead!* His father's inscription betrays a rhetorical similarity: "at your maturity you may look back and endeavor to

---

[1] Nathaniel Branden, *My Years with Ayn Rand*, (San Francisco: Jossey-Bass, 1999) p. 212.
[2] Justin Martin, *Greenspan: The Man behind Money* (Cambridge, Mass: Perseus, 2000), p. 3.
[3] Ibid., p. 2.

interpret the reasoning behind these logical forecasts and begin a like work of your own. Your Dad."[4] The book was a defense of the New Deal, a description of how government funding could end the Depression.[5]

It is not clear that Alan drew any lessons for life from this episodic parent. (Greenspan did not read *Recovery Ahead!* until years later.[6]) That he was drawn to the same occupation may have been in imitation of his father. Despite the book's losing battle against an economy that was resistant to government funding, Herbert earned a living. Accurate predictions have never mattered much in the field of economics; to forecast is the thing—publicity is essential; competence is occasional.

Alan was an obedient and well-mannered son. However, in what seems an inconsistency, he refused his bar mitzvah, even though his grandfather, whom he lived with, was cantor at a synagogue.[7]

Alan received top grades and was a "joiner" at George Washington High School. He was president of his homeroom and member of the "lunch squad," a group that broke up fights at a crowded and pugnacious school. He studied the clarinet and saxophone. He made friends with Stan Getz, a jazz musician one year his junior. He played clarinet in the school orchestra and in the school dance band. He graduated as a member of Arista, an honor society composed of top students.[8]

AFTER HIGH SCHOOL: JUILLIARD SCHOOL, ROAD MUSICIAN, AND COLLEGE

Alan next attended the illustrious Juilliard School, attesting to his musical talent. But he was only an average student, so he departed. He joined Henry Jerome and His Orchestra. Saxophonist or clarinetist as duty called, he earned $62 a week, riding buses between engagements in Memphis, Tennessee; Covington, Kentucky; and New Orleans.[9] Alan

---

[4] Alan Greenspan, *The Age of Turbulence: Adventures in a New World* (New York: Penguin, 2007), p. 21.

[5] Martin, *Greenspan*, p. 4.

[6] Ibid.

[7] Jerome Tuccille, *Alan Shrugged: The Life and Times of Alan Greenspan, the World's Most Powerful Banker* (Hoboken, N.J.: Wiley, 2002), p. 14; Martin, *Greenspan*, p. 6.

[8] Martin, *Greenspan*, pp. 7–10.

[9] Ibid., p. 15.

had little to complain about, since his classmates were strewn around the world in such exotic though unhygienic spots as Iwo Jima and Mandalay. He explained to friends that he hadn't gone to war as a consequence of a medical problem: he had a spot on his lung discovered in an x-ray. One biographer wrote: "This later turned out to be nothing."[10]

Alan decided to go back to school. He enrolled in New York University's School of Commerce, Accounts and Finance in 1945.[11] He escaped shellfire, but he was indoctrinated into the behemoth inclinations of postwar America that his high school classmates had grown accustomed to since boot camp. In Greenspan's division of NYU, known as "the factory," 9,000 students competed in business specialties, particularly real estate, sales, insurance, and public utilities management. Studies were practical; students learned a trade. Greenspan followed the less trodden and more cerebral route of economics.

Not intimidated by the anonymity of such an assembly line of students, he played clarinet in the orchestra, sang in the glee club, was chosen as president of the Symphonic Society, and was president of the Economics Society.[12] Greenspan graduated summa cum laude in 1948 with a bachelor of science degree in economics. In 1950, Greenspan earned his master's degree in economics from NYU.

Acquaintances thought Greenspan was introverted. Did he view his extracurricular activities as a way to boost his career? Whether or not that was his intention, his friendships paid dividends. Robert Kavesh was probably his best friend at NYU, and they remained close. Kavesh worked on Wall Street in the 1950s before returning to NYU to teach economics. Professor Kavesh aided Greenspan when Alan sought (and received) his doctorate in the 1970s.

To stake his future in the field was a gamble. Whether or not Greenspan had a particular insight, his talents were aligned with the direction in which economic study was moving: he could calculate. By the end of the twentieth century, economics would be consumed in mathematics. Without such talent, a budding genius stood not a chance of a degree.

---

[10] Ibid., p. 19.

[11] Ibid., p. 23.

[12] Ibid., p. 27.

There was a great urge among economists to define economics as a "science": it was a matter of respectability and legitimacy. Humanity needed a discreetly annotated and mathematically proven means to avoid another such calamity as the Great Depression.

MOVING UP—FROM NYU TO COLUMBIA UNIVERSITY

Alan Greenspan resisted any particular school of thought. Instead, he sought and captured the good graces of influential figures. Greenspan pursued his doctorate at Columbia University, which, along with Harvard and Princeton, buzzed with innovative studies.[13] In time, these theories would calcify into a dogma, the language of the trade would retreat into a catechism of symbolism, and the prescriptions of the arbiters in Washington were genuflections to the orthodoxy of the academy. Eventually, the mandates for government expansion would receive authoritative rationalizations from the universities, and the loop was closed. Anyone seeking tenure in economics inhabited the monastery garden. They bred and nurtured younger seedlings, who also blessed government policies and programs that were too entrenched to reform. The younger generation would mature and grow old, calculating ever more fantastic rationalizations of the impossible.

Columbia was only a subway ride uptown from NYU. Arthur Burns was the most prominent member of the Columbia economics faculty. Burns was coauthor of *Measuring Business Cycles* (1946), a respected text.[14] On the first day of Alan Greenspan's doctoral training, the professor asked his students, "What causes inflation?" Silence followed. This seems to have often been the case in Burns's presence. The pipe-smoking Burns enlightened the class: "Excess government spending causes inflation."[15]

Greenspan did not entirely agree with Arthur Burns's economic beliefs, but he did the important thing: he took up the pipe—Burns's trademark. Arthur Burns's own political aptitude was of the first order.

---

[13] Ibid., p. 27.

[14] Burns was coauthor of *Measuring Business Cycles* (New York: National Bureau of Economic Research, 1946) with Wesley C. Mitchell. Mitchell also wrote *Business Cycles* (1913), which was highly regarded.

[15] Martin, *Greenspan*, p. 29.

The professor moved to Washington to head President Eisenhower's Council of Economic Advisers in 1953. Burns was later appointed chairman of the Federal Reserve Board under Richard Nixon. Greenspan would also serve in both positions, rising to head the former institution at the same time Burns's reputation was sledding downhill at the latter.

THE CONFERENCE BOARD AND AYN RAND

When Burns left for Washington, Greenspan took a job at the Conference Board (which was then called the National Industrial Conference Board). He did not wait to earn his doctorate. The degree may have been secondary to his friendship with Burns. He may also have been worn out. Greenspan had worked full time at the Conference Board since 1948 while attending school at night.

The Conference Board was a private institution funded by corporations to pursue research. Greenspan immersed himself in detail about a slew of industries, including steel and railroads. He worked alongside Sandy Parker, who later became *Fortune* magazine's chief economics writer. Parker introduced economic forecasting to the magazine's readers. Greenspan's prophecies were often published, an excellent avenue for self-promotion (although many of them did not carry his signature) and an introduction to managing his personal relations with the press.

Greenspan married in 1952. He was encouraged by a friend to call Joan Mitchell for a date. They married 10 months later in the Pierre Hotel, families only. She recalled that Greenspan was not a romantic but a pleasant companion. In Mitchell's words: "He was an interesting man to talk to."[16] This seems an approximate description of his relationship with Congress 40 years later—always the gentleman, but lacking in ardor. They separated 10 months later, and their marriage was annulled.[17]

Ayn Rand would now enter Greenspan's life. More popularly known today as a novelist (*The Fountainhead* and *Atlas Shrugged*), Rand was, and still is, regaled for her philosophy of Objectivism. To simplify this

---

[16] Ibid., p. 31.
[17] Ibid., p. 33.

system of though, the pursuit of self-interest is moral, government interference with individual rights is evil. Her coterie, "the Collective" (meant
as an ironic reference to the mass culture, but the joke was on them), met
at her apartment from early evening until the cock crowed. Rand defined
and corralled good and evil. ("She abhorred facial hair and regarded anyone with a beard or mustache as inherently immoral."[18])

Alan's rise from bottom to top of Rand's group was a marvel, especially since Rand wanted no part of him. Greenspan was not sure if
he existed: "I think that I exist. But I don't know for sure. Actually,
I can't say with certainty that anything exists."[19] Rand was bemused by
the debates her top acolyte, Nathaniel Branden, held with Greenspan:
"How's the undertaker?" she'd sneer.[20] Branden played devil's advocate, so to speak, and pressed the future Federal Reserve chairman with
such queries as, "How do you explain the fact that you're here? Do you
require anything besides the proof of your own senses?"[21] Apparently,
Greenspan did.

Rand and Branden were instinctively suspicious of Greenspan's motivations. In his autobiography, Nathaniel Branden recalls a man without philosophical inclinations. At lunch, most of their discussions were
not about philosophy, but about Greenspan's disgust with the Federal
Reserve: "A number of our talks centered on the Federal Reserve Board's
role in influencing the economy by manipulating the money supply. We
talked about the Fed's destructive contribution to the Great Depression.
[Greenspan] spoke with vigor and intensity about a totally free banking
system."[22] Free banking would eliminate Federal Reserve "policy."[23] Such
an argument would hold great appeal with Rand, but elicit disclaimers
from Arthur Burns. Even then, Greenspan could talk in one direction
while moving in another.

---

[18] Tuccille, *Alan Shrugged*, p. 52.
[19] Martin, *Greenspan*, p. 40. The quote is slightly different in Tuccille, *Alan Shrugged*, p. 53:
"I *think* I exist, but I can't be certain. In fact, I can't be certain that anything exists."
[20] Martin, *Greenspan*, pp. 39–40.
[21] Ibid., p. 40.
[22] Branden, *My Years with Ayn Rand*, p. 160.
[23] Ibid.

Four decades later, Branden still can't reconcile Greenspan's temperament with the Collective: "Now, looking at [Alan], I wondered to what extent he was aware of Ayn's opinions. He rarely voiced his feelings about anything of a personal nature, and his language tended to be detached and passive." Branden recalls that in the discussions of Rand's *Atlas Shrugged*, Greenspan's contributions were meager. Complimenting Ayn on some passage, he might say, "On reading this … one tends to feel … exhilarated."[24]

Branden also recalled "[i]f Alan Greenspan mentioned a social event he had attended, Ayn would speculate about his fundamental seriousness or lack of it: 'Do you think Alan might basically be a social climber?' "[25] What specifically he acquired, or expected to acquire, from the Collective is impossible to know. He would learn later, if he did not understand already, the value of social accomplishment.

Greenspan may have been motivated for professional reasons. Objectivism appealed to those who professed free-market economics. Martin Anderson, later a member of the Reagan administration, was a fringe Randian who would prove instrumental in Greenspan's rise in the 1960s.

It is interesting that Greenspan's economic views are most often associated with a novelist, not an economist. This does not matter. There has never been a profile of Greenspan that does not mention his "attachment to Ayn Rand's free-market economics" or words to that effect. Any description of an economist to the public requires simplifications, and this was his name tag. Not one in a thousand readers would understand what this meant, which was fine. What Greenspan really believed has been probed by few and understood by none.

GREENSPAN JOINS WILLIAM TOWNSEND

While he was at the Conference Board, Greenspan was approached by William Townsend, who managed an economic consulting practice on Wall Street.[26] Townsend had been a successful bond trader in the 1920s,

---

[24] Ibid.

[25] Ibid., p. 212.

[26] Martin, *Greenspan*, p. 54.

but lost everything in the 1929 crash. Starting from the bottom, Townsend managed a firm that published statistical indexes for stock and bond market forecasting.[27] Greenspan's comparative advantage as an economist was evident to Townsend. The young economist's consumption of figures was, as one biographer wrote, "a data-head's delight."[28] In 1958, William Townsend died of a heart attack, and Greenspan, only 32 years old, was given the opportunity to buy out the Townsend family interests. He did, but he retained the firm's name of Townsend-Greenspan & Co. His clientele included U.S. Steel, Owens Corning, Weyerhaeuser, and Alcoa.[29] Greenspan continued to operate the firm until it was liquidated in 1987, when he became Federal Reserve chairman.

Fellow economists and clients assayed the future chairman's strength to be numbers. Greenspan's job was to collect data and project the demand for steel in six months' time. He was thorough and conscientious when collecting the inflow; however, the value of his forecasts is not clear. We do know that he warned *Fortune* magazine readers in March 1959 of "over-exuberance" in the stock market after the Standard & Poor's 500 (S&P 500) rose 43 percent in 1958. The market bumped and skidded for the next two years—in sum, neither making nor losing money for investors—before rocketing again in 1961.

His "over-exuberance" claim is well known (as a precursor to his "irrational exuberance" worry in 1996). More interesting is the context. He explained to *Fortune* that there were automatic stabilizers prior to World War I that held overexuberance in check. In the words of *Fortune* reporter Gilbert Bruck, Greenspan explained that "prices could not get too far out of line with real values because the supply of credit was automatically constricted by a limited money supply." These constraints, Greenspan explained, were severed once the Federal Reserve came into existence.[30]

The data that Greenspan collected were of physical properties that could be counted. As his biographer Justin Martin wrote: "The economy

---

[27] Greenspan, *The Age of Turbulence*, p. 45.

[28] Martin, *Greenspan*, p. 56.

[29] Ibid., p. 58.

[30] Gilbert Burck, "A New Kind of Stock Market," *Fortune*, March 1959, p. 201.

of the 1950s was a physical economy in very real and quantifiable terms: X number of men worked Y number of hours to produce Z tons of steel. It all got loaded onto so many railcars and wound up pounded into so many girders and aircraft struts and auto fins."[31]

But structural changes in the U.S. economy made Greenspan's specialty less authoritative. The numbers became more elusive as the economy grew less physical and more conceptual.

Greenspan's forte was staying ahead of his peers in the collection of previously under cataloged data. Yet, he was falling behind the times. Econometrics was the future.

Greenspan was skeptical of econometric modeling. In 1958, he wrote in *The American Economic Review*: "[Stephen] Taylor is right in pointing out that the basic problem in handling flow-of-funds accounts is the primitiveness of our financial theory. These accounts are extremely elaborate and extraordinarily well constructed. But unless we know what we want to use them for, they are of as much practical value as a table of random numbers. ..."[32]

Econometrics substitutes statistical tests for understanding (such as "what we want to use them for"). Greenspan was skeptical, yet, he succumbed—in his fashion. Townsend-Greenspan purchased a $100,000 computer that was the size of a car.[33] Greenspan "was especially inclined to tinker with the findings. He would often make substantial changes, certain that punch cards were no substitute for good old-fashioned observation."[34] Later, as Fed chairman, he was admired for ignoring models and conceptualizing Fed policy.

---

[31] Martin, *Greenspan*, p. 56.
[32] Alan Greenspan, *American Economic Review*, May 1958, vol. 48, (May 1958), p. 171.
[33] Martin, *Greenspan*, p. 56.
[34] Ibid, p. 59.

2

THE DARK SIDE
OF PROSPERITY

1958–1967

Mr. Greenspan declared that a rising stock market tended to put strong upward pressure on stockholder inclination to spend. If market values rise, and do not quickly fade again, he said, the gain gets built into an individual stockholder's permanent assets and his standard of living ideas change, with consumption rising accordingly.

—*"Economists Sift Jobs and Stocks,"*
New York Times, December 28, 1959

When Alan Greenspan, joined William Townsend's firm, Wall Street was the last place a bright and promising college graduate would launch his career. The Dow Jones Industrial Average would not reach its 1929 peak again until 1954. The relative attraction of launching a career at General Motors was not only obvious but necessary—only eight people were hired to work on the floor of the New York Stock Exchange between 1930 and 1951.[1] A study commissioned by Wall Street after World War II reported that, when respondents were asked their opinion of the stock market, "most people believed Wall Street was home to some of the

---

[1] John Brooks, *The Go-Go Years*: (New York: Weybright and Talley, 1973), p.113.

nation's slickest, most accomplished crooks, while a substantial segment thought the stock market was a place where cattle was sold."[2] Predictably, the best decade in the twentieth century for stock market returns was the 1950s. The period was one in which the American economy boomed.

THE FEDERAL RESERVE AT MID-CENTURY

During these early years of Greenspan's financial awareness, the Federal Reserve was fighting a battle royal with the Treasury Department. The Fed had responded to the patriotic calling of World War II by playing a sub-servient role to the needs of the U.S. Treasury. It held the 90-day Treasury bill rate at $3/8$ percent and the long-term Treasury at $2\frac{1}{2}$ percent.[3] After the war the Fed pressed for greater autonomy.

By early 1951, yields on Treasury securities began to rise. President Truman tried to coerce the Fed by issuing a statement on February 1, 1951: "The Federal Reserve Board has pledged its support to President Truman to maintain the stability of Government securities."[4] The Fed had done no such thing. Previously, Truman had decided not to reap-point Marriner Eccles, who had been chairman of the Fed from 1935 to 1948. The former chairman, who was still a Federal Reserve Board member, released his own statement that Truman's press release was a fabrication.[5] The administration stood down, but no Fed victory is long-lived. Treasury yields would rise for the next three decades, the market's response to ever-expanding government.

William McChesney Martin Jr. was an assistant secretary of the trea-sury at the time of the truce. He served as Fed chairman from 1951 to 1970. Alan Greenspan observed this Federal Reserve chairman from afar. The lunchtime conversations with Nathaniel Branden about the errant Fed were during Martin's term.

---

[2] Robert Sobel, *The Pursuit of Wealth: The Incredible Story of Money throughout the Ages* (New York: McGraw-Hill, 2000), pp. 277, 293, 300.

[3] Robert P. Bremner, *Chairman of the Fed: William McChesney Martin, Jr., and the Creation of the Modern American Financial System* (New Haven, Conn.: Yale University Press, 2004), p. 73.

[4] Martin Mayer, *The Fed: The Inside Story of How the World's Most Powerful Financial Institution Drives the Markets* (New York: Free Press, 2001), p. 89.

[5] Ibid., p. 89. The Federal Reserve chairman between 1948 and 1951 was Thomas B. McCabe.

Martin Mayer, author of several books about money and the Federal Reserve, sums up William McChesney Martin's character: "an unusually nice man, a good listener who actually heard what other people were saying, friends with just about everybody in all the financial communities where he lived or visited."[6] The economist Milton Friedman, no slouch when it came to publicity, attended the swearing-in ceremony for Arthur Burns's first term as Fed chairman. He watched the lollygagging senators mixing with Martin and pouted, "I still think Bill Martin is the best politician in the room."[7] Alan Greenspan, also in attendance, would have been equally observant.

Martin was a foe of both speculation and inflation. During the Eisenhower years, Martin's quest was largely a success. Between 1952 and 1962, the monetary base of the Federal Reserve Bank remained unchanged.[8] The Fed accommodated the rising demand in credit by reducing the reserve requirements of Federal Reserve member banks.[9] A lower reserve base allows banks to lend more, although it compromises bank stability. The Fed had been cutting reserve requirements since its formation and would continue to do so through Alan Greenspan's reign.

Americans wanted to borrow, but a problem was developing. The United States was spending more abroad than foreigners were buying from the United States. The deficit was paid for in gold, thus redistributing $1.7 billion of America's gold reserves to foreign central banks between 1950 and 1957. In 1958, foreigners bought $2.3 billion of gold from U.S. reserves (selling the dollars from the American purchases overseas). At this rate, the United States would lose all its unrestricted gold in four years; yet, in 1944, it had committed itself to honoring foreign government exchange requests.[10]

---

[6] Mayer, *The Fed*, p. 165.

[7] Charles A. Coombs, *The Arena of International Finance* (New York: Wiley-Interscience, 1976), p. 71.

[8] Richard Timberlake, *Monetary Policy in the United States: An Intellectual and Institutional History* (Chicago: University of Chicago Press, 1993), Table 21.1, p. 328.

[9] Ibid., Table 21.2, p. 330. Reserve requirements of "central reserve city banks" as a percentage of deposits were lowered from 26 percent in 1948 to 16½ percent by 1960.

[10] Bremner, *Chairman of the Fed*, pp. 144–145.

The Bretton Woods Conference of 1944 instituted the "gold exchange standard." The dollar served as monetary backstop for the world's currencies. The dollar would remain pegged to gold at the value of 35 to the ounce. Balance would be preserved by the legal authority of foreign central banks. They could redeem their dollars for gold at that rate.

One reason that Americans were spending more was that they had spent so little. GIs were marrying and needed a place to live. Only 326,000 new houses were built in 1945. By 1950, nearly two million houses were built.[11] The average size of new houses constructed in 1950 was 953 square feet, and only one-third had more than two bedrooms.[12] Government financing was instrumental. Loans were generally courtesy of Federal Housing Administration and GI Bill guarantees. The first program was a legacy of the Roosevelt administration; the latter, of the nation's support for soldiers.[13]

Credit flowed more readily, and material possessions were bought and discarded more rapidly. The *New York Times* captured the evolution on August 25, 1957: "[T]imes have changed. Owning a house is no longer so important as being able to use it while paying for it."[14] Economists classify people as "consumers." The word fit changing habits. Americans were growing more detached from ownership of property and more attached to the acquisition of things, many of which were disposable. The American temperament of the time was summed up by an economic historian of the Eisenhower years: "Although the standard of living steadily rose through the 1950s, people were not satisfied, but wanted more."[15]

NEW YORK: A LEADING ECONOMIC INDICATOR

Alan Greenspan had the advantage of working in New York. Many of the changes in America over the next 60 years were first evident in his hometown. In 1946, New York was still the "nation's largest

---

[11] Sobel, *The Pursuit of Wealth*, p. 280.

[12] National Association of Homebuilders; www.nahb.org; Source: U.S. Census Bureau, Table C-25.

[13] Sobel, *The Pursuit of Wealth*, p. 280.

[14] John Lukacs, *Outgrowing Democracy: A History of the United States in the Twentieth Century* (Garden City, N.Y.: Doubleday, 1984), p. 115.

[15] John W. Sloan, *Eisenhower and the Management of Prosperity* (Lawrence: University Press of Kansas, 1960), p. 154; quoted in Bremner, *Chairman of the Fed*, p. 148.

manufacturing town."[16] Between 1946 and 1951, five-sixths of the new factories "were built beyond the limits of the major metropolitan districts existing at the end of World War II."[17]

One who anticipated the evolution was developer William Zeckendorf. In 1956, Zeckendorf described the loss of manufacturing jobs as "magnificent.... [A]s we have lost industrial workers from the population we have gained higher paid, higher educated administrative personnel that make New York an unparalleled consumer's market."[18] In 1960 Zeckendorf told *Fortune* magazine: "[p]recisely because New York is a national headquarters, it is also a middle income as well as high-income town."[19]

The changing face of publicity was also previewed in Manhattan. Lever Brothers Chairman Charles Luckman explained: "New York is the inevitable answer to our major problem—selling."[20] By 1960, more than 25 percent of the nation's 500 largest corporations had headquarters in New York City.[21]

POPULISM DEFEATS WILLIAM McCHESNEY MARTIN'S BATTLE AGAINST INFLATION

Martin fought a valiant battle against inflation, although he was stymied by Congress. The Employment Act of 1946 committed the Fed to seek healthy economic growth—in addition to its responsibility for stable money. When the economy turns down, it does not grow. It contracts. Insolvencies and recessions are instrumental to the business cycle. Martin stood his ground before the Senate: "We are dealing with waste and extravagance, incompetency and inefficiency, the only way we have in a free society is to take losses from time to time. This is the loss economy as well as the profit economy."[22]

---

[16] Robert A.M. Stern, Thomas Mellins, and David Fishman, *New York 1960 Architecture and Urbanism between the Second World War and the Bicentennial* (New York: Monacelli: Press, 1995), p. 19.

[17] Ibid.

[18] Ibid., p. 29.

[19] Ibid., p. 29.

[20] Ibid., p. 61.

[21] Ibid., p. 29. Of those that did not, 69 percent had sales offices in New York.

[22] Bremner, *Chairman of the Fed*, p. 132; William McChesney Martin, testimony to Senate Finance Committee Hearings, April 22, 1958.

Washington, of course, did not want to hear this. "Pro-growth economists" lobbied in Washington. They spoke the words that would both appeal to the politicians' expansive tendencies and embellish their patriotic image.

The young Wall Street economist with latent political ambitions would have noted the opportunists' media presence. Harvard University professor Sumner Slichter believed that the Fed would have to accept inflation if the economy was to generate sufficient jobs. Slichter argued that costs for materials and labor were rising as "unions push up wages and fringe benefits faster than the gains from productivity of labor. The result is a continuation of the slow rise in prices."[23] For this he acquired a publicity-enhancing sobriquet: *Fortune* magazine dubbed Slichter the "father of inflation."[24] To economists of the old school, the solution was obvious: wages must meet productivity. Albert Jay Nock, who was a philosopher, not an economist, put into words what anyone with common sense knows: "It is an economic axiom that goods and services can only be paid for with goods and services."[25] America, or at least its leaders, ignored this axiom, so production migrated to where Americans were spending: overseas.

Martin lashed out at Slichter's populist appeal: "If you take [Slichter's] view, then another bust will surely come."[26] Martin, who was not a certified economist (he was a Latin scholar from Yale), knew better than the Harvard professor how empires hoodwink themselves into decline. Economists who could spin nonsensical abstractions into accepted wisdom over the course of this deterioration were amply rewarded.

GREENSPAN'S FORAYS INTO PUBLICITY AND PUBLISHING

Alan Greenspan had been born into the dark side of prosperity. The stock market boom of the 1950s was changing the way Americans behaved,

---

[23] Sumner Slichter, "Five Trends Shape the Business Future," *Nation's Business*, February 1957, p. 96.

[24] Bremner, *Chairman of the Fed*, p. 128.

[25] Albert Jay Nock, *Memoirs of a Superfluous Man* (New York and London: Harper and Brothers, 1943), p. 256.

[26] Bremner, *Chairman of the Fed*, p. 128.

and Greenspan did not approve. The *New York Times* reported Alan Greenspan's discourse at an economic conference in December 1959:

> Alan Greenspan, of Townsend, Greenspan & Co., New York financial house, presented the view that a break in stock market trends was not just a harbinger of boom or recession, as is commonly held, but a crucial factor in causing a boom or a recession.
>
> Mr. Greenspan declared that a rising stock market tended to put strong upward pressure on stockholder inclination to spend. If market values rise, and do not quickly fade again, he said, the gain gets built into an individual stockholder's permanent assets and his standard of living ideas change, with consumption rising accordingly.
>
> His general conclusion was that instability of the general economy results from the flexibility of the banking system, which supplies credit for the stock market.
>
> He questioned the theory that the enlargement of the Government's role in the national economy had brought a "new era" in which an old-fashioned financial contraction was impossible.[27]

As the stock market boomed through the first half of the 1960s, Greenspan consistently put in a bad word. For example, *Time* surveyed an ambivalent Wall Street in January 1962: "[T]he most pessimistic is Alan Greenspan of Townsend-Greenspan, who says: 'The peak of the bull market will be in the early spring, or at the latest by midyear.'"[28] His opinion was validated sooner than he expected. The S&P 500 started falling almost immediately and shed 25 percent through June. It rebounded sharply through the end of the year.

To be quoted in the *Times* was the logical route for a businessman. As such, Greenspan spent little time posturing for the academics who monopolized the status and careers of economists. Greenspan was not a prolific contributor to academic journals.

---

[27] "Economists Sift Jobs and Stocks," *New York Times*, December 28, 1959, p. 39.
[28] "Wall Street Worries," *Time*, January 26, 1962.

"The New Economics"

In 1961, John Kennedy was a fresh face in the White House. He recruited advisors who promoted the "New Economics," largely, an American version of John Maynard Keynes's beliefs. A leading proponent was Paul Samuelson: a graduate of the University of Chicago, of Harvard University, a kingpin of the Massachusetts Institute of Technology's rise as an economic think tank, and a fervent flag waver for the efficient market hypothesis (EMH).[29] In 1970, Samuelson would be awarded the Nobel Prize in economic sciences.

Samuelson was Kennedy's primary economic advisor. Viewing a sluggish economy in 1961, Samuelson wrote "what definitely is not called for is a massive program of hastily devised public works whose primary objective is merely that of making jobs and getting money pumped into the economy."[30] In November 1962, he warned Kennedy that he must cut taxes to avoid a recession: If —and only if—Congress passed a tax cut, by 1964, "events will be working clearly and strongly our way." That is, for reelection.[31] Washington politics had modified the new economics.

Walter Heller, Kennedy's Council of Economic Advisers chairman, argued that a higher rate of growth would be produced through a looser Federal Reserve monetary policy and by employing Keynesian fiscal policy in the form of a temporary tax cut. Martin was convinced that most of the data pumped out of the Council of Economic Advisers was used "to justify both an expansionary monetary policy and the Kennedy tax cut."[32]

Douglas Dillon, Kennedy's treasury secretary, introduced initiatives to close the federal deficit to $2.5 billion—an unsatisfactory result, in Dillon's opinion.[33] This may have been the last time a treasury secretary sincerely believed that the government should only spend what it received in revenue.

---

[29] Peter L. Bernstein, *Capital Ideas: The Improbable Origins of Modern Wall Street* (New York: Free Press, 1992), pp.112–125 passim.

[30] Bremner, *Chairman of the Fed*, p. 151.

[31] Ibid., p. 176.

[32] Ibid., p. 183.

[33] Ibid., p. 166.

After President Lyndon Johnson succeeded Kennedy (in 1963), spending for the Great Society and the Vietnam War raced ahead of revenues. Martin offered the public fair warning at the Columbia University commencement on June 1, 1965, where he told his audience that private domestic debt was rising, the supply of money and credit was increasing without an increase in the gold supply, and international indebtedness had risen.[34] The federal budget deficit leapt from $3.7 billion in fiscal year 1965 to $25.2 billion in 1967.[35]

Meanwhile, in addition to managing his firm, Greenspan spent considerable time with Ayn Rand. Rand was growing difficult to please: she had always been the sole arbiter of Objectivism, and her rants and excommunications grew fierce.

In 1968, Rand threw Nathaniel Branden and his wife, Barbara, out into the cold. Greenspan was a signatory. The dismissal read in part: "Because Nathaniel Branden and Barbara Branden, in a series of actions, have betrayed fundamental principles of Objectivism, we condemn and repudiate these two persons irrevocably."[36] Greenspan would say later that "he added his name hastily, unsure in the midst of all the chaos of the charges or what was at stake."[37]

It is natural to condemn Perfidious Alan, but one should note the aptitude of this future government official who abandoned and embraced contradictory positions without rancor. Illuminating is the post-Randian friendship of Greenspan and Barbara Branden.[38] Greenspan's sterile, nerveless automation might sooth or itch, but was unlikely to repel. His biographer, Jerome Tuccille, wrote: "If Alan was shocked by any of the revelations … it did not show on his face. Alan presented the same face to the world through victory and tribulation. His expression rarely changed—laconic, mostly unsmiling, somewhat hangdog.[39]

---

[34] Brooks, *The Go-Go Years*, p. 100.

[35] U.S. White House Office of Management and Budget, Fiscal Year Budget Data, October 15, 2008.

[36] Justin Martin, *Greenspan: The Man behind Money* (Cambridge, Mass.: Perseus, 2000), p. 51.

[37] Ibid.

[38] Ibid., pp. 147–148.

[39] Jerome Tuccille, *Alan Shrugged: The Life and Times of Alan Greenspan, the World's Most Powerful Banker* (Hoboken, N.J.: Wiley, 2002), p. 87.

GREENSPAN'S 1966 ESSAY: "GOLD AND ECONOMIC FREEDOM"

A few months after Martin's Columbia address in June of 1965, Greenspan wrote an essay for Rand. It may have been prodded by the collapse in the national accounts. He never discussed the undisciplined policies of Congress and the Johnson administration, but the parallels are clear.

In "Gold and Economic Freedom," Greenspan vilified the Federal Reserve's money-printing excesses of the 1920s. In Greenspan's thesis:

> When business in the United States underwent a mild contraction in 1927, the Federal Reserve created more paper reserves in the hope of forestalling any possible bank reserve shortage.... The excess credit which the Fed pumped into the economy spilled over into the stock market—triggering a fantastic speculative boom. Belatedly, Federal Reserve officials attempted to sop up the excess reserves and finally succeeded in braking the boom. But it was too late: by 1929 the speculative imbalances had become so overwhelming that the attempt precipitated a sharp retrenching and a consequent demoralizing of business confidence. As a result, the American economy collapsed.... The world economies plunged into the Great Depression of the 1930's.

Greenspan knowingly contrasted the pre-World War I gold standard to the post-1914 monetary arrangement. He also explained the relation of money and the credit system:

> Even though the units of exchange (the dollar, the pound, the franc, etc.) differ from country to country, when all are defined in terms of gold the economies of the different countries act as one—so long as there are no restraints on trade or on the movement of capital. Credit, interest rates, and prices tend to follow similar patterns in all countries.

He attacked the politicians of an earlier era and their subterfuge of the gold standard.

[T]he Federal Reserve System was organized in 1913.... Credit extended by [the Federal Reserve] is in practice (though not legally) backed by the taxing power of the federal government. Technically, we remained on the gold standard; individuals were still free to own gold, and gold continued to be used as bank reserves. But now, in addition to gold, credit extended by the Federal Reserve banks ("paper reserves") could serve as legal tender to pay depositors.[40]

The succinctness of "Gold and Economic Freedom" is quite a contrast to the labored, meandering speeches that he would make as Fed chairman.

GREENSPAN'S WARNING ABOUT THE GUNS AND BUTTER DEFICIT

The Dow Jones Industrial Average had been rising for 18 years, but it reached its peak in 1966. Greenspan coauthored a front-cover story in the January 1966 issue of *Fortune* in which he projected much higher costs than the government foretold. This article was timely, accurate, and probably not welcomed by the administration, since President Johnson and Secretary of Defense Robert McNamara were furtively spending well over budget.[41]

In "Gold and Economic Freedom," Greenspan had warned that the "gold standard is incompatible with chronic deficit spending (the hallmark of the welfare state)." In the closing paragraph, he reminded readers that "deficit spending is simply a scheme for the confiscation of wealth." To drive the nail home with a 2 × 4, he warned: "This is the shabby secret of the welfare statists' tirades against gold." Yet it was soon after this tirade against welfare statists that Greenspan changed course—he aimed his efforts toward Washington.

---

[40] Ayn Rand, *Capitalism: The Unknown Ideal*, Signet (paperback) 1967, essay by Alan Greenspan: "Gold and Economic Freedom" pp. 96–101

[41] Bremner, *Chairman of the Fed*, pp. 204, 224.

3
ADVISING NIXON: "I COULD HAVE A REAL EFFECT"

1967–1973

How Alan Greenspan, a man who believed in the philosophy of little government interference and few rules or regulations, could end up becoming chairman of the greatest regulatory agency in the country is beyond me.

—Barbara Walters, 2008[1]

Alan Greenspan entered politics during the 1968 Nixon election campaign. By different accounts, this decision was influenced by at least two old friends. Greenspan met Leonard Garment on a noontime walk. Garment was a fellow graduate of the Henry Jerome Orchestra, where Greenspan spent his wilderness years between the Juilliard School and New York University. By this time, Garment was a lawyer who also recruited volunteers for the Nixon presidential campaign.[2] Greenspan hosted Garment at the Bankers Club in Manhattan. Greenspan impressed his host with his enthusiasm for the presidential candidate.[3] Garment arranged a meeting with Nixon. The economist put on quite a performance.

---

[1] Barbara Walters, *Audition: A Memoir* (New York: Knopf, 2008), p. 262.

[2] Justin Martin, *Greenspan: The Man behind Money* (Cambridge, Mass.: Perseus, 2000), pp. 67–69.

[3] Leonard Garment, *Crazy Rhythm* (New York: Times Books, 1997), p. 107.

In Garment's recollection, Greenspan's verbal calisthenics were "Nepal Katmandu language." Nixon loved it: "That's a very intelligent man."[4]

Martin Anderson also propelled Greenspan's political career. Influential in Nixon's policy research efforts, Anderson was familiar with Greenspan through Objectivist acquaintances.[5] Greenspan served with Anderson's policy group.

As a Rand acolyte, Greenspan was forbidden to collaborate with the government. He rationalized his participation in terms that were not terribly convincing, unless one is Alan Greenspan, who had a special knack for appearing virtuous while raiding the cookie jar. He told Joseph Kraft for a 1976 profile published in the *New York Times Magazine* that he agreed to go to Washington in 1968 only when Arthur Burns at the Federal Reserve and Treasury Secretary William Simon told Greenspan "'that I could have a real effect.'"[6]

1968: Working for Nixon

Greenspan's role was coordinator of domestic policy research. It was, in the words of a Greenspan biographer, "a volunteer part-time gig, requiring just a few hours a day."[7] Greenspan gathered papers to be reviewed by different issue task forces. The task forces helped form policy for Nixon on topical issues. Most of Greenspan's research was shipped off to Nixon's staff.

After his 1968 victory, Nixon wanted Greenspan to join his administration. Greenspan soldiered on in a temporary capacity, serving as liaison with the Bureau of the Budget during the 1968–1969 transition.[8] He turned down the job of budget director.[9]

By the late 1960s, Greenspan was a millionaire. He owned an apart-

---

[4] Martin, *Greenspan*, p. 69.

[5] Ibid.

[6] Joseph Kraft, "Right, for Ford," *New York Times Magazine*, April 25, 1976, p. 27. Burns and Simon held those positions when the article was written in 1976, not in 1968. William McChesney Martin was chairman of the Fed until January 31, 1970. Arthur Burns became a member of the Federal Reserve Board on the same day and chairman of the board on February 1, 1970 .

[7] Martin, *Greenspan*, p. 71.

[8] "The Soft-Sell Charm of Alan Greenspan", *BusinessWeek*, April 28, 1975, p. 2.

[9] Martin, *Greenspan*, p. 74.

ment at 860–870 United Nations Plaza, known as "U.N. Plaza," a new and fashionable address where Walter Cronkite, Truman Capote, and Senator Robert F. Kennedy lived.[10] He seemed drawn to the celebrity culture.

The Wall Street that Alan Greenspan observed from his day job was radically different from the mortuary of gray-faced men who had moped around the stock exchange in the 1950s. The stock market attracted a Youth Movement. The 1960s would be known as "the Go-Go Years."

The fear of a "disastrous stock market break" (a possibility that Greenspan discussed with the New York Times in 1965) would elude investors for another seven years.[11] But from 1966 to 1973, the market endured a period of indecision, with sharp breaks and recoveries.

Mutual fund assets—a barometer for retail interest in the stock market—rose from $1 billion in 1945 to $35 billion in 1965, and to $50 billion by 1969.[12] Richard Jenrette, cofounder of Donaldson, Lufkin & Jenrette, called this the "great garbage market," since the public ignored old stalwarts such as General Motors and General Electric and bought Four Seasons Nursing Centers and United Convalescent Homes.[13]

By 1969, institutional investors had come to dominate the stock market: they held 60 percent of New York Stock Exchange dollar volume, roughly double their position in 1960.[14]

In short, this was the same carnival atmosphere Greenspan would see three decades later, only in the 1960s the numbers were smaller.

THE RISE AND FALL OF THE CONGLOMERATES

The serendipitous restructuring of American companies had compounded at an astounding pace since Greenspan's early professional career. Federal Reserve Chairman William McChesney Martin explained both the construction and the consequences of accelerated finance before the

---

[10] Robert A. M. Stern, Thomas Mellins, and David Fishman, New York 1960; Architecture and Urbanism between the Second World War and the Bicentennial (New York: Monacelli Press, 1995), pp. 630, 632; Martin, Greenspan, pp. 64–65

[11] Vartanig G. Vartan, "There Are Smiles on Wall Street, Smiles Are Relit," New York Times, June 17, 1965.

[12] John Brooks, The Go-Go Years Weybright and Talley, 1973, p. 101.

[13] Ibid., p. 184.

[14] Ibid., p. 260.

Senate Committee on Finance on August 13, 1957. Martin warned that "a spiral of mounting prices and wages seeks more and more financing" with a "considerable volume of the expenditure ... financed at all times out of borrowed funds."[15] The "slick and the clever" would tend to do best.[16]

Borrowed funds were rising in the 1960s because the Federal Reserve was printing too much money. Credit was increasing at double-digit rates by mid-decade. The economy was growing at a single-digit pace. What was the result? Alan Greenspan knew when he spoke to *Fortune* magazine in 1959. The reporter summarized Greenspan's concerns: "The Fed ... has recently been boxed in by a huge and partially monetized federal debt, which tends to produce an addition to the money supply, whose size is unrelated to the needs of private business."[17] And so, speculation and frenzied finance followed.

There will be three periods of abundant finance discussed over the course of this book: first, the 1960s conglomerates phase; second, the 1980s leveraged-buyout period; third, the recent buyout boom that peaked in 2007. Refinancing and merging companies is healthy, up to a point. It is when the flows of credit grow out of proportion to the economy that finance mutates companies.

During the conglomerate years, Alan Greenspan, as consultant, knew how vulnerable the Fortune 500 companies had become. There was no knowing if the biggest and strongest might fall victim to an onslaught of bank debt, convertible bonds, and warrant issues that shareholders found irresistible. It was a world turned upside down. Greenspan was Federal Reserve chairman when leveraged buyouts reached their peak in 1989, and he was still chairman in 2006, when the latest buyout scramble was building to a climax.

"Conglomerates" were unheard of during Greenspan's early years (so much so that when the structure gained hold in the 1960s, the society pages of the *New York Times* clumsily classified the victors as

---

[15] William McChesney Martin, Statement before the Committee on Finance, U.S. Senate, August 13, 1957; fraser.stlouisfedorg/historicaldocs/wmm57/download/30925/martin57_0813.pdf, pp. 8, 11.

[16] Ibid., p. 18.

[17] Gilbert Burck, "A New Kind of Stock Market," *Fortune*, March 1959, p. 201.

"conglomerateurs"[18]).

James Joseph Ling and Saul Steinberg stood at the beginning and the end of the conglomerations. In 1955, Jimmy Ling, the owner of an electrical contracting company with $1.5 million in sales, handed out prospectuses at a Texas State Fair. He sold 450,000 shares at $2.25 apiece.[19] By 1967, he ran the thirty eighth-largest industrial company in America and by 1969, the fourteenth-largest.[20] When the economy turned down in 1969, Ling-Temco-Vought collapsed, its stock falling from $167 in 1967 to $11 a share. Ling was shown the door in 1970.[21]

Saul Steinberg incorporated Ideal Leasing in 1962. In 1964, with earnings of $255,000 and revenues of $1.8 million, Steinberg renamed his company "Leasco" and took it public. From 1964 to 1968, Leasco stock appreciated 5,410 percent.[22] The 29-year-old Steinberg set his sights on Chemical Bank—the sixth-largest commercial bank in the United States.[23] He failed.

The pyramiding of securities could not be sustained. Accounting tricks, mountains of paper claims, and all of the other disguises that give cosmetic coverage to bubbles started to topple. In addition, the corporate establishment coordinated its counterattack with Washington. In 1969, the Justice Department, several members of the Senate Banking and Currency Committee, the law firm of Cravath, Swaine & Moore (Chemical Bank's counsel), and members of the Federal Reserve Board brought Steinberg's effort to an end.[24] This was within weeks of a *Time* magazine cover featuring James Joseph Ling. The cover subtitle: "Threat or Boon to U.S. Business?"[25] It has traditionally been true that politicians rediscover their populist leanings when such magazine headlines appear.

Deindustrialization, anxiety, and the general collapse of American

---

[18] Brooks, *Go-Go Years*, p. 153.

[19] Ibid., p. 165.

[20] Ibid., pp. 165–166.

[21] Fundinguniverse.com/company-histories/The LTV-Corporation-Company-History.

[22] Brooks, *Go-Go Years*, p. 238.

[23] Ibid., p. 230.

[24] Ibid., pp. 254–255.

[25] Full title of front cover: "Takeovers in High Gear: Threat or Boon to U.S. Business?" *Time*, March 7, 1969.

living standards has been the topic of thousands of books by worthy economists and sociologists. The American peak is generally considered to have been in the 1960s, with the slide commencing about 1970. John Brooks, author of *The Go-Go Years*, described the disorientation:

> The economy and amour propre of whole communities became disrupted. Conglomerates' headquarters were mostly on the two coasts, and often enough their corporate victims resided in the cities in between. The result was the repeated reduction of mid-American cities' oldest established industries from independent ventures to subsidiaries of conglomerate spiderwebs based in New York or Los Angeles.[26]

It did not help the dispirited that the median household income rose from $43,677 in 1973 to $49,968 in 2007. This is surely an overstatement, since the government's calculation of inflation exaggerates the rise in income.[27]

INCREASING INVOLVEMENT IN WASHINGTON POLITICS

When Greenspan was not advising clients, he was ready for any and all temporary shuttle assignments between New York and Washington. This arrangement fit his pattern of social and professional relationships: buzzing around the hive of activity with occasional forays to gather honey, sating his appetite, then humming into the mist.

Greenspan served on one important Washington committee: the Gates Commission (formally, the President's Commission on an All-Volunteer Armed Force), whose stated objective was to review the military draft as opposed to an all-volunteer military. Nixon appointed five pro-draft members, five anti-draft members, and five question marks; Greenspan was in the third category.

Milton Friedman is generally recognized as the catalyst toward per-

---

[26] Brooks, *Go-Go Years*, p. 177.

[27] Chapter 12 is devoted to the topic of government calculations. The figures above are from the U.S. Census Bureau, Table H-3. March 7, 2009.

suading the pro-draft contingent to its unanimous all-volunteer vote.[28] Friedman had been an acolyte of Arthur Burns (when Burns taught at Rutgers), before moving to the faculty at the University of Chicago. He was a strong advocate of abolishing the draft. Temperamentally, he and Greenspan lived on different planets. (When General Westmoreland appeared before the commission and said he didn't want to command an army of mercenaries, Freidman queried, "General, would you rather command an army of slaves?")[29] Greenspan gravitated toward the anti-draft party in typical fashion. A researcher for the Gates Commission recalls that Greenspan had not been too aware of the issues. Once he learned more about the arguments, though, he became a convert.[30] It is difficult to believe the man who coauthored the 1966 *Fortune* exposé on suspect government spending in Vietnam was so detached.

FISCAL INCONTINENCE AND MONEY MAYHEM IN 1966–1967

Alan Greenspan's participation in politics could not have begun under more interesting circumstances. Fiscal incontinence was matched by money mayhem. Federal Reserve policy added to the flood of dollars. Bank credit more than doubled from a 7.2 percent annual rate of increase in December 1965 to a 15 percent rate in April 1966.[31]

The United States was the market maker for the international monetary system. As a crisis loomed, Bundesbank President Karl Blessing stated simply and angrily: "'[I]f the deficit in the U.S. balance of payments remains large, the group's discussions [on strengthening the gold pool] might as well be brought to an end, because they would be

---

[28] One member, Roy Wilkins, did not sign the report but wrote a letter supporting the commission's decision.

[29] Martin, *Greenspan*, p. 79

[30] Ibid., p. 78. Greenspan's change of heart may have been more calculated. A RAND Report on the commission cited evidence that "the substantial powers of persuasion of economists Milton Friedman and Alan Greenspan [drove] the commission to recommend the end of conscription"; http://www.rand.org/pubs/monographs/MG263/chapter4_sec2.html.

[31] Robert P. Bremner, *Chairman of the Fed: William McChesney Martin, Jr., and the Creation of the Modern American Financial System* (New Haven, Conn.: Yale University Press, 2004), p. 215.

futile.'"[32] Blessing was correct, and the United States had no intention of dealing with deficits, credit, and money printing. The American people were not in a mood to tighten their belts, and the politicians ignored the worrywarts.

The charade went on for another three years before President Nixon officially closed the gold window on August 15, 1971, after which foreign governments could no longer receive gold payments for unwanted dollars.

PEER REVIEWS

Some of the best investment minds of the next generation did not think highly of Greenspan. Michael Steinhardt, hedge-fund manager extraordinaire for the next three decades, looked back: "Around this time [circa 1967], I first met Alan Greenspan. Then a consultant to Donaldson, Lufkin, Jenrette, he visited our offices every quarter with our DLJ salesman. I recall being disappointed ... that what he said was mostly an extrapolation of the obvious.... There were certainly no clear signs back then that he would one day rule world financial markets."[33]

Marc Faber, Hong Kong–based investor and author of the monthly *Gloom, Boom & Doom Report*, could see far enough ahead to move to Asia in the 1970s. He remembers his meetings with Alan Greenspan (when Faber still worked in New York):

> I was put in charge of research liaison for White, Weld's overseas offices.... My job entailed ... attending the monthly economic presentations [by Alan Greenspan].... When Mr. Greenspan first came on board at White, Weld as a consultant, 30 or 40 people from the firm's various departments would attend the meetings. Within a few months, however, attendance had dropped to just a handful of White, Weld employees. By then I had also learned that the easiest way for me to communicate the (to me) incom-

---

[32] Ibid., p. 240.
[33] Michael Steinhardt, *No Bull: My Life In and Out of the Markets* (New York: Wiley, 2001), p. 98.

prehensible remarks of [Greenspan] to our overseas offices was simply to summarize the previous day's news from the front page of the *Wall Street Journal*.[34]

SKYROCKETING INFLATION AND "STATISTICALITIS"

Inflation, as measured by the Consumer Price Index, rose from 3.3 percent in 1966 to 4.7 percent in 1968 to 5.5 percent in 1970.[35] For a country that thought of inflation as something that only happened "down there" (in South America), these numbers were traumatizing. Long-term government yields, which, in the not-too-distant past donned a "2" as the first digit, rose from 4.5 percent in 1966 to 6.0 percent in 1968 to 6.9 percent in 1969.[36]

The various government outposts were at a loss. Arthur Okun, President Johnson's Council of Economic Advisers chairman, found rising rates to be "disastrous and shocking."[37] Former CEA Chairman Walter Heller, in fear that "the theoretical basis for the 'new economics' would be jeopardized," wanted to increase taxes.[38] Heller argued that Lyndon Johnson needed to employ "the full use of the weapons of modern economics."[39] Economists are not reluctant to test their failing theories on entire populations.

Meanwhile, the Federal Reserve fought a pitched battle between the traditionalists and the econometricians. The latter wanted the Fed to act on predictions that were mathematically modeled by the new generation of Ph.D.s. But Fed Chairman Martin was dead set against predicting the money supply, consumption, tax revenue, and other such Keynesian aggregates, dismissing it as "statisticalitis."[40]

However, new Fed board member Sherman Maisel made history

---

[34] Marc Faber, *Gloom, Boom & Doom Report*, June 23, 2003.

[35] Ibbotson Associates, *Stocks, Bonds, Bills and Inflation, 2000 Yearbook, Market Results for 1926–1999*, 2000, p. 226, Table A-15.

[36] Ibid., p. 214, Table A-9.

[37] Bremner, *Chairman of the Fed*, p. 247.

[38] Ibid., pp. 221–222. This was mid-1966.

[39] Ibid., p. 221.

[40] Ibid., p. 269.

twice. First, he was the first academic economist to be appointed to the board since 1914.[41] Second, he pushed for (and received) board approval for model-driven decisions.

Martin lost this battle to modernism. Statisticalitis was coming to dominate every field, from political science to baseball. The Federal Reserve Open Market Committee (FOMC) would soon provide a shuttle service for academics testing their latest chalkboard theories. In 1968, the academics' machines predicted that tighter fiscal policy would slow consumer spending. Instead, consumers spent more, and economic growth shot north of 10 percent.

Yet despite such on-the-pavement evidence, the econometricians decided that the people were wrong and their machines were right. The staff warned: "It is imperative to distinguish temporary aberrations from developments of longer lasting significance."[42] With a genuflection to the machines, the Fed watched inflation skyrocket into the close of William McChesney Martin's term of office as Fed chairman. A lame duck after Nixon's election, he warned the new chief executive: "Mr. President, I have been fooled too many times by statistics. The momentum of inflation was stopped in mid-summer, but the psychology of inflation has accelerated again.[43] In 1969, wage settlements called for 30 to 35 percent increases over a three-year contract period.[44]

WILLIAM MCCHESNEY MARTIN'S PARTING SELF-EVALUATION: "I'VE FAILED"

On February 1, 1970, Arthur Burns was sworn in as the new Federal Reserve chairman. At William McChesney Martin's final Federal Open Market Committee meeting, the departing chairman offered a self-assessment: "I've failed."[45] But Martin had been fighting a battle that no human being could win. In any case, he should be complimented

---

[41] Ibid., p. 200.
[42] Ibid., p. 254.
[43] Ibid., p. 272.
[44] Ibid., p. 275.
[45] Ibid., p. 277.

for his persistent warnings and understanding of inflation throughout his term.

Martin told his farewell dinner gathering at the White House: "I wish I could turn the bank over to Arthur Burns as I would have liked. But we are in very deep trouble. We are in the wildest inflation since the Civil War."[46] After that climactic finale, a troop of singers and dancers burst into the room to stage the evening's entertainment: "The Decline and Fall of the Entire World as Seen through the Eyes of Cole Porter."[47]

On August 15, 1971, President Nixon announced the United States's unilateral decision to no longer pay gold to foreign governments for dollars. He blamed speculators.[48] He did not give blame where it was due: to the American people and, perhaps foremost, to the decision makers in the Oval Office, who had done a bang-up job of destroying the Bretton Woods agreement. At no time did Nixon acknowledge that the United States had committed the shameful act of default. Nixon also used this opportunity to place wage and price controls on practically every American. The land of the free and the brave was looking anything but. Most Americans were in favor of this initiative by the government—the same government that had shown neither the knowledge nor the backbone to avoid the financial chaos that now engulfed the free world.

From $35 an ounce (when redeemable with the U.S. government), gold rose to more than $800 an ounce within a decade, and holding paper assets was an easy way to lose a life's savings. Commodities, rare stamps, and Rembrandts were the assets to hold during the 1970s. Americans abroad found that Italian and Belgian hotels would not accept dollars. The annual inflation rate of goods (the CPI: Consumer Price Index) rose to 18 percent, short-term Treasury bills traded at 17 percent; and the 30-year bond yielded 15.6 percent.

---

[46] Ibid., p. 276.

[47] Ibid., p. 277.

[48] William Greider, *Secrets of the Temple: How the Federal Reserve Runs the Country* (New York: Simon and Schuster, 1987), p. 337.

GREENSPAN EXPANDS HIS ROLODEX

The American public was at sea. It didn't know what was coming next, so it turned to economists for answers. One who soon acquired national attention was Alan Greenspan.

Time magazine organized an illustrious Board of Economists that met four times a year. Alan Greenspan joined in 1971. He now had the opportunity to develop kinships with other members, including Otto Eckstein [formerly a member of President Johnson's Council of Economic Advisers (CEA)], Walter Heller (former chairman of the CEA), Arthur Okun (former chairman of the CEA), Beryl Sprinkel (future CEA chairman during the Reagan administration), and Robert Triffin (early forecaster of the Bretton Woods disaster). Greenspan would remain on the board until his turn as chairman of the Federal Reserve began in 1987, with the exception of his CEA years. These administration officials would come in handy during the Reagan presidency.

By 1973, Greenspan was regularly appearing in public, at least where it mattered: in the pages of the *New York Times*. He was photographed with "10 leading business and academic economists" in the January 2, 1973, issue. The group included Murray Weidenbaum, a professor of economics at Washington University who would become Nixon's assistant secretary of the treasury for economic policy and later President Reagan's first chairman of the CEA, and Albert Rees, chairman of Princeton University's department of economics. Rees had served as assistant professor of economics with Milton Friedman at the University of Chicago, where he wrote an important monograph with George Shultz when Shultz was dean of Chicago's Graduate School of Business. After serving as secretary of labor from 1969 to 1970, Schultz directed the Office of Management and Budget from 1970 to 1972, moved to head the Treasury Department from 1972 to 1974, and later was Reagan's secretary of state from 1982 to 1989. Shultz's launching pad had been his apprenticeship as senior staff economist to Arthur Burns at the CEA.[49] Clearly, the pattern of familiar faces rising up the economic stepladder was well established. Also, the

---

[49] Bremner, *Chairman of the Fed*, p. 267.

tendency to hand national policy to economists was more pronounced. This vetting of candidates for senior posts successfully relieved the pool of eccentric dispositions.

JANUARY 1973: "IT'S VERY RARE THAT YOU CAN BE AS UNQUALIFIEDLY BULLISH AS YOU CAN NOW"

On January 7, 1973, Greenspan's picture again appeared in the *Times* among a group of market forecasters, where he was described as "highly optimistic." He announced: "It's very rare that you can be as unqualifiedly bullish as you can now." The Dow Jones Industrial Average peaked at 1,051 four days later and bottomed at 571 on December 12, 1974—a loss of 46 percent during a period when the dollar lost 21 percent of its value against consumer prices.

Greenspan's inaccuracy was not important. The other economists quoted also missed the bust (although Greenspan's enthusiasm was singularly inept). His portrait was where it belonged. It is curious, though, that the man who could be counted on to give the *Times* a bearish, or at least highly qualified, stock market forecast in the 1960s was now a cheerleader when the market was highly speculative, as was the economy.

Doubts about the stock market were not hard to come by. Shortly after Greenspan's unqualifiedly bullish call, *Time* magazine discussed a chaotic series of "devaluations, revaluations and [currency] floats [that had] been coming with dizzying rapidity."[50] Living costs rose 8.8 percent in the first quarter of 1973.[51] This report prompted AFL-CIO chief George Meany to announce: "In his Inaugural Address in January, the President [Nixon] advised Americans to help themselves. It is obvious that this is what unions are going to be forced to do at the bargaining table."[52] One suspects that this was not the spirit in which the president's advice was intended, but it is difficult to fault Meany, even though successful negotiations by steelworkers, autoworkers, and airline mechanics were to reduce these industries to minor-league status. As Meany

---

[50] "The Winners and Losers from Devaluation," *Time*, February 26, 1973.
[51] "Perils of a Breakneck Boom," *Time*, April 30, 1973.
[52] Ibid.

(and Greenspan) undoubtedly knew—and *Time* reported: "[M]anufacturers decided long ago to serve foreign markets by building plants overseas rather than by exporting. The multinational corporations will profit from devaluation."[53] Federal Reserve Chairman Martin warned of "extravagance, incompetency and inefficiency" in the 1950s.[54] Ever since, the costs of production had been pricing heavy industry out of the domestic market.

Not that the presiding Fed chairman, Arthur Burns, was in the mood to lecture in such a manner. The surging inflation of 1973 was a component of Burns's decision to open the floodgates of new money in early 1972. That was an election year, and Nixon appreciated the support of his independent monetary shop, although he may have had second thoughts by 1973.

There is generally a lag between a looser Fed monetary policy and when it affects the economy. The Consumer Price Index rose 3.4 percent in 1972 and 8.8 percent in 1973.[55]

In April 1973, "Inflationary psychology [was] prodding people to buy all sorts of goods before the prices [went] up further."[56] *Time* reported that shortages of rubber, silver, aluminum, copper, and lead were frustrating producers. Nixon wanted to sell materials from stockpiles to meet demand. Competitive American businessmen could accomplish much by "speculation." A U.S. executive "may enclose a check with his order rather than wait until the steel is delivered and the dollar's value may have fallen."[57] By August, "many would-be house buyers simply [could] not get mortgage loans," and "[i]nflation and shortages are turning some people to crime. Supermarkets are reporting rising thefts from meat counters: often a shopper will stuff a couple of steaks under his belt.... Professional thieves are increasingly hijacking meat

---

[53] "Winners and Losers from Devaluation."

[54] Bremner, *Chairman of the Fed*, p. 132; Martin, testimony to Senate Finance Committee Hearings, April 22, 1958.

[55] Ibbotson Associates, *Stocks, Bonds, Bills and Inflation, 2000 Yearbook*, p. 226, Table A-15.

[56] "Perils of a Breakneck Boom."

[57] "Winners and Losers from Devaluation."

trucks."[58] California forest rangers tried to control the illegal hunting of deer, bear, and elk. In retaliation, park warden Kenneth Patrick was shot dead, with two darts from a crossbow through his chest.[59] False rumors of a rice shortage found frantic Californians dragging 50-pound bags of rice from supermarkets to their cars.[60] Shortages were not limited to food. "Newsprint, baling wire, tallow, sawdust, blue jeans, even toilets" were hard to come by. *Time* devoted a good portion of its news coverage to the inflation and to economic problems. Chicago housewife Jean Salmon told *Time*, "I don't understand what's happening. It seems to me that when one raises his prices, the other raises his in turn. It's a vicious cycle."[61] The old were particularly ill equipped in such circumstances. *Time* reported an elderly woman with a shopping basket full of cat food. She admitted to the supermarket cashier, "I'm the cat."[62]

Naturally, *Time* asked its Board of Economists for clarification of what was happening. Alan Greenspan did not have much to offer. In April 1973, he declared: "To slow this type of inflation requires strong action, and it is difficult to do that without tilting the economy down."[63] One suspects that Chicago housewife Jean Salmon could have told us as much.

Time's anonymous staff writers told us more. In February 1973, the magazine published a 4,579-word article in which the story of our times was stated clearly in a mere 24 words: "The root cause of dollar weakness is that ever since the early 1950s, the U.S. has been living beyond its means in the world."[64]

Greenspan's forbearance was noteworthy. In a search through the archives, the author of "Gold and Economic Freedom" did not say, "I told you so" (at least, not in a major newspaper or magazine). Nor, did he mention the word *gold* or discuss the inflationary consequences of the

---

[58] "The Gut Issue: Prices Running Amuck," *Time*, August 27, 1973.

[59] Ibid.

[60] Ibid.

[61] Ibid.

[62] Ibid.

[63] "Perils of a Breakneck Boom."

[64] "Winners and Losers from Devaluation."

Nixon administration's policies. He did not stick up for the little guy and instruct the nation—which was badly in need of sound instruction—that "deficit spending is simply a scheme for the confiscation of wealth" and that "this is the shabby secret of welfare statists' tirades against gold."[65]

Having demonstrated his tact, Alan Greenspan was a top candidate for a government job.

---

[65] Alan Greenspan, "Gold and Economic Freedom," in Ayn Rand, *Capitalism: The Unknown Ideal* (New York: Signet, 1967), p. 96.

4

PRESIDENT FORD'S COUNCIL OF ECONOMIC ADVISERS

1973–1976

I pretended to be somebody I wanted to be and I finally became that person. Or he became me. Or we met at some point.[1]

—Cary Grant

In 1973, Greenspan was nominated to head the President's Council of Economic Advisers. He was fortunate that Nixon's presidency disintegrated before his confirmation hearings in 1974. Whether fair or not, remnants of the Nixon administration operated under a cloud of public consternation, but the newcomers were accorded some leniency. Although Gerald Ford was under no obligation to stand by his predecessor's nominations, he decided to proceed with Greenspan's.

Greenspan phrased his detour into government service as a duty ("I could have a real effect"). He was, however, now pledging his allegiance to the administration that had dropped the gold standard. His 1966 "Gold and Economic Freedom" article read like it was written by a martinet preparing to lead a peasants' revolt. Now he was conspiring with the enemy.

---

[1] Benjamin Schwarz, "Becoming Cary Grant," *Atlantic*, January/February 2007.

THE 1970S: THE FEDERAL RESERVE AND INFLATION

As Greenspan was well aware, his pipe-smoking mentor Arthur Burns had contributed mightily to the confiscation of private wealth. Before the Joint Economic Committee in February 1972, Burns intoned that unbalancing the budget by $40 billion only "gives me some pause."[2] It was on the first day of Alan Greenspan's doctoral training at Columbia University when the professor harrumphed: "Excess government spending causes inflation."[3]

In 1970, Greenspan had explained why this is so. He told the *Times* that higher budget deficits "would force the Federal Reserve 'to at least partially accommodate, through money-supply growth, the flood of new issues emerging from the Treasury.' The cost of such actions, [Greenspan] contended 'could be devastating in terms of inflation.'"[4] Back when he spoke his own mind, Arthur Burns would have been hard pressed to offer a more lucid description.

In 1972, the monetary base grew by 10.4 percent. What banks receive, banks lend. President Nixon was reelected, but at quite a cost. (In Burns's defense, some of those close to the situation think that "honest mistakes" rather than political manipulation lay behind the Fed's zeal.)[5]

In 1973, the Fed increased the monetary base by only 2.4 percent, but credit was spilling into the economy. As mentioned in the previous chapter, there is usually a lag before the rise in money fills the channels of credit. The consumer price index rose from 3.4 percent in 1972 to 8.8 percent in 1973 to 12.2 percent in 1974.[6]

---

[2] Richard H. Timberlake, *Monetary Policy in the United States: An Intellectual and Institutional History* (Chicago: University of Chicago Press, 1993), p. 341.

[3] Justin Martin, *Greenspan: The Man behind Money* (Cambridge, Mass.: Perseus, 2000), p. 29.

[4] Thomas E. Mullaney, "Voters Will Assess Nixon's Game Plan to Revive Economy," *New York Times*, November 1, 1970, p. 139.

[5] William Greider, *Secrets of the Temple: How the Federal Reserve Runs the Country* (New York: Simon and Schuster, 1987), p. 67.

[6] Ibbotson Associates, *Stocks, Bonds, Bills and Inflation, 2000 Yearbook, Market Results for 1926–1999*, 2000, p. 226, Table A-15.

HOW THE UNITED STATES INFLATED THE WORLD

After the United States discarded the gold standard, the dollar remained the world's reserve currency. Trade around the world was still conducted in dollars even though it had depreciated against most currencies. This created havoc. Exporters to the United States received the depreciated dollars for their goods. OPEC (the Organization of Petroleum Exporting Countries), an exporter of oil to the United States, received less value for each gallon of oil exported. (The dollar fell about 50 percent against other currencies during the 1970s. This varied, depending on the foreign currency, and requires many qualifications.) Since OPEC could buy fewer goods for each gallon of oil sold, it wanted more dollars for the exchange.

Another example, the trade loop between the United States and Germany, presented a similar problem for Volkswagen. When an American bought a Volkswagen, the dollars wound their way to Volkswagen's headquarters in Germany. (This is a hypothetical case, with no knowledge of how Volkswagen operated.) The automobile manufacturer did not want dollars. It shipped them to the German central bank (the Bundesbank). In return, Volkswagen received deutschmarks at the appropriate exchange rate.

Americans were spending much more abroad than at home. Since dollars in circulation in Europe were rising in relation to deutschmarks spent on goods from the United States, cars from abroad cost more: Americans were paying for goods with less valuable dollars. The German government did not want its exporters to suffer. The Bundesbank's dollar-deutschmark transaction with Volkswagen increased the German money supply. This slowed the rise of the deutschmark's value against the dollar, but also increased German domestic inflation. In fact, the excess dollars led to inflation around the world.

This flood of dollars led to price inflation in the 1970s. More recently, the flood of dollars has led to asset inflation, including the worldwide housing bubble. This relationship will be discussed again in Chapter 24.

THE FEDERAL RESERVE'S INFLATION CALCULATIONS

Arthur Burns followed the most expeditious route to tame inflation: changing how the measure was calculated. Stephen Roach was a young economist at the Federal Reserve.[7] After oil prices quadrupled, Arthur Burns instructed his staff to calculate a CPI stripped of energy costs. Burns's rationale was the blazing Yom Kippur War, over which the Fed had no control.[8] Why the Federal Reserve's influence should matter in how the rate of consumer price inflation is calculated could be better understood by reading memoirs of the Nixon administration than by studying Arthur Burns's seminal textbook, *Measuring Business Cycles*.

Roach recalls: "Alas, it didn't turn out to be quite that simple." Burns thought the disappearance of anchovies off the Peruvian coast caused food costs to rise. They too were removed from the price index.[9] Next went used cars, children's toys, jewelry, and housing—about half the costs that consumers absorbed in their daily struggle with rising prices.[10]

Today, three decades after the anchovy shortage, without much ado from the economics guild, the media announces the monthly ex-food, ex-energy CPI, produced by the Bureau of Labor Statistics. This gently rising CPI—a charade—has compounded at a much lower rate than the true costs paid by Americans. This is one reason the collapse in living standards among the lower half remains a mystery to those who trust government press releases and the media that report them.

The science of economics as applied to national statistics was (and is) more a confiscation of the truth than a midwife to it. Incumbent and future politicians, including future Fed chairman Greenspan, introduced and nurtured such hullabaloo as "hedonics" and the "birth-death rate" in the highly publicized but little understood calculations of economic growth rates and unemployment numbers. The figures were a disgrace, and so were the parties responsible for their introduction and dissemination. Greenspan's turn at the Council of Economic Advisers was to be a screen test for a future role in the charade, a dress rehearsal for his political, acting, and dissembling talents, the inestimable qualities needed by a Fed chairman in an economy that was rocketing off its moorings.

---

[7] Roach would be chief economist at Morgan Stanley during the Greenspan years, where he used his bully pulpit to decry the Greenspan legend.

[8] *Grant's Interest Rate Observer*, July 21, 2000, p. 1.

[9] Ibid. *Grant's* quotes taken from Stephen Roach, "The Ghost of Arthur Burns," *Global: Daily Economic Comment*, Morgan Stanley, June 26, 2000.

[10] "A Nasty Whiff of Inflation," *Economist*, September 24, 2005, p. 85.

In any case, numbers cannot capture inflation. Inflation generally works hand in hand with deterioration. What was money buying?

In a 1966 Lou Harris poll, 75 percent of respondents thought that American goods were of "good" or "excellent" quality. By 1977, this had fallen to 47 percent.[11] A poll conducted by the University of Michigan in 1977 found that only 27 percent of American workers would buy the products they made.[12] Absences at Ford and General Motors had risen steadily during the 1960s, then spiked upward in 1969 and 1970. By 1970, 5 percent of General Motors's workers went fishing on any given day; more than 10 percent played hooky on Mondays and Fridays. The overpaid and disgruntled workers took to sabotaging the cars. *Fortune* magazine found that "screws have been left in brake drums, tool handles welded into fender compartments (to cause mysterious, unfindable and eternal rattles), paint scratched, and upholstery cut."[13]

At the same time, Americans were thinking big. The average size of a new house in the United States was 953 square feet in 1950; by 1970, it was 1,500 square feet. In 1950, 66 percent of new houses had two or fewer bedrooms; by 1970, that had dropped to 13 percent.[14] Americans wanted more. The "bigger is better" trend leads to other questions: if less had been OK, would oil prices and shortages have made headline news in the 1970s?

MR. GREENSPAN ESCAPES FROM NEW YORK

Greenspan's Washington tour may have been a welcome opportunity to escape New York—he was one of more than 1.1 million New Yorkers who emigrated from the city in the early 1970s.[15] Many companies fled the cities for less expensive headquarters, reversing the trend that had begun in the 1950s. By 1960, New York was the world's financial capital,

---

[11] David Frum, *How We Got Here: The 70's; The Decade That Brought You Modern Life (for Better or Worse)* (New York: Basic Books, 2000), p. 25.

[12] Ibid.

[13] Ibid., p. 21.

[14] National Association of Homebuilders; www.nahb.org; Source: U.S. Census Bureau, Table C-25.

[15] Robert A.M.Stern, Thomas Mellins, and David Fishman, *New York 1960: Architecture and Urbanism between the Second World War and the Bicentennial* (New York: Monacelli: Press, 1995), p. 32.

and much of the building over the next decade was to accommodate finance.[16] But between 1968 and 1970, 18 major corporations left New York and 14 more announced plans to leave.[17] The wave was just beginning. The financial companies generally remained in New York City. They could afford to.

Life in New York is often an exaggeration and distortion of life across America. But the texts and subtexts wearing down the nation's largest city were to define the retrenchment that evolved across America through the new millennium: production in decline; fancy finance to the forefront; the ascendancy of showbiz; the perpetual craving for entertainment and shopping; sloppy workmanship; quantity over quality; less tangible and more insecure jobs in increasingly cramped, colorless, and utilitarian offices; the rush to the suburbs for a more comfortable and affordable life, then to the exurbs when the suburbs compromised these ambitions; and the requisite obsession to make money fast enough to stay on the treadmill. By the mid-1970s, New York resembled a third-world capital, like Johannesburg or Rio, with some rich and more poor and with tension arising from transit strikes, garbage strikes, and newspaper strikes.

MR. GREENSPAN GOES TO WASHINGTON

It was Alan Greenspan's turn at bat. On August 8, 1974, he appeared before the Senate Banking Committee. (This happened to be the same day Richard Nixon announced his resignation from office.) Greenspan's Council of Economic Advisers grilling was unremarkable other than over 40 minutes of questioning by Senator William Proxmire, during which the senator "let rip."[18] Proxmire voted against Greenspan's nomination.

By the time Greenspan moved to Washington, "stagflation" (inflation and recession at the same time) was gripping the country. To read the press of the day, Greenspan was magnificent. Whatever the case, his true brilliance was managing his image. He received lengthy profiles in *BusinessWeek* and the *New York Times Magazine*. By early 1975, a "top White House official" told *BusinessWeek*, "Greenspan has a unique personal

---

[16] Ibid., p. 62.
[17] Ibid., p. 65.
[18] Martin, *Greenspan*, pp. 91–93.

relationship with the President. Alan was the only top aide to spend the entire time [at Gerald Ford's retreat] in Palm Springs during the Easter vacation."[19] The official went on to say that "[on] economic policy, Alan is a heavyweight."[20] This was high praise—especially since he didn't hold a position with tangible responsibility. According to the *BusinessWeek* profile: "Greenspan spends much of his time screening economic information to determine what gets to the President, and the quality of the material is considered 'first rate' by White House insiders."[21]

The insiders' judgment may have been sincere, but the CEA director's performance is difficult to evaluate. For instance, Greenspan's aptitude achieved a pinnacle in a November 1974 *New Yorker* analysis, in which the magazine claimed that "economists of all persuasions (with the exception of Alan Greenspan, an Ayn Rand disciple, who heads the President's Council of Economic Advisers) admit to being baffled by today's problems, the answers to which are not to be found in textbooks or in historical precedents."[22] The logic seems to run that since Greenspan was trained by Rand, he understood all. What "all" might comprise is not divulged by the *New Yorker* and apparently not by Greenspan, since the befuddled remained so.

BusinessWeek readers learned that "Greenspan's special skill as an economist is his ability to quickly recognize the changes occurring in the economy, to understand their significance, and to make the necessary adjustment. Such skills, which Greenspan honed to a fine edge as private consultant to the top executives of about 100 of the country's biggest corporations, were particularly important in recent months when the economy was collapsing with bewildering speed."[23] From the same story, Greenspan "emerged as the economist Gerald Ford listen[ed] to most often. He [had] done this through a combination of integrity, charm, pragmatism and just plain brains."[24] One might think Greenspan wrote the article himself.

---

[19] "Soft-Sell Charm," *BusinessWeek*, April 28, 1975, p. 2.

[20] Ibid.

[21] Ibid.

[22] Richard H. Rovere, "Letter from Washington," *New Yorker*, November 4, 1974, p. 170.

[23] "Soft-Sell Charm."

[24] Ibid.

Confirmation of his skills flowed from all quarters. Richard Cheney was President Ford's chief of staff. He claimed that the president attached "more weight to Greenspan's views than to those of any other among his economic advisers."[25] Yet the public record calls Greenspan's skills as an economist into question. On September 5, 1974, the day after he was sworn in as CEA chairman, Greenspan announced: "We are not about to get a dramatic decrease in economic activity."[26] With this knowledge, he urged President Ford to propose a tax surcharge—an effort to halt inflation. This was exactly the wrong time for such a tactic (which was passed into legislation). The economy contracted 5.8 percent from mid-1975 though.[27] (It probably goes without saying that raising taxes for any reason was anti-Randian.)

In April of 1975, at the time *BusinessWeek's* glowing profile was published, Greenspan pronounced to a New York audience that the worst was yet to come, when, in fact, the worst had passed.[28] According to the National Bureau of Economic Research, the recession ended in March of 1975.

Taking together Greenspan's January 7, 1973, advice that "[i]t's very rare that you can be as unqualifiedly bullish as you can now" (stated four days before the stock market commenced its 46 percent plunge) and his prediction that the worst was yet to come in April 1975 (when it had ended during his shuttle flight to New York), his public declarations validate the opinions of his former (and future) clients who found him so unenlightening.

In the fall of 1974, Greenspan was involved in the "Whip Inflation Now" marketing campaign. Participants wore WIN buttons to battle a foe that had already, at least temporarily, diminished as the leading economic problem.[29] (Consumer price inflation fell 90 percent from the fourth quarter of 1974 to the first quarter of 1975.[30])

---

[25] Joseph Kraft, "Right, for Ford," *New York Times Magazine*, April 25, 1976.

[26] Ibid.

[27] Ibid., growth rate of −5.8 percent from David E. Runkle, "Revisionist History: How Data Revisions Distort Economic Policy Research," *Federal Reserve Bank of Minneapolis Quarterly Review*, Fall 1998, pp. 3–12.

[28] Kraft, "Right, for Ford."

[29] In his autobiography, Greenspan claims the WIN Compaign was "unbelievably stupid." This was a surprise to some who remember a highly engaged CEA adviser.

[30] Ibbotson Associates, *Stocks, Bonds, Bills and Inflation, 2000 Yearbook, Market Results for 1926–1999*, 2000, p. 226, Table A-15.

In the spring of 1975 Greenspan backed a tax cut. The man who pontificated against government's ability to adjust economic policy had now proposed both a tax *increase* and a *decrease* within six months—to calibrate the economy. If Ayn Rand was watching, she may have thought she was back in the country from which she had escaped—the Soviet Union.

In 1975, *BusinessWeek* noted that "Greenspan has a reputation for being able to get along with just about everybody, including those with whom he may have serious differences.... This combination of charm and solid analytical skill" has given Greenspan the ability to capture "the ear [and possibly] the mind of the President."[31] L. William Seidman, a senior aide to Ford when he was vice president, may have understood the strange dynamic best—that Greenspan was aloof yet cordial: "He has the best bedside manner I've ever seen. He's very non-confrontational, but also very good at persuading people. Part of his mystique, I think, is he's hard to understand, but that also gives him a certain genius aspect."[32] Seidman interviewed Greenspan prior to the CEA offer: "He assured me he was pure economist and not politician. It turned out he was a better politician than any of us thought."[33]

GREENSPAN IN HOLLYWOOD

In a lengthy *New York Times* profile, Joseph Kraft described a typical day in the life of a CEA chairman: "He spends about as much time in the White House as he does in his council offices, once acknowledging that even swearing-in affairs at the White House were useful because they provided one a chance to be close to the President."[34] And a chance to impress new members of the administration with his integrity, charm, and brains.

By the 1970s, politics and publicity were merging. Washington drifted toward the rhetoric of Hollywood. *People* magazine was launched in 1974 and immediately poached *Time* magazine's readers. This was no surprise to the latter. *People* was published by Time Inc. as a spin-off from the "People" page in *Time*. The parent company pledged to "[get]

---

[31] "Soft-Sell Charm".

[32] John Cassidy, "The Fountainhead," *New Yorker*, April 24, 2000, p. 173.

[33] Ibid., p. 172. Seidman was later head of the Federal Deposit Insurance Corporation and the Resolution Trust Company, and was a commentator on CNBC.

[34] Kraft, "Right, for Ford."

back to the people who are causing the news and who are caught up in it, or deserve to be in it. Our focus is on people, not issues."[35] Participants in national issues understood that their public image was becoming as important as—maybe more important than—the policies themselves. A drawing of Secretary of State Henry Kissinger on the April 1, 1974, cover of *Time* is laid out under the title: "How Henry Does It." The very first paragraph in the cover story notes that he had "the unmistakable aura of a true celebrity" when recently in Moscow. *Time* noted, "Arab sheiks [are] fascinated ... by the machismo image of his well-publicized dates with actresses Jill St. John and Marlo Thomas."[36] Subscribers to *Time* may have wondered if they received the wrong magazine.

Greenspan's "bedside manner" went a long way in fulfilling his successful tenure at the CEA. Washington politics is chock-full of egotists, exhibitionists, dramatists, and ladder climbers. To most such domineering characters, the CEA chairman's demeanor looked inauspicious. Joseph Kraft wrote: "Everyone who has worked with Greenspan seems struck by his lack of ego, his unconcern with machismo, his disposition to emphasize his subject more than himself. Precisely because of his lack of pretension, hardly anyone has any difficulties working with him."[37]

Precisely because he appeared beneath competition, Greenspan successfully controlled situations that were well outside the CEA's authority. For example, he worked wonders in coordinating the administration's 1975 grain deal with the Soviet Union. The departments of State, Treasury, and Agriculture were the responsible parties. Secretaries Henry Kissinger (State), William Simon (Treasury) and Earl Butz (Agriculture) were strong-willed men. Nevertheless, Greenspan maneuvered himself into a negotiating role, and the Soviet grain deal of 1975 was struck: "[A] far better one than the 1972 agreement, which drove prices up."[38] This, at least, was the opinion Alan Greenspan stated to the *New York Times*; according to the *Times*, Greenspan took no credit for himself.[39]

---

[35] *Time*, March 1974.
[36] "Superstar Statecraft: How Henry Does It," *Time*, April 1, 1974.
[37] Kraft, "Right, for Ford."
[38] Ibid.
[39] Ibid.

MAGAZINE COVERS AND THE PARTY CIRCUIT

In 1975, Greenspan shone from the front cover of *Newsweek*, the first time an economist was thus celebrated. Other 1975 honorees included Jimmy Hoffa, Patty Hearst—and Henry Kissinger.[40] The publicity industry hounded Greenspan. Autograph seekers mailed him copies of the magazine to sign. (He obliged.) *Penthouse* asked for an interview. (He declined.)[41]

When he was not evading *Penthouse*, the chairman hit the party circuit. It appears this was difficult for him. The *Washington Post* social columnist labeled him a "social creeper": he "creeps through the most densely populated islands of a room saying, 'Pardon.'"[42] Whatever embarrassment Greenspan may have suffered, he persevered, and he might have echoed Cary Grant's self-analysis: "I pretended to be somebody I wanted to be and I finally became that person. Or he became me. Or we met at some point." Despite his hesitancy, he did the right thing and dated Barbara Walters, the television hostess to the good and the great. This gave him cachet in the social columns. He would later date Susan Mills in the 1980s, a producer for the *MacNeil-Lehrer Newshour*, and then married Andrea Mitchell, a political correspondent on NBC television.

After Ford lost the 1976 presidential race to Jimmy Carter, Greenspan wasted no time getting out of Washington. He caught the noon shuttle back to New York the day of President Carter's inauguration.

---

[40] Martin, *Greenspan*, p. 127.
[41] Ibid.
[42] Kraft, "Right, for Ford."

5

THE 1980 PRESIDENTIAL ELECTION: BOOSTING CARTER, REAGAN, AND KENNEDY

1976–1980

Alan Greenspan, the economist, has asserted that the translation of home-ownership equity into cash available for consumer spending is perhaps the most significant reason why the economy in 1975-1978 was consistently stronger than expected.[1]

—New York Times, February 17, 1980

As Jimmy Carter delivered his inauguration address in 1977, Greenspan resumed his publicity campaign. He also received his Ph.D. in economics from New York University in 1977. He did so under the tutelage of his former classmate, Bob Kavesh, who was now a professor at NYU. Greenspan's dissertation was peculiar. According to Jeff Madrick, writing in the *New York Review of Books*: "[H]e did not complete a conventional dissertation. Instead, he submitted published articles and other writings, some of them for publications such as *Business Economics*, which would not have met the scholarly standards for most economic

---

[1] John H. Allan, "Thrift Adrift: Why Nobody Saves," *New York Times*, February 17, 1980, p. 4.

departments."[2] Traditionally, scholarship is available to the public; however, NYU has not released Greenspan's work.[3]

The Ph.D. might or might not have aided his consulting business, but Greenspan knew it would be an asset if he were to be considered for a senior government position—such as Federal Reserve chairman. His personal relations with the press and with members of the Ford administration gave him an insider's edge, and he understood the value of constant publicity. Thus, he hired the Harry Walker Agency to line up speaking engagements. Greenspan spoke roughly once a week, for compensation ranging from $10,000 to $40,000.[4] This is an impressive fee, even today. Greenspan received glowing tributes from the press. One reason for this was his courtship: an editor of *BusinessWeek* complimented the overworked economist by saying, "No matter what he was doing, you could get him instantly."[5]

On August 16, 1977, a momentous event occurred that attested to the farsightedness of Greenspan's non-academic route to the top of his profession. Elvis Presley died. His passing caused a national ruckus. Many believed it was a hoax; some still do. "Elvis sightings" were reported by the thousands. Long before he died, Elvis ceased to exist as a person and was reincarnated into a transcendent symbol. "Elvis imitators" stumbled through their acts across America to susceptible and lachrymose audiences. They couldn't sing like Elvis but that didn't matter. This new industry embodied the image of Elvis. Likewise, the capabilities of Alan Greenspan as an economist were now transcendent; they were above examination by the press or public. He now played the role of Alan Greenspan, celebrity economist. He would never relinquish that perch.

Greenspan reassumed his position inside the womb of the press as a member of *Time* magazine's Board of Economists. The group included familiar names: Otto Eckstein, Beryl Sprinkel, Murray Weidenbaum,

---

[2] Jeff Madrick, "Mr. Fixit," *New York Review of Books*, 48, no. 12, July 19, 2001.

[3] Justin Martin, *Greenspan: The Man behind Money* (Cambridge, Mass.: Perseus, 2000), p. 138. See also: Jeff Madrick, "Mr. Fixit."

[4] Ibid., pp. 139, 276.

[5] Ibid.

Walter Heller, and Arthur Okun.[6] This was not a roll call of enlightenment. Since the solution to overindulgence was politically unpalatable, economists ignored the explosion in the fireplace and instead swatted the flies on the mantelpiece.

Charles Schultze was President Carter's chairman of the Counsel of Economic Advisers. Schultze had been director of the Bureau of the Budget during the Johnson administration. He was now on furlough from the Brookings Institution. *Time* reckoned that Schultze should steer away from the mistakes that Herbert Stein had made during his tenure at the CEA. (Stein had preceded Greenspan as chairman.) Stein "arouse[d] suspicion that politics was warping his professional judgment." The magazine offered Schultze a role model: "Alan Greenspan restored the CEA's professional respectability largely by staying out of the public eye and talking primarily to President Ford."[7] Greenspan's self-effacement proved so counterintuitive that his brand of personal publicity was continually mistaken for an absence of it.

An interview with the *New York Times* in April 1977 served to integrate the returning consultant to his hometown. Leonard Silk asked if, after "the intimate and influential relationship" he enjoyed with President Ford, Greenspan suffered "decompression pains on his return to New York." The former public servant responded, "Surprisingly few.... I haven't fundamentally changed what I am doing." This was true—the reader may not have appreciated how true.

Greenspan went on to contrast himself with former Ford aides who might find themselves adrift: "Of course, if power interests you, you would miss the change.... [M]y professional work interests me more."[8] He went on to tell Silk his initial belief that for the CEA chairman, avoiding public exposure was an error: "It is essential not to go

---

[6] "Prescriptions for a Drastic Program," *Time*, February 21, 1977. Others were Paul McCracken, chairman of the Counsel of Economic Advisers under Nixon; Robert Nathan; and Joseph Pechman.

[7] "A Starring Role for the CEA?" *Time*, February 7, 1977.

[8] Leonard Silk, "Greenspan, White House Days Behind, Picks Up as Before" *New York Times*, April 28, 1977.

completely underground.... I ought to join regular White House brief-
ings, for sheer technical reasons."[9] Silk apparently did not ask for what
technical reasons Greenspan found that "even swearing-in affairs at the
White House were useful because they provided one a chance to be close
to the President."[10]

THE CARTER YEARS: AN ECONOMY IN DECLINE

The Carter presidency may have done more to further Alan Greenspan's
rise than all his weekly speeches and exposure in *Time*. Carter was
encumbered by policies that the best minds had instituted earlier in the
decade. The break from the gold standard unleashed economic theories
that had scrimmaged on college blackboards for decades. With currencies no longer fixed to the price of gold, economic theory claimed that
the United States needed to devalue the dollar to compete with overseas
producers. The consequent cheaper dollar—in theory—would make
U.S. products less expensive abroad.

The dreary result may be summed up by reviewing the relative fortunes of domestic and foreign car producers across the decade: the
Carter administration bailed Chrysler out of a looming bankruptcy.
By 1980, 25 percent of auto sales in the United States were imports.[11] In
1950, only 500,000 automobiles were produced outside of the country
and 4,000,000 in the United States.[12]

The central problem that Carter faced was inflation. The Carter
administration aggravated the situation with larger spending deficits and
a determination to shield Americans from the consequences of higher
prices—when the only solution was to expose Americans to the reckoning for past misdeeds. Government spending and bank credit continued
to expand, delaying the insolvencies of unviable businesses. The budget
deficit reached $59 billion in 1977.[13]

---

[9] Ibid.

[10] Joseph Kraft, "Right, for Ford," *New York Times Magazine*, April 25, 1976.

[11] The Eighties Club, Chapter 5 "Car Wars"; http://eightiesclub.tripod.com/id291.htm.

[12] John Lukacs, *Outgrowing Democracy: A History of the United States in the Twentieth
Century* (Garden City, N.Y.: Doubleday, 1984), p. 110.

[13] White House Office of Management and Budget, Fiscal Year Budget Data, October 15,
2008.

Americans had learned that to stay ahead, or at least keep up, one borrowed to buy and paid later. Inflation passed 16 percent in 1979. The house-swapping frenzy of the 1970s was a precursor to the post-millennium escapade. Despite mortgage rates more than double anything in the past, residential real estate boomed. By 1979, the housing market was a national obsession. House prices had risen 8 percent or more every year since 1970. Prices were up 17.7 percent in the first nine months of 1979—from $50,200 to $57,200.[14] In 1972, membership in the National Association of Realtors first passed 100,000, and it surpassed 435,000 in 1975 (which included a merger with independent salespeople); by 1979, 761,000 Americans were selling houses.[15]

And what did Alan Greenspan make of all this? In the *New York Times*, Greenspan worried that "[p]eople no longer think a mortgage is just something to take out to buy a home. It can be a means of cashing in on your gains."[16] Between 1975 and 1978, home mortgage debt rose from $479 billion to $737 billion—a 53 percent rise. Consumer borrowing rose by 60 percent during the same period.[17]

The American middle class showed signs of fatigue and instability: the higher incidences of drug use, divorce, and single-parent homes were emblematic. A 1979 reading test showed that the reading ability of American college students at the better universities was beneath those of 1928.[18] Teachers and students were remiss. Jacques Barzun wrote "Occupational Disease: Verbal Inflation" in 1978: "How did the public school get to such a pass? The answer is: inflation—not monetary inflation, but intellectual, emotional, social, egotistical inflation. For the last fifty years American Education ... has lived by continual exaggeration of what it is for and what it can do ... Read the top-heavy curriculum plans, the twelve objectives, the twenty-three guidelines, and bring

[14] Karen W. Arenson, "Rise in Home Prices Apparently Slows," *New York Times*, November 13, 1979.

[15] Frederik Heller National Association of Realtors, "The Power of One Million," *Realtor*, May 1, 2004.

[16] Mario A. Milletti, "Inflation's Impact on Homeowners," *New York Times*, January 1, 1978.

[17] Joseph Nocera, "America's Inflation Anxiety," *Worth*, July/August 1994, p. 98.

[18] Lukacs, *Outgrowing Democracy*, p. 190.

to mind the fraudulent slogans with which the profession has gargled during the last two generations."[19] Exaggeration, abstractions, and empty vocabulary whirred through the markets: three decades later, investment managers and trading desks monitored screens while their computers exchanged securities, programmed to trade when certain words and phrases were spoken (or, more likely, shouted) on CNBC, the television network that turned investing into a football game. Alan Greenspan was the prime beneficiary of a time in which empty vocabulary was considered brilliant.

GREENSPAN WAXES NOSTALGIC FOR THE 1950S AND 1960S

Meanwhile, across America, not only were households unable to plan for the future, but the same was true of companies. In 1979, Greenspan wrote a column in the *New York Times*. He waxed nostalgic about the "halcyon days of the 1950's and 1960's" when "business investment decisions seemed appropriately focused on longer-term payoffs." But now, "it is not surprising that in recent years, business capital investments have become increasingly concentrated in assets with quick cash payoffs."

Greenspan calculated that the "[e]xpansion of manufacturing capacity has fallen short of the pattern in earlier business cycles." He thought "more ominous" the "shift in research and development budgets towards quick-payoff 'development' projects."[20]

U.S. News and World Report sounded the alarm in 1978: "The mountain of debt has grown so high in this country that many economists fear the United States is unusually vulnerable if a recession occurs.... The question now being raised is whether a day of reckoning is at hand."[21]

A time of turbulence was ahead, but not a day of reckoning. That would be postponed. In the decades ahead, price inflation would fall,

---

[19] Jacques Barzun, *A Jacques Barzun Reader* (New York: HarperCollins, 2002), pp. 392–393. Originally published in *Begin Here: The Forgotten Conditions of Teaching and Learning*, (Chicago: University of Chicago Press, 199), pp. 101–113.

[20] Alan Greenspan, "Economic Scene," *New York Times*, August 8, 1979.

[21] James Grant, *Money of the Mind: Borrowing and Lending in America from the Civil War to Michael Milken* (New York: Farrar Straus Giroux, 1992), pp. 313–314, quoting from *U.S. News & World Report*, November 20, 1978.

but never disappear. The habits and financial consciousness of the 1970s were here to stay, a consciousness that handcuffed the American imagination to a mosaic of unnecessary and unreasonable desires.

Americans would never again save as they had. Corporations would never revert to long-term capital commitments at home. The borrowing that looked so ominous to *U.S. News* in 1978 would rise to a new, permanent high plateau established in the 1980s—after which it was impossible to contract, barring a grave crisis.

What Did Alan Greenspan Learn from the 1970s?

In 1980, the *New York Times* spoke to him: "Alan Greenspan, the economist, has asserted that the translation of home-ownership equity into cash available for consumer spending is perhaps the most significant reason why the economy in 1975–1978 was consistently stronger than expected." In other words, the house-trading public prevented recession by cashing out its equity and spending it in the consumer economy.

Greenspan would have observed Arthur Burns's clashes with Congress. Monetary policy was ostensibly the Federal Reserve's mandate, but it was tethered by a short leash. Wright Patman, chairman of the House Banking and Currency Committee, was threatening to nationalize the Fed if it raised interest rates.[22] This was old hat to Patman, who had threatened to abolish the Fed when William McChesney Martin sat in the hot seat.[23]

Henry Reuss succeeded Patman as chairman of the House Banking Committee. He blamed any party other than Congress for the nation's troubles. Reuss lectured a Fed board member in 1978: "[W]e cannot stand for ruining the domestic economy just because somebody thinks it will make a few foreign bankers happy."[24] This was theater. Some bankers are always getting rich (that's the nature of leverage), but the

---

[22] Martin Mayer, *The Fate of the Dollar*, (New York Times Books, 1980), p. 206.

[23] Robert P. Bremner, *Chairman of the Fed: William McChesney Martin Jr. and the Creation of the Modern American Financial System* (New Haven, Comm.: Yale University Press, 2004), pp. 189–191.

[24] Mayer, *The Fate of the Dollar*, p. 280.

Fed was not running a $59 billion deficit. Congress is constitutionally responsible for the budget.

In August 1979, Paul Volcker was appointed Federal Reserve chairman.[25] An economist with experience inside and outside of the government, including four years as president of the Federal Reserve Bank of New York, Volcker was well versed in how markets operate. (The president of the New York Federal Reserve Bank is closer to the financial markets than the Fed chairman.) However, the markets were underwhelmed. An ounce of gold cost $282 on August 6, the day Volcker took over, the final bid of the year was $512, and gold would peak at $850 (for about two seconds) on January 21, 1980. In fact, Volcker had already turned monetary policy upside down during gold's grand ascent. On October 6, 1979, the new chairman announced that the Federal Reserve would no longer set a specific interest-rate target. He would let the market decide the correct rate for borrowing and lending. Volcker would control the supply of money. His intention was to kill inflation by reducing the money supplied by the Fed to the banking system. This, in turn, would choke the flow of credit from banks to the economy. This was what the world's economy needed, but it was not the best news for a president who was about to run for reelection. Receiving advance notice of Volcker's imminent decision, CEA Chairman Schultze telephoned Volcker from the White House. He hoped to put this genie back in the bottle, but Volcker would not budge.

Greenspan's 1980 Renomination Campaign

The Carter years found Greenspan playing both sides of the court. Leaving no stone unturned, Greenspan did his best to polish his Republican credentials while burrowing himself into the good graces

---

[25] Arthur Burns had resigned on March 31, 1978. President Carter chose G. William Miller to succeed Burns. The choice was unenlightened. Arthur Burns had his faults, but in a time of chaos, at least he smoked the familiar pipe. Upon announcement of the Miller Fed, the economist John Kenneth Galbraith expressed a common reaction: "I don't know the new guy, a surprise choice, but it's not a terribly important job." Alan Greenspan seconded Galbraith: "Critics of the Fed impute a degree of efficacy to the institution which really isn't there." Henry Scott-Stokes, "Reactions Vary for Economists on Fed Change," *New York Times*, December 30, 1977.

of the Carter administration. Hobart Rowan reported Greenspan's phlegmatic economic critique shortly after his departure from Washington: "Four months ago, conservative Alan Greenspan was President Ford's No. 1 economic adviser and confidante. Now, at the Metropolitan Club, just a block from his old office, private citizen Greenspan is taking a long, hard look at the Carter Administration. He likes what he sees.... He believes that Carter is basically less liberal on economic issues than many of his own advisers."[26] Greenspan was "tolerably pleased with President Carter's economic policies," according to the *New York Times*.[27]

After President Carter delivered an uninspiring State of the Union address in 1979, the Republican response was one of derision. Greenspan, not noted for breaking with the pack, took this occasion to wax ecstatic over Carter's performance. Carter's proposals were "an extraordinary set of documents, as Republican as I can imagine; they could just as easily have been delivered by a Republican."[28]

Later in the year, Greenspan straddled the political fence. (The Carter-Reagan presidential race in 1980 was tight until the final weeks. In late 1979, the possibility of Carter's constructing a bipartisan cabinet had an allure—if not to Carter, certainly to Greenspan.) He "affirm[ed] what some Carter aides suspect" in the *New York Times*: "that if Mr. Ford had been re-elected in 1976 his economic policy would probably have been much like Mr. Carter's.... [T]here would have been little difference and 'the rhetoric is the same.'"[29]

All candidates were potential employers. A year before the election, Greenspan had met every Republican candidate with the exception of John Connolly, as well as Democratic candidates Jerry Brown and Ted Kennedy. Greenspan organized a breakfast for candidate Kennedy with "key Wall Street figures."[30] Soon after, he told the *New York Times*,

[26] Hobart Rowen, "Carter Backed by Greenspan," *Washington Post*, May 29, 1977.

[27] Silk, "Greenspan, White House Days Behind."

[28] Warren Weaver Jr., "Carter's Address Draws a Barrage of Criticism from G.O.P. Leaders," *New York Times*, January 25, 1979.

[29] Edward Cowan, "Carter's Policy: Storm Clouds Grow," *New York Times*, June 7, 1979.

[30] Steven Rattner, "The Candidates' Economists," *New York Times*, November 18, 1979, F1.

"if only a few words were changed [in a speech by Kennedy], it could have been delivered by Gerald Ford four years ago."[31]

SUPPLY-SIDE ECONOMICS

Economic issues were central to the 1980 presidential election. With different schools of thought vying for attention, Greenspan probably choose the wisest course. He remained aloof.

Volcker's decision to control the money supply drew attention to Milton Friedman's monetarism. Putting monetarism into practice, according to Friedman's own recipe, would entail a constitutional amendment that would increase money growth at a specified, annual rate.

There was also a new school of thought: supply-side economics. Some argued that it was very old, but it did break ranks with postwar American economics by competing with, rather than rising through, the establishment.

More important, though, was that supply-side economics swept the next president off his feet. Martin Anderson, the Randian who had befriended Greenspan since the Nixon campaign, now an economist at the Hoover Institution, was Reagan's issues advisor for both his 1976 and 1980 presidential campaigns. Anderson's role included meeting and screening outside economists on behalf of the candidate.[32] Theory aside, a presidential candidate intent on halting the dismal results of the past three presidencies would be on the lookout for a new voice.

Supply-side economics emphasized the need to cut personal income taxes to stimulate the economy. Ronald Reagan was opposed to state interference in people's lives. Whether it all added up (literally—would the rising tax revenues cut the mountainous Carter budget deficits?) was never his prime concern.

Alan Greenspan was an outsider to supply-side economics. An expert juggler, Greenspan became an economic advisor to Reagan after Reagan was nominated as the Republican candidate. Martin Anderson tapped

---

[31] Edwin McDowell, "He Even Counsels Kennedy," *New York Times*, December, 9, 1979.
[32] Rattner, "The Candidates' Economists."

him for the role. Greenspan was not a sycophant. Traveling with the candidate, Greenspan told reporters that it would be a "risky proposition" to defend Reagan's proposed tax cuts on the assumption that the "supply-side" would make up for lost revenues.[33]

GREENSPAN RUNS FOR TREASURY SECRETARY

Greenspan may not have cared about economic theory. To fulfill his ambitions, he pursued a more direct strategic course: he nearly checkmated Reagan into naming him secretary of the treasury.

At 11:13 p.m. on July 16, 1980, Ronald Reagan received the Montana delegation's unanimous vote at the Republican National Convention. This ensured his nomination. He would, within the hour, stand on the stage of Joe Louis Arena and announce to the conventioneers his choice of vice-presidential running mate. The selection was still in limbo.

When Reagan and his advisors gathered in his sixty-ninth-floor suite at the Detroit Plaza Hotel on the morning of July 15, the unspoken assumption was that George H. W. Bush, Reagan's closest challenger during the campaign, would be his choice. Then Reagan queried his entourage, "What about Ford?"[34]

Several versions of the negotiations with Ford have been published. In the end, Bush was Reagan's choice. By most accounts, Reagan was predisposed to Ford as a running mate. William Casey, on Reagan's staff, asked Henry Kissinger to negotiate with Ford. Later that night, Ford and Kissinger met privately in a room in Ford's seventieth-floor suite. By luck, Alan Greenspan had been among two dozen friends who accompanied Ford on a yacht that evening and then returned to the hotel suite.[35] In less than 24 hours, Reagan would announce his choice for vice president.[36] During those 24 hours, Greenspan would play his hand for all it was worth.

---

[33] Elizabeth Drew, A Reporter At Large, "1980: Reagan," New Yorker, September 29, 1980, p. 123.

[34] Ed Magnuson, "Inside the Jerry Ford Drama," Time, July 28, 1980.

[35] Ibid.

[36] Richard V. Allen, "George Herbert Walker Bush: The Accidental Vice President," New York Times Magazine, July 30, 2000.

Reagan gave his advisors free rein to negotiate with Ford. When and how Kissinger expanded the negotiating team to include Ford's CEA chairman is not recorded, but we do know that Greenspan insinuated himself into the role of kingpin. According to *Time* magazine, "Greenspan did most of the talking for the Ford group."[37] Richard V. Allen, who was "the only person to remain in Reagan's presence throughout the adventure," remembers Reagan's summation of the first round of personal negotiations with Ford. Ford's demands included Kissinger as secretary of state and Alan Greenspan as secretary of the treasury. Reagan was unpersuaded: "I thought *that* was more than a little sacrifice."[38] (Italics in original.)

At 8:55 p.m., Reagan called the undecided Ford. In Allen's recollection, Reagan reported that "Ford had told him Kissinger 'now takes himself out' of the running for secretary of state. It was not clear that Ford and Greenspan had taken themselves out of anything."[39] At 11:30 p.m., Ford told the candidate he would not join the party ticket.[40] Shortly after, Bush agreed to be Reagan's running mate.

Greenspans' pursuit of the top spot with such determination was logical, aside from whether the ticket was in the Republican Party's best interest. The presidency could pass to the Democrats in 1984. So, Greenspan abandoned his reticent demeanor and promoted himself ruthlessly. In the pinch, Greenspan pursued his personal interest more aggressively than Henry Kissinger.

Greenspan had no reason to despair, if despair he did. Most presidential cabinets shuffle jobs every couple of years. Reagan might win a second term, during which time the treasury secretary post or the chairmanship of the Fed might be available (presumedly, the positions Greenspan sought). Greenspan's job was to retain a high profile in the media, maintain his reputation as a much-respected consulting economist, and wedge his persona into the new administration.

---

[37] Magnuson, "Inside the Jerry Ford Drama."
[38] Allen, "George Herbert Walker Bush," pp. 36, 38.
[39] Ibid., p. 39.
[40] Magnuson, "Inside the Jerry Ford Drama."

6

PARTIES, PUBLICITY, PROMOTION—AND LOBBYING FOR THE FEDERAL RESERVE CHAIRMANSHIP

1980–1987

With some urgency, Mr. Greenspan says the recent trend toward short-lived investment means that a higher percentage of the nation's plant and equipment wears out each year. "What happens if you have inadequate capital investment, is you wind up with lower standards of living than you otherwise would."[1]

—New York Times, *1984*

Many seeds of the 2007 financial collapse either were planted or bloomed in the 1980s. The 1970s had been a period of financial experimentation. The leveraged buyout and the junk bond were tested. The Carter administration initiated deregulation in several industries.

Standards fell in the eighties. Investment banks converted from partnerships to publicly traded companies; the chase for higher profits was on.[2]

---

[1] Steven Greenhouse, "Pitfalls in the Capital Spending Boom," *New York Times*, June 3, 1984.

[2] Donaldson, Lufkin & Jenrette was the first to go public in 1970.

Financial discipline decayed, and the excesses snowballed into the present. Instability grew as a result of government, corporate, and consumer borrowing. Bailouts of the largest commercial banks, the unfortunate abuse of junk-bond financing (a welcome development turned into a destructive weapon), and stock-option cash-out plans for those at the top are legacies of the decade.

The setting is important. Nothing mattered more than the decline of interest rates. The falling inflation rate was crucial, but there may be no more important reason for recovery than the pricing of the United States: it was selling at liquidation prices. Long-term government bond yields peaked at 15.78 percent in May 1981, the highest rate paid on bonds by the United States in the nation's history. By 1986, long-term Treasuries yielded 7.37 percent.[3] Prime corporate bond yields fell from 15.49 percent in September 1981 to 10.18 percent in November 1982.[4] At 10 percent, companies initiated long-delayed financing needs.

In August 1982, the Dow Jones Industrial Average was at the same level as in 1964. In "real" terms—accounting for price inflation—the Dow had fallen 75 percent from its 1966 peak. On August 12, 1982, the Dow Jones Industrial Average closed at 776—a loss of 275 points, or 26 percent (before inflation), since Alan Greenspan had made his "unqualifiedly bullish" buy recommendation in January 1973. From that 1982 low, the Dow rose to 2,722 on August 25, 1987. Since buying America was a good deal, the dollar shot up against foreign currencies.

Alan Greenspan kept his face in the public's mind with television appearances on *Wall Street Week with Louis Rukeyser* and *Today* immediately after Reagan's 1980 election. In addition to Greenspan's speaking engagements, there were his contributions to Time's Board of Economists, consulting relationships, and corporate board memberships. He had a bird's-eye view of the radical changes in American finance from the board of J. P. Morgan.

---

[3] Sidney Homer and Richard Sylla, *A History of Interest Rates*, 4th ed. (Hoboken, N.J.: Wiley 2005), pp. 386 (May 1981), 384 (1986).

[4] Ibid.

Greenspan in the Eighties: From Expert Forecaster to "Notes on Fashion"

Greenspan was a regular in Washington, both appearing before congressional committees and serving Reagan's White House. He was interviewed by the *New York Times* on March 24, 1981. This would have been read by those who wield influence: "Alan Greenspan, the New York–based economist, has emerged as a major influence on the [Reagan] Administration's new economic policies.... [H]is expertise as a forecaster and consultant through his firm, Townsend-Greenspan & Company, [has] enhanced his influence in Washington and his stature in the business and financial community."[5] Whether the *Times* reporter interviewed Townsend-Greenspan's clients is not clear.

A 1983 *Times* profile was accompanied by a three-quarter-page picture of Alan Greenspan leaning forward from the edge of his seat aside his office desk. He bears the determined look of a man with little time for picture taking. The story noted: "For high fees, his clients can buy into a wide array of computerized services, data banks and consultations with the senior economists—or even with Mr. Greenspan himself. His time is the firm's scarcest resource and, as a consequence, a high-priced commodity. Client lunches with him can run $2,000, a speech for nonclients, $10,000."[6]

The profile followed with his curriculum vitae—board memberships, 200 clients—and the two characteristics common to past interviews: his wizardry with numbers and the enduring image of an ascetic monk huddled like a prophet in a cave: "Mr. Greenspan says he is most comfortable not on television or at fashionable dinner parties, but at work in his New York office....where he is in easy reach of the Townsend-Greenspan library and all its blue binders full of statistical data—'Livestock' to 'Loan Activity'.... to 'Mobile Home Sales.' Work is so central to Mr. Greenspan's life, in fact, that little else, except perhaps baroque music, really seems to engage him."

---

[5] "Talking Business with Alan Greenspan," *New York Times*, March 24, 1981.

[6] Tamar Lewin, "The Quiet Allure of Alan Greenspan," *New York Times*, June 5, 1983.

And, as always, his detachment from the corridors of power: "Those who know him say they think he would take the job at the Fed if asked, although several thought it would be hard for him to leave Townsend-Greenspan."[7]

For one described as being so disengaged from the world, Greenspan had his fill of flirting with it. In the same newspaper that published the 1983 profile, Greenspan was a fixture on the society pages, in the fashion columns, and in television and radio listings. Some names will be known to readers, some have drifted into anonymity. That is the nature of social striving: the chosen are gods and goddesses, the discarded are broken on the wheel of fortune.

Greenspan joined "some 60 chums" of Malcolm Forbes on Forbes's yacht to celebrate the publisher's birthday. Others who sailed included Happy Rockefeller, Gloria Vanderbilt, Arthur Ochs Sulzberger (publisher of the *Times*), Dina Merrill, and New York City Mayor Ed Koch.[8] On another occasion, Greenspan joined Norman Mailer and United Nations delegates from the Netherlands, New Zealand, and Spain to ponder why Carl Bernstein was "wearing a white scarf with his black-tie ensemble at table?"[9] Greenspan attended Barbara and Allen Thomas's annual dessert party: "Among the 65 guests [was] Alan Greenspan, the economist. A chocolate chip cookie freak, Mr. Greenspan was devouring the selection from David's Cookie Kitchen."[10]

The simple introduction is a demonstration of his rise. Earlier in his career, the *Times*'s business page noted his firm, Townsend-Greenspan, to anchor its source to an entity. Now the *Times* only mentioned "the economist." In the chatty, worldly-wise style of "The Evening Hours" and "Notes on Fashion," *Times* readers would have felt insulted by a full introduction to the regular partygoers.

Greenspan turned out at Happy Rockefeller's gala in honor of Nancy and Henry Kissinger. "[T]he limousines were double-parked on Fifth Avenue, and they stretched around the corner to 62nd Street.... Theodore H.

---

[7] Ibid.

[8] Enid Nemy, "The Evening Hours," *New York Times*, August 21, 1981.

[9] John Duka, "Notes on Fashion," *New York Times*, December 29, 1981.

[10] Susan Heller Anderson, "The Evening Hours," *New York Times*, December 31, 1981.

White, the author ... summed up the event this way: 'This is the top 10 percent of every A guest list in town—banking, industry, social and media.'" The A team included Brooke Astor, Felix Rohatyn, Laurence Rockefeller, Art Buchwald, Pierre Salinger, Jerry Zipkin, and Robert McNamara.[11] When the 21 Club was reopened after renovations in 1987, the *Times* reporter thought the restaurant would "go on as it always has: being the frat house, the club, the first aid station of the city's power brokers." The *Times* predicted that Greenspan "will get the same warm greeting [he has] come to expect over the years."[12]

Only a handful of guests were mentioned in a typical "Evening Hours" column, and Greenspan's name appeared regularly. For most attendees, a mention in the *Times*'s society pages was more important than an invitation to the party. Given the names present, mention of an economist seems an odd interest on the part of readers. That he often escorted Barbara Walters helped, but he received mention on his own merit. In a long *Times* magazine feature, "Living Well Is Still the Best Revenge," "the economist Alan Greenspan" is discussed as being among "the very rich, very powerful and very gifted," even though Barbara Walters was unable to attend this rendezvous at the home of Oscar and Françoise de la Renta. Others mentioned in this tribute to the anointed include Ahmet and Mica Ertegun, French director Louis Malle (escorting Candice Bergen), Norman Mailer, Diana Vreeland, Jerzy Kozinski (author of *Being There*), and Giovanni Agnelli (who asked Mailer on Greenspan's arrival if that "was indeed Alan Greenspan 'the famous economist'").[13] He was even quoted in a cooking column, as a gourmet judge of chocolate desserts.[14]

The inflation in prices during the 1980s was at least matched by the inflation of words, but it does appear that the economist Alan Greenspan was indeed "famous." In a 1983 *Times* article about the speaking circuit ("The Superstars"), the *Times* reader learned: "Mr. Greenspan has emerged as the

[11] Judy Klemesrud, "The Evening Hours," *New York Times*, March 26, 1982.

[12] Frank J. Prial, " '21' and El Morocco: 2 Legends Reopen," *New York Times*, April 29, 1987.

[13] Francesca Stanfill, "Living Well Is Still the Best Revenge," *New York Times Magazine*, December 21, 1980.

[14] Marian Burros, "Dessert Party: A Feast of Sumptuous Treats," *New York Times*, November 2, 1983.

most sought-after economist by lecture audiences worldwide." Whether or not this evaluation is inflated is not as important as that it is stated: the Newspaper of Record established reputations. Despite 80 or so speeches a year, Greenspan told the *Times*, "Speech-making isn't my business." More than a few who sat through congressional testimony in future decades would agree, but the man seemed to spend quite a bit of time disavowing what he did the most.

The opening paragraph of the 1983 *Times* profile tipped off the attentive reader as to its timing: "Just last weekend, Alan Greenspan attended Henry Kissinger's lavish 60th birthday party accompanied by Barbara Walters. When not attending such elegant affairs, he can be found on television or in Washington or in the most powerful of corporate boardrooms offering his views on economic affairs, politics and the social issues of the day. At age 57, Greenspan is one of the most popular guests on New York's party circuit—and one of America's leading and most sought after economists. Now, however, the bespectacled, softspoken Mr. Greenspan is being talked about for what would be his most lofty position. He is nearly everybody's first choice for chairman of the Federal Reserve Board, should Paul Volcker ... be asked to step aside."[15]

VOLCKER LOSES SUPPORT

While the gourmet economist bettered his reputation, Paul Volcker lost popularity with the people. He was doing the job he was hired to do. He was unpopular in the White House for the same reason. Industrial production did not rise for three years—from mid-1979 to mid-1982. Blue-collar unemployment was over 16 percent.[16] The supply-siders and the neo-somethings who set administration policy knew the inflation menace had to be subdued, but choking it to death was proving costly. It was feared that the coming redistribution of congressional seats in the 1982 midterm elections would be directly correlated with the rising unemployment rate. (Higher unemployment would probably benefit

---

[15] Lewin, "Quiet Allure of Alan Greenspan."
[16] Barrie A. Wigmore, *Securities Markets in the 1980s*, vol. 1 (New York: Oxford University Press, 1997), p. 39.

the Democrats.) The rising unemployment rate was thought to be a consequence of tight money, so it was time to loosen up. As current voting members of the Fed board stepped aside, the Reagan White House appointed members who would be known as "doves." They didn't like inflation, but they were even less enthusiastic about double-digit unemployment.

Jimmy Carter had opened the path to financial deregulation in the 1970s.[17] The Federal Reserve reduced the reserve requirements of banks (after congressional authorization).[18] This helped to expand credit. Total credit market debt—government, corporate, and consumer—grew by $533 billion in 1981 and by $1.1 trillion in 1985.[19] The eighties would later be known as the Decade of Greed.

The greedy federal government spent $128 billion more than it received from taxes in 1982; by 1983, the federal budget deficit swelled to $221 billion. Two decades earlier, Treasury Secretary Dillon considered the $2.5 billion deficit unpardonable.

Technological developments such as complicated derivative structures and colorful, action-packed computer-trading screens channeled America's fast-buck energies (the tempo of moneymaking never slowed down after the seventies) into financial solutions rather than the slow, awkward development of production capacity. Internal corporate growth, sometimes called "organic growth," places limits on how fast a company can get big. A solution that was growing more palatable was to borrow and buy growth. The value of the top 100 mergers by S&P industrial companies rose from 19 percent of gross capital expenditures in 1979 to 66 percent in 1984.[20]

---

[17] For instance, caps on interest rates paid by financial institutions were eliminated. Changes that would follow include increasing savings and loan (S&L) deposit insurance from $40,000 per customer to $100,000 and authorization to invest in a broader range of assets.

[18] Congress authorized the Fed to set requirements for all depository institutions in 1980. After passage of the Monetary Control Act of 1980, required reserve balances fell from over $30 billion in 1980 to $20 billion in 1984. Joshua N. Feinman, *Federal Reserve Bulletin*, June 1993, pp. 569–589.

[19] Federal Reserve Flow of Funds Z.1 files, historical tables. Available at http://www.federalreserve.gov/releases/z1/Current/data.htm.

[20] Wigmore, *Securities Markets in the 1980s*, pp. 147–148.

Most of the excitement was in New York, but the city's demographics told a sober story. Manufacturing jobs fell from 16.8 percent in 1976 to 11 percent in 1986. The proportion of New Yorkers living under the poverty line rose from 15 percent in 1975 to 23.9 percent in 1985.[21]

PRECURSOR TO THE "GREENSPAN PUT"

At the beginning of the 1980s, commercial banks were tottering. In the 1970s, they had plowed into the rising market: banks lent to commodity-producing countries. When commodity prices collapsed, so did the loans. Walter Wriston, chairman of Citicorp, led the charge into the Southern Hemisphere. He declared that sovereign governments never defaulted and, to prove himself correct, beggared the U.S. government to bail out Argentina, Brazil, and Mexico after Citicorp's loans to those countries were on the edge of default.[22] The government complied.

Commercial banks also lent without a thought toward the future in local markets that suffered when price inflation eased: agriculture and home loans. The lenders needed help, so the federal government rescued the hapless banks. Banks came to expect government coddling.

The Continental Illinois National Bank and Trust bailout is an important precursor to the American financial crack-up. Continental Illinois was the nation's sixth-largest bank and was overloaded with oil and gas loans and neck deep in sovereign loans.[23] On May 17, 1984, a new era of financial collectivism was ushered into being. The Federal Deposit Insurance Corporation (FDIC) decided that the nation's (by now) ninth-largest bank was "too big to fail." The FDIC announced a $2 billion capital injection into the holding company. The government followed with other initiatives that are all too familiar today, including $3.4 billion borrowed

---

[21] Robert A. M. Stern, David Fishman, and Jacob Tilove, *New York 2000: Architecture and Urbanism between the Bicentennial and the Millennium* (New York: Monacelli Press, 2006), pp. 19–20.

[22] The U.S. government did so through advances from the Federal Reserve, the Treasury, the Department of Energy, and the Department of Agriculture. These sums were advanced to Brazil (among others) so that Brazil could repay its debt to Citicorp. James Grant, *Money of the Mind: Borrowing and Lending in America from the Civil War to Michael Milken* (New York: Farrar Straus Giroux, 1992), pp. 339, 341, 343.

[23] Wigmore, *Securities Markets in the 1980s*, pp. 44–45.

from the Fed's discount window.[24] The government committed itself to insuring all deposits, not merely the $100,000 deposit limit.[25] In addition, it also protected creditors of the holding company.[26] This and other wrinkles of the bailout are interesting precedents, too involved to discuss here. A distinction is that of treasury secretaries, then and now. In 1984, "Treasury Secretary Donald Regan blasted the plan as 'unauthorized and unlegislated expansion of federal guarantees in contravention of executive branch policy,'" but he was ignored."[27] Today, treasury secretaries Hank Paulson (did) and Timothy Geithner (does) hand billions of dollars to the most negligent banks and brokerages.

The Citicorp and Continental Illinois bailouts happened during Paul Volcker's term at the Fed. What would later be called the "Greenspan put" preceded the future Federal Reserve chairman. (The Greenspan put was the belief that if the markets ever stumbled, Fed Chairman Greenspan would flood the market with money, which would trancate investors' downside risk while launching a new speculative fury.)

From a business perspective, it is unfathomable why banks, which are consistently incompetent in the lines of business in which they are authorized to transact, are continually given permission to expand and to enter new lines of business in which they lack experience.

Leveraged Buyouts and Junk Bonds

The conglomerate form of financing was dead. In the 1970s, private-equity investments, more the province of insurance companies in the past, were being managed by independent companies. Kohlberg Kravis Roberts & Co. (KKR) was a young private-equity firm in the

---

[24] Ibid., pp. 44–51. In turn, the FDIC took over.

[25] During the 1980s, financial institutions were granted the authority to cross lines of monopoly. Savings and Loans (S&Ls) lost their monopoly on home mortgages (hitherto, commercial banks had been barred from this market), and competition grew by leaps and bounds. (As mentioned in footnote 17, the S&Ls received broader authority.) Commercial bank entry broadened the residential mortgage market; the growing junk-bond appetite of savings and loans, insurance companies, and mutual funds extended the ability of investment banks to underwrite more junk bonds.

[26] Wigmore, *Securities Markets in the 1980s*, pp. 50–51.

[27] Ibid.

1970s, when the "the notion of a buyout was not well understood" (as KKR informs the public on its Web site). In 1979, Kohlberg Kravis Roberts negotiated the first *leveraged* buyout (LBO) of a public company by a private-equity firm.[28] It took KKR over a year to find financing, as well it might. The idea of buying a company by loading its balance sheet with debt (the "leverage" in LBO) was new. This was the means by which the 1980s form of hostile bids for companies took wing, in conjunction with another development.

Michael Milken's group at the investment-banking house of Drexel Burnham (later to be Drexel Burnham Lambert Inc.) educated the world, and then dominated it, in the fertile laboratory of junk bonds.[29] (Junk bonds are those that are rated below investment grade by the rating agencies.) Early buyers of Drexel's junk bonds had acquired valuable experience in the conglomerate years—Carl Lindner of American Financial Corporation and Saul Steinberg of Reliance Insurance.[30]

After his initial success with "fallen angels"—companies that had fallen on hard times and been downgraded—Milken gravitated toward "new-issue" junk bonds. Drexel performed an admirable service by finding investors for some promising companies, with Turner Broadcasting and Humana being early success stories.[31]

It was not long before the weapon (junk bonds) and the strategy (hostile bids) discovered each other. One other component was needed: a willing buyer. The mutual fund industry offered 11 junk-bond funds before 1980.[32]

The early financings were responsibly packaged to permit the companies so structured to cover their debt payments out of projected earnings. By 1983, however, future annual profits (before depreciation and taxes) were projected to be 20 percent *less* than annual debt payments.[33] The deterioration was laid out in clear terms to the buyers, but they were

---

[28] Ibid., p. 303.

[29] Ibid.

[30] Ibid., p. 280. Milken did not invent junk bonds, as is often claimed. There were precedents: railroad and REIT (real estate investment trust) junk bonds.

[31] Ibid., p. 282.

[32] Ibid., p. 283.

[33] Ibid. p. 282. Between 1980 and 1982 the ratio of earnings before interest and taxes (EBIT) divided by debt payments was about 2.0. The ratio dropped to 0.8 in 1983.

often buying for reasons not explained by the efficient market hypothesis. (This has been the dominant precept in finance and economics over the past few decades: that market prices reflect all known information. This is the backbone of economists' models, the consistent failure of which would seem to deter them from constructing new models.) Barrie Wigmore, author of a seminal financial study of the period, found that this was one development he could not quantify: "How much the surge in junk bond new-issues in 1983 and 1984 was due to expanded savings and loan powers and the merger boom and how dependent it was on under-the-table incentives to money managers will probably never be resolved."[34]

THE DECADE OF GREED

The explosion of finance initiated a new Youth Movement. In July 1986, a *BusinessWeek* cover story quoted a Harvard Business School professor who compared Mike Milken to J. P. Morgan.[35] The comparison was taken to heart: the Harvard Business School class of 1985 included 65 members who were prosecuted for securities violations.[36]

Some of the corporate restructuring was productive, although much was driven by the call to "align management incentives with shareholder value." To boost shareholder value—the stock price—every quarter, financial channels combined with clever accounting were necessary. The balance sheet expanded, often through the allure of debt and buying back equity.

In 1985, Franco Modigliani won the Nobel Prize in economics. The Modigliani-Miller theorem holds that the value of a business does not decrease when its capital structure is geared toward debt (we are incorporating the efficient market fantasy dementia here.) Impatient CEOs applied the superficial gloss of this hypothesis to borrow in frightful quantities and boost profits.[37]

---

[34] Ibid., p. 287.

[35] Grant, *Money of the Mind*, p. 393.

[36] Philip Delves Broughton, *Ahead of the Curve: Two Years at Harvard Business School* (New York: Penguin Press, 2008), p. 157.

[37] Merton Miller, the other party to the theorem, was awarded the Nobel Prize in 1990.

VOLCKER'S RENOMINATION

Paul Volcker's term as Fed chairman ran until 1983. Alan Greenspan consistently supported Volcker, in public statements and private conversations. Some of Greenspan's forecasts warned of dire times, but he was generally discussing the problems of the economy as a whole. He put at least as much blame on federal budget deficits as on problems caused by monetary policy—a money mishap that Greenspan inferred was caused by misdeeds prior to Volcker's term. As a member of *Time*'s Board of Economists, Greenspan warned in 1981 that "towering interest rates are threatening the survival of many American financial institutions."[38] The American people blamed Paul Volcker for the high interest rates, but Alan Greenspan did not. Instead, he told *Time* in December of 1982, "The Fed is in a box." He supported Volcker's increasingly lonely policy by reminding readers that bond buyers thought a rapid expansion of the money supply could eventually reignite inflation (raising long-term bond rates).[39] When the press was full of tattletale gossip on the acerbic relations between Volcker and the White House (specifically, Donald Regan), Greenspan told the *Times*: "It's counterproductive and it's unfortunate. The Fed is doing as good a job as it can do in these circumstances."[40] Regan was a tough cookie. Greenspan put the Fed and Volcker ahead of his own interests.

Greenspan's campaign for Fed chairmanship was subtle. Paul Volcker's four-year term as chairman expired in August 1983, but it appears that the White House could not make up its mind about a successor. Wall Street put pressure on the White House to reappoint Volcker. A survey of 702 business executives published in the *Wall Street Journal* on June 8 revealed that 77 percent wanted Volcker to be reappointed. In second place was Greenspan: 37 percent expressed special confidence in him.[41] With such support, he was in a commanding position to succeed Volcker, should the opportunity arise.

---

[38] Charles P. Alexander, "Will Reagan's Plan Work?" *Time*, February 23, 1981.

[39] Charles P. Alexander, "The Elusive Recovery," *Time*, December 27, 1982.

[40] Jonathan Fuerbringer, "Reagan vs. Fed: The Fallout," *New York Times*, January 30, 1982, p. 29.

[41] William Greider, *Secrets of the Temple: How the Federal Reserve Runs the Country* (New York: Simon and Schuster 1987), p. 572. The survey was by A. G. Becker Paribas.

This expression of confidence in Greenspan is notable. The comings and goings in Washington are an open book to Wall Street. When Greenspan was not speaking or attending galas, he was working the White House. His biographer Jerome Tuccille writes: "According to several White House insiders, Alan made a point of regularly massaging the people who mattered."[42] Martin Anderson told Tuccille: "I don't think I was in the White House once where I didn't see him sitting in the lobby or working the offices. I was absolutely astounded by his omnipresence.... He was always huddling in the corner with someone."[43] Greenspan's campaign made an impression on Wall Street, as did his likable disposition. A Fed chairman who gave Wall Street "the opinion you needed"[44] and was a director of J. P. Morgan would be apt to see the world from the creditor's perspective.

The consulting economist orchestrated a media blitz. He made television appearances on the *Today* show in May 1983 and "The Editor's Desk" on June 12, 1983.[45] The *Times* profile (quoted earlier) appeared on June 5, 1983. The June 6, 1983, edition of *U.S. News & World Report* published an interview.[46]

Also on June 6, Volcker arranged a private meeting with Reagan. In the Oval Office, the Fed chairman told the president: " 'This has dragged on too long and you ought to settle it one way or the other.'" Reagan announced Volcker's reappointment during his weekly radio broadcast on June 18.[47] Greenspan wound down his campaign with another "From the Editor's Desk" appearance on June 19.

ALAN GREENSPAN: CHAIRMAN OF THE NATIONAL COMMISSION ON SOCIAL SECURITY REFORM

Greenspan was well positioned for a senior position—not only in the White House but also with Congress. He headed a group that reformed

---

[42] Jerome Tuccille, *Alan Shrugged: The Life and Times of Alan Greenspan, the World's Most Powerful Banker* (Hoboken, NJ.: Wiley, 2002), p. 157.

[43] Ibid., pp. 157–158.

[44] Martin Mayer, *The Greatest-Ever Bank Robbery: The Collapse of the Savings and Loan Industry* (New York: Scribner's, 1990), p. 140

[45] *New York Times* TV listings, June 12, 1983.

[46] "The Long-Term Boom Now in Prospect," *U.S. News & World Report*, June 6, 1983.

[47] Greider, *Secrets of the Temple*, pp. 572–574.

social security. This was one of the most delicate political issues during the early 1980s. The argument went that social security was the largest government expense, and the system would be bankrupt by 1984. Social security had to be cut. Taking money away from old people does not win votes. The nation's elected representatives did what they always do when a difficult decision needs to be made: they ran for the hills and appointed a commission.

Never one to hop off a fence if he could sit on it, the appointed chairman of the National Commission on Social Security Reform moved the deck chairs sufficiently to delay action for another few years. There was room to think that the commission had succeeded.[48] The fix was temporary; as Federal Reserve chairman, Greenspan would once again permit the politicians to avoid responsibility. (This is the subject of Chapter 12.)

The United States continued to buy far more from overseas than it produced. The deficit in goods reached $145 billion in 1986. This was quite a splurge, as were the federal deficit and the debt-stuffed corporate balance sheets.

Alan Greenspan saw dark clouds. This is noteworthy, since, as Fed chairman, Greenspan would say that it did not matter if the United States produced things. In 1984, speaking to the *Times*, he had taken a more traditional view: "With some urgency, Mr. Greenspan says the recent trend toward short-lived investment means that a higher percentage of the nation's plant and equipment wears out each year. Thus, a larger amount of investment is needed each year just to replace this depreciated capital stock, and more investment yet is needed to increase the nation's net capital stock." Greenspan stated the consequence: "What happens if you have inadequate capital investment, is you wind up with lower standards of living than you otherwise would."[49]

Given his views, Alan Greenspan would seem as well suited as anyone, in an official Washington posting, to warn of a dire future. Instead, he mumbled for 18 years and evaded such discussions.

---

[48] In brief, the commission did not touch the age at which a person is eligible for benefits; it taxed beneficiaries if their income was above a certain level, it required federal employees to contribute to the system, and it retained the formula for adjusting benefits for inflation.

[49] Steven Greenhouse, "Pitfalls in the Capital Spending Boom," *New York Times*, June 3, 1984.

7

LINCOLN SAVINGS AND LOAN ASSOCIATION

1984–1985

Charles Keating's S&L was *the* example of how the industry had spun out of control. [Seidman's italics.][1]

—*L. William Seidman,* Full Faith and Credit:
The Great S&L Debacle and Other Washington Sagas

Greenspan was fortunate that his nomination for Federal Reserve chairman preceded the unwinding of Lincoln Savings and Loan. The infamous "Keating Five" scandal was hatched at Lincoln. Five U.S. senators lost credibility in its wake—Alan Cranston, Donald Riegle, Dennis DeConcini, John Glenn, and John McCain. Greenspan was hired by Charles Keating in 1985 to write a letter to regulators on Lincoln's behalf. The government bailout of the savings and loan industry cost American taxpayers $124.6 billion.[2] Lincoln alone cost at least $2.0 billion.[3]

---

[1] L. William Seidman, *Full Faith and Credit: The Great S&L Debacle and Other Washington Sagas* (New York: Times Books, 1993), p. 229.

[2] Different assumptions produce different totals; http://www.gao.gov/archive/1996/ai96123.pdf.

[3] www.fdic.gov/bank/historical/s&l/.

Savings and loans (also called "thrifts") had suffered whiplash from the rise and fall of interest rates. Many were in danger of extinction. Alan Greenspan had warned of their vulnerability in 1981when he told *U.S. News & World Report* that high interest rates were suffocating S&Ls: they "can only exist in a non-inflationary environment."[4] He told the *New York Times* "[t]here are now a bunch of moribund cases out there." Greenspan was not sure if "any" of the savings and loans had equity, but that was not the real problem: "The problem is cash flow . . . there are a number of institutions that are barely able . . . to pay their liability side of the balance sheet]."[5]

Lincoln before Keating: One of the Best Managed Savings and Loans

What Greenspan said seems overstated, but there was much truth in it. Notably, his concern did not apply to Lincoln Savings and Loan of Irvine, California. It was run by the Crocker family, which owned 40 percent of the shares. Like most S&Ls, it lost money in 1981 and 1982, but it returned to profitability in 1983 (with the decline of interest rates). Donald Crocker, son of the founder, had nursed Lincoln back to health and was ready to sell. Charles Keating offered to pay $51 million in 1983—two and a half times its over-the-counter market price.[6] Michael Milken at Drexel, Burnham helped broker Keating's acquisition.[7]

Keating inherited a thrift institution with the lowest ratio of delinquent mortgages of any large thrift institution in California.[8] When seeking approval from the Federal Home Loan Bank (FHLB) of San

---

[4] "Are Americans Going Too Deep into Debt? Interview with Alan Greenspan," *U.S. News & World Report*, August 3, 1981.

[5] "Talking Business with Alan Greenspan," *New York Times*, March 24, 1981, p. D2.

[6] Martin Mayer, *The Greatest-Ever Bank Robbery: The Collapse of the Savings and Loan Industry* (New York: Scribner's, 1990), p. 171.

[7] Martin Mayer, *The Bankers: The Next Generation* (New York: Truman Talley Books, 1997): "Charles Keating acquired Lincoln Savings and Loan with the help of Mike Milken of Drexel Burnham," p. 370.

[8] Mayer, *Greatest-Ever Bank Robbery*, p. 171.

Francisco,[9] Keating stated that he would continue with the current management in place and that he would concentrate on California home mortgages. Having received approval from the FHLB, he jettisoned Lincoln's senior management. Keating would later say he fired them because they were incompetent and that Crocker had told him to do so. Crocker had said nothing of the sort.[10] Keating's new board was not on the payroll of Lincoln. Instead, board members were paid by Keating's holding company that owned the bank.[11]

LINCOLN, KEATING, AND DREXEL BURNHAM'S DAISY CHAIN

A consultant hired to review Lincoln's books should have looked upon Keating and his connections with some curiosity. Since Alan Greenspan devoted great energy to knowing those who wielded the levers of power, it would have been a strange lapse if he was uninterested in his client. Keating had been executive vice president of Carl Lindner's American Financial Corporation. Lindner's reputation rose from the financing boom of the 1960s. Between 1961 (when the company went public) and 1979, American Financial Corporation produced a compound annual return of 19.2 percent.[12] During the 1970s, Lindner was an investor in Milken's early junk-bond offerings. In 1979, the SEC had charged Keating with making improper loans to insiders and friends (of Lindner's Provident Bank of Cincinnati), plus failing to report a pattern of loans to purchasers of assets that Lindner wished to sell. "Keating had consented to a permanent injunction with the SEC, which should have barred Keating forever from ownership of an insured" deposit-taking institution.[13]

---

[9] There are 12 regional Federal Home Loan banks. Lincoln Savings and Loan was in the San Francisco district. Until 1989, the FHLBs were the "principal supervisory agents" responsible for the solvency and honesty of ther local S&Ls. Mayer, *Greatest-Ever Bank Robbery*, pp. xi–xii.

[10] Ibid., p. 171.

[11] Ibid., p. 170.

[12] Thomas C. Hayes, "The 'Money Merchant' of Cincinnati," *New York Times*, June 24, 1979, F7.

[13] Mayer, *Greatest-Ever Bank Robbery*, p. 169.

In 1978, Keating had bought a Phoenix house-building company from Lindner. This was renamed American Continental Corporation (ACC). ACC was the holding company that later purchased and owned Lincoln Savings and Loan.[14] Keating leveraged it and then expanded into several western cities; all of these efforts failed between 1982 and 1987. Martin Mayer, author of *The Greatest-Ever Bank Robbery: The Collapse of the Savings and Loan Industry*, wrote: "There is every reason to believe that Keating went after an S&L because he had lost access to other sources of funds and needed government-insured deposits to finance his operations."[15]

S&Ls were an attractive platform for a businessman with a certain turn of mind. Deregulation of the industry permitted a panorama of investment classes that had previously been forbidden. William Seidman, who had interviewed Greenspan before his Council of Economic Advisers appointment, learned that "S&Ls could raise nearly unlimited amounts of funds through brokered deposits at low [interest] rates because the money was insured by the government. They could ... make their profit on the spread between the low and high rates of interest."[16]

Charles Keating needed money. He needed yield from the securities bought by Lincoln. He needed capital gains from the trading of land and securities. He bought the riskiest junk bonds, land, and takeover stocks.[17] Keating's first big investment was $132 million in the common stock of Gulf Broadcast Company. He bought the stock from Lindner's American Financial Corporation, which had accumulated 19 percent of Gulf Broadcast shares.[18]

In *Securities Markets in the 1980s*, Barrie Wigmore wrote that Carl Lindner and Saul Steinberg "ran small insurance companies and dealt repeatedly in borderline investment tactics."[19] In Wigmore's opinion, the evolution of the pair's "activities illustrates the combination of native cunning and access to leverage that made them effective."[20]

---

[14] Ibid., p. 167.

[15] Ibid., p. 173.

[16] Seidman, *Full Faith and Credit*, pp. 235–236.

[17] Mayer, *Greatest-Ever Bank Robbery*, p. 174.

[18] Ibid.

[19] Barrie A. Wigmore, *Securities Markets in the 1980s*, vol. 1 (New York: Oxford University Press, 1997), p. 360.

[20] Ibid., p. 356.

Regarding the relationship of Lindner and Steinberg, Wigmore wrote: "[i]t is tempting to conclude they also represented a cabal, who worked through Michael Milken's group."[21]

When Seidman was appointed to head the Resolution Trust Corporation (RTC)—the agency created to resolve problems in the S&L industry—he faced a mystery: why was the heaviest financial carnage among the largest holders of junk bonds sold by Michael Milken? These included Lincoln; Centrust Savings Bank of Miami, Florida; and Columbia Savings and Loan of Beverly Hills, California. Among them, the three banks held $2.5 billion of junk bonds by the end of 1984—which was equal to 35 percent of the amount held by all mutual funds.[22] (William Seidman later wrote that of the more than 900 convictions initiated by RTC enforcement actions, those of the chairmen of Centrust, Columbia, and Charles Keating were "key."[23])

Later in the decade, Seidman's investigators discovered that Michael Milken had "rigged the market by operating a sort of daisy chain among the S&Ls to trade the bonds back and forth across his famous X-shaped trading desk at his headquarters in Beverly Hills. By manipulating the market, he maintained the facade that the bonds were trading at genuine market prices. . . . When he [Milken] was brought down, and his trading operation with him, so were the S&Ls that depended on the value of his bonds to stay afloat."[24] Of note: the in-house pricing of derivatives, such as collateralized debt obligations (CDOs), was essential to the current financial collapse.

Between 1983 and 1984, Lincoln's assets more than doubled, from $1.1 billion to $2.24 billion.[25] From the time Keating took control of Lincoln in

---

[21] Ibid., p. 346. Wigmore includes one more "old hand" from "the merger wave of the late 1960s": Meshulam Riklis and his Rabid American Corporation.

[22] Ibid., p. 286.

[23] Seidman, *Full Faith and Credit*, p. 226.

[24] Ibid., p. 236. An example of how the daisy chain worked: Drexel put Keating into Playtex stock which Lincoln bought for $420,000. Lincoln sold the shares to American Continental Corporation, Keating's holding company, for $2.1 million. Lincoln booked the $1.7 million profit. ACC sold most of the shares to Centrust Savings Bank of Miani for $12.47 million. ACC booked a $10.37 million profit. Source: Mayer, *Greatest-Ever Bank Robbery*, p. 175.

[25] Nathaniel C. Nash, "Greenspan's Lincoln Savings Regret," *New York Times*, November 20, 1989.

February 1984 through the end of the year, he "had switched virtually all of its activities to real estate development and speculative investments."[26]

Savings and loans that had "exploited California's liberal thrift industry regulations" were profiled on the front page of the *Times*'s business section on November 15, 1984. Alan Greenspan's hometown newspaper reported that "Columbia Savings and Loan Association of Beverly Hills nearly quintupled in size" to $4.9 billion over the past two years.[27] The *Times* referred to a *Forbes* magazine article that explained Columbia's growth was aided by ties to a "confederation of fast-stepping financiers, such as Carl Lindner [and] Saul Steinberg, who buy and sell low-grade commercial paper through the head of Drexel Burnham's Beverly Hills office, Michael Milken."[28]

The savings and loan industry was not yet "the worst public scandal in American history," as Martin Mayer wrote in 1990.[29] But, catastrophes were already piling up. Not too far from Lincoln's headquarters in Irvine, California, San Marino Savings and Loan Association of San Marino, had grown from $23.9 million in 1980 to $841 million in 1984 by compounding collusive real estate partnerships.[30] In February 1984, it was seized by the government.

This brings us up to December 1984. Alan Greenspan wrote his letter in support of Lincoln in February 1985.

GREENSPAN'S LETTER ON BEHALF OF CHARLES KEATING

Seidman discovered that "Keating's highly paid law firms, accounting firms, and appraisers were also very much a part of what turned out to be a huge fraudulent operation."[31] In 1984, Keating hired the four largest law firms in New York. Arthur Liman (of the law firm Paul, Weiss, Rifkind, Wharton & Garrison) recommended that Keating hire

---

[26] Wigmore, *Securities Markets in the 1980s*, p. 360.

[27] Thomas C. Hayes, "New Curbs on Industry Under Study," *New York Times*, November 15, 1984, p. D1.

[28] Ibid.

[29] Mayer, *Greatest-Ever Bank Robbery*, p. 1.

[30] Ibid., p. 127.

[31] Seidman, *Full Faith and Credit*, p. 233.

Alan Greenspan to write a bill of good health. Martin Mayer wrote that Greenspan was "then a private consultant heading a not very successful firm."[32] In his 1969 book, *New Breed on Wall Street*, Mayer wrote that Greenspan specialized in "statistical espionage." Mayer later wrote: "the book on him in that capacity was that you could order the opinion you needed."[33] Whether Greenspan was catering to his clients or was simply obtuse is not known.

On February 13, 1985, Greenspan wrote a letter to Thomas F. Sharkey, the principal supervisory agent at the Federal Home Loan Bank of San Francisco. Most of the letter addressed the direct investments of Lincoln. Greenspan informed Sharkey that Lincoln had "adequate capitalization, sound business plans, managerial expertise and proper diversification." Greenspan stated that Lincoln's management "is seasoned and expert in selecting and making direct investments." Greenspan's report also stated that Lincoln "has developed a series of carefully planned, highly promising, and widely diversified projects" and that "denial of the permission Lincoln seeks would work a serious and unfair hardship on an association that has, through its skill and expertise, transformed itself into a financially strong institution that presents no foreseeable risk to the Federal Savings and Loan Corporation."[34]

In William Seidman's words: "The Greenspan report failed to note that Keating's savings and loan had simply exchanged interest rate risks for much greater asset quality risks—that is, the old-fashioned, hair-curling risk of speculative real estate investments."[35] While in Keating's employ, Greenspan also suffered a lapse when writing a letter to Edwin Gray, the Federal Home Loan Bank chairman. Greenspan, the man who would become the nation's leading bank regulator in 1987, notified Gray that deregulation was working as planned. Greenspan cited 17 thrifts that had reported record profits and were prospering under the new rules. By 1989, 15 of those 17 thrifts would be out of business and would cost the Federal Savings and Loan Insurance Corporation several

---

[32] Mayer, *Greatest-Ever Bank Robbery*, p. 140.
[33] Ibid.
[34] Ibid., p. 326, Appendix C: "The Greenspan Letter."
[35] Seidman, *Full Faith and Credit*, p. 232

billion dollars.[36] The television show *Frontline* reported that Keating paid Greenspan \$40,000.[37]

It cost the government (so, the taxpayers) at least \$2.0 billion to clean up Lincon Savings and Loan.[38] Yet Alan Greenspan was not held to account for his previous endorsement. The political establishment was in no position to cross-examine him. When Keating was asked whether the money he contributed to the Keating Five had influenced them, his response was refreshingly honest: "I certainly hope so."[39] In 1988, when the hemorrhaging S&Ls had already cost several politicians their credibility, 333 House members and 61 senators listed "significant donations from the industry."[40] Donald Regan, who was President Reagan's chief of staff from 1985 to 1987, had been trying to oust Ed Gray from his position (as chairman of the Federal Home Loan Bank Board) since 1984, when Regan was treasury secretary. One reason for this may have been that many of the S&Ls that Gray shut were large contributors to President Reagan's 1984 reelection campaign. Donald Regan "believed in helping contributors to the party."[41]

Looking Back in 1989: Greenspan Had No Regrets

The media did not enlighten the public. Greenspan evaded the *New York Times* in its interrogation. The 1989 article, "Greenspan's Lincoln Savings Regret," was poorly titled. The chairman expressed no regret. If Greenspan had received the same assignment in 1989 with the same evidence he had in 1984, "his conclusions about Lincoln ... would be very much the same."[42]

---

[36] Stephen Pizzo, Mary Fricker, and Paul Muolo, *Inside Job: The Looting of America's Savings and Loans* (New York: McGraw-Hill, 1989), p. 266; "Greenspan wrote the letter while he was paid consultant for Lincoln Savings and Loan of Irvine, California, owned by a Charles Keating, Jr., company."

[37] Mayer, *Greatest-Ever Bank Robbery*, p. 140.

[38] www.fdic.gov/bank/historical/s&l/.

[39] Margaret Carlson: Interview with Charles Keating, "Money Talks," *Time*, April 9, 1990.

[40] Mary Fricker and Steve Pizzo, "The S. & L. Scandal: The Gang's All Here," *New York Times*, July 27, 1990.

[41] Mayer, *Greatest-Ever Bank Robbery*, p. 139.

[42] Nathaniel C. Nash, "Greenspan's Lincoln Savings Regret," *New York Times*, November 20, 1989.

Alan Greenspan loathed to admit a mistake. Like a mother hen defending her offspring, Greenspan had developed highly successful defenses. In this case, he took a defiant stand, and it put an end to the interrogation. He seemed to reserve such defiance for instances when his actions were indefensible.

Greenspan told the *New York Times* reporter in 1989 that the issue "was whether the ownership by savings and loan associations in real estate projects and other commercial ventures posed excessive risk."[43] These are topics that Greenspan addressed to Edwin Gray. They are general subjects, not the specific issues of a bank balance sheet filled with risky loans and junk bonds. Greenspan reviewed its "application [for direct investments] and its audited financial statements" (according to his letter to Thomas F. Sharkey).[44] By the end of 1984, Lincoln's investments included raw land in the boondocks even as it betrayed an insatiable appetite for junk bonds.[45]

Such carelessness is important, given the fact that by 1989, Greenspan was the country's leading bank regulator. He had had considerable relevant experience when he was hired by Charles Keating. Greenspan was a director of J. P. Morgan. He had been on the board of directors of Trans-World Financial, a savings and loan holding company, from 1962 to 1974.[46] Moreover, Greenspan would later reminisce about his assiduous grounding in analyzing bank loans: "When … I was on the loan committee of [J. P. Morgan], … we actually went through the loan portfolio major client … by major client. The review was quite thorough."[47]

Chances are, the Lincoln junk-bond portfolio that Greenspan presumably reviewed was full of Drexel Burnham issues. The 1984 annual report of Columbia Savings and Loan—one of the "big three" that held $3.5 billion of junk at the end of the same year—shows that every issue was sold by Milken's group.[48]

---

[43] Ibid.

[44] Mayer, *Greatest-Ever Bank Robbery*, p. 325.

[45] Nash, "Greenspan's Lincoln Savings Regret."

[46] Greenspan's "Statement for Completion by Presidential Nominees" under "Qualifications."

[47] FOMC transcript, September 29, 1998, p. 106.

[48] Wigmore, *Securities Markets in the 1980s*, p. 286.

The *New York Times* reporter also told his readers in 1989 that "no one in Washington is saying that Mr. Greenspan has compromised either his integrity or that of his office." Probably so. But the question is whether there was anyone left in Washington who dared raise the issue of integrity.

In the end, Greenspan compromised something. Maybe it was his obligation or ability to think. The evidence from Ayn Rand to the present was of a mind detached from its surroundings and unburdened by intellectual curiosity. He would soon be Federal Reserve chairman.

8

"THE NEW MR. DOLLAR":
CHAIRMAN OF THE
FEDERAL RESERVE

1987

SENATOR PROXMIRE: "Every one of the other chairmen of the Council of Economic Advisers had the same problem, and they didn't miss by as much as you did, not nearly as much."

ALAN GREENSPAN: "I feel sorry for me and happy for them."[1]

—Senate Committee on Banking, Housing and Urban Affairs transcript, July 21, 1987

Paul Volcker decided not to seek a third term in 1987. If President Reagan had pressed him to stay on, Volcker might have relented, but the Federal Reserve chairman did not receive enthusiastic support.[2]

Volcker's purported independence from political considerations had been diluted. By the fall of 1986, Reagan had replaced all voting Fed governors. Previous appointees had resigned or their terms had expired.[3]

---

[1] Senate Committee on Banking, Housing and Urban Affairs transcript, July 21, 1987, p. 42.

[2] In 1987, "[t]he Administration wanted a Fed chairman who would ... collaborate more intimately with the White House." William Greider, *Secrets of the Temple: How the Federal Reserve Runs the Country* (New York: Simon and Schuster, 1987), p. 713.

[3] Senate Committee on Banking, Housing and Urban Affairs transcript, July 21, 1987, p. 4.

The *Wall Street Journal* wrote that this would "put a supply-side stamp on the central bank ... [and] may enhance the chances for easier credit."[4] The supply-side movement had developed, politically, with similarities to the New Economics policy makers of the 1950s and 1960s. The supply-siders seamlessly wrapped expansive tendencies inside a pro-growth American flag. As in the 1950s, the mandate for growth swamped considerations that a closer relationship between credit and production was needed to approach a more balanced economy.

When Greenspan learned of his nomination to head the Fed, "he struggled inwardly to control his glee."[5] His biographer Jerome Tuccille writes: "*This* was the role he had been training for his entire life."[6]

When the nomination was announced, Greenspan's face was on the front cover of *Time*, with the caption "The New Mr. Dollar."[7] This was prophetic—both the omnipresent Greenspan image and the man who printed more dollars than all of his predecessors combined. Opinions in the *Time* profile varied. Robert Hormats, vice chairman of Goldman Sachs (International), predicted a sharp reversal in the new chairman's ability to communicate: Volcker's "banker's jargon" was difficult to understand; Greenspan had "a gift for rendering economic concepts in ... uncomplicated language."[8] This raises the question of how well Wall Street knew Greenspan in 1983, when 37 percent had expressed special confidence in him as Volcker's heir.

THE NOMINATION HEARING: PROXMIRE'S QUEST FOR AN INDEPENDENT FED

Greenspan's nomination hearing before the Committee on Banking, Housing and Urban Affairs took place on July 21, 1987. It was chaired by Senator William Proxmire, a Democrat from Wisconsin. The senator

---

[4] Paul Blustein, "Fed Governor Emmett Rice Resigns Position," *Wall Street Journal*, October 3, 1986.

[5] Jerome Tuccille, *Alan Shrugged: The Life and Times of Alan Greenspan, the World's Most Powerful Banker* (Hoboken, N.J.: Wiley, 2002), p.163.

[6] Ibid.

[7] George Russell, "The New Mr. Dollar," *Time*, June 15, 1987.

[8] Ibid.

told the candidate that he had voted against Greenspan's nomination for chairman of the Council of Economic Advisers in 1974. Proxmire chided the candidate for a "dismal forecasting record" when Greenspan was chairman of the CEA. The senator reviewed the forecasts made by the CEA between 1976 and 1986. Proxmire was most interested in the CEA's forward-looking projections for the years after Greenspan's tenure. In Proxmire's words, the forecasts made by the candidate were "way off." Of the Treasury bill interest-rate forecasts made by the Council of Economic Advisers (for the years 1976 through 1986), Greenspan's "were wrong by the biggest margin of any in the 11 years." (The senator is referring to all of the CEA chairmen who served during the 11 years.) Proxmire went on: "There you broke all records for the entire period in error." Moreover, the man whose opinions President Ford weighed more heavily than "those of any other economist" had prophesied the Treasury bill rate would be 4.4 percent in 1978. It was 9.8 percent.

Of inflation: "[T]here again, you broke all records." The only CEA chairman to adorn the front cover of *Newsweek* estimated that the Consumer Price Index would rise 4.5 percent in 1978. Instead, it soared 9.2 percent.

In later years, Greenspan would control such quibbles, but not this day. He replied to Proxmire: "[T]hat is not my recollection of the way the forecasts went." Proxmire then read the projections to Greenspan. The candidate admitted: "Well, if they're written down, those are the numbers."

Greenspan had an excuse:

GREENSPAN: "There is a very substantial difference, Senator, between forecasting in the Administration and forecasting outside."
PROXMIRE: "I sure hope so!"

Greenspan then embarked on the gobbledygook so familiar during his chairmanship. Proxmire waited patiently and then responded:

PROXMIRE: "[E]very one of the chairmen of the Council of Economic Advisers had the same problem, and they didn't miss by as much as you did, not nearly as much."
GREENSPAN: "I feel sorry for me and happy for them."

Proxmire, perhaps having anticipated Greenspan's public sector–private sector line of defense, had done his homework:

> PROXMIRE: "[Y]ou had an opportunity to be a forecaster with Greenspan & O'Neill [sic]. As you know, you put your forecasts to a direct test in the private sector."

(The firm of "Greenspan O'Neil Associates" referred to a joint venture between Greenspan and C. Roderick "Rory" O'Neil that provided money management services to pension funds.) Proxmire next quoted a then-recent issue of *Forbes* magazine:

> PROXMIRE: "'Greenspan & O'Neill turned in one of the least impressive records of all pension fund advisers.'"

Greenspan did not throw out an illusory defense this time:

> GREENSPAN: "All I can say is, I acknowledge that that did not work very well, and I take my share of the responsibility."
> PROXMIRE: "I hope … when you get to the Federal Reserve Board everything will come up roses. You can't always be wrong."
> GREENSPAN: "All I can suggest to you, Senator, is that the rest of my career has been somewhat more successful. [Laughter]"[9]

Proxmire did not respond and let other senators question the candidate. Greenspan knew—if not on this day, then soon enough—that he could run out the clock with his own form of filibustering. Like a caterpillar that huddles into a ball when its back is touched, Greenspan would change a specific point into a vague assertion that would leave his questioner unsure of how to pry him open.

The other senators had their own concerns. Senator Jim Sasser (D-Tenn.), who was also chairman of the Senate Budget Committee, was

---

[9] Dialogue between Greenspan and Proxmire about Greenspan's record: Senate Committee on Banking, Housing and Urban Affairs transcript, July 21, 1987, pp. 41–42.

concerned with debt accumulation. He thought the rising corporate debt associated with mergers and acquisitions was troubling, particularly the capacity of business to operate in the next downturn. Greenspan agreed. The United States would be more vulnerable in such a circumstance. Greenspan believed that fixed charges could be a problem, "specifically, debt service, which obviously does not decline when gross operating incomes fall, and the so-called 'coverage' of the interest becomes insufficient. ... We are increasing debt at levels which should make us all uncomfortable. It certainly makes me uncomfortable."[10] Greenspan apparently grew more comfortable. During the late housing boom, the Fed chairman gave many speeches extolling Americans' rising wealth (house prices) while not addressing the fixed debt "which obviously does not decline" that home buyers acquired when buying those houses.

The Leveraged Too-Big-to-Fail Megabank Foretold

Dismal as Greenspan's forecasting record was, Proxmire seemed more concerned about another topic: the growing concentration in banking. Greenspan was testifying during the great deregulation of banking. Initiatives, other than those mentioned in previous chapters, included authorization for commercial banks to cross state lines, to enter the brokerage business, and to change themselves into conglomerates offering all of the above services and more. The pressure to grow also pushed from the other end—investment banks ran brokerages, brokerages became investment banks; and so on. And from the outside there were nonbank banks such as Sears.

Proxmire was concerned with Greenspan's lobbying efforts. Among other ventures, a top project was Sears's attempt to offer banking services. Proxmire addressed the candidate: "[Y]ou think, if you erected Chinese walls, you can still merge banking and commerce. And that shocks this Senator, and I think it should shock many others. You, in my judgment, favor an increased concentration of banking."[11]

---

[10] Senate Committee on Banking, Housing and Urban Affairs transcript, July 21, 1987, pp. 36–37.

[11] Ibid., p. 60.

Proxmire had a second reason for concern. Prior to the nomination hearing, Greenspan submitted a statement to the White House and Congress, a full disclosure of relationships that might present conflicts of interest. In that statement, Greenspan did not disclose either Sears, Roebuck and Company or Lincoln Savings and Loan.[12] In the public record, there is an attachment to Greenspan's disclosure, a "response to a query by Chairman Proxmire."[13] Greenspan responded to Proxmire's request for "information about certain client relationships."[14] The attachment (a letter dated June 30, 1987, from Greenspan to Proxmire) distinguished Sears and Lincoln from the relationships listed in his full disclosure by slipping them in the side pocket of "advocacy projects." He was paid by each to lobby for banking deregulation.[15]

Proxmire reminded Greenspan that the Federal Reserve was acquiring greater control of the banking system: "[A]s Chairman of the Federal Reserve Board ... you are the country's leading bank regulator. The Fed, as we know, regulates a large number of State member banks ... [and] the bank holding companies that control an increasing proportion of all the commercial banking in our country. You take over this position at a time when there's a headlong drive toward increasing bank concentration."[16]

Proxmire tutored Greenspan on the menace of financial concentration: "As Chairman of the Federal Reserve Board you and your agency play the key role in approval or disapproval of these massive bank mergers.... I would feel much better about this appointment if there was somewhere in your record an indication of your awareness of the dangers to our economy of excessive financial concentration. Maybe you can reassure us that you understand that banking should be separated from commerce and the unique multiplicity of banking in this country is an immense source of strength for our small businesses."[17]

---

[12] Nathaniel C. Nash, "Greenspan Says He'd Sit Out Some Federal Reserve Votes," *New York Times*, July 11, 1987.

[13] Senate Committee on Banking, Housing and Urban Affairs transcript, July 21, 1987, p. 73.

[14] Ibid., p. 78.

[15] Ibid., pp. 78–79.

[16] Ibid., p. 5.

[17] Ibid., pp. 5–6.

The candidate and director of J. P. Morgan and Company as well as its banking subsidiary, Morgan Guaranty Trust Company, was not Proxmire's ideal central banker in this regard. Large banks are generally indifferent to small business.

Proxmire knew what to expect from Greenspan. Proxmire described Greenspan elsewhere in the hearing as a "get along, go along, comfortable" CEA chairman.[18] Over the course of Greenspan's term at the Fed, banks would merge and expand until they were no longer banks. They take deposits, make loans, trade for their own accounts, manage private-equity funds, manage hedge funds, serve as brokers for competing hedge funds, offer mortgages, securitize mortgages, sell securitized mortgages, then sell credit derivative swaps to protect the buyer against default from the securitized mortgages they previously sold. The chairman's statements and questions were spoken to Greenspan, but may have been directed as much at members of the Senate Banking Committee. Proxmire saw danger ahead and found few kindred spirits among his fellow legislators. He resigned himself to a lonely outpost: "It seems to me that banking in this country and finance in this country is … likely to move very sharply … in the direction of concentration…. I think, most Senators, if they thought very long about it, might be very concerned about it. And I think the American people would be too." (He also spoke as a man with little use for the Federal Reserve: "You will move in with a Board of clones—not clowns, clones.")[19]

Proxmire concluded: "[T]his nomination should result in a slam-bang debate in committee and on the floor. It won't. And it is startling, in view of what you have told us."[20]

Senator Proxmire did not run again for the Senate. His term expired in 1989. Later in 1989, the Federal Reserve permitted J. P. Morgan to underwrite Xerox debt, the first such issue from a commercial bank since 1933, the year of the Glass-Steagall Act. (That legislation had separated commercial from investment banking.) In what *Time* magazine called

---

[18] Ibid., p. 4.
[19] Ibid., p. 60.
[20] Ibid., pp. 59–60.

"the widest breach of Glass-Steagall yet,"[21] the Federal Reserve permitted J. P. Morgan to underwrite stock in 1990.[22]

Today, Greenspan's forbearance from regulating banks and derivatives is ascribed to his Ayn Rand–free-market beliefs. Greenspan has no such beliefs. Senator Proxmire understood competitive banking. Competition was disappearing. After the Glass-Steagall Act was repealed in 1999, the largest banks devoured the minnows until the supermarket-megabanks were so large that they did not compete. The behemoths kept adding leverage. They deflected criticism ("we're hedged") until they grew so large, leveraged, and reckless that they were capable of devouring the world economy.

THE DEATH OF TOWNSEND-GREENSPAN

The Townsend-Greenspan firm died quietly on July 31, 1987. The government asked Greenspan to remove his name from the firm, and he complied.[23] The furniture and computers were sold at the beginning of August.[24] Greenspan was required to place his $2.9 million of assets in a blind trust.[25] The White House request was fortuitous. Pierre Rinfret, a New York consulting economist (who had served with Greenspan on Nixon's 1968 economic advisory panel), refuted the common perception: "Everyone thinks that Greenspan gave up a lucrative consulting business to go to work in the public sector. In actuality, his business had been losing clients steadily to the point where he hardly had any left by the middle of the nineteen eighties."[26] The new Fed chairman had spent the past few years lobbying at 1600 Pennsylvania Avenue in lieu of studying livestock and mobile home sales. Townsend-Greenspan had been hollowed out.

---

[21] "American Notes: Banking," *Time*, October 1, 1990.

[22] "History of J. P. Morgan Chase, 1799 to the Present"; www.jpmorgan,com/pages/jpmorgan/investbk/about/history.

[23] "Greenspan's Firm Is Closing," *New York Times*, July 30, 1987, p. D5.

[24] Ibid.

[25] Justin Martin, *Greenspan: The Man behind Money* (Cambridge, Mass.: Perseus, 2000), p. 156.

[26] Tuccille, *Alan Shrugged*, p. 154.

INTRODUCTION TO PART 2
THE PINNACLE OF POWER

1987–2006

A permanent Governor of the Bank of England would be one of the greatest men in England. He would be a little 'monarch' in the City.... He would be the personal embodiment of the Bank of England; he would be constantly clothed with an almost indefinite *prestige*.... Practical men would be apt to say that it was better than the Prime Ministership, for it would ... have a greater jurisdiction over that which practical men would most value,—over money.

—*Walter Bagehot,* Lombard Street *(1873)*

On August 11, 1987, his hand placed on the Torah, the economist who had refused his bar mitzvah was sworn in as Federal Reserve chairman.[1] Shortly after Greenspan revealed himself as a man who could keep a straight face no matter what he said.

Greenspan was tested immediately by the stock market crash on October 19, 1987. In retirement, Alan Greenspan would declare the 1987 stock market crash was a key educational experience during his tenure.[2] Among the lessons not learned was to distrust derivative sales pitches. The derivative product that set off this crash was excused by

---

[1] Justin Martin, *Greenspan: The Man behind Money,* (Cambridge, Mass.: Perseus, 2000), pp. 157–158. "Cousin Wesley brought along the copy of the Torah used at Greenspan's CEA swearing in that was signed by Gerald Ford."

[2] Anthony Massucci, "Greenspan Cites 1987 Stock Crash, 9/11 as Key Education at Fed," *Bloomberg,* June 1, 2007.

one of its inventors, Mark Rubinstein: "[A] day like this wouldn't be expected to happen during the lifetime of the universe."[3] We would hear other "once in the lifetime of the universe" excuses in 1994 (discussed in Chapter 10), 1998 (the topic of Chapter 15), and again in 2008. Each time, Greenspan followed by singing the virtues of derivatives. He seemed to be a slow learner.

The most charitable interpretation of Americans' love affair with Greenspan would acknowledge people's mental laxity. It is not too strong a description to say that many Americans worshipped Greenspan. At the very least, most Americans who listened to Greenspan took him at his word—even though they did not know what he was saying. This included the Washington politicians, Washington-oriented economists, and Wall Street strategists.

They were well served by Greenspan. All interests inflated. Expansion surrounded us: the stock market, stock-option payouts, Fannie Mae, the reputation of central banking, and the growing opportunities to become a CNBC celebrity. This contrasted with the deflation of the middle class and the industrial economy.

A striking characteristic of Greenspan's term at the Federal Reserve was how his reputation grew as the influence of the Fed diminished. Finance had become much bigger than the banking system. The Federal Reserve historically had acted to expand or contract the economy by adding bank reserves to or subtracting them from the banking system.

Alan Greenspan contributed to the Fed's loss of control. He ceded the Federal Reserve's mandate to regulate and rein in financial excess. He reduced or eliminated many reserve requirements for bank deposits. He effectively renounced the Federal Reserve's authority over stock market margin requirements. While devolving the Fed's real authority, he spent much of his term acquiring a mystical hold on the American imagination.

Whether by accident or design, his open-mouth policy averted attention from his deficiencies. He missed the recession of the early 1990s. Yet, before Congress in 1994, he reconstructed his heroic anticipation and foresighted action that had averted a deeper recession—the same recession that he never mentioned until it was over. The significance of this recession may not be appreciated.

---

[3] http://www.derivativesstrategy.com/magazine/archive/1999/0799qa.asp.

The recovery was a unique one. It owed more to finance than to work. Banks had bungled in the late 1980s, making real estate loans that left them incapacitated. With the banks unable to lend, the Greenspan Fed cut the funds rate from 9.5 percent in early 1989 to 3 percent by late 1992. That rate sat at 3 percent until February 1994. Banks borrowed at 3 percent and bought long-term Treasuries yielding 6 percent. This refloated their balance sheets, but at a cost.

Banks were no longer the financial traffic cop for the economy. The bond market and derivatives played larger roles. The bank credit system would struggle and recover, but it would not reclaim its predominant role. Savings and investment assets were leaving the banking system and entering markets. The Federal Reserve controls only money supplied to and from the banking system; here again, it lost influence.[4] Markets are more fickle than bank lending; thus, the financial machinery was less stable.

Greenspan gave his often quoted "irrational exuberance" speech in December 1996. This was his ever-so-muted warning that the stock market might be overpriced: "how do we know when irrational exuberance has unduly escalated asset values?"

Yet, he claimed he had popped a bubble in 1994. "I think we partially broke the back of an emerging speculation in equities. We pricked that bubble [in the bond market] as well."[5] He offered to pop the bubble at the September 1996 FOMC meeting: "I recognize that there is a stock market bubble problem at this point.... We do have the possibility of raising major concerns by increasing margin requirements. I guarantee that if you want to get rid of the bubble, whatever it is, that will do it."

After his "irrational exuberance" speech, Greenspan gave a couple of warnings in early 1997. Critics told him that he should not make stock market predictions. He never addressed the bubble again—that is, until he decided that he could not identify one before it blew up. Greenspan donned his flak jacket before Congress in June 1999: "bubbles generally are perceptible only after the fact."[6] The same man had claimed credit for popping bubbles at four Federal Open Market

---

[4] Peter Warburton, *Debt and Delusion: Central Bank Follies That Threaten Economic Disaster* (Princeton, N.J.: WorldMeta View Press, 2005), p. 9.

[5] FOMC meeting, February 28, 1994, p. 3.

[6] Joint Economic Committee, *Monetary Policy and the Economic Outlook*, June 17, 1999.

Committee meetings in 1994. His see-no-evil, hear-no-evil bubble claim would become known as the Greenspan Doctrine among economists.[7] His open money spigot policy whenever the stock market buckled became known as the "Greenspan put" among speculators. This was a government welfare program with consequences we continue to delay and magnify.

One of the most dismaying developments during the Greenspan era was the silence of professional economists. As a whole, they nodded their heads in agreement, no matter what the man said. Greenspan's most enduring fabrication was productivity. The chairman's cheerleading for productivity and technology was essential to the stock market bubble, and to Fed policy. Greenspan hypothesized that the stock market was not overpriced; it simply reflected improvements in productivity. Therefore, stocks were worth whatever the market considered the appropriate New Era price.

The gruesome contortions of the productivity calculation are addressed in Chapter 12. It was from this platform that Greenspan launched his tortured justifications for the Nasdaq trading at 200 times earnings by early 2000.[8] Central banks around the world aligned their policies with the New Era. That central bank policy was driven by such effervescent claims shows the bankruptcy of economic thought among those making policy today.

Greenspan enthusiastically endorsed this road to the poorhouse. At one FOMC meeting in 2002, Greenspan remarked: "We know ... that the average extraction of equity per sale of an existing home is well over $50,000. A substantial part of the equity extraction related to home sales, which is running at an annual rate close to $200 billion, is expended on personal consumption and home modernization, two components, of course, of GDP."[9]

On February 23, 2004, the Federal Reserve chairman addressed the Credit Union National Association. Greenspan observed: "Many homeowners might have saved tens of thousands of dollars had they

---

[7] A headline in the March 28, 2008, *Financial Times* for an article by Krishna Guha read: "Greenspan Doctrine on Asset Prices Questioned." First sentence: "The Federal Reserve may have to rethink the Greenspan Doctrine that a central bank should not try to target asset prices."

[8] Fred Hickey, *High-Tech Strategist*, January 4, 2000.

[9] FOMC meeting transcript, September 24, 2002, p. 78.

held adjustable-rate mortgages."[10] By early 2004, many house buyers could meet monthly payments only with an adjustable-rate mortgage. (These were sold at a low rate that would adjust to a higher rate in later years.) When those became unaffordable, "interest-only" and "negative-amortization" mortgages were necessary. In 2002, 2 percent of California residential mortgages were interest only. This rose to 47 percent in 2004 and 61 percent in January and February of 2005.[11]

Greenspan also elevated the housing boom by telling Americans how rich they were. He very rarely used the word *debt*—that is, the payments required to pay down mortgage principal. Instead, he threw out multitrillion-dollar figures for the "wealth" that Americans had accumulated through the rising values of house prices.

Shortly before retirement, Greenspan, seemed more forthcoming: "[W]e can have little doubt that the exceptionally low level of home mortgage interest rates has been a major driver of the recent surge of home building and home turnover and the steep climb in home prices."[12] In the same speech, he claimed that if house prices cooled, "these borrowers, and the institutions that service them, could be exposed to significant losses."[13]

Greenspan stepped down from the Federal Reserve on January 31, 2006.

---

[10] Alan Greenspan, "Understanding Household Debt Obligations," speech at the Credit Union National Association 2004 Governmental Affairs Conference, Washington, D.C., February 23, 2004.

[11] "Consumer Finance," speech at Ruth Simon, "Concerns Mount About Mortgage Risks," *Wall Street Journal Online*, May 17, 2005.

[12] Alan Greenspan, "Mortgage Banking," speech at the American Bankers Association Annual Convention, Palm Desert, California (via satellite), September 26, 2005.

[13] Ibid.

9

THE STOCK MARKET CRASH
AND THE RECESSION THAT
GREENSPAN MISSED

1987–1990

Modern particle physics is, in a literal sense, incomprehensible. It is grounded not in the tangible and testable notions of objects and points and pushes and pulls but in a sophisticated and indirect mathematical language of fields and interactions and wave-functions.... Even within the community of particle physicists there are those who think that the trend towards increasing abstraction is turning theoretical physics into recreational mathematics, endlessly amusing to those who can master the techniques and join the game, but ultimately meaningless because the objects of the mathematical manipulations are forever beyond the access of experiment and measurement.

—*David Lindley,* The End of Physics *(1993)*[1]

[A] day like this wouldn't be expected to happen in the life of our universe, which is 20 billion years. Indeed, it wouldn't even happen if you were to live through 20 billion of those universes.[2]

—Mark Rubinstein, an architect of portfolio insurance, discussing the failure of his product on October 19, 1987

---

[1] David Lindley, *The End of Physics: The Myth of a Unified Theory* (New York: Basic Books, 1993), pp. 18–19.

[2] http://www.derivativesstrategy.com/magazine/archive/1999/0799qa.asp.

Looking back, there were several good reasons the stock market crashed in 1987. (Looking back, there always are.) Secretary of the Treasury James Baker enjoined the Germans to devalue the deutschmark. Congressman Dan Rostenkowski had threatened a bill that would hamper leveraged buyouts. Stock prices were too high (the Dow had risen 350 percent over the previous five years). A derivatives strategy had blown apart.

The last topic will be discussed, since that is Alan Greenspan's legacy. The chairman was to extol the virtues of derivatives over the next 18 years and forever praise their ability to diffuse risk. This first widespread failure of a derivatives strategy demonstrated that when such a product is universally employed, it concentrates risk.

The derivative strategy that came a cropper was portfolio insurance. It was the brainstorm of Mark Rubinstein and Hayne Leland, professors at Berkeley, who formed the firm of Leland O'Brien Rubinstein Associates (LOR).[3] The basic concept was to insure investors against losses in the stock market.[4] The thesis was fine, but the execution could be applied on a wide scale only after the introduction of financial derivatives.[5]

Leland O'Brien Rubinstein's success bred imitators—oodles of them. As with most investment ideas, success draws too many participants, and it ends in tears.[6] A distinguishing flaw was the assumption of a

---

[3] Peter L. Bernstein, *Capital Ideas: The Improbable Origins of Modern Wall Street* (New York: Free Press, 1992), pp. 269–274.

[4] A simplified example: XYZ company's pension plan wants to protect against losing more than 8 percent of its principal in any calendar year. The Treasury bill rate is 5 percent. All of its assets are invested in the S&P 500. The stock market falls 13 percent on the first day of the year. The portfolio insurer shifts 100 percent of the money out of stocks and into Treasury bills. At the end of the year, the 5 percent earned on the principal will leave the fund with an 8 percent loss for the year.

[5] A futures contract on the S&P 500 was inaugurated in 1983. By buying (or selling) an S&P 500 futures contract, the insured would hold a position equal to that resulting from buying (or selling) the 500 stocks. Based on the actual asset mix and portfolio performance of the pension plan (our assumed purchaser of the product), LOR instructed the client to buy and sell the requisite number of contracts to meet the objective.

[6] If all pension plans set the line in the sand at an 8 percent one-year loss, it would be impossible for all the portfolio insurers to sell stocks at the same moment.

"continuous market."[7] There had to be a buyer at a price linked to the previous price. It would not work if buyers for the "underlying" security disappeared. (The *underlying* is the physical item being delivered: corn, for instance, or the 500 stocks in the Standard & Poor's index.) A derivative "derives" its price from the physical item. In the case of financial derivatives, the derivative derives its price from the price of a stock, bond, or currency. For example, a derivative gives the buyer the option to purchase a share of General Electric stock for $10. If GE stock is trading at $8 when the option is sold, the contract has no immediate value: why pay $10 when the stock can be bought for $8? If GE stock rises to $40, the option owner is owed (at least) $30 by the broker who sold the derivative.

OCTOBER 19, 1987

On August 25, 1987, the Dow Jones Industrial Average peaked at 2,722. This was a 43 percent rise since the beginning of the year. The DJIA suffered a 10 percent loss over the four days leading up to October 19, 1987. In lockstep with the mathematical formulas, each day portfolio insurers sold the S&P 500 futures contracts and bought Treasury bills. The stocks underlying the S&P 500 Index (or the S&P 500 futures contract) were sold.

On Monday, October 19, 1987, sell orders for stocks overwhelmed the market before it opened. The Dow finally opened at 2,047, a 200-point drop from the Friday close. Markets were not continuous. The most basic of premises was wrong, and it was wrong largely because portfolio insurance overwhelmed the markets.

It was impossible to calculate the S&P 500 Index. The comparative option contracts traded at as much as a 20 percent discount to the stocks; dealers refused to buy stocks; market makers would not answer their telephones; mutual fund shareholders could not sell because of the overloaded telephone lines; brokers sold their clients' stock without

---

[7] From Bernstein, *Capital Ideas*, p. 285: "For the strategy to be fully effective, the investors without portfolio insurance must accommodate the investors with portfolio insurance, at all times and under all conditions. Changes in stock prices must be continuous—a stock must not close at $25 and open the next day at $22....The events of October 1987 shattered the underlying assumptions of how markets, and therefore, portfolio insurance would work in practice."

telling them, often at a price far below the bid. So many had jumped into the product (Chase Manhattan Bank; Morgan Stanley; Aetna Life & Casualty; Exxon's and General Motors's pension plans) that a record number of S&P 500 index options were traded. The failure of portfolio insurance to deliver as promised was self-fulfilling.[8]

The result was that on October 19, the Dow fell 22.6 percent, and the S&P 500 dropped 20.5 percent. S&P 500 futures fell nearly 29 percent—cash selling (of stocks) could not keep pace with futures selling.[9]

LOR's business had seen its best days. Rubenstein claimed that "a one-day decline of 29 percent ... wouldn't happen in the life of our universe, which is 20 billion years. Indeed, it wouldn't even happen if you were to live through 20 billion of those universes."[10] The calculations differed, but this was the general view of efficient market theorists, a group that suffers from innocence, self-absorption, and tenure. The strategy had been marketed as the culmination of theories produced by Nobel Prize–winning economists. The guild stuck to its models and assumptions of continuous markets, so an event that was impossible, given these assumptions, was dismissed as such.

The stock market crash was a trial by fire for the new Fed chairman. He reassured markets that the Fed would supply unlimited funding to the banking system. This soothed nerves, and the stock market started to recover. Comparisons to 1929 were inevitable. The black cloud obscured the generally upward trend of stock market prices for the year: the S&P 500 rose 5.2 percent in 1987. The economy was growing. In 1929, it was slowing.

Greenspan was generally lauded for his response to the market crash. The greatest criticism was of his September 4 decision to raise the discount rate from 5.5 percent to 6.0 percent, about six weeks before the crash.[11]

Greenspan's decision to raise the discount rate had been more than justified—it was redundant. Paul Volcker, in maybe the only comment

---

[8] Robert Sobel, *Panic on Wall Street* (New York: Dutton, 1988), pp. 440–479.

[9] Richard Bookstaber, *A Demon of Our Own Design*, (Hoboken, N.J.: Wiley, 2007), p. 13,

[10] http://www.derivativesstrategy.com/magazine/archive/1999/0799qa.asp.

[11] Steven K. Beckner, *Back from the Brink: The Greenspan Years* (New York: Wiley, 1996), pp. 32–33.

the former chairman made about the Greenspan Fed, fully endorsed the September 4 rate decision.[12] The fed funds rate—which is far more influential than the discount rate—was already rising on September 4. It would continue to rise afterward. The 30-year Treasury yield leapt from 9.0 percent in August to 9.75 percent.[13] A stock market that had risen 43 percent between January 1 and August 25 faced a rash of complexities.

There is a tendency now to recall the entire Volcker chairmanship as an Arcadian paradise, but Alan Greenspan assumed office at a difficult time. Imbalances were rising. The balance of payments with foreign countries had increased from a deficit of $5 billion in 1982 to one of $147 billion in 1986.[14] The federal budget deficit had risen from $127 billion in 1982 to $221 billion in 1986.[15] Corporate and consumer debt were also rising.

LESSONS FROM THE CRASH

Greenspan appeared before the Senate Banking Committee in February 1988. He thought that "[e]ven if that last surge in long-term [interest] rates had not occurred, the [stock] market would have topped out and come down anyway, and I find it difficult to perceive how actions of the Federal Reserve were material factors in the market."[16]

He may have been right. However, it is unfortunate that this real-world, real-time opportunity to understand the misleading promises of derivative manufacturers passed him by. Not only had the strategy failed, but the practitioners and apologists dismissed it. This was recreational mathematics in a rich medium. Greenspan had every reason to ban complex derivative strategies from his banks. He would serve as chief regulator of the financial system as it grew to a size far beyond the requirements of the economy it purportedly served. The strategies grew more inventive, impressive, exhilarating, perplexing, and finally unintelligible.

The crash afforded Greenspan his first opportunity to open the money spigot, and he did so with relish. He received general support.

---

[12] "Volcker Hails Fed Rate Rise," *New York Times*, September 11, 1987, p. D14.

[13] Steven K. Beckner, *Back from the Brink: The Greenspan Years*, p. 34.

[14] OECD.StatExtracts.

[15] Congressional Budget Office.

[16] Beckner, *Back from the Brink*, p. 62. This testimony was on February 24, 1988.

During Greenspan's 1987 nomination hearing, Democrats had warned Greenspan not to attempt an Arthur Burns money-printing effort to elect Republicans in 1988. If it hadn't been for the crash, cutting the funds rate would have placed Greenspan in the dock. However, Democrats did not fault Greenspan for his efforts to calm the markets.

The stock market crash punched a hole in the 1980s asset inflation. Rather than a bubble popping, it was more like an automobile tire with a slow, steady leak. The savings and loan crack-up caused a drain on credit. Commercial banks, too, incapable of restraining themselves during a splurge—any splurge—were about to reduce lending.

WHEN CITICORP LENDS—WE ALL PAY

After the foreign loan mishap of the early 1980s, it did not take long for big banks to again drive themselves into penury. Real estate lending accounted for 60 percent of the net loan growth of the U.S. banking system between 1984 and 1989.[17]

In the first quarter of 1990, real estate lending grew 20 percent in New York.[18] Yet, by 1990, there was more vacant office space in midtown Manhattan than the total office space of Portland, Oregon; Tampa, Florida; and Seattle, Washington.[19] Having divorced itself from any sense of reason, the financial industry was due for a douse of reality. In the recession that was now leaving the nursery, 25 percent of the jobs lost nationally would be in New York City.[20] By 1991, 60 percent of the city's residents claimed they would leave New York if they could.[21]

The bellwether of ignorance, Citicorp, once again led the charge to the bottom. The chairman, John Reed, admitted: "We were warned about real estate two years ago, and we pooh-poohed it. Now I'm damned

---

[17] James Grant, *Money of the Mind: Borrowing and Lending in America from the Civil War to Michael Milken* (New York: Farrar Straus Giroux, 1992), p. 418.

[18] Ibid., p. 417.

[19] Robert A. M. Stern, David Fishman, and Jacob Tilove, *New York 2000: Architecture and Urbanism between the Bicentennial and the Millennium* (New York: Monacelli Press, 2006), p. 24.

[20] Ibid., p. 28.

[21] Ibid.

embarrassed because the critics were right and we were wrong."[22] By July 1991, Congressman John Dingell from Michigan stated that Citigroup was "technically insolvent."[23] Greenspan did not opt for a noninterventionist approach. Even if he had wanted to, the Continental Illinois precedent would have been difficult to contradict.

Greenspan might differ from Volcker in many ways, but one thing was the same: the Federal Reserve chairmanship had evolved into a brokerage operation for insolvent financial institutions. Whatever claims Greenspan might make (or Paul Volcker had made) about the stability and resiliency of the American financial system, former Fed Chairman William McChesney Martin would find it unrecognizably frenetic.

Finance and financial institutions were more fluid than when the gold standard existed. Alan Greenspan explained the traditional reserve currency's balancing properties in "Gold and Economic Freedom" (discussed in Chapter 2). The world bond market increased from less than $1 trillion in 1970 to $23 trillion by 1987.[24] Without a gold standard, there was no ultimate settlement, so unredeemable currency and bond claims grew. Asset inflation and concentration of credit gave those who possessed "native cunning and access to leverage" an opportunity to apply their skills.

THE PANDERER AND HIS MASTERS

Early in Greenspan's term, the chairman of the House Banking Committee, Democratic Congressman Henry González of Texas, fumed about the "tremendous power" of the Fed. The institution should be "accountable."[25] Gonzáles had attempted to impeach Volcker. Such a campaign was in the tradition of grandstanding politicians in Washington. It also suggests a reason for the outsized prestige of the Federal Reserve. Were it not for Greenspan's testimony before hectoring politicians, the man and his board

---

[22] Grant, *Money of the Mind*, p. 430; Reed was quoted in "Citicorp Faces the World: An Interview with John Reed," *Harvard Business Review*, November–December, 1990.

[23] Ibid.

[24] Peter Warburton, *Debt and Delusion: Central Bank Follies that Threaten Economic Disaster* (Princeton, N.J.: WorldMeta View Press, 2005), p. 3.

[25] Beckner, *Back from the Brink*, p. 111.

might have been cast into the dull blur of other federal bureaucracies. As it is, the willingness of the Senate and Congress to shift blame from their mendacious and inflationary budgets has cemented their incumbency far more than their legislation has served the country.

Greenspan would be entreated to inflate by a phalanx of political interests—the executive branch as well as Congress, Democrats and Republicans alike. The inundation will not be discussed here in equal proportion to its influence. However, as an example of its constant presence, one can turn to Steven K. Beckner's *Back from the Brink: The Greenspan Years*. The book serves as a catalog of unseemly intrusions.[26] Greenspan's weakness of character was only too apparent, but it should not be forgotten that he served the interests of politicians who used the loquacious chairman as an air-raid shelter.

THE PREDATORS CRASH

After the 1987 crash, the stock market recovered, but easy liquidity did not. The deals grew larger, though, with riskier bonds to finance these monuments to braggadocio. In early 1989, Kohlberg Kravis Roberts paid $30.9 billion for RJR Nabisco Inc. This was a big number. It is difficult for an outsider to assess the efficiencies of such combinations, but they cause anxiety and disorientation. Sneaker jobs were going to Asia. This jumble of numbers and worries is often what we live by. The smorgasbord did not appeal to the tastes of either the public or the politicians.

The temper in Washington was growing hostile.[27] Kohlberg Kravis Roberts gathered 400 dealmakers and lawyers at the Pierre Hotel in New York to celebrate the RJR Nabisco LBO on lobster and Dom Perignon. The dealmakers from Drexel Burnham, Merrill Lynch, Morgan Stanley, and Wasserstein Perella and the lawyers from Davis Polk & Wardwell and Skadden Arps, Slate, Meagher & Flom were congratulated for making over $1 billion in fees. This did not include the junk-bond sales and

---

[26] From this author's unsystematic notes, see, pp. 111, 119, 141–145, 156, 163, 219, 231, 236, 243, 270, 272, 285–286, 291, 293, 294, 298, 302, 306, 310, 312, 313, 314, 315–327, 331–333, 348, 364, 366, and 370. This covers only the years 1987–1994.

[27] The term *financial buyer* was used to differentiate these deals from "corporate buyers" or "strategic buyers." Corporations were being priced out of the merger business.

bank loans. Given the times, the dinner received publicity. It was also seen as being in poor taste. *Predator's Ball*, a bestselling book about Drexel Burnham, encased Michael Milken's already famous client parties in perpetuity.

Even as the borrowing bubble was peaking, it had already started to deflate. Integrated Resources, a financial services company that seemed to dabble in everything, but specialized in selling tax shelters and absorbing Drexel Burnham issues, met its maker on June 13, 1989. That was the day when no bank would roll over its commercial paper. It was also the day that Michael Milken resigned from Drexel.[28] The daisy chain that had bloomed from the X-shaped desk in Los Angeles was withering.[29]

In fact, it started to gasp for water in late 1988 when Drexel Burnham Lambert agreed to settle insider trading investigations. Early in 1989, Michael Milken was indicted on 98 counts of fraud and racketeering. The market had been flooded with worthless paper: junk-bond issues rose from $2 billion in 1980 to over $200 billion issued in 1988. In December 1989, KKR placed one of its companies into Chapter 11 proceedings—Hillsborough Holdings Corporation, the first bankruptcy filing by a large company owned by Kohlberg Kravis Roberts.[30] The LBO mystique was gone.

The changing times were evident when Saul Steinberg spent $1 million at a Southampton summer party in 1989. This was half the cost of his daughter's 1988 wedding at the Metropolitan Museum of Art's Temple of Dendur, which had passed unnoticed. Southampton party guests told an inquiring press of their outrage. Other guests noted that the outraged looked mighty pleased at the party. Soon after, a bestselling book would immortalize the KKR and RJR Nabisco deal: *Barbarians at the Gate.* [31] Milken and Charles Keating were headed to jail.

---

[28] James Grant, *Minding Mr. Market: Ten Years on Wall Street with Grant's Interest Rate Observer* (New York: Farrar Straus Giroux, 1993), pp. 262–266.

[29] Drexel Burnham Lambert Inc. filed for bankruptcy, on February 13, 1990.

[30] "Chapter 11 for Kohlberg Kravis Unit," *New York Times*, December 28, 1989.

[31] Bryan Barfrough, *Barbarians at the Gate: The Fall of RJR Nabisco* (New York: Harper, 1990).

GREENSPAN NEVER SAW THE RECESSION—THEN PROMOTES
HIS FORESIGHT

Meanwhile, Chairman Greenspan was a busy man. In a 1989 *New York Times Magazine* profile, Louis Uchitelle met the chairman in his office. He observed that Greenspan "has been Fed chairman for almost a year and a half, but the built-in bookcases are still mostly empty." Uchitelle also noted that Greenspan's desk was strewn with newspapers, reports, statistics, and "even a paperback novel." [32] Senator Proxmire would probably not be surprised at his dishevelment.

Greenspan's audiences soaked up his subpar predictions as if they were front-page news. In fact, they were. A front-page headline from the January 31, 1990, *New York Times* read: "Recession Chances Have Diminished, Greenspan Says." [33] In August of 1990, he pronounced, "'those who argue that we are already in a recession are reasonably certain to be wrong.'" [34] The recession's official starting date was July 1, 1990. [35] Greenspan never mentioned the existence of a recession until four years later.

In 1994, Alan Greenspan produced a history lesson that served the interests of Alan Greenspan. He spoke of a credit crunch in the spring of 1989. The Federal Reserve chairman had anticipated the problem: "In an endeavor to defuse these financial strains, we moved short-term rates lower in a long series of steps in the summer of 1992, and we held them at unusually low levels until the end of 1993—both absolutely, and, importantly, relative to inflation." [36]

Greenspan's reconstruction of his own actions grew more heroic: "Lower interest rates fostered a dramatic improvement in the financial condition of borrowers and lenders. Households rolled outstanding

---

[32] Louis Uchitelle, "Caution at the Fed," *New York Times*, January 15, 1989, p. SM18.

[33] Robert D. Hershey Jr., "Recession Chances Have Diminished, Greenspan Says," *New York Times*, January 31, 1990, p. A1.

[34] Prakash Loungani, "The Arcane Art of Predicting Recessions," *Financial Times*, December 18, 2000.

[35] The National Bureau of Economic Research dates recessions.

[36] James Grant, *The Trouble with Prosperity: The Loss of Fear, the Rise of Speculation, and the Risk to American Savings* (New Year: Times Books, 1996), p. 195. Greenspan's reconstruction is covered in depth.

mortgages and consumer loans into much lower-rate debt.... And banks, which had cut back on credit availability partly because of their own balance sheet problems, were able to strengthen their capital positions."[37]

In *The Trouble with Prosperity*, James Grant wrote. "A search of the literature for examples of the personal and institutional foresight to which the chairman had alluded was unavailing."[38]

Despite the fevered attention commanded by the Federal Reserve chairman when he appeared before this or that committee, Greenspan's ignorance of the recession had gone unnoticed. The media would rather embellish a González-Greenspan feud. It made better copy.

The relationship between Greenspan, the politicians, and the press is not dissimilar to the rise of Chauncey Gardner in Jerzy Kosinski's novel *Being There*. Chauncey is a slow-minded gardener whose only recreational activity is watching TV. Chauncey cannot read or write. Louis Uchitelle's description of Greenspan's office is from a visual age. Greenspan was said to watch CNBC in his office. Chauncey becomes a mystical seer in Washington. His fame rising, he meets the president. Chauncey tells him that growth in the garden comes in the spring and summer, but then we have fall and winter: "As long as the roots are not severed all is well and will be well again." The president interprets this to be an economic forecast, and he "must admit ... [it] is one of the most refreshing and optimistic statements I've heard in a very, very long time."[39]

The parallel is of a man who mesmerized large pockets of seemingly intelligent people, not by any complete thought, but by phrases and words, such as "irrational exuberance," "conundrum," "measured," "soft spot," and "productivity". His forecasting record was abysmal, yet his face would adorn the front pages of newspapers the day after he issued another meandering statement. As the Fed continued to lose control of money, Greenspan's monetary policy seemed to be all that mattered. As his forecasts grew worse, he moved markets all the more.

Greenspan succeeded in a visual culture that was limited to short bursts of attention and limited memories.

---

[37] Ibid., p. 195.
[38] Ibid.
[39] Jerzy Kosinski, *Being There* (New York: Grove Press, 1999), p. 54.

10

RESTORING THE ECONOMY—
GREENSPAN UNDERWRITES
THE CARRY TRADE

1990–1994

I think we partially broke the back of an emerging speculation in equities.... We pricked that bubble [in the bond market] as well.... We also have created a degree of uncertainty; if we were looking at the emergence of speculative forces, which clearly were evident in very early stages, then I think we had a desirable effect.[1]

—*Alan Greenspan, February 28, 1994*

The sluggish economy was probably more of a burden to Alan Greenspan than similar downturns had been to his predecessors. The failure of the New Economics (managing the economy by adjusting spending and taxes) in the 1960s and 1970s had discredited fiscal policy as a means of managing the economy. Paul Volcker received wide acclaim for reviving the economy in the early 1980s. Thus, monetary policy was thought to be capable of stimulating the American economy in the early 1990s. Why the government needed to prevent a capitalist economy from recession was rarely discussed, least of all by the so-called capitalists who expected Washington to solve their problems.

---

[1] FOMC meeting transcript, February 28, 1994, p. 3.

The finger pointing was not only from the White House and congressional committees, but also from members of the FOMC. Federal Reserve Governor Wayne Angell thought that problems could have been averted if the Fed had recognized the recession sooner. Angell explained the consequences of the Fed's late start: "[I]f we hadn't had the recession then we wouldn't have ended up with a three percent fed funds rate."[2] The funds rate had briefly flirted with 10 percent in early 1989. It encountered no headwinds as it plummeted to 3 percent by late 1992.

Bank solvency improved and capital was restored with a nod of thanks to Greenspan. The Fed cut the funds rate 24 consecutive times between 1989 and 1993.[3] Banks refinanced their balance sheets by borrowing short and lending long. In this case, they were lending to the government—buying long-term Treasury securities. This preference for 10-year Treasuries meant the marginal dollar was not lent to business: "Greenspan and others took every chance they could to urge, if not beg, banks to lend."[4] Tacitly, Greenspan approved the banks' preferred strategy by steadily cutting the funds rate. A surprise rate increase during this tumble might have frightened the brazen. Political pressure may have deterred Greenspan from initiating a change in direction. Both Greenspan and George Bush were running for reelection.

GREENSPAN'S 1991 REELECTION

Greenspan's term as Fed chairman was to expire on August 11, 1991.[5] President Bush did not divulge his inclinations. The Fed cut the discount

---

[2] Steven K. Beckner, *Back from the Brink: The Greenspan Years* (New York: John Wiley & Sons, 1996), p. 215.

[3] James Grant, *The Trouble with Prosperity: The Loss of Fear, the Rise of Speculation, and the Risk to American Savings* (New York: Times Books, 1996), p. 192.

[4] Beckner, *Back from the Brink*, p. 245. In early 1991, Greenspan told the Senate Banking Committee that the Fed had seriously considered buying commercial bank loans to ease the credit crunch. The looming question, Greenspan explained, was whether the Fed should become "effectively a commercial banker." Ibid., p. 226.

[5] Ibid., p. 432: "Bush made what is known as a *recess appointment* while Congress was not in session. Greenspan's term as chairman expired on August 11, 1991, and his term as governor on January 31, 1992. Announced August 9, the recess appointment took effect August 10. Not until March 2, 1992 was Greenspan formally designated to a second four-year term, expiring March 2, 1996. He was also given another full 14-year term as a member of the Board of Governors, expiring January 31, 2006."

rate on August 6, 1991. Bush reappointed Greenspan to a new term as Fed chairman on August 9.[6] Normally, changes in monetary policy (such as increasing or decreasing rates) are made at meetings of the Federal Open Market Committee (FOMC). The FOMC meets about every six weeks. It had last met on July 2–3, and it would next meet on August 20, 1991. In this case, the FOMC held a conference call between meetings, and its decision to reduce the discount rate was announced the next day, August 7. At the July 2–3 meeting, the FOMC had voted unanimously "to stay on hold and in neutral."[7] The committee may have been anxious (legislators had introduced a bill to strip Fed presidents of their vote on monetary policy), but the next meeting was only two weeks after the conference call.[8] The chairman's stars were aligned: the timing of the conference call, the decision to cut the discount rate, the president's reappointment, and the date on which Greenspan's term was to end were a fortunate combination.

This was a recess appointment, since Congress was not in session. The legislators would vote on the president's choice in 1992. On December 17, 1991, President Bush, who had been talking cheerfully about the economy, spoke bluntly: "I am less interested in what the technical definition [of recession] is. People are hurting. When there's this kind of sluggishness and concern—definitions—heck with it. Let's get on with the business at hand."[9] The next day, General Motors announced that it was laying off 70,000 workers and closing 21 manufacturing plants.[10] Two days later, on December 20, 1991, the Fed cut the discount rate by a full percent (from 4½ percent to 3½ percent) and the funds rate by one-half of one percent (from 4½ percent to 4 percent).[11]

The Senate Banking Committee delayed Greenspan's reconfirmation. On January 29, 1992, the senators grilled Greenspan, then gave him a long list of questions to answer in writing.[12] It looked as if they were keeping the Federal Reserve chairman after school for punishment.

---

[6] Ibid., p. 244.

[7] Ibid., p. 243

[8] Ibid.

[9] Ibid., p. 260.

[10] On 21 plants and Bush quote, ibid.; on 70,000 laid off, Doron P. Levin, "General Motors to Cut 70,000 Jobs; 21 Plants to Shut," *New York Times*, December 19, 1991.

[11] Beckner, *Back from the Brink*, p. 261.

[12] Ibid., p. 269.

Congress had little to complain about. The lack of credit extended by the banking system stymied the economy, but it is not clear that the conduits of a recovery—businesses and households—wanted to borrow. Nonfinancial businesses reduced their debt loads in 1991 and 1992. Consumers continued to borrow more, but at a slower rate than in the 1980s. The Fed had cut reserve requirements for banks in late 1990, an unusual move for the Federal Reserve Board and certainly indicative of the Fed's efforts to get the machinery moving.[13]

A more orthodox approach is for the Fed to pump money into the banking system. Banks then lend and the economy grows. Usually. There was a snag though—the banks were short of capital, so lending was constrained.

But the relationship between banking and business was changing The bond market and derivative growth played a larger role in refloating the American economy in the 1990s. The bank credit system would recover, but it would not reclaim its predominant role in the economy. In 1980, banks handled 58 percent of savings and investment assets in the U.S. economy. This had faded to 33 percent by 1994.[14] Since the Fed is directly involved in the money supplied to the banking system but has limited sway over the bond market, monetary policy would have less influence over the economy.

Financial innovation played a larger role in nonfinancial corporations. Since the 1970s, corporate treasury departments had embraced derivatives to survive interest-rate and exchange-rate volatility (after the gold standard was abandoned). These were the real McCoy—derivatives used by a manufacturer to hedge against currency losses when, for instance, a company sold soap in a country other than where its production plant was located.

LEVERAGED SPECULATION RESTORES THE ECONOMY

Investment banks, most of them publicly traded companies by now, took more risk. They sold complicated derivative products to their clients, who

---

[13] Ibid., p. 209. On December 4, 1990, the Fed announced that it was eliminating the 3 percent requirement on nonpersonal time deposits and net eurocurrency liabilities by December 27, 1990. This added $13.6 billion to the credit system.

[14] Peter Warburton, *Debt and Delusion: Central Bank Follies That Threaten Economic Disaster* (Princeton, N.J.: WorldMetaView Press, 2005), p. 9.

absorbed much of this risk, often unwittingly. In the early 1990s, treasury departments of the largest department stores and computer manufacturers used such strategies to heal wounded balance sheets.

As the Fed dropped the overnight funds rate to 3.0 percent, the spread between short- and long-term yields grew more profitable. Commercial bank borrowing of government securities leapt from $30 billion in 1989 to over $100 billion in 1991 and 1992.[15] In both these latter years, commercial banks reduced both commercial and consumer credit lending.[16]

The investment banks had gone beyond underwriting and now acted as an alternative source of credit. They expanded their balance sheets, leveraging the capital that stood behind their solvency. They were extending more credit to the brokers and hedge funds that were buying the profitable derivative products created by the investment banks.

Bear Stearns was one investment bank that lent to speculating hedge funds. William Michaelcheck, a senior managing director of the firm, analyzed the market: "We think that there has got to be $100 billion to $200 billion of this right now, of investment partnerships, going from the biggest to the smallest, buying one-, two- and three-year Treasuries and financing them day to day, speculating on interest rates. And the people who have done this over the past year have made a fortune."[17]

Michaelcheck was quoted in October 1991, when the funds rate was 5¼ percent. Fortune making grew in magnitude, and apparent ease, as the Fed lowered the funds rate to 3.0 percent a year later. It would sit at 3.0 percent until February 1994, when it was raised to 3¼ percent.

There are no margin requirements in the government bond market.[18] If the lender is willing, the borrower's leverage is unlimited. In *The Trouble with Prosperity*, James Grant tells of meeting with an investor who had earned $300,000 over the previous weekend. Every dollar contributing to this return had been borrowed—all $769 million of them.[19] This was to be known as the "carry trade." Speculators borrowed at a cheap rate—such

---

[15] Federal Reserve Flow of Funds Accounts Z.1, http://www.federalreserve.gov/releases/z1/Current/data.htm.

[16] Federal Reserve Flow of Funds Accounts Z.1

[17] Grant, *The Trouble with Prosperity*, p.191.

[18] Ibid., p.187.

[19] Ibid.

as a Treasury bill, yielding 3 percent. They bought higher-yielding securities, such as Japanese government bonds that yielded around 6 percent. They expected (or hoped) that the borrowed asset would not rise in price. They leveraged the 3 percent spread at 10:1 or 100:1. Up to the present, the carry trade has funded fortunes in New York, London, Tokyo, and Shanghai. The securities that were borrowed and lent would change, but the strategy did not. This was another reason that central banks had less influence than they had during the chairmanship of William McChesney Martin. Financial flows were channeled away from funding potentially profitable enterprises. The FOMC's calibration of interest rates could not keep pace with the evolving motivations of borrowers.

Congress did not quibble. Maybe it did not understand the economy was bound together with leveraged finance. In any case, it had reason to keep quiet: the federal deficit rose from $155 billion in Ronald Reagan's final year of service to $290 billion in 1991.[20] Demand for Treasuries from speculators held the cost of government borrowing down. (In 1991, long-term Treasury yields fell from 8.3 percent to 7.3 percent.)

HOW CAN ONE SAVE?

Americans are admonished for not saving, but it was difficult to save when being propelled along the roller coaster of volatile interest rates, inflation, and the stock market. During the 1970s, the middle class had been jarred by inflation. As the Federal Reserve loosened its monetary policy in the early 1990s, interest rates fell across the spectrum of maturities. An investor might have been too frightened to step into the stock market during the 1980s (memories of the 1966–1982 swoon remained vivid) but could earn 13 percent on a certificate of deposit.[21] By 1992, CDs yielded only 4 percent. In 1990, food prices rose at the fastest rate since 1980.[22] Saving looked more and more like the losing proposition of the 1970s.

---

[20] research/stlouisfed.org/fred2/data/FYFSD.txt.

[21] Maggie Mahar, *Bull! A History of the Boom, 1982–1999* (New York: HarperBusiness, 2003), p. 114.

[22] Food and beverage inflation was 4.6 percent in 1990; www.bls.Gov/opub/ted/1999/Jun/wk5/art01.txt.

This does not seem like the time the population at large would embrace the stock market. The recession led to a slowing of consumer borrowing, yet net cash flows into stock mutual funds rose from $8 billion in 1985 to $13 billion in 1990 to $79 billion in 1992 and to $127 billion in 1993. In 1992 and 1993, money market funds suffered net outflows.[23] The stock market was about to replace the bank deposit system (and money market funds) as the backbone of household wealth.

THE RECOVERY: CUTTING WORKERS AND INVESTMENT

The economists declared the recession was over in March 1991, but there was little evidence of a recovery. Moreover, the large layoffs that followed were different from previous recessions; now, management was dismissed en masse. When 70,000 workers were laid off from General Motors in December 1991, CEO Robert Stempel announced that GM's salaried workforce (that is, management) was being cut from 140,000 in 1985 to 70,000 by 1995.[24]

The median household income fell from $46,670 in 1989 to $44,665 in 1994. It would start to rise again, but this was not much above the $43,677 median income in 1973.[25] More important than the data were the mass firings that made a "career" seem more a wish than a pursuit.

Layoffs and capital spending reductions had a salutary effect on companies that had bulked up on debt in the 1980s. Squeezing costs to raise profits may be just what any one company needs. When applied across the economy, however, the capacity for real economic growth withers. This recovery lacked investment in capital equipment.

On December 19, 1991, GM announced that it would cut $1.1 billion from its previous 1992 capital spending plans. Coincidentally or not, Chairman Greenspan spoke on the same day. He declared that "the essential shortcomings of this economy is [sic] the lack of savings

---

[23] Investment Company Institute, "Mutual Fund Assets and Flows in 2000," *Perspective*, February 2001.

[24] Levin, "General Motors to Cut 70,000 Jobs; 21 Plants to Shut."

[25] U.S. Census Bureau, *Current Population Reports, Consumer Income*, p. 41, Table A-3.

and investment.... Investment is the key to enhanced productivity and higher living standards."[26]

That depends on where you sit. "Shareholder value" was paying off. Corporate profits fell 21 percent during 1991, a year in which the S&P 500 rose 31 percent.[27] The winnings were rising to the top. The CEOs of the largest 100 companies in America received an average of $2.63 million from grants and options in 1991 when their companies were losing money as if it was 1932.[28] In 1976, a CEO had been paid 36 times the average worker's salary. In 1993, average CEO pay was 131 times that of the average worker.[29]

THE COCK CROWS: GREENSPAN PRICKS THE BUBBLE

Alan Greenspan gave a clear warning that the carry trade was coming to an end. On January 31, 1994, before the Joint Economic Committee, he stated "Short-term interest rates are abnormally low in real terms"[30] It was no secret that the borrow short and lend long strategy had refinanced the banking system. By early 1994, banks were liquid and lending.

The Fed raised the funds rate from 3.0 percent to 3.25 percent on February 4. This was the first of several increases, the consequence of which was the most traumatic financial convulsion since the 1987 crash. Margin calls drove prices lower, prompting more margin calls and more selling. Long-term Treasury yields rose from 6.3 percent in January to 8.0 percent in December 1994.

Greenspan may not have anticipated how derivatives had leveraged the financial system. Still, he could not have been completely surprised by the deleveraging. At the December 1993 FOMC meeting, Federal

---

[26] "Excerpts from the Fed Chief's Testimony," *New York Times*, December 19, 1991.

[27] Steve Lohr, "Recession Puts a Harsh Spotlight on Hefty Pay of Top Executives," *New York Times*, January 20, 1992.

[28] Ibid.

[29] Joann S. Lublin and Scott Thurm, "Behind Soaring Executive Pay—Decades of Failed Restraints," *Wall Street Journal*, October 12, 2006.

[30] Beckner, *Back from the Brink*, p. 348. Greenspan was testifying before the Joint Economic Committee, January 31, 1994.

Reserve Governor Lawrence Lindsey warned: "[W]e all agree that the 3 percent [funds] rate is unsustainable. We all know we always act too late."[31] Lindsey talked about a rush into $1 million home mortgages since, at current interest rates and forthcoming tax rates, this was "like borrowing money free for 30 years."[32]

On a February 28, 1994, FOMC conference call, Chairman Greenspan declared: "I think we partially broke the back of an emerging speculation in equities. ... We pricked that bubble [in the bond market] as well. ... We also have created a degree of uncertainty; if we were looking at the emergence of speculative forces, which clearly were evident in very early stages, then I think we had a desirable effect."[33]

The Fed raised the funds rate from 3.25 percent to 3.5 percent on March 22. On an April 18 FOMC conference call, the chairman ventured: "[T]he sharp declines in stock and bond prices since our last meeting, I think, have defused a significant part of the bubble which had previously built up. We let a lot of air out of the tire, so to speak."[34] The Fed, Greenspan believed, could not stop here: "While we have defused a goodly part of the bubble, we have an awful lot left in there."[35] The need to defuse was so compelling that the FOMC decided to raise the funds rate from 3.50 percent to 3.75 percent during the call, rather than wait until the next meeting.

At the May 17 FOMC meeting, the chairman decided to tighten again: "[W]e have taken a very significant amount of air out of the bubble. ... I think there's still a lot of bubble around; we have not completely eliminated it.... [T]he only way we're going to pierce it is essentially to create a degree of uncertainty.... [W]e have the capability I would say at this stage to move more strongly than we usually do."[36] The FOMC voted to raise the funds rate from 3.75 percent to 4.25 percent.

---

[31] FOMC meeting transcript, December 21, 1993, p. 28.

[32] Ibid., p. 27.

[33] FOMC meeting transcript, February 28, 1994, p. 3.

[34] FOMC meeting transcript, April 18, 1994, p. 7.

[35] Ibid., p. 9.

[36] FOMC meeting transcript, May 17, 1994, p. 32.

At the August 16 meeting, Greenspan expressed satisfaction: "I think we clearly demonstrated that the bubble for all practical purposes has been defused."[37] The FOMC raised the funds rate another 0.50 percent at this meeting, to 4.75 percent. (It would follow with two more rate increases, to 6.0 percent, by February 1, 1995.)

Greenspan was also forthright in public. On May 27, 1994, he told Congress that depositors had shifted their money out of banks and from money market funds into stocks and bonds, "and some of those buying the funds perhaps did not fully appreciate the exposure of their new investments to the usual fluctuations in bond and stock prices."[38] The Federal Reserve chairman was obviously well versed in the novice investor's exposure to unfamiliar territory.

DERIVATIVE LESSONS

Greenspan witnessed derivative mayhem when he raised the funds rate from 3.00 percent to 3.25 percent. Askin Capital Management was a $600 million hedge fund that lost all of its money by April 7, 1994.[39] The Piper Jaffrey Institutional Government Income Portfolio lost 28 percent of its principal.[40] It happened that 93 percent of the Piper Jaffrey fund was invested in mortgage derivatives called collateralized mortgage obligations (CMOs). The mortgages were all rated AAA because the government backed them.[41] This would not be the last time derivative strategists and their models sank the ship by misestimating the risks of AAA rated mortgage securities.

Companies groping for shareholder value included Air Products and Chemicals (which lost $113 million) and Dell Computer (which lost $35 million).[42] Securities and funds sold by NationsBank, Fidelity

---

[37] FOMC meeting transcript, August 16, 1994, p. 32.

[38] Beckner, *Back from the Brink*, p. 365.

[39] Frank Partnoy, *Infectious Greed: How Deceit and Risk Corrupted the Financial Markets* (New York: Henry Holt, 2003), p. 128.

[40] Ibid., p. 130.

[41] Ibid., p. 122.

[42] Ibid., pp. 114, 136.

Investments, the Vanguard Group, Fleet Financial, and United Services Advisors suffered unexpected losses.[43]

Financial derivatives were born to serve a need—to hedge the currency and interest-rate risks of companies. As the market grew, they served desires. Instead of hedging, companies often speculated. Banks were willing to help. Derivative sales were very profitable. Between 1990 and 1993, Merrill Lynch earned more than $3.1 billion, topping the total profits of its previous 18 years as a public company. Over $100 million of its 1993 earnings were from derivative sales to a single client: Orange County, California, which lost $1.7 billion on the trades and filed for bankruptcy.[44]

CONGRESS TRUSTS GREENSPAN, IGNORES SOROS

Congress held hearings on the derivatives maelstrom in April 1994. George Soros appeared before the House Banking Committee on April 13. Soros was the one hedge fund manager who was famous, and would have been known to Congress. He told the legislators: "There are so many [new financial instruments], and some of them are so esoteric, that the risks involved may not be understood even by the most sophisticated investors."[45]

After the congressional study was completed, Alan Greenspan dismissed it as unnecessary. He described the risk of derivatives as "negligible."[46] Congress chose to believe Greenspan and ignore Soros.

Worse than misapprehending the derivative menace, Greenspan, Congress, and probably most economists did not contemplate the possibility that such an unbalanced economy would eventually not respond to Federal Reserve money stimulus.

At the October 6, 1992, FOMC meeting, Federal Reserve Governor Wayne Angell addressed the attenuating influence of finance on an economy. "Since we have watched the Fed funds rate come down from

---

[43] Ibid., pp. 131–132.

[44] Ibid., p. 117.

[45] Ibid., p. 114.

[46] Hubert B. Herring, "Business Diary," *New York Times*, May 29, 1994.

9.9% to 3.0%—that's 690 basis points—and it has had less than the intended effect upon credit and upon spending, then it seems very appropriate for us to look again at this model."[47]

In early 2009, the Federal Reserve and Treasury attempted to rouse the economy by extending trillions of dollars to banks and industries. It is want of imagination to fill the patient with ever larger doses of the same medicine. Yet, this remains the Federal Reserve's modus operandi.

---

[47] FOMC meeting transcript, October 6, 1992, p. 21.

II

CUTTING RATES AND RUNNING FOR ANOTHER TERM AS CHAIRMAN

1995–1996

I think the downside risks are basically coming from the possibility of significant increases in stock and bond prices.... Ironically, the real danger is that things may get too good. When things get too good, human beings behave awfully.[1]

—*Alan Greenspan, March 1995*

The back half of the 1990s looked gloomier than the first half. In early January 1995, the *Wall Street Journal*, *New York Times*, and *Barron's* published annual reviews and forecasts, all of which agreed that Wall Street and Main Street were in a funk. Top brokerage firm analysts were interviewed. One was David Shulman, chief equity strategist at Salomon Brothers, who confirmed that "cash is in a bull market right now." Most of the experts expressed caution; about half of those interviewed expected the stock market to fall in 1995.[2]

---

[1] FOMC meeting transcript, March 28, 1995, pp. 42–43.
[2] David Kansas, "Analysts Figure Either Stocks or Bonds Must Give Ground to the Other This Year," *Wall Street Journal*, January 3, 1995, p. R3.

The *New York Times* special section "Outlook 1995" captured the consensus: "Rarely since World War II have … citizens [of the world's most powerful economies] been so worried that the good times are about to end before they get their share of the bounty." The *Times* observed that the United States had suffered 20 years of job stagnation, and "workers [are] convinced that economic upturns benefit everyone but them."[3]

The gloominess may have been overdone. The refinancing of corporate balance sheets was rewarded—corporate earnings more than doubled between 1992 and 1997.[4] From 1989 to 1994, business debts grew by just 5.6 percent ($204 billion). On the other hand, the combination of downsizing and offshoring was grinding down the middle class. Consumer debts grew by 36 percent over the 1989 to 1994 period ($1.2 trillion)—six times the growth of business debts.[5]

CONSTRAINING MONEY GROWTH AND BOOSTING CREDIT

What tided over the indebted was the rise in available credit. The Federal Reserve has a direct hand in the size of the monetary base. Through the mid-1990s, the Fed was slowing down this contribution to the economy. (The monetary base rose by 10.2 percent in 1993, by 8.1 percent in 1994, and by 3.9 percent in 1995, and would increase 4.0 percent in 1996.[6]) This showed discipline, but the Fed was ceding control over the monetary aggregates that are more responsive to commercial bank lending policies. It had reduced reserve requirements (mentioned in Chapter 10)

---

[3] David E. Sanger, "Global Prospects Brighten for Most," *New York Times*, January 3, 1995, p. C1.

[4] Jim Rogers, "For Whom the Closing Bell Tolls," welling@weeden, http://www.welling. weedenco.com, August 8, 2003. The 15 largest mergers in 1994 were stock or cash transactions. The LBO was dead. From: Greg Steinmetz, "Mergers and Acquisitions Set Records but Lacked that '80s Pizazz," *Wall Street Journal*, January 3, 1995, p.R8.

[5] *Richebächer Letter*, July 2003, p. 4.

[6] Federal Reserve Statistics and Historical Data, H.3, Table 1: "Aggregate Reserves of Depository Institutions and the Monetary Base (Adjusted for Changes in Reserve Requirements—SA and NSA)"; http://www.federalreserve.gov/releases/h3/hist/.

and permitted banks to "sweep" assets from retail checking accounts. This latter practice reduced bank reserve requirements by about $4.5 billion (around 8 percent) in 1995.[7]

A much broader measure of growth—one that is more attuned to *credit* than to *money*—is M3. The rate of credit creation within the limits of M3 rose 2.6 percent in 1994, 6.2 percent in 1995, 9.9 percent in 1997, and 10.4 percent in 1998.[8] The Fed interest rate increases through 1994 and early 1995 were for naught, since banks' lower reserves permitted them to lend more. To an extent, borrowed funds went into the stock market and other speculative activities.

This was the period when Alan Greenspan became a household term (*term*, since "Alan Greenspan" seemed as much a thing as a person). It was also the period when credit decisions beyond bank lending—such as securitizing subprime assets—further reduced the influence of the Fed (should it wish to restrain the economy).

BAILING OUT MEXICO—WITH AN EYE TO GREENSPAN'S 1996 REELECTION

The bailout of a foreign country is a political decision made by Congress and the executive branch of the government, which is not a topic for this book. However, Alan Greenspan's insertion of the Federal Reserve requires an abbreviated peso detour.

Through the 1980s and early '90s, Mexico had been spending too much. The peso was pegged to the dollar. In late December 1994, the Mexican government devalued and let the peso float. It fell 42 percent

---

[7] In 1990, the Fed eliminated the 3 percent requirement on nonpersonal time deposits and net eurocurrency liabilities. In 1992, the Fed lowered the required reserve ratio transaction deposits from 12 percent to 10 percent. See Joshua N. Feinman, "Reserve Requirements: History, Current Practice, and Potential Reform," *Federal Reserve Bulletin*, June 1993, pp. 569–589. In 1995, banks took more advantage of "sweeping" depositors' checking account balances into money-market deposit accounts that earn interest. Since no reserves are required to be held against the deposit account, the bank can then lend against the sweep. This reduced bank reserve requirements by about $4.5 billion in 1995. *New York Federal Reserve Annual Report 1995*, pp. 13–30; www.newyorkfed.org/aboutthefed/annual/annual95/omkt.pdf.

[8] St. Louis Federal Reserve, Economic Data, Monetary Aggregates, M-3 and Components.

in a matter of days. The possibility of political upheaval and a drop in trade (the United States ran a trade surplus with Mexico in 1994) served as an incentive to bail out the Mexican government.[9]

Treasury Secretary Robert Rubin led the bailout effort. Congress rebelled. President Clinton diverted funds for the bailout. Rubin took his case to the legislators. He had only recently been installed as treasury secretary. Alan Greenspan carried more political weight on Capitol Hill. Greenspan accompanied Rubin to the Senate and House office buildings "testifying and lobbying in support of the package."[10]

This was quite a compromise by the Federal Reserve chairman. Federal Reserve Governor John LaWare put it bluntly: "'It politicized the Fed to the extent that we were asked to endorse a political settlement or agreement. ... It was a compromise of Federal Reserve independence and something that we have obviously jealously guarded for a long, long time.'"[11] But LaWare understood that Greenspan was playing a more important political game. Greenspan needed to be "'a friend of the guy who has the power to keep him in power.'"[12] Keeping him in power probably refers to Greenspan's reappointment in 1996. FOMC decisions in 1995 may have been influenced by Greenspan's reelection campaign.

1995: A MIDYEAR ABOUT-FACE

To many, 1995 was the year when the financial system inflated beyond redemption.

In February, the Fed raised the funds rate to 6 percent.[13] Then, in July, the Federal Reserve cut the rate to 5¾ percent. Such a quick turnabout is unusual. The Fed runs the risk of looking like a chicken with its head cut off. The FOMC was motivated to loosen money by slowing retail

---

[9] Steven K. Beckner, *Back from the Brink: The Greenspan Years* (New York: John Wiley & Sons, 1996), p. 379.

[10] Ibid., p. 382.

[11] Ibid.

[12] Ibid.

[13] Ibid., p. 389.

[14] Ibid., pp. 396–401.

sales and car sales, rising unemployment claims, and a lower purchasing managers' index.[14] At the July meeting, Greenspan told the committee: "[T]he data of the last few weeks clearly are moving in the direction that ... we at least seem to have reached the maximum risk potential and probably are now somewhat on the other side"[15] (meaning that recessionary risks had abated). He recommended a 25 basis point cut even while stating: "[S]ince the risks are beginning to ease slightly, there is no urgency here."[16]

The decision was Greenspan's. FOMC members had plenty of time to air their views (71 pages of transcript), but a clue to Greenspan's grasp on the committee arises from a plaintive question after the decision had been made. An unidentified speaker asks, "Is there a press release?" Greenspan responded, "I am sorry. The draft reads as follows: 'Chairman Alan Greenspan announced today that the Federal Open Market Committee decided.'"[17] Greenspan had brought the committee's communiqué to the meeting.

"THE GREENSPAN FED" WAS EXACTLY THAT

When Volcker ruled, the board was not a rubber stamp. There was no such unruliness under Greenspan. There was rarely an interesting discussion.

Alan Blinder was appointed to the vacant post of vice chairman of the Federal Reserve in 1994. A Princeton undergraduate, he earned his Ph.D. at MIT, where his dissertation was supervised by Robert Solow (also one of Ben S. Bernanke's thesis sponsors).[18] Blinder served on the Council of Economic Advisers in the first Clinton administration (where his greatest contribution may have been as algebra homework consultant to Chelsea Clinton).[19] Blinder was filling the home stretch of a 14-year term vacated by David Mullins. Clinton wanted to reappoint

---

[15] FOMC meeting transcript, July 5–6, 1995, p. 56.

[16] Ibid., p. 59

[17] Ibid., p. 72.

[18] Bernanke's thesis sponsors at MIT were Stanley Fischer, Rudiger Dornbusch, and Robert Solow; http://econ-www.mit.edu/about/economic.

[19] John Cassidy, "Fleeing the Fed" ("Annals of Finance"), *New Yorker*, February 19, 1996, p. 39.

Blinder to a full 14-year term in 1996, but Blinder declined. Instead, he returned to Princeton. Blinder did not speak publicly about his decision, but when Felix Rohatyn, investment banker from Lazard Frères and "Evening Hours" companion of Alan Greenspan, decided to pursue the opening, Blinder asked: "Why are you doing it? I'm leaving because I can't stand it."[20]

Laurence Meyer served as a Federal Reserve governor from 1996 to 2002. In *A Term at the Fed*, Meyer wrote that Greenspan drafted the statements about the economy and economic policy that the FOMC issued after it met. In Meyer's words: "[T]he fact that the statements were prepared by the Chairman without any real input from the Committee, created a degree of tension ... that never diminished during my term."[21] The July 1995 transcript shows how the Greenspan FOMC operated.

Alan Blinder was most surprised that when decisions were to be made, most often, the board was offered only one option: the staff recommendation.[22] When Janet Yellen resigned as governor in 1997, she considered it a "great job, if you like to travel around the country and read speeches written by the staff."[23] Earlier, Yellen had met with the staff to understand the process used in its economic forecast. Greenspan "became concerned when he saw Yellen talking to the staff, fearing she might 'impurify' the staff forecast."[24] Such control may be explained by another aspect of Greenspan's character. Bert Ely, a consultant on federal involvement in the credit system, believed: " 'The chairman is not a secure man. He has to be the one in the spotlight, and he doesn't want competition. Blinder was somebody who was extremely well qualified to challenge Greenspan.' "[25]

---

[20] William D. Cohan, *The Last Tycoons: The Secret History of Lazard Frères & Co.* (New York: Doubleday, 2007), pp. 376–377.

[21] Laurence H. Meyer, *A Term at the Fed: An Insider's View* (New York: HarperBusiness, 2004), p. 75.

[22] Ibid.

[23] Martin Mayer, *The Fed: The Inside Story of How the World's Most Powerful Financial Institution Drives the Markets* (New York: Free Press, 2001), p. 304.

[24] Beckner, *Back from the Brink*, p. 372.

[25] Cassidy, "Fleeing the Fed," p. 42.

The chairman—at least Chairman Greenspan—controlled the topics under discussion, the structure of an argument, the conclusion of a debate that never existed, and the vote. As vice chairman, Blinder sat in the office next to Greenspan's, yet they often went a week at a time without speaking to each other. In Laurence Meyer's autobiography, he has little of a personal nature to say about Greenspan, since they were barely acquainted, despite his 5½ years of service.[26] It is fair to say that when decisions of the Greenspan Fed are evaluated, it was Alan Greenspan who set policy.

Greenspan Feeds a Frenzy

Greenspan's decision in July 1995 to cut the funds rate was a mistake. It was made in the midst of a credit and stock market boom. The S&P 500 had risen 20 percent in the year through June; the Nasdaq had risen 24 percent. Between the May 23 and July 6 FOMC meetings, the Nasdaq rose 7.5 percent. Yet, the stock market was barely discussed in July. This was quite a change from recent meetings.

At the March 28, 1995, meeting, Greenspan had warned: "I think the downside risks are basically coming from the possibility of significant increases in stock and bond prices. If you remember, some of our discussions about the necessity of moving in early 1994 recognized that we were beginning to get wealth effects that were unsustainable and potentially creating bubbles. Ironically, the real danger is that things may get too good. When things get too good, human beings behave awfully."[27]

At the May 23, 1995, meeting, Greenspan mused: "The way I put it is that I am more nervous about the asset bubble than I am about product prices."[28] Earlier in the meeting, he had stated his nervousness regarding an asset bubble in starker terms: "The disequilibrium that is implicit in this forecast is an asset price bubble, and I am not sure at this stage that we know how or by what means we ought to be responding to that, and whether we dare. There is always the question, if we make a preemptive

---

[26] Meyer, *A Term at the Fed*, p. 219.
[27] FOMC meeting transcript, March 28, 1995, pp. 42–43.
[28] FOMC meeting transcript, May 23, 1995, p. 34.

strike against an asset bubble, of whether we could blow the economy out of the water."[29]

Why the aftermath of a bursting bubble scared him at this point is not clear. We would hear such hand-wringing again and again in later years, but the May meeting may have been the first time he expressed such doubts. Yet, at the same meeting, Greenspan patted himself on the back for the Fed's earlier foresight: "[W]hen we moved in February 1994, one of the reasons was that an asset price bubble was building up.... In retrospect, it was terribly fortunate that that bubble got pricked at the appropriate time."[30] Was the bubble of 1995 so much bigger than the one in 1994 that popping it now might "blow the economy out of the water"? If so, cutting rates certainly wasn't the answer. Greenspan did not mention his fear of a bubble at the July meeting—a fear that was clearly present at the May meeting.

Reading sequential FOMC transcripts from the Greenspan years can be most revealing by following topics as they reach a peak, then simply disappear when the danger grows acute.

Two More Fed Fund's Cuts: For "Insurance"

This was only the beginning of the cuts, but much was happening outside the Federal Reserve headquarters on Constitution Avenue, the Eccles Building (named after former Federal Reserve Chairman Marriner S. Eccles). Jeff Vinik, manager of the Fidelity Magellan Fund, was the June 6, 1995, celebrity attraction at Salvatore Ferragamo on Fifth Avenue.[31] It was at about this time that Jean-Marie Eveillard, star stock picker for SoGen mutual funds, could no longer take a leisurely lunchtime stroll in New York without autograph and photograph seekers nipping at his heels.[32]

Inside the Eccles Building, the Fed cut the funds rate 0.25 percent in December 1995 and again in January 1996—to 5¼ percent. Greenspan

---

[29] Ibid., p. 33.

[30] Ibid., p. 32.

[31] *Grant's Interest Rate Observer*, May 26, 1995, p. 2.

[32] *Grant's Interest Rate Observer*, May 10, 1996.

called the January reduction "insurance" against recession.[33] It was more an incitement to madness.

At the December 19, 1995, FOMC meeting, Greenspan answered his own question of the possible risks incurred by cutting the funds rate: "The real danger is that we are at the edge of a bond and stock bubble."[34] Two weeks before, Molly Baker at the *Wall Street Journal* reported, "every time someone points out the Internet stocks are absurdly overvalued, the stocks seem to double again in a matter of days or weeks."[35]

Cathy Minehan, president of the Boston Federal Reserve, was a voice of reason: "Mr. Chairman, it is hard for me to believe that real interest rates are too high. It is also hard for me to think about easing credit in the face of the kinds of financial markets that we have right now. The costs of being wrong, both in terms of stock and bond market bubbles … clearly are much higher if upside risks are realized as opposed to downside risks."[36] The vote to cut the funds rate was unanimous.

The S&P 500 index would rise 33 percent in 1995, 23 percent in 1996, and 33 percent in 1997.[37] This was the greatest three-year boom of the twentieth century, or so we thought.

The Internet Runs Amok

Outside of the FOMC conference room, innumeracy and euphoria were running amok. In the January 3, 1994, *New York Times*—the year before the edition discussed earlier—a novelty was mentioned. In an article about the "information superhighway," the word *Internet* may have crossed readers' paths for the first time: "[C]ommonly known as the Net, [it] is going mainstream, even trendy … [but] the Net is seen as a nerdy prototype for the information superhighway."[38]

---

[33] Beckner, *Back from the Brink*, p. 400—July 6, 1995, rate cut from 6 percent to 5¾ percent; p. 411—December 19 rate cut from 5¾ percent to 5½ percent; p. 413—rate cut on January 31, 1996, "what Greenspan called 'insurance.'"

[34] FOMC meeting transcript, December 19, 1995, p. 40.

[35] Molly Baker, "Stargazers Abound While Internet Stocks Skyrocket," *Wall Street Journal*, December 7, 1995, p. C1.

[36] FOMC meeting transcript, December 19, 1995, p. 41.

[37] Jim Rogers "For Whom the Closing Bell Tolls" October 22, 2002, Jimrogers.com.

[38] Steve Lohr, "The Road from Lab to Marketplace," *New York Times*, January 3, 1994, p. C11.

Yet 20 months later, on August 9, 1995, Netscape went public and set the world ablaze. The Web-browsing company had never produced a profit. It was rare for a reputable underwriter to take a company public without a string of quarterly earnings. Netscape filed for an offering of 3.5 million shares; investors placed orders for 100 million. Expected to go public at $14 a share, it rose to $71, closed the first day at $58, and ended the year at $139. On December 1, Jim Clark, the founder of Netscape, told Bloomberg News: "[Y]ou could argue there's something of an Internet bubble developing."[39]

This was when "IPO" was introduced to the American vocabulary. Until now, initial public offering was simply a legal term for a security offering.

Speculation chased the rising market. Net inflows to stock, bond, and money market mutual funds rose from $76 billion in 1994 to $242 billion in 1998.[40] (For the five years from 1985 through 1989, total inflows were $216 billion.)

GREENSPAN'S REELECTION

Greenspan entered the homestretch of his "reelection" campaign. In his book on Greenspan's years at the Fed, market analyst Steven Beckner reported: "[Greenspan's] term as chairman was to expire March 2, but repeated questions from reporters about his fate were greeted with week after week of ambiguity and ambivalence from Clinton and his aides. Nor had they uttered a word of praise for the job Greenspan had done. He was left to twist slowly in the wintry wind."[41]

The Economic Report of the President, released on February 13, 1996, was presented under the tutelage of Joseph Stiglitz, then chairman of the Council of Economic Advisers. It argued that lower interest rates would not induce inflation.[42]

---

[39] From interview with Bloomberg Business News, *San Francisco Chronicle*, November 30, 1995, p. D1.

[40] Sean Collins, "Mutual Fund Assets and Flows in 2000," *Perspective*, Investment Company Institute, February 2001.

[41] Beckner, *Back from the Brink*, p. 414.

[42] The Clinton Administration, or Stiglitz, had great faith in NAIRU, the nonaccelerating inflation rate of unemployment. NAIRU postulates that there is a point at which the unemployment rate and the inflation rate are in balance. If the unemployment rate

President Clinton followed with a speech on February 15, 1996. He called for a "national debate" on "whether the economy could grow at faster than 2-½% without accelerating inflation."[43] Treasury Secretary Robert Rubin followed Clinton. He told the National Press Club that he welcomed a "vibrant debate" at the Fed on the economy's ability to grow.[44] Larry Summers, Rubin's deputy secretary of the treasury, gave a speech that steamrolled Greenspan. Only an accredited economist could think it made sense: "We cannot and will not accept any 'speed limit' on American growth."[45] No speed limit was applied to either the stock market or to the house mortgage market, the engines for growth over the next decade. The MIT- and Harvard-trained Summers, nephew of Nobel Prize–winning economist Paul Samuelson, leads the Obama administration's brain trust.

Beckner continued: "Fed officials deny these election-year attempts to pressure them had any impact, but thereafter Greenspan and others went to great lengths to deny they wanted to restrain growth."[46] Magnifying glass in hand, Beckner sniffs the trail: "In his February 20, 1996 ... testimony, Greenspan ... said the Fed would 'welcome' faster growth."[47] Beckner spoke to a "former Fed official" shortly before Clinton blessed Greenspan's third term as chairman: "Alan Greenspan is so dedicated to trying to get himself reappointed that he is willing to compromise some of his independence in order to do so. He desperately wants to be reappointed."[48]

"THANK GOD FOR ALAN GREENSPAN"

"Thank God for Alan Greenspan" proclaimed the March 18, 1996, issue of *Fortune*: "No recession. No inflation. No voodoo."[49] Robert Ferrell,

---

goes below this level, inflation will rise, and vice versa. The Stiglitz team proposed that NAIRU was lower than believed; thus, the Fed could cut rates, which would (in the CEA's mind) reduce unemployment without risking higher inflation.

[43] Beckner, p. 414.
[44] Ibid., pp. 416–417.
[45] Ibid., p. 417.
[46] Ibid., p. 414.
[47] Ibid., p. 439.
[48] Ibid., p. 415.
[49] *Grant's Interest Rate Observer*, March 15, 1996.

then senior investment officer at Merrill Lynch, offered a more down-to-earth assessment: "If this is the biggest bull market of the century, or maybe the biggest bull market we have ever seen, then maybe the speculation is bigger than we have ever seen."[50] *Reader's Digest* published an article with the title "You Can Make a Million." According to the author: "[I]t can be done on a modest salary, even on retirement income."[51]

Comparator Systems. Presstek. Diana Corporation. Iomega. These rocket ships were headed straight to the moon but ran out of fuel. For those who were there, the flesh may crawl. For those who weren't, it was just beginning. The Great Garbage Market of 1968 was invoked as comparison. But the garbage grew more expensive from 1996 to 2000. There were boosters other than Greenspan. Professor Jeremy Siegel had written a best seller: *Stocks for the Long Run*. He theorized that stocks are always the best-performing asset if you wait long enough. Or something like that. It didn't matter. They bought the book and bought stocks.

In *The Autumn of the Middle Ages*, Johan Huizinga wrote: "[T]he whole of intellectual life [of the late Middle Ages] sought concrete expression, as if the notion of gold was immediately minted into coin. There is an unlimited desire to bestow form on everything.... This tendency towards pictorial expression is constantly in jeopardy of becoming petrified."[52]

In the autumn of the current age, the mind sought and found a new symbol: Alan Greenspan. Next, he would mint gold by bestowing form on an abstract concept: productivity.

---

[50] *Grant's Interest Rate Observer*, May 10, 1996, p. 1.

[51] *Grant's Interest Rate Observer*, July 19, 1996, p. 4.

[52] Johan Huizinga, *The Autumn of the Middle Ages*, trans. Rodney J. Payton and Ulrich Mamnitzsche (Chicago: The University of Chicago Press, Chicago, 1996), p. 173. (Orig. pub. in 1919 as *Herfsttij der Middeleewen*).

12

THE PRODUCTIVITY MIRAGE
THAT GREENSPAN DOUBTED

1995–1997

[T]he concept of the general price level is extremely vague and we cannot even speak of a very approximate determination of the average price level. Every index number is to a certain extent arbitrary: the selection of the commodities that are to be included, the choice of the weighting, the base from which the index starts, and, lastly, the mathematical processes applied, are all arbitrary."[1]

—*Wilhelm Röpke*, Crises and Cycles, *1936*

The stock market became a national obsession in the late 1990s. Brokerage firms were more than happy to cheer prices higher, but they needed an explanation: *why* was the stock market doubling, tripling, or, in the case of the Nasdaq Index, up thirteen-fold from early 1991? The formulation needed to be simple, and it was—it was captured in one word: productivity.[2]

Alan Greenspan was the leading productivity mythologian, whipping up enthusiasm in practically every speech. His repetitious cheerleading

---

[1] Wilhelm Röpke, *Crises and Cycles* (London: William Hodge & Co., 1936), p. 149.
[2] William A. Fleckenstein and Frederick Sheehan, *Greenspan's Bubbles: The Age of Ignorance at the Federal Reserve* (New York: McGraw-Hill, 2008), p. 36

for the "more rapid-pace of IT innovations," which eliminated the "doubling up on materials and people" that had caused "inevitable misjudgments.... Decisions were made from information that was hours, days, or even weeks old" was grounded in the productivity improvements that never existed.[3] In 2001 and 2002, when the superstars of the miracle wrote off $100 billion or $200 billion of nonexistent value, it was obvious that the emperor wore no clothes.

The steps by which the productivity calculation entered the fat farm and exited a superstar model will be described by component. The government inflation calculation plays a large role, since productivity is a measure of "real" improvement. To calculate real improvement, the inflation rate is subtracted from the increase in production. If the government understates the inflation rate (the government's CPI is 1 percent, when it really was 4 percent), it is overstating productivity.

THE BOSKIN COMMISSION

Alan Greenspan's 1983 Social Security Commission did not solve the problem of funding benefits. (See Chapter 6.) The insiders knew this at the time. The chairman of the commission had wrapped its conclusions in vagaries that politicians then draped in platitudes. A decade later, the funding problem was too big to ignore. The Federal Reserve chairman offered a solution. Testifying before the Senate and House Budget Committee on January 10, 1995, he told the committee that the inflation rate was overestimated.[4] He suggested that the anomaly be investigated.

If Greenspan was correct (or if his assumption could at least be rationalized), this would be a godsend. Benefits could be cut, and congressional

---

[3] Greenspan gave this speech many times. These specific quotes are from "Technology and the Economy," at the Economic Club of New York, New York, January 13, 2000.

[4] Statement by Alan Greenspan, Chairman, Board of Governors of the Federal Reserve System, before a Joint Hearing of the Senate and House Committees on the Budget, January 10, 1995: "The present budget scoring process is already partly dynamic but tends to underweight the impact of supply-side changes and relies on a consumer price index that may overstate inflation by 0.5% to 1.5%. The likely benefits of reduced spending and tax cuts are difficult to calculate, but should nonetheless at least be estimated and considered as Congress debates its courses of action. Overoptimism is dangerous in budgeting, but so is willful ignorance of a program's positive fiscal effects."

constituencies would never know it. After Greenspan passed the baton to the politicians, Congress passed it to Michael Boskin. The Boskin Commission (officially, the Advisory Commission to Study the Consumer Price Index) was duly formed.

Boskin was the right man for the job. He had served as chairman of President Bush's Council of Economic Advisers from 1989 to 1993. He proved a worthy successor to CEA functionaries Arthur Burns and Alan Greenspan. The Boskin Commission found that inflation was overstated by 1.1 percent. Several recommendations were made by the commission to the Budget Committee. These were instituted by the Bureau of Labor Statistics (BLS) with great efficiency—with too much efficiency.

There was no pretense on the Boskin Commission's part that its mandate was other than to reduce the *measurement* of the annual Consumer Price Index (CPI).[5] The Bureau of Labor Statistics' CPI is applied to social security benefits each year. It is used to compensate recipients for the increasing cost of living: if the CPI rises 3 percent, the next year's benefit checks rise by 3 percent. Also, inflation-indexed U.S. Treasury bonds are indexed to the annual rise in the CPI. The lower the CPI, the less the government has to pay holders of these bonds. A synopsis of the commission's mandate precedes the report: "The Advisory Commission to Study the Consumer Price Index (a.k.a. The Boskin Commission) was appointed by the Senate Finance Committee to study the role of the CPI in government benefit programs and to make recommendations for any needed changes in the CPI."[6] The purpose was *not* to improve the government's measurement of changes in consumer costs. The purpose was to measure the influence of the CPI on the cost of government programs. The Boskin Commission was to "make recommendations for any needed changes in the CPI."

The government wanted to reduce the cost of social security. Therefore, the recommended changes reduced the consumer price index, as reported by the civil servants to the people they serve. Greg Mankiw, chairman of President Bush's Council of Economic Advisers from 2003 to 2005, said at

[5] Fleckenstein and Sheehan, *Greenspan's Bubbles*, p. 39.
[6] http://www.ssa.gov/history/reports/boskinrpt.html#exec.

the time, "[T]he debate about the CPI was really a political debate about how, and by how much, to cut real entitlements."[7] Barry Bosworth of the Brookings Institution called the revised CPI an "'immaculate conception' version of deficit reduction, in which spending is cut without Congress taking the blame."[8] Jack Triplett of the Brookings Institution extended the argument: "What I liked least about the Commission Report was exactly what made it so influential—its guesstimate of 1.1 percentage points of bias.... The Commission (and others that have followed) used ad hoc reasoning to come up with a number.... [T]his seemingly so precise 1.1% number caught the eyes ... of the press and the politicians, and also of economists."[9] Triplett went on to chide the report for succumbing "to the lure of political statements in its choice of language to describe the effect of CPI measurement errors on Social Security expenditures."

Despite such criticisms, there was little public discussion of the Boskin Commission or its influence. One reason is the complexity of the parts. It is difficult to launch a coherent critique if the method by which the government has underestimated inflation (or underestimated the unemployment rate, or overstated productivity) is not understood. What follows is not a blow-by-blow analysis of methodologies. Rather, it is an explanation of some (but by no means all) of the larger distortions that, in themselves, show how government calculations are divorced from the reality of how we live and pay our bills.

Before the Boskin Commission, period-to-period CPI changes were calculated arithmetically. The Boskin Commission recommended that they be calculated geometrically. The change was made to account for "substitution effects." For example, if the price of beef rises relative to the price of chicken, consumers will substitute chicken for the beef they previously ate. Since the price of chicken rose less than the price of beef, the CPI will be relatively lower. That the consumer might want to eat beef rather than chicken is not a consideration.

---

[7] Jack E. Triplett, "The Boskin Commission Report After a Decade," *International Productivity Monitor*, no. 12, spring 2006, p. 56.

[8] Barry P. Bosworth, "The Politics of Immaculate Conception: Congress Should Set the Budget, Not the CPI," *Brookings Review*, spring 1997, pp. 43–44.

[9] Triplett, "The Boskin Commission Report," p. 46.

Jack Triplett wrote: "It is merely a mechanical fact that an unweighted arithmetic mean of positive quantities will be greater than an unweighted geometric mean. The difference between the two is not evidence of substitution bias. [Meaning: That consumers actually bought chicken instead of beef—author's note] No inference ... can be drawn from the fact that the geometric mean basic component gives a lower estimate of price change than the arithmetic mean, since this will always be the case."[10] In other words, the mathematics of using the geometric calculation will always be lower, but the statisticians had no knowledge of whether consumers substituted chicken for beef.

Here is an example of how these calculations differ. The price of a hog rises from $100 to $161 over five years. The "annualized" rise—this is the geometric calculation—is 10 percent a year. The change each year—the arithmetic calculation—is a little over 12 percent: 61 divided by 5. Using the new math, 2 percent is lopped off the consumer price index.[11]

And what has been the result? John Williams, author of *Shadow Government Statistics*, who has reconstructed and made the comparison, calculates that the geometric figure reduces the CPI by about 2.7 percent annually. The effect of compounding at a lower-than-accurate rate, year after year, has had a devastating effect on social security payments.[12] Williams calculates payments today would be double the current checks if the government had not changed methodologies.[13]

Geometric averaging is the most straightforward of the changes suggested by the Boskin Report. Without a key to the magicians' locker at the BLS, quantification of other distortions is difficult. They are more a matter of intuition. For instance, the BLS reduces the price we pay for products by quality or a "hedonic" adjustment.[14] (This is the same

---

[10] Triplett, "Boskin Commission Report," p. 53.

[11] Fleckenstein and Sheehan; *Greenspan's Bubbles*, p. 39.

[12] Williams is author of the electronic newsletter *Shadow Government Statistics*, "Analysis Behind and Beyond Government Economic Reporting." www.shadowstats.com

[13] Williams, "The Consumer Price Index," *Shadow Government Statistics*, October 1, 2006

[14] *Quality* is used here for what readers may know as "hedonic" adjustments. The two are not synonymous, but they are close enough for this discussion.

concept as that used in the "real" cost of computers, which distorts productivity and GDP measurements. This will be discussed later in the
chapter; see "Productivity.")

According to Steve Leuthold, founder and chief investment officer of
the Leuthold Group, a research firm in Minneapolis, the average price
paid for a new car in the United States has risen from $6,847 in 1979
to $27,940 in 2004, a 308 percent increase. Over those years, the Con-
sumer Price Index assumed that car prices rose 71 percent, to $11,708.
Thus, the government-calculated CPI eliminated 82 percent of the price
increase.[15] The Consumer Price Index does not measure the cost of
goods in dollars, yet, a consumer must pay $27,940 for a new car.

Such quality adjustments are used to reduce prices in the areas of
apparel, air fares, gasoline, hospital services, television sets, microwave
ovens, television sets, washing machines, clothes dryers, and textbooks.
Discount air fares do save money, but no adjustment is made for
cramped and dirty seats and endless delays: What is the cost of lousy
service in a service economy?[16]

Another fanciful figure is house-price appreciation. House prices
are about one-fifth to one-quarter of the CPI. The Bureau of Labor
Statistics does not include house price sales in the CPI. Instead, it
calculates the "owners' equivalent rent."[17] (The data are gathered by
survey—basically, by asking homeowners how much they would pay
to rent their own house.) In 2005, the change in the cost of purchasing a house rose 3.1 percent, according to the BLS and calculated in
the CPI. According to OFHEO (Office of Federal Housing Enterprise
Oversight), another government agency, house prices rose by 13.3 percent in 2005. The cumulative effect over the decade from 1995 to 2005
can be viewed in Table 12-1.[18]

---

[15] Fleckenstein and Sheehan, *Greenspan's Bubbles*, p. 40.

[16] Ibid., p. 41.

[17] Boskin Commission Report discusses the history of owners' equivalent rent on pages
8 and 41; http://www.ssa.gov/history/reports/boskinrpt.html-ref.

[18] These data were gathered from www.OFHEO.gov. OFHEO (the agency) was replaced
by the Federal Housing Finance Agency in 2008. The historical OFHEO house price
indexes do not seem to be on the FHFA site.

Table 12-1

Index	OFHEO "Real" House Price Change	BLS "Rent Equivalent"	Housing as a % of CPI
2005	13.33%	3.1%	23.4%
2004	11.99%	2.9%	23.2%
2003	7.85%	2.2%	23.4%
2002	7.43%	3.1%	22.2%
2001	7.53%	4.7%	22.1%
2000	7.55%	3.4%	20.5%
1999	5.13%	2.4%	20.5%
1998	4.98%	3.1%	20.5%
1997	4.59%	3.8%	20.2%
1996	2.58%	3.1%	19.6%

Note: Over this period the rent equivalent was first called the "owners' equivalent rent," then the "owners equivalent rent of primary residence," and now, "rent of primary residence." It is a subset of "shelter," which runs about 10% higher (in total proportion of the CPI) than rent equivalent/house price appreciation.

There are two periods within this decade to isolate. The first period is 1998 to 2001, the years when Greenspan touted productivity. The second period is 2002 to 2004, when Ben Bernanke led the Federal Reserve's deflation campaign, which will be discussed in Chapter 23. Low inflation was the Federal Reserve's rationale for cutting interest rates to 1 percent. According to a recent study, owners' equivalent rent reduced the reported CPI by 2.9 percent in 2004.[19] On April 23, 2004, Federal Reserve Governor Ben S. Bernanke stated: "[M]y own best guess is that core inflation has stopped falling and appears to be stabilizing in the vicinity of 1-½ percent, comfortably within my own preferred range of 1 to 2 percent."[20]

John Williams, calculates that if the 1980 methodology for measuring inflation were still used in March 2009, the reported CPI would have

---

[19] Steven Gjerstad and Vernon L. Smith, "From Bubble to Depression?" *Wall Street Journal*, April 6, 2009, A15. The authors used the Case-Shiller 20-city composite index for house price appreciation.

[20] Ben S. Bernanke, "The Economic Outlook and Monetary Policy," speech at the World Economy Laboratory Spring Conference, Washington, D.C., April 22, 2004.

been 7.3 percent. The Bureau of Labor Statistics releases six measurements of CPI. In March 2009, the highest of these was 1.8 percent; the measurement that the media generally discusses fell 0.4 percent.[21]

The economy functions exactly the same way, whatever the BLS's methodology. (That is, leaving aside how a higher reported inflation rate changes consumption and market behavior.) This and other changes (productivity, gross domestic product, and so on) are not of the real world, but exist in an abstract, mathematician's universe.

GREENSPAN ENDORSES BOSKIN COMMISSION RECOMMENDATIONS

Alan Greenspan debriefed the Senate Finance Committee on January 30, 1997. He approved of the changes recommended by the Boskin Commission, then threw his weight behind an effort to allot new resources, particularly to quality adjustments: "[M]ost of the needed developments will require time, effort, and quite possibly additional resources. It is important that the Congress provide the Bureau with sufficient resources to pursue the agenda vigorously."[22]

The Federal Reserve chairman seemed to be in a hurry.

PRODUCTIVITY

"Productivity," as defined by the Bureau of Labor Statistics, is measured by comparing the amount of goods and services produced to the inputs that were used in production."[23] The BLS goes onto explain the calculation:

---

[21] *Shadow Government Statistics*, April 20, 2009, p. 18; http://www.shadowstats.com/article/33, under the heading "Alternate Realities."

[22] Testimony of Chairman Alan Greenspan before the Committee on Finance, United States Senate, "The Consumer Price Index," January 30, 1997; http://www.federalreserve.gov/boarddocs/testimony/1997/19970130.htm.

[23] Bureau of Labor Statistics, "People Are Asking ... : How is Productivity Measured by BLS?" last modified November 9, 2004; http://www.bls.gov/lpc/peoplebox.htm. For a more formal explanation of the government process for calculating productivity, see Lucy P. Eldridge, Marilyn E. Manser, and Phyllis Flohr Otto, "Alternative Measures of Supervisory Employee Hours and Productivity Growth," *Monthly Labor Review*, April 2004, p. 10. For a more formal explanation of what productivity is, see Eldridge et al., "Alternative Measures," pp. 9–10.

"Labor productivity is the ratio of the output of goods and services to the labor hours devoted to the production of that output."[24]

The numerator (the number on top of the ratio) is "real" goods produced. ("Real" subtracts inflation. If the goods produced and sold increased by 10 percent but inflation also rose 10 percent, there would be no increase in "real" production. If inflation rose by 1 percent, the real increase would be 9 percent.)

The most notorious maneuvering during Greenspan's productivity obsession was with computers. In 1998, sales of computers to businesses were calculated at $95.1 billion. This was the money actually spent. However, when the Bureau of Economic Analysis relayed the output to the Bureau of Labor Statistics, it stated that sales ("real" sales) were $351.8 billion. What the BEA called "real" was unreal because the real expenditures—dollars spent—were $95 billion. The $256 billion boost to the numerator ($351 − $95) not only increased the productivity number, but also artificially lifted the gross domestic product by $256 billion of unreal dollars. This permitted Greenspan—and practically every other government official, CEO, and sell-side analyst—to make inflated claims for the enormous amount of capital investment that was gunning the Miracle Economy. Yet, this investment never existed. For what it's worth, the Bureau of Economic Analysis stopped hedonically adjusting computer prices in 2003.

The denominator (the number on the bottom) is the measurement of hours worked. The methodology for calculating how many hours all Americans worked is a parody of how government bureaucracies operates.[25] Since the denominator includes extrapolations from estimates made in 1978, the productivity figure is worthless.

---

[24] Bureau of Labor Statistics, "People Are Asking … : How is Productivity Measured by BLS?" last modified November 9, 2004; http://www.bls.gov/lpc/peoplebox.htm.

[25] The substantive part of the denominator is derived from a BLS survey. The BLS asks businesses how many hours their employees worked in the previous week. The BLS does not collect hours for nonproduction and supervisory workers. It assumes that the "average weekly hours for supervisory workers are the same as those for nonsupervisory workers." It would be quite a coincidence if this were true. That still leaves nonproduction workers at manufacturing companies. These are extrapolations "from an estimate for 1978." And so on.

Even Alan Greenspan did not seem to believe the new calculations. On March 31, 1998, Greenspan told the FOMC: "The productivity numbers are very rough estimates because we are measuring a whole set of product outputs from one set of data and a whole set of labor inputs from a different set. That they come out even remotely measuring actual labor productivity is open to question in my view."[26]

Greenspan seemed to be thinking along the same lines on August 22, 1995: "We are all acutely aware that there has been a shift toward increasingly conceptual and impalpable value added and that actual GDP in constant dollars is becoming progressively less visible."[27]

Speaking before the Charlotte, North Carolina, Chamber of Commerce on July 10, 1998, he discussed "an ever increasing conceptualization of our Gross Domestic Product—the substitution, in effect, of ideas for physical matter in the creation of economic value."[28] Most economists consider productivity to be a measurement of economic value.

Alan Greenspan was more reticent about government social security calculations when he was abroad. In his autobiography, Greenspan recalls telling a Soviet Union government official that a Soviet "inflation-fighting program that revolved around indexation" was likely to be unsuccessful. Greenspan discussed the U.S. problem with having indexed social security and advised the minister that indexing inflation "is likely to cause even more serious problems."[29]

The Soviet official understood Soviet indexation for what it was: bureaucratic central planning.[30] Greenspan then reveals his inner self: "Years before becoming Fed chairman, I'd actually tried picturing myself in the central planner's job."[31] Since he now fixed the world's interest rate, he was living rather than picturing it.

---

[26] FOMC meeting transcript, March 31, 1998, pp. 76–77.

[27] FOMC meeting transcript, August 22, 1995, p. 6.

[28] Alan Greenspan, "The Implications of Technological Change," speech at the Charlotte, North Carolina, Chamber of Commerce, July 10, 1998; http://www.federalreserve.gov/boarddocs/speeches/1998/19980710.htm.

[29] Alan Greenspan, *The Age of Turbulence : Adventures in a New World* (New York: Penguin, 2007) p. 125.

[30] Ibid.

[31] Ibid., p. 129.

It would be difficult to overstate the influence of the quarterly productivity announcement in the great bull market in the late 1990s. During the technology boom, anticipation of this news release emptied pharmacies of antacid tablets. Yet, it was a hoax.

The geometric averaging and quality adjustments inspired by the Boskin Commission were—and still are today—only a few of the false adjustments to inflation. The mathematical hijinks increased the "real" gross domestic product calculation, but GDP itself is not real. It overstates growth by adding "real" adjustments, as is true with the "productivity" calculations.

Entering the second half of the nineties, the stage was set: the Federal Reserve chairman, who had been wrong on almost every prediction he had ever made, would lift markets to heights never before achieved, largely because of his predictions. These were not even of the stock market itself, but of a supposed link between the government's rising productivity measurement and the correct price for the stock market. The measurement was false and was probably not believed by the Federal Reserve chairman. Nevertheless, the productivity calculation and its link to the stock market dominated headlines once the Federal Reserve chairman emphasized its importance. There was little rebuttal. Those who rebutted (and there were vocal dissenters) were shouting into a gale.

13

"IRRATIONAL EXUBERANCE" AND OTHER DISCLOSURES

1995–1998

Federal Reserve Board Chairman Greenspan isn't talking about the stock market these days. In fact, the word among Fed officials is: don't use the word "stock" and "market" in the same sentence. No one wants the blame for the crash.[1]

—*Wall Street Journal*, November 25, 1996

In tandem with his recommendations to Congress that government inflation calculations be changed, Greenspan used the FOMC as a sounding board for his productivity claim. At the August 1995 FOMC meeting, Greenspan alerted committee members to "a major statistical problem." He also offered a solution: "[W]e are getting increasing evidence that we probably are expensing items that really should be capitalized. This is the issue with software."[2]

Software was the perfect boost to the productivity measurements. Just before Greenspan spoke, a Fed staffer said: "At present, when software is not bundled with the computer, it is counted as an intermediate product."[3]

---

[1] "The Outlook: Worried Fed Watches Markets Climb," *Wall Street Journal*, November 25, 1996, p. A1.

[2] FOMC meeting transcript, August 22, 1995, p. 6.

[3] Ibid.

Intermediate products are not included in the national product—the GDP. The staffer had explained that reclassifying software as final output would increase productivity. (More accurately, it would boost the government's *measurement* of productivity. The government's accounting categories do not affect the productivity of the economy.) The staffer tutored the FOMC novices. He explained the relationship between higher GDP and productivity: "If output of software has been growing faster than other output, that would push up 'true' output growth.... [I]t may well be that productivity is growing faster and that we just are not measuring output properly."[4]

Greenspan explained the relationship between his inference and the stock market: "We have all seen, as I think you are aware, a number of industries in which the ratio of the stock market value to book value is much higher than one.... The stock market is basically telling us that there has indeed been an acceleration of productivity if one properly incorporates in output that which the markets value as output."[5]

It is a brave man who declares "what the stock market is ... telling us." Another interpretation would consider the Netscape initial public offering two weeks before this meeting, calculate the Nasdaq's 36 percent year-to-date rise, reflect on the Fed's July decision to loosen money, and postulate that the stock market had decided the Fed was throwing fuel on the fire and it was time to make fast money.

Greenspan's interpretation was bound by an airtight equation: the stock market price is always correct. It is the known quantity. The economy is a menagerie of variables. In the years to come, Greenspan would introduce, interpret, reinterpret, reconstruct, and abandon particular variables. Here, at the unveiling, it is an understated book value that must be reconstructed by turning an expense into a capital investment.

The infallibility of the stock market was most important to Greenspan, since he was retreating from responsibility, or even a discussion of asset bubbles. The entire miracle economy consisted of a series of abstractions: stock market prices; software output; productivity; a "conceptual economy."

---

[4] Ibid.
[5] Ibid.

In November, two meetings later, Michael Prell, the director of research at the Fed, tried to enlighten the chairman: "On the trend of potential output growth ... recent evidence of surprises in productivity growth disappears. We seem to be running on a trend that has been in place for well over a decade.... It doesn't suggest that there has been a radical revolution over this decade relative to where we were running before."[6] At the same meeting, Alan Blinder, vice chairman of the Federal Reserve, warned the FOMC not to "get excited about something that is not there."[7] Daniel Sichel, an economist on the Fed staff, who resigned and wrote a book. *The Computer Revolution*, published in 1997, rebutted the acceleration of productivity: it was a myth.[8]

Greenspan was not to be deterred. Years later, the *Wall Street Journal* reviewed the chairman's campaign:

> Alan Greenspan began to push a reluctant Federal Reserve to embrace his New Economy vision of rapid productivity growth and rising living standards.... In October 1995, a group of supply managers from various industries visited the Fed to discuss the latest in high-efficiency "just-in-time" inventory management....
> [One of the] executives described routing goods to drugstores: "They would load up a truck and without having orders send the truck out. The drugstore computer system would call the supplier, which would call the truck on the road and say, 'Go to such-and-such store and deliver the following items'" ... To [Edward] Kelley, the retiring Fed governor ... who referred to himself as "an old inventory manager" ... this was like "going to Mars."[9]

THE GREENSPAN HYPOTHESIS

The Fed chairman presented his proposal as a coherent whole at the December 19, 1995, FOMC meeting. He raised "a broad hypothesis

---

[6] FOMC meeting transcript, November 15, 1995, p. 16.

[7] Ibid., p. 18.

[8] Daniel E. Sichel, *The Computer Revolution* (Washington DC: Brookings Institution, 1997).

[9] Greg Ip and Jacob Schlesinger, "Did Greenspan Push US High-Tech Optimism Too Far?" *Wall Street Journal*, December 28, 2001.

about where the economy is going over the longer term and what the underlying forces are."[10] Greenspan was puzzled: "One would certainly assume that we could see [the acceleration of technological change] in the productivity data, but it is difficult to find it there. In my judgment there are several reasons, the most important of which is that the data are lousy.... [W]e are not capitalizing various types of activities properly.... That creates economic value in the stock-market sense, and we are not measuring it properly."[11] He had been looking at business cycles since the late 1940s, and "there was just nothing like this earlier."[12]

The Federal Reserve chairman might control the debate, but he did not control the government numbers. It would be best if the productivity figures supported his hypothesis. The reclassification of software as a capital expenditure in 1999 helped.

The gestation of his productivity brainstorm approximated the period in which he was cutting the fed funds rate during his 1995–1996 reelection campaign. Greenspan broached his productivity rationalization at the August 1995 meeting and turned it into a hypothesis at the December 1995 meeting. The Federal Reserve cut the funds rate by 0.25 percent on July 6, 1995, December 19, 1995, and January 31, 1996.

IRRATIONAL EXUBERANCE

Alan Greenspan's speeches will not tax the editors of *Bartlett's*, but one phrase has stuck: his warning of "irrational exuberance" on December 5, 1996. That it struck such a nerve is more important than the phrase itself. He could not have raised the possibility in a more tentative fashion. ("But how do we know when irrational exuberance has unduly escalated asset values, which then become subject to unexpected and prolonged contractions as they have in Japan over the past decade?"[13]) There was no mention of manias or crashes. He used the word *bubble* only to imply that he was not anxious: "We as central bankers need not

---

[10] FOMC meeting transcript, December 19, 1995, p. 35.

[11] Ibid., p. 37.

[12] Ibid.

[13] Speech available at http://www.federalreserve.gov/boarddocs/speeches/1996/19961205.htm.

be concerned if a collapsing financial asset bubble does not threaten to impair the real economy, its production, jobs, and price stability."

He was speaking in the midst of a stock market bubble, and almost everyone feared it or knew it, including the Federal Reserve. On November 25, 1996, the *Wall Street Journal* had reported: "Federal Reserve Board Chairman Greenspan isn't talking about the stock market these days. In fact, the word among Fed officials is: don't use the words 'stock' and 'market' in the same sentence. No one wants the blame for the crash."[14] Two days later, the Bank for International Settlements (the central bankers' central bank) warned about the "prevailing euphoria" in global credit markets.[15]

At the September 24, 1996, FOMC meeting, Greenspan said: "I recognize that there is a stock market bubble problem at this point.... We do have the possibility of raising major concerns by increasing margin requirements. I guarantee that if you want to get rid of the bubble, whatever it is, that will do it. My concern is that I am not sure what else it will do."[16] Of course he couldn't know what else it would do, but he had identified a stock market bubble and that he could burst it. He would later deny that he could do either.

Splicing his statements from the September 24, 1996, meeting to the December 5, 1996, speech, the drama of how the Fed would respond to a bubble was over. At the September FOMC meeting, the chairman would not act, since he was "not sure what else it will do." On December 5, Greenspan stated that the Fed would only act if "a collapsing financial asset bubble does not threaten to impair the real economy." Since any popped asset bubble will not only threaten but also to some degree impair the real economy, his dilemma could never be resolved. He spent the next 10 years talking.

GREENSPAN RAISES THE FUNDS RATE—ONCE

Greenspan raised rates in 1997 once: from 5.25 percent to 5.50 percent in March. It would have been far better if he had not raised rates the Fed

---

[14] "The Outlook: Worried Fed Watches Markets Climb," *Wall Street Journal*, November 25, 1996, p. A1.

[15] *Grant's Interest Rate Observer*, December 5, 1996, p. 1.

[16] FOMC meeting transcript, September 24, 1996, pp. 30–31.

Funds rate at all. At the March 1995 meeting, Federal Reserve Governor Lindsey reminded the FOMC of its tentative communiqués in the spring of 1993. (That was when the Fed held the funds rate at 3 percent, funding the carry-trade recapitalization of the banking industry). Lindsey had said, "I have to conclude that doing that, if anything, cemented the market's view that we were stuck at a particular rate. It only built the market's confidence that they could borrow at 3 percent and lend at 6 percent, which is literally what they were doing." Lindsey warned the FOMC not to sound tough (in the form of an "asymmetric" public statement, asymmetric being any meaningful change in language from the Fed's previous statements) if it did not have the courage to stick to its convictions (in which case it should release a "symmetric" statement, indicating no change in the Fed's outlook): "[I]f what we fear is a bubble, we should not in my view go asymmetric unless we really expect to raise rates.... [Meaning—once the Fed started raising rates, and indicated publicly that it intended to pursue an objective, it should keep raising rates until the stock market's speculative atmosphere disappeared.—author's note] Given what we did in 1993 ... I am afraid we would only strengthen the conviction of the market and maybe actually exacerbate the bubble."[17]

Lindsey resigned in early 1997. The FOMC made the one-time hike in 1997 without the benefit of Cassandra's wisdom. As in the Greek myth, Lindsey was right. After the FOMC it tightened once in 1997 and then backed off, speculators had no fear. The market never looked back. The statements by Greenspan at the early 1994 FOMC meetings show he knew that one-time rate hikes were not enough. What had changed by 1997?

The politicians may have frightened Greenspan. In January 1997, he told the Senate Committee on the Budget that "the stock market continued to climb at a breathtaking rate."[18] Before the Senate Banking Committee on February 26, 1997, Greenspan did warn, in his fashion, that the stock market was overpriced: "[R]egrettably, history is strewn with

---

[17] FOMC meeting transcript, March 28, 1995, p. 48.
[18] Senate Committee on the Budget, "Performance of the U.S. Economy," January 21, 1997.

visions of such 'new eras' that, in the end, have proven to be a mirage. In short, history counsels caution. Such caution seems especially warranted with regard to the sharp rise in equity prices during the past two years."[19] Responding to a senator's question, he repeated his most famous phrase, making a distinction that a three-year-old would understand: "It's not markets that are irrational. It's people who become irrationally exuberant."[20] That he thought it was worth mentioning signifies his timidity.

Senator Phil Gramm from Texas disagreed with the errant forecaster: "I think people hear what you are saying and conclude that you believe equities are overvalued. I would guess that equity values are not only *not* overvalued but may still be undervalued."[21] On March 4, Greenspan spoke before the House Committee on the Budget.[22] Congressman Jim Bunning from Kentucky told Greenspan that the chairman's stock market forecast was "misguided."[23] This may seem like a topic that was beyond the congressman's brief, but he was vectoring toward the most destabilizing influence of Greenspan's freelance opinions: his inflammation of the stock market. "'My question to you,'" Bunning said, "'is why have you, on two occasions, taken to jawboning the U.S. stock market and the U.S. bond market with your comments to affect a free and open market as head of the Federal Reserve Board, which is in charge of setting monetary policy?'"[24]

Chairman Greenspan replied that markets have a direct influence on monetary policy.[25] This is true. Greenspan would deny this link— and the Federal Reserve's responsibility—as the bubble grew fearsome. While stocks rose, there was no one person who was more responsible

---

[19] Senate Committee on Banking, Housing, and Urban Affairs, "The Federal Reserve's Semiannual Monetary Policy Report," February 26, 1997.

[20] Floyd Norris, "A Warning Investors Have Ignored Before," *New York Times*, February 27, 1997, p. D1.

[21] Jerome Tuccille, *Alan Shrugged: The Life and Times of Alan Greenspan, the World's Most Powerful Banker* (Hoboken, N.J.: Wiley, 2002), p. 226. Tuccille also gives comments from Jim Bunning, writing as if Bunning were a senator and speaking at the same meeting as Gramm. Bunning was a congressman at the time.

[22] House Committee on the Budget, "Bias in the Consumer Price Index," March 4, 1997.

[23] Tuccille, *Alan Shrugged*, p. 226.

[24] Richard W. Stevenson, "Terse Congressman Questions Greenspan's Market Motives," *New York Times*, March 5, 1997.

[25] Ibid.

for the stock market mania. The chairman disowned his personal influence when he responded to Bunning: "'Nobody can affect [markets] in a fundamental way.'" This may be true, but Bunning questioned Greenspan because the chairman's influence was anything but fundamental. It was—take your pick—emotional, abstract, spiritual, or absurd, but not fundamental. Richard W. Stevenson, a reporter at the *New York Times*, wrote the next day that Bunning was "clearly not satisfied with Mr. Greenspan's protestations of innocence and impotence."[26] This is a remarkable summation of Greenspan's road to success. Congressman Bunning, a former major league pitcher, winner of 224 games and member of baseball's Hall of Fame, achieved that success by preying on hitters' weaknesses. Greenspan's self-effacing innocence and impotence was obvious to the hurler, who hit more batters than all but 10 pitchers in the history of baseball.

The day after the chairman's February 26, 1997, testimony before the Senate, he was in the headlines of the *New York Times*: "Greenspan Warns Again that Stocks May Be Too High." If that didn't upset the markets, there was another headline in the same newspaper "Greenspan Speaks and Stocks Plunge." The *Times* published seven articles that mentioned Greenspan on February 27.[27] The following day, it published seven more, including an editorial: "Wise Warnings to Giddy Investors."[28]

Whether it was fear of politicians or not, Greenspan did not raise the funds rate again. He worked on his productivity hypothesis instead.

THE SUBPRIME WARNING

Other markets were running amok. Asset-backed derivatives had spread beyond the homely mortgage and credit card receivables. The market was buying untested securities such as future receipts of Pakistan Telecommunication Corporation, credit card transactions in Mexico, airline-ticket payments for TACA International (an El Salvadorian airline), automobile installment payments in Thailand, and David Bowie's future album

---

[26] Ibid.

[27] Source for *New York Times* articles: proquest.bpl.org.

[28] The seven articles include "If Groundhogs Were Boastful: 'I Hate to Say I Told You So.'"

receipts (a rock star who had peaked in the 1970s).[29] Closer to home, the fastest growing subprime lenders were filing for bankruptcy (e.g., Jayhawk Acceptance), suffering downgrades (e.g., Olympic Financial), and disclosing fraud. (In February, Mercury Finance Company, "the Mercedes-Benz of the subprime auto lending industry," disclosed that 50 percent of its 1996 net income never existed.[30])

Over the coming months, this cycle of subprime lending unwound. Nonpayment on mobile-home loans produced default charts that looked like hockey sticks. These loans would never have been offered if the financier had not been able to sell them to an investment bank. The investment bank acted as a veteran second baseman in a double play—it bought the mortgage (from the financier) and sold it (in an asset-backed security) as quickly as possible to an investor. A pension fund or mutual fund investor now owned the trailer (through the purchase by its yield- and bonus-chasing money manager). Each of the participants along the assembly line profited. Bankers earned fees and pension plans earned interest until the defaults swelled. The pension plan bore all the losses. (The evicted trailer owner was none the better, either.)

"Bulldog," a 325-pound automobile repo man and "credit adjuster" from Dallas, explained the inevitable consequence of lending in the subprime loan market: "Aw, it's just a bunch of Wall Street intellectuals showing how dumb they are. How are you going to make money off people that don't have any money? I don't think these Wall Street folks have any idea what they are dealing with."[31] Nor did the Fed.

At the time Bulldog shared his sound banking philosophy, subprime home lenders were sprouting wings. Ameriquest Mortgage, New Century Financial Corporation, and Countrywide Credit Industries Inc., were busy selling subprime mortgages to Wall Street firms. It was not a coincidence that they were based in or around Irvine, California, home to Lincoln Savings and Loan and other detritus of the previous decade's savings and loan fraud.

---

[29] *Grant's Interest Rate Observer*, February 14, 1997, p. 9.
[30] Ibid., p. 2.
[31] Ibid., p. 4.

At the December 1996 meeting, two weeks after the chairman's irrational exuberance speech, Lindsey broadened the FOMC's concerns beyond
stocks. He warned that 1997 would be a "very good year for irrational exuberance" in credit.[32] Bank lending had exploded. Broad credit expansion
as calculated in the Fed's M3 measurement was rising at the fastest rate
since 1987, and before that, at the fastest rate since the early 1970s.[33] A large
proportion of the 1970s' growth rate included price inflation. In 1987, M3
growth veered toward asset inflation—stocks, bonds, and derivatives. This
was also true in 1997, a year in which the Nasdaq rose 22 percent.

The carry trade was a giant of its former self. Net borrowings of government bond dealers doubled between early 1994 and early 1998.[34] Dealers borrow so that they can lend to investors and to speculators, or to
leverage their own positions. Commercial banks, over which the Federal
Reserve had regulating authority, played an important role.

"As I Noted Earlier"—When? Where?

As the Greenspan Fed withdrew from monitoring asset bubbles and
bank lending, the chairman's hypothesis was about to go public. The
chairman revealed it to Congress at intervals. Before the House Committee on the Budget on October 8, 1997, Greenspan claimed: "Clearly,
impressive new technologies have imparted a sense of change in which
previous economic relationships are seen as being less reliable now....
An acceleration of productivity growth, *should it materialize*, would put
the economy on a higher trend growth path than [federal agencies] have
projected"[35] [author's italics]. Later in October, Greenspan told Congress: "While productivity growth does appear to have picked up in the
last six months ... it will take some time to judge the extent of a lasting
improvement."[36]

---

[32] FOMC meeting transcript, December 17, 1996, pp. 28–29.

[33] M3 grew 7.3 percent in 1997, 9.9 percent in 1998, and 10.4 percent in 1999.

[34] *Grant's Interest Rate Observer*, February 27,1998, chart, p. 2.

[35] House Committee on the Budget, "Economic and Budgetary Outlook,"
October 8, 1997.

[36] Before the Joint Economic Committee ("Turbulence in World Financial Markets") on
October 29, 1997.

He continued to discuss productivity in this tentative form before Congress in late January and early February 1998.[37] In testimony before Congress in February 1998, he shifted from the future tense to the here and now: "*As I noted earlier,* our nation has been experiencing a higher growth rate of productivity—output per hour worked—in recent years. The dramatic improvements in computing power and communication and information technology appear to have been a major force behind this beneficial trend"[38] [author's italics].

"As I noted earlier" was presumptuous. His only previous theorizing before Congress was in the test-tube stage ("should it materialize").[39] His discourse also diluted such otherwise urgent questions as: "Are you concerned with the stock market?" Bubble talk was everywhere, including to the FOMC, but the chairman ignored it.

---

[37] Senate Committee on the Budget, "The Current Fiscal Situation," January 29, 1998; House Committee on Banking and Financial Services, "The Current Asia Crisis and the Dynamics of International Finance," January 30, 1998; he repeated this testimony before the Senate Committee on Foreign Relations, February 12, 1998.

[38] House Subcommittee on Domestic and International Monetary Policy of the Committee on Banking and Financial Services, *The Federal Reserve's Semiannual Monetary Policy Report,* February 24, 1998.

[39] At the January 29, 1998, appearance before the House Budget Committee he thought, "productivity appears to have accelerated sufficiently last year to damp increases in unit labor costs."

14

IN A BUBBLE OF HIS OWN

———

1998

———

I won't take up your time with the umpteenth restatement of our skepticism regarding the sustainability of these valuation levels.[1]

—Michael Prell, Federal Reserve economist, in presentation to the FOMC, at June 30–July 1, 1998, meeting

It might be forgotten now, but the astounding close to the second millennium was preceded by an already astonishing run. Between 1992 and 1997, the S&P 500 Index compounded at 27 percent a year.

Southeast Asia had drawn investment flows in the early 1990s. Foreign investment then stalled. In mid-1997, Asian markets buckled. Investment exited, and many of the Asian stock and currency markets had collapsed by the end of the year.

The U.S. stock and bond markets were a natural outlet for funds. This boosted the dollar. U.S. interest rates fell, and lower interest rates fueled more borrowing and leveraging. The atmosphere fed on itself: there grew a cadre of enthusiasts who sometimes quit their jobs to "day trade." A late 1997 Montgomery Securities poll showed that investors expected a 34 percent annual stock market return over the next decade. Upon such an achievement, the Dow Jones Industrial Average would top 151,000.[2]

---

[1] FOMC meeting transcript, June 30–July 1,1998, p. 14.

[2] Centurion Counsel Market Neutral N-30D, for December 31, 1997; www.secinfo.com The DJIA was 7,908 on December 31, 1997 and 13,264 on December 31, 2007. It fell to 6,457 on March 9, 2009 before its recent recovery.

Yet Greenspan was deaf and blind to the manic mood, or at least he pretended to be. He needed to certify his productivity thesis to deter bubble talk. At the December 16, 1997, FOMC meeting, Jerry Jordan (president of the Cleveland Fed) tried to steer the conversation toward inflating asset prices: "Some Board members referred earlier to the dichotomy between the prices of services and the prices of goods.... [T]he notion of dichotomy also has to be applied in the case of asset prices."[3] Jordan drew a conclusion that contradicted the Fed's myopic concentration on a steady price level of goods and services. Jordan proposed that in the 1920s, "U.S. monetary policy was ... too expansionary for asset prices."[4] Putting words in Jordan's mouth, this led to the 1929 stock market crash. He continued: "I think that it's a useful reminder of what can go wrong if we are too narrow in thinking about words like 'inflation' or 'deflation'.... What do [people] mean by the word 'inflation?' Clearly, it cannot refer simply to the current prices of goods."[5]

When Jordan finished speaking, Greenspan called on another board governor (Ned Gramlich) to speak. This was a common tactic of Greenspan's to stifle any topic he'd rather not discuss.

Greenspan thought that "[s]omething very different is happening."[6] The "something" that Jerry Jordan had identified was never addressed by the chairman. Somethings that differed from Greenspan's somethings were never discussed by the chairman, if he could avoid them. He usually succeeded.

At the December meeting, Greenspan grew excited over his coagulating thesis: "[W]e keep getting reams of ever-lower CPI readings that seem outrageous in the context of clearly accelerating wages and an ever-tighter labor market. ... I was startled by this morning's CPI report. We cannot keep getting such numbers and continue to say that inflation is about to rise."[7] Jordan had just told Greenspan that prices were rising. In more colloquial terms, it was the share price of Microsoft rather than the store price of mayonnaise that was inflating.

---

[3] FOMC meeting transcript, December 16, 1997, pp. 57–58.
[4] Ibid., p. 58.
[5] Ibid.
[6] Ibid., p. 68.
[7] Ibid., pp. 68–69.

The lower CPI readings were not startling. The chairman should have expected them. Of everyone in the room, he, at least, should have remembered that the Bureau of Labor Statistics was adapting the Boskin Commission's recommendations to reduce the government-sanctioned inflation rate. The crisis in Asia had sparked an export surge. Indonesians were selling goods at any price for the privilege of importing a hard currency.

The Fed's data hound apparently did not know Asian currencies had fallen against the dollar by over 30 percent in the past two years, the sharpest fall being in the weeks lending up to the December 1997 FOMC meeting.[8] Goods exported from Asia to the United States were bought with fewer dollars. Yet Greenspan was "startled" that dollars bought more goods. Greenspan had good reason to ignore deflationary Asia: ignorance boosted his productivity argument.

"NOBODY CHALLENGED HIM OR DARED SAY ANYTHING"

The FOMC met again on February 3 and 4, 1998. This was about three weeks before Greenspan's "As I noted earlier, our nation has been experiencing a higher growth rate of productivity" congressional performance. He lectured: "Productivity gains clearly have kept increases in unit labor costs at a very modest level."[9] (What happened to the "clearly accelerating wages and an ever-tighter labor market" that he asserted at the December meeting?) Maybe they had, but the FOMC was not convinced. In *Maestro*, Bob Woodward's biography of Greenspan, the author wrote that the chairman's "language was highly idiosyncratic, often not fully grounded in the data. He was prone to take leaps. At the FOMC, [Federal Reserve governor Janet] Yellen noticed the Ph.D.s on the committee, or some of the members of the staff, would be nearly rolling their eyes as the chairman voiced his views about how the economy might be changing. Nobody challenged him or dared say anything, but it weakened his hold on the committee."[10]

How this "weakened his hold" is not clear, since the FOMC always voted as Greenspan wished. At the February 1998 meeting, Fed Governor

---

[8] Andy Lees, UBS, "Terms of Trade," January 7, 2008.

[9] FOMC meeting transcript, February 3–4, 1998, p. 112.

[10] Bob Woodward, *Maestro: Greenspan's Fed and the American Boom*. (New York: Simon and Schuster, 2000), p. 169.

Jerry Jordan might have weakened Greenspan's hold when he queried a Fed staffer about "a wide array of other financial indicators that do not suggest a restrictive monetary policy at all."[11] If indeed the Fed's monetary policy was loose, a lively debate concerning Greenspan's productivity gains should have been in order. There was no discussion.

Three weeks later, on February 24, 1998, Greenspan appeared before Congress.[12] He expanded on his productivity revelation. He observed that "computing power and communication and information technology" were now "available to as many homes, offices, stores, and shop floors as possible, [having] produced double-digit annual reductions in prices of capital goods embodying new technologies."[13]

Many (though not all) of these reductions were from hedonic pricing (for example, the annihilation of true computer prices had been adopted) and from the flood of Asian goods. This was so obvious that it apparently didn't deserve mention. Currencies had collapsed and prices had soared in Asia. By August 2008, Indonesian food prices had doubled.[14] President B. J. Habibie asked his people to fast two days a week—an unnecessary request, given their already shrinking

[11] Ibid., p. 102. Jordan then listed a series of exuberant markets: "These include not just the ample availability of credit from the banking industry but from the financial services industry more broadly, the relatively rapid growth of various measures of money, and the ongoing strength in various asset markets."

[12] Greenspan was so busy that a chronology of his early 1998 speeches and testimony might be helpful: a January 29 appearance before the Senate Budget Committee, *The Current Fiscal Situation*; a January 30 appearance before the House Committee on Banking and Financial Services. *The Current Asia Crisis and the Dynamics of International Finance*; a February 12 performance before the Senate Foreign Relations Committee (same testimony titled slightly differently: *The Current Asian Crisis ...*); a February 24 lecture to a subcommittee of the House Committee on Banking and Financial Services, *The Federal Reserve's Semiannual Report on Economic Conditions and the Conduct of Monetary Policy*, a March 3 appearance before a subcommittee of the Senate's Committee on Appropriations, *The Current Asian Crisis*; and a March 4 appearance before the House Committee on the Budget, *Coming Budgetary Challenges*. The FOMC met on February 3–4. It next met on March 31.

[13] House Subcommittee on Domestic and International Monetary Policy of the Committee on Banking and Financial Services, *The Federal Reserve's Semiannual Monetary Policy Report*, February 24, 1998.

[14] Steven R. Tabor, World Bank Institute, "General Food Price Subsidies in Indonesia: The 1997/1998 Crisis Episode," December 8, 2000 presentation, World Bank Institute, Washington, DC, p. 5.

waistlines.[15] Financial collapse spread around the globe. Russia defaulted on its debt obligations in August 1998, and bond markets around the world scurried for cover.

The United States benefited from these calamities in obvious ways. The dollar rose against currencies that fell. These countries would sell anything, at any price, to get dollars. This was disinflationary in the United States. Lower inflation and the global flight to quality created an obsession with a single destination for global assets. The elephants in the room that Alan Greenspan failed to see outnumbered those in the Kalahari Desert. That this public servant received such applause from economists is unpardonable.

In his February 24 testimony before Congress, Greenspan linked productivity to the extremely ambitious IPO and stock market: "Critical to this process has been the rapidly increasing efficiency of our financial markets.... Capital now flows with relatively little friction to projects embodying new ideas. Silicon Valley is a tribute both to American ingenuity and to the financial system's ever-increasing ability to supply venture capital to the entrepreneurs who are such a dynamic force in our economy."[16]

Wall Street firms that had opened offices in Silicon Valley during the IPO mania could not have hired a better public relations representative. Their behavior was often scandalous (that, we knew at the time) and criminal (as the courts would decide, in due course). Greenspan capped off his ode to the venture capitalists who lined Sand Hill Road in Menlo Park, California, in a stellar summation: "More recent evidence remains consistent with the view that this capital spending has contributed to a noticeable pickup in productivity."[17] Within weeks, Michael Wolff, an entrepreneur who had taken full advantage of the pickup in productivity, published his memoir. He described Silicon Valley companies that had nothing to sell, other than common stock. In *Burn Rate: How I Survived the Gold Rush Years on the Internet*, Wolff admitted: "Optimism is our

---

[15] Seth Mydans, "Vote Places Habibie in Firm Control of Indonesian Politics," *New York Times*, July 12, 1998.

[16] House Subcommittee on Domestic and International Monetary Policy of the Committee on Banking and Financial Services, "The Federal Reserve's Semiannual Monetary Policy Report," February 24, 1998.

[17] Ibid.

bank account; fantasy is our product; press releases are our good name."
His book was intended as "a sort of anti-press release."[18] Wolff, applying
his American ingenuity, diverted capital flows, or "dumb money" (his
words), from the rich.[19] This was the most prominent dynamic force in
Silicon Valley.

Greenspan was not as innocent as he might seem. He had shown some
knowledge of how markets work three years earlier, at the December 19,
1995, FOMC meeting: "The sharp decline in long-term yields has struck
me as quite extraordinary.... [W]e are getting issues of 100-year bonds....
The fact that some borrowers are issuing these bonds is terrific. Until you
get somebody dumb enough to buy them."[20] By 1998, Greenspan's productivity circumlocutions were drawing ever dumber money into the
chairman's efficiently priced stock market.

Dot-com IPOs exited Silicon Valley at a rate comparable to the speed
at which they went out of business. A few of the forgettable gimmicks
for raising $100 million to $1 billion from the summer and fall of 1998
include NetGravity, Broadcast.com, GeoCities, Fatbrain.com, NBCi,
and uBid. They couldn't even spell, how were they going to sell? In fact,
they didn't; these companies either burned through their cash or had
been acquired by late 2001.[21]

Such exuberance might have frightened the investing public. However,
Abby Joseph Cohen, market strategist at Goldman Sachs, was second
only to Greenspan in relieving market anxieties. When Cohen spoke, it
was widely and immediately reported. She referred to her model quite
often; it was a happy model, happy with the world and the stock market
alike. She spent much of her time on television and, like Greenspan, was
invariably courteous, pleasant, and vague. It was often said she reassured
investors because she looked like a middle-class housewife. This became
a cliché, yet the cliché itself was reassuring.

---

[18] Michael Wolff, *Burn Rate: How I Survived the Gold Rush Years on the Internet* (New
York: Simon and Schuster, 1998), pp. 11–12. "Burn rate" means the need to continually raise more money before a company burns through its earlier funding.

[19] Ibid., p. 51.

[20] FOMC meeting transcript, December 19, 1995, p. 38.

[21] John Cassidy, *Dot.con: The Greatest Story Ever Sold* (New York: HarperCollins, 2002),
pp. 350–351

She rebranded American affluence as Supertanker America.[22] The United States was a flagship of such unsinkable construction that the world's problems were, well, the world's problems. Ms. Cohen, earnest to the core, could not have understood the irony of designing such a label in the same year that the movie *Titanic* won 11 Oscar awards. This is not a singular characteristic of Cohen's: if Wall Street was long on irony, the stock market would be short on exuberance.

GREENSPAN VS. THE FOMC

The FOMC next met on March 31, 1998. Federal Reserve staff economist Michael Prell reviewed current conditions: "[T]he gravitational pull of valuation may no longer be operating. The PE ratio for the S&P 500 recently reached 27 ... even as companies were issuing warnings and analysts were lowering their 1998 profit forecast."[23] At the same meeting, Fed Governor Jerry Jordan reminded Greenspan: "I also continue to be concerned that we may never see the effects of monetary excesses in output prices, but rather we will see them in asset prices."[24]

Cathy Minehan, president of the Boston Fed, was also worried: "This speculation is fed by financial markets, which are extremely accommodative. From every perspective that we can see in our region and nationally, monetary policy is not tight; it is not even neutral. It is accommodative to an increasingly speculative environment."[25] Nor was board member Susan Phillips attuned to the productivity miracle: "The situation is starting to feel a bit surreal, perhaps even unbelievable...."[26]

A case for raising the fed funds rate—or margin requirements—was clear. The S&P 500 had risen 46 percent for the 12-month period ending on March 31, 1998. Greenspan's response to these comments was mixed. He seemed to understand that the economy was now driven by the stock market: "We have an economic policy that is essentially unsustainable.... There is no credible model of which I am aware that embodies all of

---

[22] Patricia Lamiell, "Is the Stock Market a Supertanker or the *Titanic?*" Associated Press, March 31,1998.

[23] FOMC meeting transcript, March 31, 1998, p. 14.

[24] Ibid., p. 30.

[25] Ibid., p. 46.

[26] Ibid., p. 68.

this."[27] Since the stock market was beyond his ability to model, the logic of his productivity boom is suspect. Greenspan had hung his hat on stock prices always reflecting correct prices. The variables on the other side of the equation, particularly productivity, changed as need be. Of course, he complained that productivity was not measured properly. In any event, Greenspan did not raise the funds rate.[28]

Two months later, at the May 1998 meeting, the FOMC was rebellious, or as rebellious as this period piece from the Age of Etiquette dared to be. Jerry Jordan weighed in again by reporting what was happening in his district, in Cleveland: "Bankers complain a lot that pension funds and insurance companies are doing deals that no sensible banker would be willing to consider."[29]

Several other members grumbled, to no effect. Greenspan carried the vote, although he felt compelled to say: "I have been giving a lot of thought to the question of whether we are experiencing a stock market bubble, and if we are, what we should do about it. If the market were to fall 40 to 50 percent, I would be willing to stipulate that there had been a bubble!"[30] Was this a new model? After the market did fall 50 percent, in 2000–2001, Greenspan did not admit to a bubble—he wouldn't even discuss it.

At the May 1998 meeting, he gingerly tested the waters for his "can't see a bubble" act: "[T]he stock market is significantly overvalued.... But"—there had to be a but—"do I really know significantly more than the money managers who effectively determine the prices of these individual stocks? I must say that I, too, feel a degree of humility about my present ability to make such a forecast." Others would substitute another word for humility. Taking a step back, if he was too humble to venture a stock market forecast, how could he sit at a table where his committee fixed the world's short-term borrowing rate?

Greenspan closed the argument on whether the Fed would act on Jerry Jordan's long-running warning when he declared: "I have concluded that

---

[27] Ibid., p. 78.

[28] He did not think it was "appropriate to move at this stage. Were we to do so, I believe we would create too large a shock for the system, which it would not be able to absorb quickly." Ibid., p. 79.

[29] FOMC meeting transcript, May 19, 1998, p. 58. Ibid., p. 64.

[30] Ibid., p. 84.

in the broader sense we have to stay with our fundamental central bank goal, namely, to stabilize product price levels."[31] This was only four months after he had told the American Economic Association (in January 1998): "The severe economic contraction of the early 1930s, and the associated persistent declines in product prices, could probably not have occurred apart from the steep asset price deflation that started in 1929."[32]

Greenspan's malleable model, which had broken down at the March 1998 meeting, was once again in tip-top shape. The stock market once again knew all. To justify productivity as the missing variable, Greenspan kept jettisoning unseemly measures. He first ignored his favored price/book ratio (which he had extolled three years earlier, at the August 1995 FOMC meeting). After such warnings as Michael Prell's at the March 1998 meeting, the chairman steered clear of price/earnings ratios. His speeches became more emphatic in their propositions—for example, in July 1998: "The implications of today's *relentless* technological changes are my subject matter this afternoon"[33] [author's italics]. It seems a good bet that Greenspan was not calculating productivity as much as he was watching the Nasdaq Composite Index, which is heavily weighted with technology darlings. It had risen 21 percent between these two statements, 30 percent over the past year, and 99 percent over the last three years. In July, the Nasdaq burst through the 2,000 level—only three years after first piercing 1,000. More than 50 percent of the Nasdaq 1000-point rise was due to only three stocks: Microsoft, Cisco Systems, and Intel.[34]

PRODUCTIVITY GAINS A CREW MEMBER: STOCK MARKET ANALYSTS

The chairman's latest brainstorm was to cite stock analysts' earnings to justify the stock market. The unveiling was at the FOMC meeting of June 30 and July 1, 1998. At the top of the midyear meeting, Michael

---

[31] Ibid., p. 85.

[32] Alan Greenspan, "Problems of Price Measurement," speech at the Annual Meeting of the American Economic Association and American Finance Association, Chicago, Illinois, January 3, 1998.

[33] Alan Greenspan, "The Implications of Technological Changes," speech at the Charlotte Chamber of Commerce, Charlotte, North Carolina, July 10, 1998.

[34] Andrew Bary, *Barron's*, July 20, 1998, p. mw 4.

Prell presented two profit forecasts: both Wall Street's and the internal (Federal Reserve) projected rate of earnings growth. Both predicted a profit decline.[35] (Prell did not help the chairman by stating, "I won't take up your time with the umpteenth restatement of our skepticism regarding the sustainability of these valuation levels."[36]) Greenspan, in a bubble of his own, thought that "the crucial error in our forecast models has been the productivity numbers."[37] This humble central banker further asserted: "Everyone has been wrong by underestimating domestic demand and wrong in the other direction by overestimating inflation." Having been wrong, "[t]his has created a major increase in stock prices and a virtuous circle wealth effect." [38]

This is quite a list of insights, each contingent on either a previous insight (by Greenspan) or a previous flaw by "everyone." It was the prior meeting when he admitted his humility.

After Prell's introductory discussion of poor projected earnings growth, this would not seem the time for Greenspan to mention profit forecasts to justify the current level of the stock market. He introduced his new diversion by discussing five-year earnings expectations by analysts.[39] Prell told the committee projected earnings growth was expected to slow by the end of 1998. So, the chairman discussed only analysts' predictions for 2003, five years later.

Although the public generally took Wall Street "buy" recommendations at face value, and would pay dearly for its innocence, anyone with the slightest experience knew that the raison d'etre of these ratings was to hock stocks for their employers. Fed Governor Ned Gramlich alluded to their deficiency at the September 1998 meeting by labeling them "so-called stock market analysts."[40] He thought that their forecasts were still

---

[35] FOMC meeting transcript, June 30–July 1, 1998, pp. 13–15. Wall Street earnings are I/B/E/S operating earnings per share; Federal Reserve earnings are NIPA after-tax book profits.

[36] Ibid., p. 14.

[37] Ibid., p. 35.

[38] Ibid.

[39] Ibid.

[40] FOMC meeting transcript, September 29, 1998, p. 69.

"on the high side by all measures"—specifically mentioning their over-indulgent longer-term projections.[41] Greenspan did not take the bait.

The chairman's mind may have been elsewhere. Long-Term Capital Management had failed and threatened the financial system.

---

[41] Ibid.

15

LONG-TERM CAPITAL
MANAGEMENT: A LESSON
IGNORED

1998

It is one thing for one bank to have failed to appreciate what was happening to [Long-Term Capital Management], but this list of institutions is just mind boggling.[1]

> —*Alan Greenspan, FOMC meeting, September 29, 1998,*
> *upon learning that the counterparties that lent to Long-Term*
> *Capital Management did not monitor LTCM's balance sheet*

In the first three weeks of September 1998, Long-Term Capital Management (LTCM), a Greenwich, Connecticut, hedge fund, lost half a billion dollars a week, and everyone knew it.[2] Except, possibly, Alan Greenspan. In mid-September, in the midst of the turmoil, he told the House Banking Committee that "hedge funds [are] strongly

---

[1] Alan Greenspan, "Financial Derivatives," speech at the Futures Industry Association, Boca Raton, Florida, March 19, 1999.

[2] Nicholas Dunbar, *Inventing Money: The Story of Long-Term Capital Management and the Legends Behind It* (New York: Wiley, 2001), p. 210.

regulated by those who lend the money."[3] He ignored the Federal Reserve's responsibility, which is to regulate those who lend the money. The central bank had not done its job.

Four and a half months earlier, on May 2, 1998, Greenspan had given a speech in which he emphasized the advantages of "private market regulation."[4] Greenspan explained, "[R]apidly changing technology has begun to render obsolete much of the bank examination regime established in earlier decades. Bank regulators are perforce being pressed to depend increasingly on ever more complex and sophisticated private market regulation.... [O]ne of the key lessons from our banking history [is] that private counterparty supervision is still the first line of regulatory defense."

"Counterparty" may need an explanation. Banks have counterparty risk to their borrowers: the borrower may not repay a loan. That was a concern when the value of LTCM's collateral fell below the amount of money it had borrowed. There is also counterparty risk in a derivative contract. A hypothetical example: when Citigroup and J. P. Morgan enter an interest-rate swap, Citigroup will receive floating-rate interest payments every six months, and J. P. Morgan will receive fixed-rate interest payments at the same time.[5] The interest-rate payments are computed based on a principal amount upon which the interest is earned: $100 million, for instance. The "counterparty" risk is that one of the participants fails and cannot pay back the $100 million of principal.

In his May speech, the chairman also noted that "[t]he complexity and speed of transactions and the growing complexity of the instruments have required both federal and state examiners to focus more on supervising risk management procedures, rather than actual portfolios." The Fed now evaluated how banks monitored bank risks (e.g., their modeling techniques, the process used to supervise counterparties) in lieu of examining specific securities. It apparently never occurred to Greenspan, at least in any public statement, that maybe derivative structures should be reined in

---

[3] U.S. General Accounting Office, *Long-Term Capital Management: Regulators Need to Focus Greater Attention on Systemic Risk*, GAO/GGD-00-3, October 29, 1999, p. 15, quoted in *Martin Mayer, The Fed: The Inside Story of How the World's Most Powerful Financial Institution Drives the Markets* (New York: Free Press, 2001), p. 267.

[4] Alan Greenspan, "Our Banking History," speech at the Annual Meeting and Conference of the Conference of State Bank Supervisors, Nashville, Tennessee, May 2, 1998.

[5] Citicorp was renamed Citigroup Inc. after it merged with Travelers Group in 1998.

a bit, since government regulators could no longer understand the holdings in bank portfolios.

THOSE DAFFY NOBELS

There had been plenty of warnings that not much had changed since the derivative failures in 1994. Ignorance was essential to derivative operations. We need look no further than Long-Term Capital Management and two of its employees, Robert Merton and Myron Scholes. The pair received the Nobel Prize in economic sciences in 1997 "for a new method to determine the value of derivatives." Upon receiving his award in Stockholm, Myron Scholes "singled out two companies—General Electric and Enron—as having the ability to outcompete existing financial firms. He noted, 'Financial products are becoming so specialized that, for the most part, it would be prohibitively expensive to trade them in organized markets.' According to Scholes, Enron's trading of unregulated over-the-counter energy derivatives was a new model that someday would replace the organized [and regulated] securities exchanges."[6] Enron's specialized derivatives left the company bankrupt in 2001, and General Electric's financial ventures led it to government life support by 2008. The year after Merton and Scholes received their Nobel Prizes, the firm where they applied their theories collapsed.

John Meriwether had anticipated the derivatives boom by forming his Arbitrage Group at Salomon Brothers in 1977.[7] Meriwether left Salomon in 1991. In 1993, he formed Long-Term Capital Management (LTCM). He hired his top Salomon colleagues, including Merton and Scholes. By 1997, LTCM employed 25 Ph.D.s, who manufactured highly quantitative arbitrage trades. The fund rose 59 percent in 1995 and 44 percent in 1996, but then the law of diminishing returns kicked in.[8] The firm was managing much more money. The Ph.D.s were finding less opportunity to apply their skills. LTCM produced a 17 percent return in 1997.

---

[6] Frank Partnoy, *Infectious Greed: How Deceit and Risk Corrupted the Financial Markets* (New York: Times Books, 2003), p. 303.

[7] Roger Lowenstein, *When Genius Failed: The Rise and Fall of Long-Term Capital Management* (New York: Random House, 2000), p. 9.

[8] Partnoy, *Infectious Greed*, pp. 254–255. It is not clear if the 1995 and 1996 returns are gross or net. The 1997 returns are after fees.

Its strategy "moved from highly quantitative arbitrage trades to outright gambling on currencies and stocks."[9]

LTCM proved to be too big to fail. The reason for its salvation was the same reason that its fortunes looked so dire: everybody who was anybody had a large stake in its solvency. If LTCM failed, the securities it held would not appeal to a very scared and skeptical market that showed no inclination to buy.

On September 21, 1998, LTCM lost $553 million in a virtuoso rejection of the Nobel laureates' diversification models: all security prices went down.[10] The scientists from the classroom held a loose grip on the human mind. They forgot that "[d]uring a crisis, the correlation always goes to one."[11] This is the normal, time-tested reaction in such circumstances— everyone sells. This correlation never fails. This correlation is never modeled; if it were incorporated, banks would not trade leveraged derivatives.

THE FED COULD HAVE TAKEN MORE REGULATORY INITIATIVE

The FOMC held a meeting on September 29, 1998. The staff and Fed governors briefed Greenspan on Long-Term Capital Management's counterparties—the banks and brokers that lent to and traded with LTCM. When it became apparent to Greenspan that the risk management apparatus of the institutions he regulated operated at the level he should have expected (that is, expected from their history with loans to less-developed countries in the seventies and to commercial builders in the eighties), he was at a loss: "The question is why it happened in this case. Is it just that the lenders were dazzled by the people at LTCM and did not take a close look?"[12]

From there, it grew worse. He was told that none of the banks, with the exception of Bankers Trust, had an up-to-date balance sheet for LTCM. Even Bankers Trust's was "a relatively small piece of the whole action because so much of the latter is off-balance-sheet."[13]

---

[9] Ibid., p. 255.

[10] Lowenstein, *When Genius Failed*, p. 191.

[11] Martin S. Fridson, "Review of *When Genius Failed*, by Roger Lowenstein," *Financial Analysts Journal*, March/April 2001, p. 81.

[12] FOMC meeting transcript, September 29, 1998, p. 107.

[13] Ibid.

The need for supervision of the banks was obvious when a staffer commented: "It was something of a signature for [LTCM] to insist that if a counterparty wanted to deal with them, there would be no initial margin. Not many other firms have gotten away with that."[14] For this reason alone, the Fed should have geared up its watchdogs to monitor the banks. There may be exceptions, but regulators should assume that large banks care more about profit than about risk. Banks chase the hot market until either the government bails them out (Citigroup—again and again) or they fail (Texas banks in the 1980s).

A staff member told the FOMC that LTCM's counterparties only required the hedge fund to post collateral equal to the amount it had borrowed. Greenspan, a former director of J. P. Morgan, with 50 years of Wall Street experience, shared his perspective on collateral: "If I am a bank lender and I lend $200 million to a hedge fund, ordinarily I would be over-collateralized. I would hold more than $200 million in, say, U.S. Treasury bills."[15] A staffer told the FOMC that LTCM's collateral included "U.S. Treasuries, Danish government bonds, BBB credits— you name it."[16] With all prices falling, BBB credits were weak collateral. Greenspan was learning how the "private counterparty supervision" actually functioned. It must have been obvious to the chairman that banks took a more casual approach to collateral than they did in his J.P. Morgan days.

Continuing with Greenspan's example, suppose the value of LTCM's collateral had fallen to $180 million, $20 million less than the amount it had borrowed. The counterparties would have demanded the hedge fund post $20 million more. By September 29, LTCM was unable to meet counterparty demands for additional collateral.

Greenspan was to receive more lessons in this application of modern finance. On September 21, when it seems (interpreting the transcript) the Fed first read LTCM's balance sheet, its leverage was 55 to 1. A staffer offered more bad news: "The off-balance-sheet leverage was 100 to 1 or 200 to 1—I don't know how to calculate it."[17] The staffer wasn't alone.

---

[14] Ibid., p. 118.
[15] Ibid., pp. 110–111.
[16] Ibid., p. 108.
[17] Ibid., p. 108.

Greenspan's "first line of regulatory defense" didn't know whether LTCM was trading interest-rate swaps or stolen cars.

Greenspan expressed his exasperation several times during the meeting: "It is one thing for one bank to have failed to appreciate what was happening to [LTCM], but this list of institutions is just mind boggling."[18] So boggled was the man that Greenspan (and his successor Ben Bernanke) allowed the commercial banking system to leverage as never before, writing over $100 trillion worth of derivatives contracts between then and 2008—without so much as a dollar bill of reserves for these off-balance-sheet structures.

The FOMC discussed the adequacy of its own bank examinations. It was told that the Fed had not examined the banks since December 1997.[19] Vice Chairman McDonough said (at another point in the meeting): "It is not as if we were asleep."[20] But possibly they were dazzled. A Federal Reserve staff member mentioned banks' risk management processes, but "[t]he question is how effectively the banks were implementing those policies and procedures."[21] To the knowledge of the staffers at the meeting, no one at the Fed had taken the initiative to check.

In Greenspan's remaining time at the helm, these gaps were left to fester despite the probability that the banks did have the information. The banks were often buying and selling on the trades made by LTCM. The trading desks of the banks had a good idea what the hedge fund owned.

THE RESCUE

Nicholas Dunbar, physicist, derivatives master, and author, described the atmosphere on the LTCM trading floor in the firm's final week of independence: "Thirty years of financial theory has proved itself useless. Billion dollar track records and Nobel Prizes are now meaningless.... All that is left is a poker game."[22] As the poker game unfolded, Nobel Prize winner Robert Merton kept breaking into tears. He worried that

---

[18] Ibid.

[19] Ibid., p. 103.

[20] Ibid., p. 114.

[21] Ibid., p. 103–104.

[22] Nicholas Dunbar, *Inventing Money: The Story of Long-Term Capital Management and the Legends behind It* (New York: Wiley, 2000). p. 214.

LTCM's fall would ruin the standing of modern finance.[23] He had no need to worry. Americans worship experts, even when they are dismal failures. The reputations of Merton, Scholes, and the Nobel Prize in economic sciences were not in the least dented.

William McDonough coordinated the LTCM bailout. Twelve banks pledged $3.65 billion.[24] The firm remained intact, although it was tethered to a short leash. Meriwether remained.

Greenspan's decision to ignore what he had learned on September 29 was perplexing. It is common now to ascribe Greenspan's neglectful regulation to his free-market principles. But the transcript shows he was amazed that the banks did not monitor the hedge funds. From that moment forward, he knew that no one effectively regulated the hedge funds—not the government, and not the financial counterparties.

JUSTIFYING A RATE CUT? OR TWO? OR THREE?

By the end of the September 29 meeting, the FOMC voted to cut the funds rate by 0.25 percent, to 5.25 percent, with little concern for the economy. Greenspan later wrote, "it was highly likely that the U.S. economy would continue expanding at a healthy pace."[25] According to Greenspan's book, the reason for the rate cuts (there were to be three, each of 0.25 percent) was the "small but real risk that the default might disrupt global financial markets enough to severely affect the United States."[26]

The September 29 rate cut boosted the stock market, although that was not the ostensible reason for the reduction. The stock market had peaked in July and had fallen about 10 percent since. Stocks continued to drift lower. Between September 29 and October 14, 1998, the Nasdaq fell another 10 percent and the S&P 500 by 4 percent.

Still, this was a gain of 3.5 percent for the year. From the end of 1994 to the high in July 1998, the market had risen 160 percent.[27]

---

[23] Lowenstein, *When Genius Failed*, p. 176.

[24] Ibid., p. 207.

[25] Alan Greenspan, *The Age of Turbulence: Adventures in a New World* (New York: Penguin, 2007), p. 196.

[26] Ibid.

[27] William A. Fleckenstein with Frederick Sheehan, *Greenspan's Bubbles: The Age of Ignorance at the Federal Reserve* (New York: McGraw-Hill, 2008), p. 51.

The FOMC held another conference call on October 15, 1998. At 3:14 p.m., it announced the second 0.25 percent fed funds rate cut. This reduction was a surprise to the markets. Normally, although not always, such announcements are made after meetings of the FOMC. The New York Stock Exchange would close 46 minutes later. The rate cut came the day before October option contracts closed. The bond market had already shut. Holdings of stocks, stock options that hedge those holdings, bond positions, and related options are calibrated with careful precision. Market makers were bewildered. Given the potential for enormous losses, a frenzy of buying pushed the S&P 500 futures up 5 percent in five minutes.[28]

There was not a compelling case for cutting the funds rate only 16 days after the previous rate cut. The transcript of the October 15 conference call shows that opinions about the state of the markets from Fed district presidents were mixed.[29] The discussion turned to whether the FOMC should act now or wait until the next scheduled meeting in November. The decision was made to cut the funds rate to 5.0 percent. Fed Governor Ned Gramlich summed up the reason: "From the standpoint of the real economy, it probably doesn't matter too much; four weeks is not that long a period when we consider all the lags in the real economy. But for the financial markets, four weeks could be a long time."[30]

By November of 1999, the Nasdaq Composite had doubled in price.[31]

Nowhere in the October 15 FOMC transcript does a member mention the timing of a rate-cutting press release. Greenspan states that his own point of view had been formed "after 50 years of looking at the economy on almost a daily basis."[32] He surely had an inkling of how the markets would respond to a surprise announcement. FOMC Secretary Kohn said that the FOMC is "not constrained by the practice followed after regularly scheduled FOMC meetings [when the release time is known by outsiders].... I would expect [the press release] to be out within the hour." According to the transcript, Chairman Greenspan next thanked everyone, which is followed by "END OF SESSION."[33]

[28] Ibid., p. 56.
[29] Ibid., pp. 53–54, gives the views of the district presidents.
[30] FOMC conference call transcript, October 15, 1998, p. 26.
[31] Fleckenstein and Sheehan, *Greenspan's Bubbles*, p. 56.
[32] FOMC conference call transcript, October 15, 1998, p. 29.
[33] Ibid., p. 37.

There was no question, in most participants' minds, that Greenspan would always support the stock market. Following the LTCM rescue, the head of the largest hedge funds in the world told Martin Mayer, "If I get into big trouble, the Fed will come and save me."[34] Retail investors, too, were confident the "Greenspan put" was integrated into Federal Reserve policy.

Pandering to the Money Changers

In March 1999, Greenspan gave a speech on derivatives. He might have wandered onto the podium from Mars: derivatives "are an increasingly important vehicle for unbundling risk."[35] He also doused post-LTCM regulation reform: "Some may now argue that the periodic emergence of financial panics implies a need to abandon models-based approaches to regulatory capital and to return to traditional approaches based on regulatory risk measurement schemes. In my view, however, this would be a major mistake." The regulators' risk models "are much less accurate than banks' risk measurement models."[36]

In this speech, Greenspan asserted that "notional values are not meaningful measures of the risks associated with derivatives."[37] Notional values (e.g., the $100 million of principal discussed in the "counterparty" explanation earlier) became quite important when investment banks started falling like ducks in a shooting gallery.

Maybe Greenspan couldn't distinguish a derivative from a Botticelli, but he did know his audience. This March 1999 speech was before the Futures Industry Association. He congratulated the trade group: "It should come as no surprise that the profitability of derivative products ... doubtless is a factor in the significant gain in the overall finance industry's share of American corporate output during the past decade. In short, the value added of derivatives themselves derives from their ability to enhance the process of wealth creation."[38] This is bureaucratese for: "You are making more money than all of industrial America. The GDP needs you. Keep it up."

---

[34] Martin Mayer, *The Fed*, (New York: The Free Press, 2001) pp. 138–139.

[35] Alan Greenspan, "Financial Derivatives," speech at the Futures Industry Association, Boca Raton, Florida, March 19, 1999.

[36] Ibid.

[37] Ibid.

[38] Ibid.

Greenspan also stated that "derivatives are mainly a zero sum game."[39] He appeared inattentive to the scandal and joke of Wall Street bookkeeping. This would be expressed by Paul Volcker in 2006. In mock confusion, Volcker asked why it was that derivatives were the only financial instrument with no losers. Everyone wins.[40] He was referring to Wall Street earnings reports, which consistently showed banks profiting from derivatives trading quarter after quarter. The banks' pricing models were bonus generators.

After 1998, derivatives exploded into more complex and incomprehensible forms. They permitted the world's financial debt to balloon in a manner that forestalled another financial catastrophe for nine years. LTCM was small in scope compared to the size of the banking system a few years later. That no other similar miscalculation on the part of a hedge fund or bank—large or small—occurred for almost a decade was not because derivative shops had learned from their mistakes. The methodology of derivative construction remained the same. The acronyms compounded, but the models remained flawed.

LTCM's models calculated that the likelihood of the actual event—the loss of the firm's capital—was so remote that it would take several billion times the life of the universe for it to actually transpire.[41] However, these once-in-the-history-of-the-universe events were growing in frequency. The 1987 portfolio-insurance implosion, the 1994 derivative failures, and the 1998 LTCM bailout were all miscarriages that fell under the responsibility of the same Federal Reserve chairman. He showed no inclination to rein in derivative excesses. Instead, he gave speeches lauding the derivatives' virtues and congratulating the practitioners who were making so much money.

---

[39] Ibid.

[40] Paul Volcker, "Central Banker for the World: Challenges Ahead," speech at Grant's Interest Rate Observer Conference, St. Regis Hotel, New York City, March 29, 2006.

[41] Joe Kolman, "LTCM Speaks," *Derivatives Strategy*, April 1999; http:// www.derivativesstrategy.com/magazine/archive/1999/0499fea1.asp.

16

GREENSPAN LAUNCHES
HIS DOCTRINE

November 1998–May 1999

Once the Federal Reserve was set up, Greenspan reasons, the money supply never really got short. With one eye necessarily cocked towards politics, the Fed has always maintained a more than adequate money supply even when speculative booms threaten.[1]

—Fortune *magazine, March 1959*

The reduction of borrowing costs after the Long-Term Capital Management bailout was instrumental in the repricing of common stocks. From October 8, 1998, to December 31, 1999, the Nasdaq rose 178 percent.

The Fed's largesse fired deluded behavior that cannot be captured by market returns alone. On November 13, 1998, TheGlobe.com went public at $9 and closed the day at $63.50. How could an investor make 600 percent returns in less time than it takes to cook a turkey? TheGlobe.com was worth (if that's the right word) $5 billion.[2] Cofounder Stephan Paternot had plenty to celebrate. Soon after the IPO, the 25-year-old entrepreneur was filmed by CNN dancing in leather pants

---

[1] Gilbert Burck, *Fortune*, "A New Kind of Stock Market," March 1959, p. 201
[2] William A. Fleckenstein with Frederick Sheehan, *Greenspan's Bubbles: The Age of Ignorance at the Federal Reserve* (New York: McGraw-Hill, 2008), pp. 58–59.

(with his model girlfriend) on top of a nightclub table: "Got the girl. Got the money. Now I'm ready to live a disgusting, frivolous life." True to his word, on August 8, 2001, TheGlobe.com filed for bankruptcy.[3]

Four days after TheGlobe.com's IPO, Greenspan introduced bubble talk at the FOMC, apparently for the sole purpose of strangling it. The chairman admitted that "concerns about an asset bubble are not without validity, and that is where I have my greatest concerns about easing. Let me first, however, address the inflation issue."[4] He never did return to the asset bubble. Cathy Minehan and Thomas Hoenig, presidents of the Boston and Kansas City Federal Reserve Banks, subsequently tried to rouse the crowd, but to no avail. Greenspan chose a strange way to express his "greatest concern" about easing: he eased once again, another 0.25 percent. This was the last of the post–Long-Term Capital Management Fed funds cuts, a total of 0.75 percent—from 5.50 percent to 4.75 percent.

Greenspan lived in Neverland. The *Financial Times* would conclude that 1998 was "a year when it was pretty hard to sustain the belief that markets are perfectly rational."[5] Alan Greenspan may not have suffered doubts since his productivity equation defined the market as always being rational. Even so, the chairman threw a monkey wrench into his hypothesis by suggesting the stock market might be overpriced. He told the FOMC: "I do know that the presumption we have discussed in the last year or so that we can effectively manage a bubble is probably based on a lack of humility. *As I've said before*, a bubble is perceivable only in retrospect"[6] (author's italics).

As with his "as I noted earlier" productivity claim before Congress (in February 1998), he had never said such a thing to the FOMC, nor anywhere else, on the record. His Uriah Heep act of not knowing the consequences of popping a bubble was, by now, a long-running play.

---

[3] Andres Pinter, "A Star Is Rebooted," *New York Observer*, March 30, 2003; Anita Jain, "Flying at High Attitude," *Crain's New York Business*, May 31, 2004.

[4] FOMC meeting transcript, November 17, 1998, p. 89.

[5] Philip Coggan, "Sentiment Shifts to Low Inflation and Low Growth," *Financial Times*, January 4, 1999, p. 28.

[6] FOMC meeting transcript, December 22, 1998, p. 61.

The Fed chairman had test-run his humility at the March 1998 meeting when he said he would know there had been a bubble after the market fell 50 percent. He had now stated what would become known as the Greenspan doctrine.

His is a contorted form of humility. Greenspan is humble while telling the FOMC that, despite what the members might think, he knew that "a bubble is perceivable only in retrospect." He might have come to believe this, but it was still only his opinion. It certainly was not the opinion of Cleveland Federal Reserve Bank President Jerry Jordan, who said at the same meeting: "I have seen—probably everyone has now seen—newsletters, advisory letters, talking heads on CNBC, and so on saying that there is no risk that the stock market is going to go down because if it ever started down, the Fed would ease policy to prop it back up.... I think there are more and more people coming to that belief and acting on it."[7]

Greenspan may have been prompted into his absolute declaration by his very own hobbyhorse: stock market analysts. Several Federal Reserve staff members and FOMC participants warned earlier in the December meeting of poor corporate earnings predictions. Staff economist Michael Prell spoke of "a continuation of crummy earnings and poor returns." Cathy Minehan, president of the Boston Fed, said, "[D]eclining corporate profits could cause the stock market to decline sharply."[8]

Falling corporate profits should have diminished Greenspan's productivity thesis; instead, he found them inspiring. He told the FOMC: "[Although] security analysts have dramatically reduced their earnings expectations for the year 1998, they have not decreased their earnings expectations for the longer run.... This effectively explains how the stock market can rise with earnings expectations falling."[9]

It may require a moment to digest Greenspan's logic. The chairman believed, or, at least said, that since current earnings were falling, and analysts had not changed their estimates for 2003, the *rate* of growth

---

[7] Ibid., p. 38.
[8] Ibid., pp. 13, 30.
[9] Ibid., p. 60.

had to be higher over the next five years to meet the five-year estimate. Greenspan was selling the Brooklyn Bridge. Michael Moskow, president of the Chicago Federal Reserve Bank, stated what anyone with experience knows:

> MR. MOSKOW: I also want to make a brief comment about your description of the earnings forecasts by Wall Street analysts, with the short-term earnings forecasts coming down but the long-term forecasts staying where they were before. It reminds me of my years when I was in private industry and looked at many, many business plans, as I am sure you did as well. The head of a business would often come in and say, "Earnings this first year are going down, but wait until two, three, four, and five. They are going to go right up." We called this the hockey-stick approach because we saw it so frequently. So, I would be very skeptical about the forecasts that the Wall Street analysts are making about long-term profits.
>
> CHAIRMAN GREENSPAN: I tried not to convey a view that was other than that. President Stern.[10]

By calling on Gary Stern, president of the Minneapolis Federal Reserve Bank, Greenspan avoided Moskow's comment. While Greenspan had acknowledged that Moskow was correct, he effectively dismissed the observation from FOMC discussions. Profit projections for 2003 were Greenspan's sole lifeline at the December meeting. (For now: profits fell for the next few years, and Greenspan would hone his hypothesis accordingly.) His tactic of cutting off an uncooperative FOMC member (Moskow) by calling on someone else (Stern) was old hat.

In retrospect, this was the meeting at which Greenspan conceded his productivity argument. Maybe he didn't realize it; maybe nobody realized it. He would continue with his merry-go-round of justifications for the stock market, but the chairman had now introduced his escape hatch: even if he was wrong about productivity, about analyst earnings, and about all the other hokum that blessed the price of stocks, it no

---

[10] Ibid., p. 67.

longer mattered from a practical sense. Having declared that a central bank could not see a bubble until after it burst, the Federal Reserve would do nothing, whatever the circumstances.

The Federal Reserve was not alone in funding the stock market: 34 central banks cut rates 66 times in the last three months of 1998.[11] Central bankers, by and large, wanted to debase their currencies.

"THE CENTRAL BANKER AS GOD"

Alan Greenspan was now God, according to the *Economist*. On November 14, 1998, the hallowed periodical published an article entitled "The Central Banker as God," which stated: "Today, Alan Greenspan … is revered as a god by most investors." Yet his holiness was debated in financial periodicals. On September 29, 1998, financial writer James Grant offered a more earthly view in the *Wall Street Journal*'s lead op-ed, with the title: "Alan Greenspan Isn't God."

No, but unquestioned faith was a dangerous gamble. This productivity thing was, of course, beyond most investors, since it was beyond Alan Greenspan. They knew about it, though, and as long as Greenspan was reported to be pleased with it, and with analysts and projections and technology and whatever else he was talking about, they bought stocks. Bob Woodward put it well: "He has become both a symbol and a means of explaining and understanding the economy."[12]

One Greenspan biographer, Justin Martin, summed up the average American's verdict. Martin wrote of the post–Long-Term Capital Management atmosphere: "During the nervous days of 1998, Greenspan showed infallible instincts in steering the U.S. economy. It was a masterful performance, and a crucial one."[13]

Martin captured the idiom of the moment: "Greenspan's deft handling of the Asian Contagion [the collapse of Asian markets in 1997] turned him into a bona fide celebrity. Years in the future, social historians will

---

[11] John Kirton, University of Toronto, "Canada as a Principal Financial Power," 2000; http://www.g7.utoronto.ca/scholar/kirton2000/phase2.htm.

[12] Bob Woodward, *Maestro: Greenspan's Fed and the American Boom* (New York: Simon & Schuster, 2000), p. 227.

[13] Justin Martin, *Greenspan: The Man behind Money* (Cambridge, Mass.: Perseus, 2000), p. xvii.

look back on the heady days of economic prosperity that immediately followed the crisis as Greenspan's defining moment. The Fed chairman was promoted to iconic status and joined the ranks of Harry Houdini, General Douglas MacArthur, and Madonna."[14]

The New Economy and the Old Economy were fashionable terms. Technology was New; nontechnology was Old. Stephen Koffler, an analyst at Donaldson, Lufkin & Jenrette, explained why: "[The] Internet changes valuation standards because it's a pivotal point to changes in the economy. The Internet ... is driving tremendous gains in productivity. It's hard to find other times in history where that's been true."[15] He might have considered the lightbulb, the steam engine, or the wheel.

In March 1999, apparently losing ground with his analyst rationale, and certainly having lost credibility with Chicago Federal Reserve President Michael Moskow at the December 1998 meeting, Greenspan took the next step: "[S]ecurity analysts ... are speaking to corporate management and getting an excess dose of optimism."[16] Greenspan expounded: "[Their expectations] are obviously not independent observations."[17] Yet, analysts remained his crutch. Greenspan noted the "extent of the acceleration in productivity" by relying on "that terribly flawed number we often discuss, the expected long-term growth in earnings per share of the S&P 500 as estimated by security analysts."[18] The admission that analyst predictions were terribly flawed was new. With any such retreat, though, a forward advance generally followed. These bursts of insight that reversed setbacks might be likened to Marshal Foch's message during the Battle of the Marne: "My center is giving way, my right is retreating, situation excellent. I am attacking!" That was in 1914. In March 1999, Marshal Greenspan thrust analyst

---

[14] Ibid., p. 221.

[15] Ibid., Greg Ip, "Internet Valuations Explode, Sparking Debate," *Wall Street Journal,* December 28, 1998.

[16] FOMC meeting transcript, March 30, 1999, p. 54.

[17] Ibid., p. 55.

[18] Ibid., "acceleration in productivity," p. 53; "terribly flawed number," p. 54.

forecasts into the breach by "presum[ing] that the bias in those numbers has not changed significantly over the years."[19]

Why would Greenspan presume that? His new consistent bias theorem had never been measured; at least, the Fed chairman cited no evidence other than his own assertion. He would repeat this refrain about bias over the next few meetings. The "we" who "presumed" the consistent bias was one Alan Greenspan (although some others were starting to hop aboard). Consistent bias was enough of a fig leaf to control the board's tactless suggestions that productivity as justification for current stock prices was a tall tale.

There was a more straightforward measure of productivity that Greenspan could have consulted: corporate profits. If he had pursued such a route, he would probably have consulted the Bureau of Economic Analysis (BEA) corporate profit calculations.[20]

In fact, at the February 1999 FOMC meeting, Federal Reserve Economist Michael Prell emphasized the divergence between recent corporate profits the BEA had calculated, which were falling, and profit projections from Wall Street strategists, which were shooting up. Prell showed the committee a chart that displayed the two trends.[21] The Wall Street projections were from I/B/E/S, the Institutional Broker's Estimate System. To quote Alan Greenspan from a forthcoming speech, I/B/E/S is "a Wall Street research firm that compiles these estimates for the S&P 500.[22] The 1999 I/B/E/S forecast looked like a hockey stick.[23]

There are problems with any collection of data, but in an era when government data accentuate the positive, BEA calculations looked bleak.

---

[19] Ibid., p. 54.

[20] These are the National Income and Product Accounts (NIPA) produced by the Bureau of Economic Analysis.

[21] On the Federal Reserve Web site with FOMC transcripts, "Presentation Materials" are also stored. Prell's chart can be found on p. 10, chart 3, with the heading "Earnings Outlook," for the February 2–3, 1999 meeting.

[22] Alan Greenspan, "The American Economy in a World Context," speech at the 35th Annual Conference on Bank Structure and Competition of the Federal Reserve Bank of Chicago, Chicago, May 6, 1999.

[23] FOMC meeting transcript, February 2–3, 1999, pp. 22–23.

Profits in the United States had peaked back in 1997. Nonfinancial profits had fallen from $508.4 billion in 1997 to $470.1 billion in 1998. This
was a 7 percent drop. Given Greenspan's remarkable history of hopping
on a wagon just as it explodes, it is not surprising that the computer
industry fared far worse than America as a whole: computer company
earnings had fallen 84 percent, from $25.3 billion in 1997 to $3.9 billion
in 1998.[24]

Stock market analysts were another exploding bandwagon. They
were front-page news by 1998. There was, for instance, Henry Blodget, a
rookie analyst at CIBC Oppenheimer. On December 15, 1998, Amazon.
com common stock traded at $242 per share. Blodget predicted that it
would rise to $400 per share. On December 30, Amazon reached $350;
on January 7, 1999, it opened trading at $411, and on the next day, Janu-
ary 8, 1999, it rose again to $597.[25] The idea that analysts would issue
"price targets" was unheard of a few years back. Now, both the analysts
and their firms thrived on publicity from such predictions.

A landmark that was more noteworthy for celebration than for
substance was the Dow Jones Industrial Average crossing 10,000 on
March 30, 1999. CNBC turned the studio into a replica of the New
Year's countdown in Times Square. The *Wall Street Journal* prepared
a next-morning edition stuffed with ads congratulating the stock
market. Traditional measurements, such as price/earnings ratios,
could no longer be calculated. Often the bellwethers had no earnings;
sometimes they had no sales. This opened the way for a book that captured the latest American dream, *Dow 36,000*, by James K. Glassman
and Kevin A. Hassett. They posted a preview on the editorial page of
the *Wall Street Journal* on March 17, 1999: "Our calculations show that
with earnings growing in the long-term at the same rate as the gross
domestic product and Treasury bonds below 6%, a perfectly reasonable level for the Dow would be 36000—tomorrow, not 10 or 20 years
from now."[26]

---

[24] *Richebächer Letter*, July 2004, p. 11.
[25] These prices are adjusted to negate a 3:1 stock split on January 5, 1999.
[26] James K. Glassman and Kevin A. Hassett, "Stock Prices Are Still Far Too Low," *Wall
Street Journal*, March 17, 1999.

GREENSPAN'S "VERITABLE ARMY OF TECHNICIANS": STOCK MARKET ANALYSTS

Greenspan spoke at a conference sponsored by the Federal Reserve Bank of Chicago on May 6, 1999. He heralded a new era—that of a century before: "I do not say we are in a new era.... There was far greater justification to view the future with the unbridled optimism of a presumed new era a century ago.... In a very short number of years the world witnessed an astounding list of new creations: electric power and light, radios, phonographs, telephones, motion pictures, x-rays, and motor vehicles, just to begin the list."[27] This is an impressive start.

The chairman then listed reasons that the current non-New-Era New Era was so exciting: "[I]nformation access in real-time resulting from processes such as, for example, checkout counter bar code scanning and satellite location of trucks, fostered marked reductions in delivery lead times."[28] In the words of retired Federal Reserve Governor Edward Kelley, Greenspan and his space-age delivery system were still "going to Mars."[29] Greenspan offered further evidence: before this "veritable avalanche of IT innovations, most of twentieth century business decisionmaking had been hampered by limited information."[30] Given the current price of the stock market, some would say that the more limited information was preferred to the veritable avalanche, but Greenspan held the opposite opinion: "Owing to ... the ... emergence of more accurate price signals and less costly price discovery, market participants have been able to detect and to respond to finely calibrated nuances in consumer demand."[31]

For the first time, Greenspan rolled out his own finely calibrated nuance in public (before, only the FOMC had been exposed to this

---

[27] Greenspan, "The American Economy in a World Context." He avoided "New Era" in public but was more colloquial in private. For example, at the March 30, 1999, FOMC meeting (transcript, p. 54): "I think the question on the table is whether we are looking at an aberration or at emergence of a new era."

[28] Ibid.

[29] Greg Ip and Jacob M. Schlesinger, "Did Greenspan Push His Optimism About the New Economy Too Far?" *Wall Street Journal*, December 28, 2001.

[30] Greenspan, "The American Economy in a World Context."

[31] Ibid.

aberration): "[My] view is reinforced by securities analysts who presumably are knowledgeable about the companies they follow. This veritable
army of technicians has been projecting increasingly higher five-year
earnings growth, on average, since early 1995, according to I/B/E/S, a
Wall Street research firm that compiles these estimates for the S&P 500."
Greenspan did not mention the divergence on Michael Prell's chart
between I/B/E/S predictions and BEA profits.

The chairman continued: "In January 1995, the analysts projected
five-year earnings to rise on average by about 11 percent annually. After
successive upward revisions, the March 1999 estimate was set at about
13.5 percent.... While there are ample data to conclude that these estimates are biased upward, there is scant evidence to suggest the bias has
changed.... [C]ompanies are apparently conveying to analysts that, to
date, they see no diminution in expectations of productivity acceleration. This does not mean that the analysts are correct, or for that matter
the companies."[32]

Here his confidence in the amazing American economy is checked
by disclaimers—"presumably are knowledgeable," "apparently conveying"—and then he states that his cadre of informants and the
companies they relied upon for information might know nothing
at all. Reading FOMC transcripts, there is no record of companies
expressing a view on productivity, accelerating or not. In summation,
the speech was a catalog of platitudes: claims were disclaimed; abso-
lutes were qualified; enthusiasm was contingent; veritable armies of
technicians may be wrong or right. The speech was a smash hit.

Coincident with the chairman's remarks was the Royal Society for the
Arts publication of *Opening Minds: Education for the 21st Century*. It
quoted science historian James Burke. The author prophesied: "Instead
of judging people by their ability to memorize, to think sequentially
and to write good prose, we might measure intelligence by the ability to
pinball around through [*sic*] knowledge and make imaginative patterns
on the web."[33] Burke's view of the future was speaking at the Federal

---

[32] Ibid.

[33] Royal Society for the Arts, *Opening Minds: Education for the 21st Century* (London:
Royal Society for the Arts, 1999), p. 7. The study quoted from James Burke, *The Pinball
Effect*, (Boston: Back Bay Books, 1997), Introduction, no page numbers.

Reserve Bank of Chicago on May 6, 1999. Greenspan's mental pinging was not lost on his critics, one of whom referred to the Federal Reserve chairman as "Pinball Al" in his weekly commentary.[34]

It is unimaginable that Messrs. Volcker, Burns, and Martin would consider such hypotheses about the future of technology a suitable topic for the Federal Reserve chairman. It is both inappropriate and beyond the Federal Reserve's brief. Yet, he spoke as the expert. Greenspan styled his mental doodling as hypotheses, knowing that the public accepted them as dogma.

His admission that analysts' projections were biased upward with "scant evidence to suggest the bias has changed" is divorced from historical evidence (analysts grow more optimistic the longer a boom booms[35]). Making five-year guesses is an impossible task. Most important, though, this is a very strange train of thought by which to set central bank policy. (It is also a very strange reason to buy stocks.)

VOLCKER EXPRESSES SKEPTICISM

One who differed on the interpretation of corporate profits was Paul Volcker. On May 14, 1999, the former Federal Reserve chairman spoke at American University. His message resonates and contrasts for its succinct and timely qualities: "The fate of the world is dependent on the stock market, whose growth is dependent on about 50 stocks, half of which have never reported any earnings."[36]

To borrow from Volcker and expand on his summary: Productivity is the lifeblood of the economy. It is productivity, more exactly, the belief in rising productivity, that prevents an otherwise manic stock market from collapsing. It is the stock market that now runs the economy, rather than the market functioning as a mechanism to finance business.

---

[34] Christopher Wood, author of *Greed & fear*, his weekly market commentary to clients of CLSA (Credit Lyonnais Southeast Asia).

[35] At the end of the eighties' boom—in September 1990—analysts predicted 22 percent earnings growth for the following year; instead, profits *fell* 11 percent over that period. *Gloom, Boom & Doom Report*, February 1, 2008, p. 1.

[36] Fleckenstein and Sheehan, *Greenspan's Bubbles*, p. 67. Volcker's speech was the commencement address at American University, School of Public Affairs/Kogod School of Business.

It is the accelerated tendencies of the enriched American consumer and their outsized spending that keeps a downsized Asia working. It is the upwardly biased Wall Street forecasts—that we have decided are no more upwardly biased than in the past—that validates productivity, the U.S. stock market, the U.S. economy, provokes U.S. consumption, and which feeds and shelters most of humanity.

17
"This Is Insane!!"

I'm not saying [security analyst] forecasts are any good as far as earn-ings projections are concerned. Indeed, they're awful. They are biased on the upside, as they are made by people who are getting paid largely to project rising earnings in order to sell stocks, which is the business of the people who employ them.[1]

—Federal Reserve Chairman Alan Greenspan,
October 5, 1999, FOMC meeting

The chairman had not told the public or Congress about the Federal Reserve's bubble trouble. His contention of Federal Reserve impotence still snoozed at the FOMC conference table. Until Chairman Greenspan took his central bank vision public (i.e., we can't see a crash before the carcass has fallen off a cliff), this academic constraint brayed through Ivy League common rooms. As for Wall Street, this was to be a gift from God, the god who hypothesized in the Eccles Building.

June 17, 1999, was the day that Greenspan disclosed his doctrine to Congress: "The 1990s have witnessed one of the great bull stock markets in American history. Whether that means an unstable bubble has devel-oped in its wake is difficult to assess. A large number of analysts have judged the level of equity prices to be excessive, even taking into account

---

[1] FOMC meeting transcript, October 5, 1999, p. 48.

the rise in 'fair value' resulting from the acceleration of productivity and the associated long-term corporate earnings outlook."[2]

Assuming that he was speaking logically (and not just pinballing), Greenspan was acknowledging that the stock market was now accelerating at a faster pace than analysts' five-year projections. Apparently, Greenspan's equation—stock market price gains are justified by productivity—was breaking down. Had reality run ahead of his ability to dissemble? No, Greenspan was on top of his game. He next advanced his case for impotency: "But bubbles generally are perceptible only after the fact. To spot a bubble in advance requires a judgment that hundreds of thousands of informed investors have it all wrong. Betting against markets is usually precarious at best."[3]

The claim was ridiculous—but it worked. Betting against markets may be precarious, but that is exactly what an investor does with each portfolio decision. Just as he had sprung "can't see a bubble" on the FOMC in December 1998, Greenspan now announced this central bank restriction to Congress. The next day, a *New York Times* editorial expressed its tentative acceptance of Greenspan's most outlandish claim: "The new Greenspan is brimming with self-assurance. Let us hope the market does not test his new confidence."[4] If only the *New York Times* had brimmed with enough self-confidence to state that the Federal Reserve chairman was abandoning the Federal Reserve's responsibility.

Maybe the *Times* was too stunned for such a response. In one gulp, it learned that the Fed did not, and could not, see the hot-air balloon it had so generously expanded—mostly with Greenspan's hot air. The editors had long trusted the chairman. When Greenspan had issued his stock market warning in February 1997, the *Times* stood by Greenspan in an editorial with the title: "Wise Warnings to Giddy Investors." (This was when Congress reprimanded Greenspan for jawboning the stock market down.[5]) In the editors' words: "To ward off the bad outcome,

---

[2] Joint Economic Committee, "Monetary Policy and the Economic Outlook," June 17, 1999.

[3] Ibid.

[4] Editorial, "Hints of a Mild Fed Action," *New York Times*, June 18, 1999.

[5] *Jawboning* is giving a verbal warning or threat.

Mr. Greenspan gently reminded investors that stock prices fall as well as rise. ... He also reminded them that the Fed will not shrink from raising interest rates—which will draw money out of stocks." The 1997 editorial went on to remind readers that those on Wall Street who "contend that the American economy is heading toward unprecedented prosperity" lack perspective: "like any story that says the future will be unlike the past, the predictions are probably wrong."[6]

The *Times* did not know that between 1997 and 1999 Greenspan would echo the giddy cheerleaders on Wall Street—that this *was* an unprecedented moment in history. Once Greenspan declared our good fortune, he had no reason to monitor the stock market. The June 1999 speech simply informed the public of the chairman's decision to do nothing.

Greenspan's brimming nonchalance was evident throughout his "don't worry, be happy" testimony on June 17, 1999: "While bubbles that burst are scarcely benign, the consequences need not be catastrophic for the economy." He told the (presumably) puzzled congressmen: "[W]hile the stock market crash of 1929 was destabilizing, most analysts attribute the Great Depression to *ensuing* failures of policy" [author's italics].[7]

This directly contradicted what he had written in 1966. In his essay "Gold and Economic Freedom," Greenspan had placed the blame entirely on Fed policy *before* the crash. (From his 1966 article: "The excess credit which the Fed pumped into the economy [in 1927] spilled over into the stock market—triggering a fantastic speculative boom.")

The detachment of the FOMC from reality grew worse. Between May 29 and June 29, 1999 (the month leading up to the June 29–30, 1999, FOMC meeting), the *New York Times* discussed the stock market bubble in 10 separate articles. (A headline on May 30: "Pop! Goes the Bubble."[8]) The word *bubble* was used only once at the June 29–30 conclave. The stock market was mentioned 21 times at this meeting.

---

[6] Editorial, "Wise Warnings to Giddy Investors," *New York Times*, February 28, 1999.

[7] Alan Greenspan, "Monetary Policy and the Economic Outlook," Joint Economic Committee, June 17, 1999.

[8] Gretchen Morgenson, "Pop! Goes the Bubble," "Market Watch," *New York Times*, May 30, 1999.

The FOMC raised the fed funds rate from 4.75 percent to 5.00 percent—the first change since the three interest rates cuts following the LTCM troubles in late 1998 (described in Chapter 15). If the stock market was the reason the FOMC tightened, it was well disguised. Forty pages of the transcript prattle on about the FOMC communiqué: should it be of a symmetric or an asymmetric nature? A Fed staffer then read the draft statement. This had been handed out before the meeting started. It passed with a single dissent (Dallas President Robert McTeer).[9]

The chairman's sole contribution to stock market analysis at this meeting lifted the bar of either banality or understatement to a new level: "We are observing market capitalizations that are telling us something very interesting even as we simultaneously argue that stock market prices are overvalued. We are seeing a very dramatic shift in the changing capitalizations of high-tech versus low-tech companies."[10] Whatever argument he referred to was not made at this meeting. In the past 10 years of transcripts, there had never been an FOMC argument.

On August 27, 1999, in Jackson Hole, Wyoming, Greenspan talked about assets. Greenspan's talk confirms that he still understood markets are not always efficiently priced and that the consequences of market crashes are substantial. In his speech, the Federal Reserve chairman explained: "[W]hen events are unexpected, more complex, and move more rapidly than is the norm, human beings become less able to cope." The failure "to be able to comprehend external events almost invariably induces fear." This induces "disengagement from an activity." The "attempts to disengage from markets ... means bids are hit and prices fall."[11] In his roundabout way, Greenspan had described a market crash.

Such waves of emotional instability beg the question of how derivative models can successfully anticipate fear that causes bids to be hit and prices to fall. Greenspan told his audience that models fail in unusual circumstances: "Probability distributions that are estimated largely, or exclusively,

---

[9] FOMC meeting transcript, June 29–30, 1999, p. 113.

[10] Ibid., pp. 84–85.

[11] Alan Greenspan, "New Challenges for Monetary Policy," speech at a symposium sponsored by the Federal Reserve Bank of Kansas City, Jackson Hole, Wyoming, August 27, 1999.

over cycles excluding periods of panic will underestimate the probability of extreme price movements because they fail to capture a secondary peak at the extreme negative tail that reflects the probability of occurrence of a panic."[12] Yet, he seemed content to let bank models monitor risk.

At about the same time Greenspan delivered his speech, Fred Hickey was preparing the September 1999 edition of his monthly *High-Tech Strategist*, a highly regarded newsletter devoted to technology investing. The probability of a rising "secondary peak at the extreme negative tail" grew more obvious upon reading Hickey's letter.

Hickey noted that the Philadelphia semiconductor index tripled from October 1998 through August 1999. Yet, semiconductor sales had peaked at $150 billion in 1995. Money poured into the fastest-rising mutual funds, which then funneled the flows into the largest stocks. Hickey wrote: "The six biggest capitalization tech stocks (Microsoft, Intel, IBM, Cisco, Lucent, Dell) are now valued at $1.65 trillion, up $460 billion this year.... [T]here's been no revenue growth in the world P.C. [personal computer] industry in 2½ years." Hickey went on: "Just today, on September 3, 1999, the melt up caused by the 'favorable' unemployment report added $63 billion to the market valuations of the 'Big 6.' *One* day's gain. At their lows in late 1990, all of the stocks in [Hickey's top-10 model technology portfolio: IBM, Hewlett-Packard, Intel, Microsoft, Motorola, Cisco, Sun Microsystems, Texas Instruments, Oracle, and Micron Tech] could have been purchased for a grand total of $52 billion. Essentially, most of the technology industry in 1990 is an even swap for one day's gain of 6 stocks today. This is insane!!"[13]

THE ROAD TO FAME: TELL THE PEOPLE WHAT THEY WANT TO HEAR

James Glassman and Kevin Hassett, celebrities now, were on the editorial page of the *Wall Street Journal* touting *Dow 36,000*: "[W]hy should certain P/Es constitute a ceiling? ... When you apply our model, the market looks like a very good deal, even at today's prices."[14]

---

[12] Ibid.

[13] Fred Hickey, *High-Tech Strategist*, September 3, 1999.

[14] James K. Glassman and Kevin A. Hassett, "Bursting Mr. Greenspan's Bubble," *Wall Street Journal*, September 3, 1999.

Greenspan spoke five days later at the Gerald R. Ford Foundation in Grand Rapids, Michigan. Before the former president, Greenspan made a sweeping and unverifiable claim: "It is safe to say that we are witnessing this decade, in the United States, history's most compelling demonstration of the productive capacity of free peoples operating in free markets."[15] Soon after, Abby Joseph Cohen gave a speech at the Waldorf-Astoria. Its title: "Supertanker America, Still on Course."[16] This competing celebrity was as repetitious as Greenspan, which was why she was so valuable. In the words of another legendary self-promoter, Jim Cramer: "Every time she spoke, she turned around the futures, or broke the nasty selling waves, as she explained why panicking was wrong and we were in a rip-roaring bull market. In a market that had come to see this frumpy curly-haired nerd as a double-hulled supertanker herself.... Cohen had stayed bullish ... not wavering for an instant from her Supertanker America thesis."[17]

The kinetoscope of images, incessant noise, and juvenile vocabulary exploded like shrapnel in the face of a world that had already run out of superlatives. Television ads promoting Internet companies featured a college student belching the alphabet, ravenous wolves attacking a high-school band, gerbils shot from cannons, children tattooed in day-care centers, a world in which "practically no bodily function is too private and no rude behavior too coarse to be featured in a spot."[18]

FROM THE HORSE'S MOUTH: ANALYSTS ARE PAID TO SELL STOCKS

The Fed raised the funds rate another 0.25 percent in August 1999, in November 1999, in February 2000, and in March 2000 to 6.00 percent.

---

[15] Alan Greenspan, "Maintaining Economic Vitality," speech in the Millennium Lecture Series sponsored by the Gerald R. Ford Foundation and Grand Valley State University, Grand Rapids, Michigan, September 8, 1999.

[16] Abby Joseph Cohen, "Supertanker America, Still on Course," speech at the Financial Executives International (FEI), Current Financial Reporting Issues Conference, Waldorf-Astoria Hotel, New York City, November 15, 1999.

[17] James J. Cramer, *Confessions of a Street Addict* (New York: Simon & Schuster, 2002), p. 222.

[18] Patricia Winters Lauro, "Dot-Com Companies Have Built Their Brands by Using More Ads, in Good Taste or Not. Often Not," "The Media Business: Advertising," *New York Times*, September 30, 1999.

There is little in the transcripts to suggest that the stock market played a role in these decisions, although it is probable that some worrywarts who had warned of a crash latched onto any rationale expounded (no matter how trivial) to slow the supply of credit into the stock market.

But credit was not slowing. The markets barely noticed these rate hikes. The expected rate of return by borrowers—Americans and foreigners alike—was far greater than 6 percent. The enthusiasm spilled over into the real economy, which was building more houses and selling more cars. In a March 1999 speech to the Mortgage Bankers Association, Greenspan had told the congregation: "The past few years have been remarkable for your industry."[19]

Greenspan's productivity miracle was so calcified by the October 1999 meeting that it was no longer controversial. He informed the FOMC: "[W]e are seeing a remarkable acceleration in economic activity now, which under our old regime ... would lead us to say that this expansion is getting dramatically out of hand."[20] The "old regime" was an addition to the Greenspan lexicon, presumably in lieu of the "old era/new era" construction. The new regime would be shooed into the tumbrels within six months. Security analysts were no longer enough; he juggled farther out on the gangplank: "I'm not saying [security analyst] forecasts are any good as far as earnings projections are concerned. Indeed, they're awful. They are biased on the upside, as they are made by people who are getting paid largely to project rising earnings in order to sell stocks, which is the business of the people who employ them."[21] (This inside information never reached a wider audience. Greenspan would, in the future, admit that analysts were prone to optimism, but not that they were corrupt, until he scolded the bunch of them after the Enron affair.)

Greenspan plunged on by introducing a new measurement: corporate executives were lowering their costs. The new metric is corporate executives, who apparently could be taken at their word. This was another bandwagon Greenspan grabbed hold of just in time for it to explode.

---

[19] Alan Greenspan, "Mortgage Finance," speech at the Mortgage Bankers Association, Washington, D.C., March 8, 1999.

[20] FOMC meeting transcript, October 5, 1999, p. 49.

[21] Ibid., p. 48.

A year before, *BusinessWeek* had published an advertising supplement that addressed the priorities of corporate executives. Chief financial officers responded to the question: "As CFO, I have fought off other executives' requests that I misrepresent corporate results." In response, 55 percent replied, "Yes, I fought them off," while 12 percent answered: "I yielded to the requests."[22] In *Bull! A History of the Boom and the Bust, 1982–2004*, Maggie Mahar writes: "That two-thirds of these CFOs freely admitted that they had been asked to goose the numbers suggested that the type of person who might blanch at such a suggestion had probably fallen off the corporate ladder early on in the bull market."[23] That Greenspan would still take the word of corporate executives at face value is difficult to believe.

GREENSPAN'S Y2K FEAR: ANOTHER DOG THAT DID NOTHING IN THE NIGHTTIME

Greenspan's Y2K fear ("Year 2000") was contributed by technology companies, the same experts who were compressing information from months to minutes. Computers built 20 or 30 years earlier were not capable of calculating the "2" digit to succeed the "1" when "1999" came to a close. We were doomed: the developed world would cease to function at midnight on New Year's Eve. Planes and elevators would fall from the sky; sewage plants would burst, ruining water supplies; financial calculations (in statements and security prices) would make us all billionaires, or broke.

Greenspan may have believed the prophecies, or he may have feared that panic ahead of the millennium would drain the banking system of cash. Whatever the case, he told the Senate Banking Committee that the Fed was preparing to let loose $50 billion into the banking system.[24]

---

[22] *BusinessWeek*, July 13, 1998, p. 113 "The Seventh Annual *BusinessWeek* Forum of Chief Financial Officers," polling provided by Meridia Audience Response, Plymouth Meeting, Pennsylvania.

[23] Maggie Mahar, *Bull! A History of the Boom and the Bust, 1982–2004* (New York: Harper Business, 2004), pp. 269–270.

[24] Jerome Tuccille, *Alan Shrugged: The Life and Times of Alan Greenspan, the World's Most Powerful Banker* (Hoboken, N.J.: Wiley, 2002), pp. 244–245.

The gates were so wide open that there was nothing the Fed could do to slow the market's ascent. Yet there was very little talk of Y2K in FOMC meetings. It had been discussed a couple of times at meetings over the previous two years, but never in reference to monetary policy.[25] No one mentioned the $50 billion. Given the amount of time the FOMC debated symmetric and asymmetric communiqués, a word or two about $50 billion dropped into the banking system would seem appropriate.

"THE MOST FASCINATING PERSON OF 1999"

The chairman sounded no worse for wear at the FOMC meeting on December 21, 1999. "I see no overheating other than in the stock market."[26] Maybe so, but he was viewing the world through the clogged end of a drainpipe: the stock market *was* the economy.

Greenspan prefaced his stock market assessment with a lesson in stock market aesthetics: "To talk in terms of momentum, or price/sales ratios, or, even better, how much in losses a firm has experienced as reasons for higher stock prices is clearly just nonsense. The fundamental consideration is that a buyer is purchasing claims against future cash."[27] This was not true. Day trading was sweeping the nation—teachers and lawyers quit their jobs and traded stocks from their bedrooms. Their future was lunchtime.

Greenspan's dyspeptic (for him) outburst was probably in reaction to staff economist Michael Prell's earlier discussion of an IPO prospectus. The indefatigable Prell had discussed VA Linux, which entered the carnival on December 9, 1999. VA Linux jumped 700 percent on its first day of trading. It was valued at $9 billion. Prell compared the current atmosphere to that of England's South Sea Bubble fiasco in 1720 which so devastated Isaac Newton, he would not discuss it for the rest of his

---

[25] For FOMC comments, see William A. Fleckenstein with Frederick Sheehan, *Greenspan's Bubbles: The Age of Ignorance at the Federal Reserve* (New York: McGraw-Hill, 2008), pp. 78–79.

[26] FOMC meeting transcript, December 21, 1999, p. 49. This FOMC meeting is discussed at greater length in Fleckenstein and Sheehan, *Greenspan's Bubbles*, pp. 76–79.

[27] FOMC meeting transcript, December 21, 1999, pp. 46–47.

life. He quoted from the South Sea share offering: "'A company for carrying on an undertaking of great advantage, but nobody to know what it is.'"[28]

Greenspan had taken to ignoring—not even mentioning—warnings from the FOMC and the staff. Why he felt a need to respond (that is, assuming that he was responding to Prell's specific claim with: "how much in losses a firm has experienced") would be conjecture, but his insistence that stocks were bought for their estimated profits in 2004 (five years hence) must have left some FOMC members wondering why they were spending their time listening to his malarkey.

There were real Internet businesses pulling in real revenue, the accomplishment of which turned traditional business planning on its head. The *New York Times* reported in October 1999 that the top 10 online brokers (those that facilitate stock and bond trading on the Internet) had dedicated $1.5 billion to their advertising budgets for the next year. This was approximately the same as Ford's annual advertising allowance and far above those of Coca-Cola and Walt Disney combined.[29] Deciding that the Internet ruckus was more fun than making a buck, American Express offered free trading; E*TRADE paid $150 per person to convert one competitor's customers' brokerage accounts; and Ameritrade gave new customers two round-trip tickets to London, Mexico, or Hawaii.[30]

The A&E Biography television network named Greenspan the "most fascinating person of 1999." He even appeared on the cartoon shows: "[A] suitably dour animated likeness of the Fed chairman appeared on [*The Simpsons*].... Bart tries to high-five the Fed chairman, but

---

[28] Ibid., p. 10.

[29] Joseph Kahn, "The On-Line Brokerage Battle," "The Media Business: Advertising," *New York Times*, October 4, 1999.

[30] Patrick McGeehan, "Latest Lure on the Web: Free Trades," "Investing," *New York Times*, November 14, 1999. AMEX offered "commission-free stock purchases for anybody who deposited $25,000." E*TRADE's offer applied to Discover Brokerage Direct (of Morgan Stanley Dean Witter). Ameritrade offered the free round-trip flights to anyone who opened an account with a minimum balance of $5,000 (from full-page advertisement in the *Wall Street Journal* October 27, 1999, p. C9).

Greenspan ignores him."[31] The CNBC financial network (which was more whimsied than *The Simpsons*) "took to providing live coverage even of some of the Fed chairman's minor testimony, with the tag line: 'Greenspan Speaks.' It also introduced a wildly popular and widely imitated feature called the Briefcase Indicator"[32]: as Greenspan walked to his office in the Eccles Building on the mornings of FOMC meetings, CNBC would stake out his path. The premise: if his briefcase was thin, the chairman was in harmony with the world; if it was thick, a conundrum brewed. In the latter instance, CNBC deduced that a change in policy was on the table. CNBC anchors rattled on with step-by-step commentary during his stroll, to background music such as the theme song from *Mission: Impossible*.[33]

The question hung heavy: was Greenspan aware of the pageantry? A CNBC producer observed: "This is one of the most powerful men in the world. Why doesn't he just get dropped off at the front door?"[34] Although Greenspan claimed to be an introvert, he certainly was an exhibitionist.

---

[31] Justin Martin, *Greenspan: The Man behind Money* (Cambridge, Mass.: Perseus, 2000), p. 225.

[32] Ibid., p. 223.

[33] Ibid.

[34] Ibid.

18

GREENSPAN'S POSTBUBBLE
SOLUTION: TIGHTEN MONEY

January–May 2000

I would not only reappoint Mr. Greenspan; if Mr. Greenspan should
happen to die, God forbid ... I would prop him up and put a pair of
dark glasses on him.[1]

—Presidential candidate John McCain, 2000

The millennial media coverage fed the growing consensus of one world
converging—unless it collapsed on New Year's Eve. The dire Y2K predictions by technology experts went unfulfilled. Not an elevator plunged
nor a computer failed. The experts contended that never-ending over-
time work had corrected any potential problems. There is no question
that late-night shifts by computer programmers modified and improved
computer systems. Nevertheless, that not a single silicon wafer anywhere
failed sowed seeds of doubt about the expertise of the experts.

In preparation for panic, Alan Greenspan stuffed the banks with
money. This was prudent, but it once again calls into question why he
was roaming the country making speeches about technology.

Money chases an inflating asset. The Nasdaq average rose 54 percent
from mid-October 1999 through January 3, 2000. The Nasdaq average

---

[1] "Excerpts from New Hampshire Debate Involving G.O.P. Presidential Candidates,"
New York Times, December 3, 1999.

had risen 907 percent over the previous five years. Japan's Nikkei index, widely considered the largest stock market bubble in a major industrialized country, had appreciated only 230 percent in the five-year run-up before it burst a decade before. The price/earnings ratio of the Nasdaq was now around 200:1. Japanese stocks had peaked on December 31, 1989, at 80:1.[2]

In January 2000, the Federal Reserve started to absorb the dollars it had printed in 1999. The Fed expanded the monetary base at an annualized rate of 44 percent between October 20, 1999, and December 29, 1999. It reduced the base by 20.4 percent from December 29, 1999, to February 23, 2000.[3] This doomed the stock market.

A trio of waves peaked and then collapsed in 2000. The Internet silliness topped off in March. The telecommunications wave carried mutual fund managers into the fall, and the optical networking mania finally ran out of energy in early winter.

Corporate earnings, the neglected story of the past two years, continued to tumble. Profits of the big five technology companies (Microsoft, Cisco, Intel, Oracle, and Dell) were falling, even as their stock prices skyrocketed. These five stocks now comprised 25 percent of the Nasdaq average.[4] Their ascent fed on itself as flows into mutual funds demanded that they be invested in technology.

The Y2K scare formed the peak of the stock market cycle for a second reason. Companies had been frightened into buying the latest computer gear beforehand. They were also scared to death that the Internet would compromise their businesses. They had spent extravagantly on technology equipment. The corporate shopping cycle was over.

Greenspan's third term as Fed chairman was drawing to an end. In contrast to the cat-and-mouse games of 1996, President Clinton gleefully nominated Greenspan on January 4, 2000. The president was star-struck. Federal Reserve Chairman Greenspan's "devotion to new technologies has been so significant, I've been thinking of taking

---

[2] Fred Hickey, *High-Tech Strategist*, January 4, 2000.

[3] St Louis Federal Reserve, U.S. Financial Data, "Adjusted Monetary Base" chart, March 2, 2000.

[4] Hickey, *High-Tech Strategist*, January 4, 2000.

Alan.com public—then we could pay off the debt even before 2015."[5] It was a time of infinite extrapolation.

In January, the town of Halfway, Oregon, changed its name to Half.com.[6] In February, James Wolfensohn, president of the World Bank, told the *Financial Times*: "In Ethiopia, I met a man who was trading goats over the internet with Ethiopian taxi drivers in the US."[7] The nutters could only applaud, missing the point that there was a screw loose.

This was true in the nation's financial capital, as reported by a morning stroller: "I went downstairs to Fifth Avenue to get a pretzel.... and a rainbow-colored double-decker bus rumbled past me ... with the following message plastered along its length: 'IPOS FOR EVERYONE! EVERYONE CAN WIN! COME SEE US AT MAINSTREETIPO.COM!' The bus stopped a block down the avenue ... and people came off the sidewalks on both sides of the avenue and surrounded the driver-side window asking questions."[8]

GIVING GREENSPAN "CREDIT FOR THE GOLDEN AGE"

On January 26, 2000, the Senate Banking Committee held its quadrennial deposition of Greenspan as candidate for another term as Fed chairman. The senators did not so much interrogate him as they did worship him. "Members of both parties heaped praise on Mr. Greenspan," recorded the *New York Times*.[9] The generosity of Republican Senator Phil Gramm from Texas flowed over: "If you were forced to narrow down the credit for the golden age that we find ourselves living in, I think there are many people who would be due credit, and there are more who would claim credit. But of those who are in a position of authority, I think your name would have to be at the top of the list."[10] Such adulation was a sure sign

---

[5] http://money.cnn.com/2000/01/04/markets/greenspan/AG.

[6] William A. Fleckenstein, *The Contrarian*, siliconinvestor.com, January 24, 2000.

[7] Alexandra Nusbaum, "Bridge to Span Technology Gap: Interview with James Wolfensohn," *Financial Times*, February 15, 2000.

[8] William A. Fleckenstein, *The Contrarian*, siliconinvestor.com, March 1, 2000.

[9] Richard W. Stevenson, "Greenspan Holds Forth before a Friendly Panel," *New York Times*, January 27, 2000.

[10] Ibid.

that the stock market was peaking. When a "golden age" is proclaimed, it is time to sell.

Greenspan kicked off his 2000 speaking tour on January 13, with a speech entitled (what else?): "Technology and the Economy." He had nothing new to say, but in the tradition of the best publicists, he knew that "[p]olitical propaganda ... is aimed at the broad masses.... Its task is the highest creative art of putting sometimes complicated events and facts in a way simple enough to be understood by the man on the street."[11] Serenading the Economic Club of New York, the accomplished musician simplified his composition to a variation on "Chopsticks": "Before this revolution in information availability, most twentieth-century business decisionmaking had been hampered by wide uncertainty.... Decisions were made from information that was hours, days, or even weeks old."[12] Greenspan seemed never to tire of repeating this refrain, despite growing evidence of the worst decision making seen in generations.

Inevitably, he leaned on his crutch: "[S]ecurity analysts, reflecting detailed information on and from the companies they cover, have continued to revise *upward* long-term earnings projections."[13] He went on to tell the economists that "the American economy was experiencing a once-in-a-century acceleration of innovation, which propelled forward productivity, output, corporate profits, and stock prices at a pace not seen in generations, if ever."[14]

The economists gushed. They should at least have known that corporate profits, having peaked in 1997, continued to fall. The data from the Bureau of Economic Analysis (BEA), which Greenspan did his best to ignore, were diverging more than ever from Wall Street forecasts. Staff economist Michael Prell would not let Greenspan ignore the "rosy earnings forecasts of security analysts" (in February 2000) that, in Prell's view, were "rather wacky" (in March 2000).[15]

---

[11] Joseph Goebbels, speech at 1934 Nuremburg rally, translation by Randall Bytwerk; http://www.calvin.edu/academic/cas/gpa/goeb59.htm.

[12] Alan Greenspan, "Technology and the New Economy," speech at the Economic Club of New York, New York, January 13, 2000.

[13] Ibid.

[14] Ibid.

[15] FOMC meeting transcript, February 1–2, 2000, p. 16; FOMC meeting transcript, March 21, 2000, p. 30.

The BEA calculated that machinery profits had fallen from $209.0 billion in 1997 to $150.6 billion in 1999. Of the current obsession, computer industry profits peaked at $25.3 billion in 1997. By 1999, the industry was losing $6.5 billion.[16] This never received much publicity: technology companies in the aggregate had turned from profit-making to loss-making enterprises during the most fevered years of the technology stock bubble.

The stock market was still rising. The Dow Jones Industrial Average (which is not oriented toward technology companies), peaked on January 14, 2000, when it closed at 13,722. The Nasdaq rose another 20 percent and peaked on March 10, with a closing price of 5,048.

MARGIN DISCUSSIONS THAT NEVER HAPPENED

During the January 26, 2000, Senate Coronation, the politicians could at least imagine black clouds. Total margin debt had risen 45 percent between October 1999 and February 2000.[17] A chart comparing the parabolic rise of borrowed shares and the stock market warned of a close linkage. The Federal Reserve has the authority to raise margin requirements at any time.[18] Current requirements were 50 percent—in other words, for every $50 paid for stock (cash payment to the broker), an investor could borrow $50 from the broker. But the Fed could wave its wand and dictate a 60 percent or 100 percent cash payment for a $100 exposure to the stock market.

Democratic Senator Chuck Schumer of New York thought the stock market might be speculative. He asked Greenspan if the recent surge in borrowed shares was a concern. Greenspan told Schumer the Fed was studying the problem. The Fed Chairman said that such an increase would have little effect on the stock market. Yet, Greenspan did express concern over rising margin purchases: "They have moved up at a pace which has

---

[16] *Richebächer Letter*, July 2004, p. 11; from Bureau of Economic Analysis, Commerce Department Survey of Current Business.

[17] William A. Fleckenstein with Frederick Sheehan, *Greenspan's Bubbles: The Age of Ignorance at the Federal Reserve* (New York: McGraw-Hill, 2008), p. 87. This is New York Stock Exchange Margin debt.

[18] The Securities Exchange Act of 1934 delegated the authority to regulate broker loans to the Federal Reserve.

created a good deal of evaluation on our part and, obviously, the supervisory regulators."[19]

Just who was doing the evaluating remains unknown. There had been no discussion at the FOMC about margin requirements over (at least) the previous three years. Greenspan went on to tell the committee that "all of the studies have suggested that the level of stock prices have nothing to do with margin requirements."[20] The Federal Reserve Web site posts one study of margin requirements, in 1997.[21] If this was read by FOMC attendees, it was never mentioned at their meetings. Greenspan, possibly concocting his spiel on the fly, discovered that he was an ardent populist: limits on borrowing would hurt small investors more than institutions.

In his best bedside manner, Greenspan soothed the committee by claiming: "We, obviously, have also been discussing what alternatives there are.... I don't want to suggest that we're about to do anything at this stage, but I would confirm that we obviously are doing a good deal of thinking about the whole process."[22] If alternative thinking was ever a topic at the FOMC, it must have been by semaphore.

Greenspan claimed that margin requirements would not change behavior, but there was, in fact, another regulatory authority that thought differently. Just two days prior to the chairman's testimony, the New York Mercantile Exchange had raised margin requirements on heating oil, effective immediately, by 80 percent.[23]

Henry Kaufman, who moved markets when he spoke from Salomon Brothers in the 1980s, and whose opinion was worth whatever his private clients now paid, disagreed with Greenspan: "When you raise margin requirements, you express concern that is telegraphed to the market

[19] Stevenson, "Greenspan Holds Forth before a Friendly Panel."

[20] Senate Committee on Housing, Banking, and Urban Affairs, "Nomination of Alan Greenspan, of New York, to Be Chairman of the Board of Governors of the Federal Reserve System," January 26, 2000, p. 30.

[21] Paul H. Kupiec, *Margin Requirements, Volatility, and Market Integrity: What Have We Learned Since the Crash?* Finance and Economics Discussion Series 1997-22, Federal Reserve Board, April 1997.

[22] Stevenson, "Greenspan Holds Forth before a Friendly Panel."

[23] Fleckenstein and Sheehan, *Greenspan's Bubbles*, p. 88.

at large. You express a concern about speculation, and the inappropriate use of credit and risks that it may expose to the financial system."[24] Kaufman was dismissive of Greenspan's comment that he had asked security regulators to study the issue: "Does that mean that to do something, we have to have a long experience with it and a major problem?"[25] Under Greenspan's new regime, the answer would always be yes.

Paul Volcker was interviewed by the *New York Times*. He was forthcoming about the stock market: "I think it is a kind of casino. It's all the rage, trading certificates that have no intrinsic value."[26] There is no hint that Volcker had anyone specifically in mind when he told the interviewer: "I was so proud of being in government all my life. [P]ublic service at almost all levels has come into various disrepute. You don't get the people in government that you should."[27]

A sign of mental instability was another Youth Movement. R. W. Huntington Jr., a veteran of several decades in the insurance industry, observed the scene from his investment post at Connecticut General Life Insurance Company in 1929: "We old fogies have been told time and again that we have entered a new era which we were incapable of understanding; that the past used to be the best guide for the future ... but [is] no good now." Huntington acknowledged the capacity for youth to make a fortune during a bull market, since it was not inhibited by knowledge: "[F]or the last six years the prudent and experienced have not made money on paper ... as much as the rash and inexperienced who have never seen hard times or severe recessions."[28]

In the Go-Go Years, 26-year-old conglomerateurs made fortunes. In April 2000, there was Tom Hadfield. The 17-year-old entrepreneur had floated his second Internet start-up (Schoolsnet.com). The *Financial*

---

[24] Gretchen Morgenson, "Something Borrowed May Leave Market Blue," "Market Watch," *New York Times*, January 30, 2000, p. B1.

[25] Ibid.

[26] Alex Berenson, "After the Fed, a Large Presence," *New York Times*, January 23, 2000, p. B2.

[27] Ibid.

[28] R. W. Huntington, "The Company's Investment Policy," in Charles D. Ellis and James R. Vertin (eds.) *Classics: An Investor's Anthology* (Homewood, Ill.: Dow Jones-Irwin, 1989), pp. 61–62.

Times noted that Hadfield had founded his first Web site, Soccernet, when he was only 12. It was owned by Walt Disney at the time of this second flotation.[29]

The *Wall Street Journal* introduced its readership to Justin Hendrix, a "spike-haired, 19-year-old freshman at Seattle University with a messy bedroom and a summer job maintaining ice-making machines at local supermarkets." Known as "Dr. Wall Street," he offered up-to-the-minute advice: "This is the new economy, and you can learn as much about Wall Street on the Internet in two years as you could in the 10 or 15 years it used to take others."[30] Strictly speaking, Hendrix was correct, given the advice that Wall Street firms were offering their clients and the public.

Harvard Business School opened an office in Silicon Valley to develop Internet start-up case studies.[31] A March 2000 KPMG International poll of college seniors found that 74 percent of the students expected to become millionaires.[32]

Instead of sounding like "Dr. Wall Street" himself, Greenspan might have dampened the future carnage. Among his other storied accomplishments was that of an economic advisor who made stock market predictions for more than 50 years.

BASKING IN ADULATION: "LET'S HEAR IT FOR A GREAT CHAIRMAN"

Yet Greenspan continued to root for the Nasdaq. This was the mirror image of the world rooting for Greenspan. The praise was unremitting. He basked. He glowed. *Der Spiegel* chimed in with the continental view: "Greenspan is the new magic man of the Millennium."[33]

---

[29] Andrew Ward, "Schoolboy to Float Second Startup," *Financial Times*, April 17, 2000.

[30] Jeff D. Opdyke, "Paging 'Dr. Wall Street': Teen Prescribes Stock Winners," *Wall Street Journal*, July 10, 2000.

[31] Ross Kerber, "Internet Boom Reverberating in Business Schools," *Boston Globe*, February 4, 1999.

[32] James P. Miller, "A Special News Report About Life on the Job—and Trends Taking Shape There," "Work Week," *Wall Street Journal*, March 28, 2000.

[33] Albert Wimmer, Professor, Notre Dame University, "'Bullman Forever': Teaching Students How to Be Wall Street Watchdogs," www.krannert,purdue.edu/centers/cibers/publications/gbl, p. 157.

On March 6, 2000, Greenspan attended a "New Economy" conference at Boston College. It was his birthday. He was presented with a cake and a cheery round of "Happy Birthday" from the packed house. Before his lecture, the local congressman, Ed Markey, primed the star-struck audience: "Let's hear it for a great chairman, ladies and gentlemen." They responded exactly as the warm-up crowd for a TV-game show should.[34]

The New Economy conference received the standard pep talk: "At a fundamental level, the essential contribution of information technology is the expansion of knowledge and its obverse, the reduction in uncertainty."[35] On and on he went, the music man inevitably concluding: "Decisions were made from information that was hours, days…"[36]

Greenspan offered the Boston College audience a vision of the third millennium: "I see nothing to suggest that these [high-rate-of-return, productivity-enhancing investments] will peter out any time soon."[37] The great chairman did not disappoint the shareholders in attendance.

Arthur Levitt, chairman of the SEC, also gave a speech at the conference, in which he warned that retail investors did not fully understand markets and "may fall victim to their own wishful thinking."[38] These would be the investors whom Greenspan had told the senators would find it difficult to leverage their Internet stocks if the Fed raised margin requirements.

Julian Robertson, a hedge fund manager who produced at least 27 percent annual returns for close to two decades, threw in the towel. "The current craze in Internet stocks was creating a Ponzi scheme and that makes the process self-perpetuating until the pyramid eventually collapses under its own excess." He closed his career by telling the *New York Times*: "I'm 67 years old, who needs this?"[39]

---

[34] John Cassidy, "The Fountainhead," *New Yorker*, April 24, 2000.

[35] Alan Greensan, "The Revolution in Information Technology," before the Boston College Conference on the New Economy, Boston, MA, March 6, 2000.

[36] Ibid.

[37] Ibid.

[38] Arthur Levitt, "The New Economy," speech at The Finance Conference 2000, Boston College, Boston, March 6, 2000.

[39] Gretchen Morgenson, "A Onetime Highflying Hedge Fund Appears Likely to Shut Down," "Market Place," *New York Times*, March 31, 2000.

The Federal Reserve chairman did not seem to be influenced by the dissonance, which is not surprising. Greenspan had recast the job. A review of his speeches and testimony from this period is full of technology and productivity fluff. He did not speak much about money and credit. These had been the main concerns of previous Fed chairmen. The government had designed the Federal Reserve System to monitor money and credit. Greenspan rarely discussed either.

He may have enjoyed his superstar status to such a degree that he preferred to speak about a hot topic. Or, he may have avoided discussions of money if he came to realize he was illequipped to mention it. One confirmation of the latter flows from a congressional hearing in February 2000:

> Mr. GREENSPAN. Our problem is not that we do not believe in sound money; we do.... The difficulty is in defining what part of our liquidity structure is truly money.... [A]s a consequence of that we ... have downgraded the use of the monetary aggregates for monetary policy purposes....
>
> Dr. [Ron] PAUL. So it is hard to manage something you can't define?
>
> Mr. GREENSPAN. It is not possible to manage something you cannot define.[40]

Since Greenspan's responsibility was to peg the price of money at the correct interest rate, this was an important admission. It passed without notice.

WHAT TO DO AFTER A "SPECULATIVE BUBBLE OF EXTRAORDINARY PROPORTIONS"? TIGHTEN MONEY

In the end, Greenspan's words were of no intrinsic value. At the close of trading on April 14, the Nasdaq Composite closed at 3,321, a fall of 35 percent from March 10. Massive buying interests did what they could

---

[40] House Committee on Banking and Financial Services, *Conduct of Monetary Policy: Report of the Federal Reserve Board Pursuant to the Full Employment and Balanced Growth Act of 1978 P.L. 95–523 and The State of the* Economy, February 17, 2000, p. 30.

to restore the market, but it was exhausted, particularly the technology companies.

There was no doubt that, after inflating for the past decade, the stock market was now deflating. Since the stock market ran the economy, there was a good chance that the GDP would follow. This was an odd time for the Federal Reserve to raise the funds rate. Two years earlier, at the May 19, 1998, FOMC meeting, Greenspan claimed: "If the market were to fall 40 or 50 percent, I would be willing to stipulate that there had been a bubble!"[41] The Nasdaq fell 35 percent in a month. Greenspan never said in 1998 what action the Fed would take when the market wobbled on the windowsill. Now we found out: he tightened money. The Fed raised the funds rate from 6.0 percent to 6.5 percent in May 2000.

At the FOMC meeting on May 16, Michael Prell commented, "[W]e've experienced a speculative bubble of extraordinary proportions."[42] Greenspan was not interested in stocks. Instead, he spent considerable time on the relationship between productivity and oil: the "lighter distillates" being used in Germany had caught his attention.[43]

Greenspan had obviously decided before the meeting to raise the fed funds rate by 0.50 percent: "I think the evidence indicates that productivity, indeed perhaps underlying GDP, is still accelerating."[44]

He mentioned that "the network externalities effect of our high-tech system is creating a major underlying acceleration of our economy."[45] Whatever this meant, it was part of Greenspan's pitch to tighten money. The FOMC voted unanimously to target a 6.50 percent fed funds rate. The Fed had raised the funds rate by 0.25 percent in February and 0.25 percent in March. It was now 1.00 percent higher than at the beginning of 2000.

---

[41] FOMC meeting transcript, May 19, 1998, p. 84.
[42] FOMC meeting transcript, May 16, 2000, p. 23.
[43] Ibid., p. 87.
[44] Ibid., p. 82.
[45] Ibid.

19

THE MAESTRO'S
OPEN-MOUTH POLICY

June–December 2000

If something can't go on forever, it will stop.[1]

—*Alan Greenspan, September 13, 2000*

The Senate Banking Committee held a series of hearings in early 2000, "The Emerging Structure of U.S. Securities Markets and the Appropriate Role for Regulation." The Federal Reserve chairman spoke on April 13, 2000, about one month after the Nasdaq had peaked. Greenspan tried to steer clear of a stock market discussion. What the Federal Reserve chairman wanted to ignore, Republican Senator Jim Bunning from Kentucky wished to pursue.

Bunning asked if Greenspan's jawboning had contributed to the recent 25 percent fall in the Nasdaq index. The Federal Reserve's role was a long-running feud between the two. This was really a long-standing grievance about the role of Alan Greenspan. Bunning's frustration may have been with Alan Greenspan, the showman, rather than with Alan

---

[1] Alan Greenspan, quoting Herbert Stein, chairman of the Counsel of Economic Advisers under President Nixon. Of Stein's statement, Greenspan said that he "got it just right." At the Herbert Stein Memorial Luncheon, sponsored by National Association for Business Economics, in conjunction with the Federal Reserve Bank of Dallas, Annual Meeting, National Association for Business Economics, Drake Hotel, Chicago, September 13, 2000. www.nabe.com/am2000/grnspnvid.

Greenspan, the Federal Reserve chairman. The chairman responded as if he were the Fed's legal counsel: "Senator, I continue to deny and insist upon continuing to deny that our goal is to jawbone the stock market. It is not."[2]

Greenspan's reply veered away from the transgression that really irked Bunning, which was Greenspan's outsized reputation and influence on American life. The senator had not asked Greenspan to define the Fed's job. There was no miscommunication between the two: Bunning wanted Greenspan to receive no more publicity than an undersecretary of transportation.

Greenspan understood how his own words had become a major influence on the markets. In a January 2001 FOMC conference call, Greenspan would note that "years ago presumptions about what the Fed would or would not do didn't have much effect on the marketplace. Now we just whisper or open our mouths or smile or something and the markets go berserk."[3] As Bunning knew, it wasn't "we." It was Greenspan's theatrics that had remodeled the American mind.

Bunning went on to ask if the losses in the Nasdaq had eliminated the so-called bubble in the economy.[4] The chairman's response dodged self-incrimination:

> Chairman GREENSPAN: Senator, ... I don't believe we can know that there has been a bubble.... When you think of the fact that there are millions of very intelligent investors out there ... to basically presume that you know a great deal more than that general wisdom, I think is, first, presumptuous, and second, invariably wrong.[5]

The chairman's hypothesis somehow equates "intelligent investors" to "general wisdom," but intelligent investors such as Julian Robertson

---

[2] Senate Committee on Banking, Housing, and Urban Affairs, "The Emerging Structure of U.S. Securities Markets and the Appropriate Role for Regulation," February 29, 2000; April 13, 2000; and May 8, 2000. Greenspan spoke at the April 13, 2000, hearing. Quote is on p. 154.

[3] FOMC conference call transcript, January 3, 2001, p. 25.

[4] Senate Banking Committee, "Emerging Structure of U.S. Securities Markets," p. 159.

[5] Ibid.

sent money back to their clients in the same month. "General wisdom" was dumb enough to buy Nasdaq stocks, as it had been "dumb enough to buy 100-year bonds" in 1995.[6]

Bunning would not accept the general wisdom hypothesis:

> Senator BUNNING: Well, I could argue all day about that because I don't think there are an awful lot of sophisticated investors, as you might suspect.
>
> Chairman GREENSPAN: There are enough, Senator.

Greenspan kept talking. He had said it all before. Bunning could not win, even with experience as an investment broker.[7]

IGNORING THE STOCK MARKET

By the spring and summer of 2000, stock market woes were as much a topic of conversation as IPOs had been six months earlier. Chairman Greenspan avoided the subject. He seemed to speak of nothing except technology, although this perception is partly due to the media's obsession with any utterance by Greenspan on the topic. A speech in June 2000 was typical: "Substantial increases in U.S. capital investment, and the accompanying faster growth of our capital stock relative to labor input ... explain a large part of the pickup in underlying growth in output per hour over the past five years, *irrespective of how measured*"[8] [authors' italics]. This was in a speech titled "Business Data Analysis," before, of all groups, the New York Association for Business Economics.

He also told his audience: "That there has been some underlying improvement in the growth of aggregate productivity is now generally conceded by all but the most skeptical."[9] By 2000, mathematical

---

[6] FOMC meeting transcript, December 19, 1995, p. 38.

[7] Michael Barone and Richard E. Cohen, *Almanac of American Politics, 2008* (Washington, D.C.: National Journal Group, 2007), p. 682. Bunning had been an investment broker and agent from 1960 to 1986.

[8] Alan Greenspan, "Business Data Analysis," speech via videoconference, New York Association for Business Economics, New York, June 13, 2000.

[9] Ibid.

innovations attributable to the Boskin Commission Report had hedonically lowered the price of software sales, television sets, washing machines, microwave ovens, and textbooks (textbooks that included more color graphics increased the nation's GDP). Those business economists who had read the May 2000 *Survey of Current Business* published by the Bureau of Economic Analysis would have seen that businesses had spent $97.8 billion in 1999 on computers but that "real" spending, according to the BEA, had been $220 billion.[10] That is, computers bought in 1999 had cost businesses $97.8 billon. The $220 billion included the Bureau of Economic Analysis's adjustment for how much the $98 billion of spending contributed to the economy. The $220 billion was used when the government calculated GDP growth and productivity. The $122 billon difference was fictional; those dollars never existed. The $122 billion of fiction was more than 1 percent of the gross domestic product in 1999.

It would seem that all but the most skeptical would question whether the recreational mathematics that the bureaucrats at the BEA applied accurately calculated GDP growth.[11] "Irrespective of how measured" would also dismiss a study published by the Congressional Budget Office in June 1999. Robert J. Gordon, a professor at Northwestern University, was the author. Gordon wrote: "There has been *no productivity growth acceleration* in the 99% of the economy located outside the sector which manufactures computer software.... Indeed, far from exhibiting productivity acceleration, the *productivity slowdown* in manufacturing has gotten *worse*"[12] [authors' italics].

---

[10] Bureau of Economic Analysis, *Survey of Current Business*, May 2000. The comparison is between Table 5.4, Private Fixed Investment by Type, and Table 5.5, Real Private Fixed Investment by Type.

[11] Skepticism was at the top of the list when the National Research Counsel published a 2002 committee report. Under the direction of Charles Schultze (CEA director under President Carter), the "Schultze panel" noted the considerable literature on estimating hedonic functions; however, "researchers are much less experienced using them across a variety of goods." The Schultze opinion was, depending on the source, either *the* reason or *a* reason that the BEA dropped its hedonic adjustments to computers in September 2003.

[12] Robert J. Gordon, "Has the 'New Economy' Rendered the Productivity Slowdown Obsolete?" Northwestern University and National Bureau of Economic Research, revised version, June 14, 1999; http://research.stlouisfed.org/conferences/workshop/gordon.pdf.

The FOMC met two weeks after this speech, on June 27 and 28, 2000. Greenspan admitted that "the economy is slowing to a certain extent."[13] He claimed "the evidence of an actual recession at this point is belied by the fact that there is no evidence of which I am aware that suggests any significant deterioration in productivity growth."[14] Hedonics at the Bureau of Economic Analysis and Gordon's study at the Congressional Budget Office had placed the burden of proof on Greenspan to validate *any* productivity improvement over the past decade.[15]

Aside from that, this contention that rising productivity prevents recession was new. No doubt, the calligraphy of deltas and epsilons on assorted campus blackboards has tested the hypothesis, but now the New York University Ph.D. was running the ship of state on such conjecture.

Greenspan leaned on analysts again to support his contentions, despite contrary evidence in the press.[16] The May 2000 issue of *Red Herring*, a widely read technology magazine, quoted from a speech by Keith Benjamin (a former Robertson Stephens analyst who had moved to venture-capital firm Highland Capital Partners): "Let's get real. I mean I used to actually have to … justify these valuations. Now, I think I did a pretty good job of fooling at least some of you in the audience, but OK, today I can step back and say there's no way I could have ever really justified any of the valuations.… What can I say? God bless America and the capitalist system."[17]

At the August 22, 2000, FOMC meeting, Greenspan cited security analysts' higher long-term earnings projections with a qualification: "As I have mentioned before, the latter may not be very knowledgeable

---

[13] FOMC meeting transcript, June 27–28, 2000, p. 104.

[14] Ibid., p. 106. William A. Fleckenstein with Frederick Sheehan, *Greenspan's Bubbles: The Age of Ignorance at the Federal Reserve* (New York: McGraw-Hill, 2008), p. 102, discusses the CBO paper in more detail.

[15] In 2000, business computer sales of $101 billion were inflated to hedonically adjusted "real sales" of $290 billion—the difference being about 2 percent of GDP growth. Data from *Survey of Current Business*, Bureau of Economic Analysis, December 2001.

[16] "Long-term expectations of the security analysts, which we presume reflect the views of corporate management, have not diminished. Indeed, they continue to move up for both the high-tech and the old economy firms." FOMC meeting transcript, June 27–28, 2000, p. 106.

[17] Duff McDonald, "Investor The First Annual Price Target Awards," *Red Hessing*, May 2000.

about what is going on in the business world, but they are reasonably good reporters of what the companies that they follow are saying about their longer-term outlooks."[18]

The wonder is why they would be "reasonably good reporters," since Greenspan had previously acknowledged (in the October 1999 FOMC meeting, discussed in Chapter 17) that "[earnings projections] are biased on the upside, as they are made by people who are getting paid largely to project rising earnings to sell stocks, which is the business of the people who employ them."[19] In fact, just three months before the August 2000 meeting, on June 3, 2000, Merrill Lynch had published a "buy" recommendation on Excite@Home (ATHM). Yet the firm's superstar Internet analyst, Henry Blodget, wrote to a Merrill comrade: "ATHM is such a piece of crap!"[20]

Wall Street and Greenspan spared no effort to prop up prices. Critics called this Greenspan's open-mouth policy. Wall Street voices pumped up the buying opportunity. The most revered, Abby Joseph Cohen from Goldman Sachs, wrote a note to clients (and thus the nation) on October 13, 2000, that the stock market was 15 percent undervalued. The Nasdaq rose almost 8 percent that day, its second-largest one-day percentage gain ever.[21] It then fell 25 percent by the end of the year.

At the October 3, 2000, FOMC meeting, Greenspan was perplexed by "some really bizarre stock price movements among some of the larger and fairly well established high-tech firms," but consoled himself with "long-term forecasts of earnings by securities analysts."[22]

---

[18] FOMC meeting transcript, August 22, 2000, p. 73.

[19] FOMC meeting transcript, October 5, 1999, p. 48.

[20] "Vested Interest," *Now with Bill Moyers*, PBS, May 31, 2002. From John Cassidy, *Dot.con: The Greatest Story Ever Sold* (New York: HarperCollins, 2002), table on pp. 348–349: Excite@home went public on July 11, 1997. The IPO raised $2 billion. On March 10, 2000, its market cap was $10.8 billion. On August 31, 2001, its market cap was $172 million. Cassidy, p. 308: "Of all the money-eating Internet companies, the Excite/At Home combine was probably the most ravenous. Since 1995, it had gone through almost $10 billion." This was in January 2001.

[21] Jonathan Fuerbringer, "Nasdaq in Comeback, Surging Almost 8%," *New York Times*, October 14, 2000, p. C1.

[22] FOMC meeting transcript, October 3, 2000, p. 76.

In late 1998, a cheery Mary Meeker, star technology analyst at Morgan Stanley, graced the front cover of *Barron's* with the title: "Queen of the 'Net." In December 1999, a *Wall Street Journal* editorial chastised her: "When Web companies openly admit they gave their IPO business to Morgan Stanley hoping to get a favorable tout from Mary Meeker, you have to wonder whom the analysts are really working for."[23] The *Journal* was not thrilled with how other analysts composed their "Buy" lists: "The news last week, moreover, wasn't that Jack Grubman, Salomon [Smith Barney]'s top-rated telecom analyst, had become a believer in AT&T's cable strategy.[24] The news was that his change of heart came just as Salomon was pitching for work as an underwriter of AT&T's wireless tracking stock."[25] In May 2000, Grubman told *BusinessWeek* the conflict of interest that so disturbed the *Journal* had been resolved: "What used to be a conflict is now a synergy."[26]

At the November 15, 2000, meeting, Greenspan cited analysts, with reservations: "If we take the I/B/E/S data, which is really the best we have on profit expectations, real or crazy, those numbers have not changed." The next day (November 16, 2000), Kirsten Campbell, assistant vice president, Merrill Lynch Internet Research, sent an e-mail to Henry Blodget: "I don't want to be a whore for f-king mgmt. If 2-2 means that we are putting half of Merrill retail into this stock because [Merrill is] out accumulating it then I don't think that's the right thing to do. We are losing people and money and I don't like it. John and Mary Smith are losing their retirement because we don't want [a colleague] to be mad at us the whole idea that we are independent from banking is a big lie."[27] Campbell lacked Greenspan's refinement, but a guest appearance at an FOMC meeting might have added the spark it lacked.

---

[23] Editorial, "Analyze This," *Wall Street Journal*, December 17, 1999.

[24] Salomon Brothers had been bought and merged with Smith Barney.

[25] Editorial, "Analyze This."

[26] Peter Elstrom, "The Power Broker," *BusinessWeek*, May 15, 2000, p. 74.

[27] "Vested Interest," *Now with Bill Moyers*, PBS, May 31, 2002.

Greenspan Clears His Throat

On December 5, 2000, Alan Greenspan spoke at the America's Community Bankers Conference. After a few paragraphs, the chairman cleared his throat and queried the audience: "Why, then, one might ask, is this process of reassessment taking place now?" He noted: "The orders and output surge this past year in a number of high-technology industries, amounting in some cases to 50 percent and more, was not sustainable."[28]

Greenspan told FOMC members the bad news at their December 19, 2000, meeting. The economic expansion had "very clearly and unambiguously moved down dramatically from its pace of earlier this year, which was unsustainable."[29] The chairman continued: "The key question, and one we really cannot answer, is whether the growth rate has stabilized. At this point we cannot know.... The problem, as I've indicated on numerous occasions and as a number of you have commented, is that we do not have the capability of reliably forecasting a recession."[30]

Oh, those models! Greenspan couldn't see a bubble and now sat on his hands waiting for a recession. When a problem confronted the chairman, he walked away from it. The Federal Reserve, like a ship's captain, is expected to act *in extremis*; once again, Greenspan deserted the bridge. Greenspan pinned the model problem on oil: "[W]e have never been able to use our model structures to forecast a recession out of an oil shock. We've had three oil shocks in recent decades that were followed by recessions."[31] Given this observation, why did he need a model at all to prepare for a recession? The definition of a recession is debated and redefined by committees. The simplest (though not official) measurement of recession is whether the GDP has contracted for two

---

[28] Alan Greenspan, "Structural Changes in the Economy and Financial Markets," speech at America's Community Banker's Conference, Business Strategies for Bottom Line Results, New York, December 5, 2000.

[29] FOMC meeting transcript, December 19, 2000, p. 69.

[30] Ibid., pp. 69–70.

[31] Ibid., p. 70.

consecutive quarters. Real GDP fell −0.1 percent in the second quarter of 2000, rose +0.5 percent in the third quarter, and fell −0.1 percent in the fourth quarter. Recession or not, the economy lacked get-up-and go-from the time the stock market started falling.

Greenspan also washed his hands (temporarily) of the productivity–stock market–analyst–corporate management hoax at the December meeting. He acknowledged: "I have gotten calls from a number of high-tech executives who are telling me that the market is dissolving rapidly before their eyes. But I suspect that a not inconceivable possibility is that what is dissolving in front of their eyes is their own personal net worth! [Laughter.] That does bias one's view of what is happening in the world. So, we have to be a little careful about being seduced by those types of evaluations."[32]

Greenspan had good reason to laugh off CEOs. They were modern-day court jesters. On November 19, 2000, Intel Corporation's chairman, Craig Barrett, pronounced, "We're very bullish on our core business and expect it to continue to grow.... [N]ext year is going to be very exciting and continue to give us positive growth."[33] On December 4, 2000, Cisco Systems Chairman John Chambers delivered his annual speech to Wall Street analysts. "I have never been more optimistic about the future of our industry as a whole, or of Cisco."[34]

Intel and Cisco were two of the most revered technology companies. They were both entering freefalls. In April 2001, John Chambers admitted, "[T]his may be the fastest any industry our size has decelerated."[35] Chambers was paid $279 million in 1999 and 2000 for his foresighted leadership.[36]

By the end of 2000, the Nasdaq Composite had fallen 51 percent and the Philadelphia Internet Index had lost 77 percent from its peak. All

---

[32] Ibid., pp. 71–72.

[33] "Is the Chip Slowdown Overblown?" *Investor's Business Daily*, November 21, 2000, p. A6.

[34] The Center for Future Studies, *Developing and Using Scenarios*, p. 15; http://www.futurestudies.co.uk//images/scenarios_presentation.pdf.

[35] Fred Hickey, *High-Tech Strategist*, May 4, 2001, p. 6.

[36] Ibid., November 6, 2003, p. 1.

told, investors in U.S. stocks had lost trillions of dollars and were constantly reminded of this by the wonder of technology's multicolored screens that flashed instant calculations of their attenuated portfolio holdings.

One index was rising: a biography of Alan Greenspan, *Maestro*, written by Bob Woodward. It was number three in the December 24 *New York Times Book Review* nonfiction best-seller list. On its tail was *The Darwin Awards*, a chronicle of characters whose behavior was spectacularly inept. It trailed at number four.[37]

---

[37] Best Sellers, *New York Times Book Review*, December 24, 2000.

20

STOCKS COLLAPSE AND AMERICA ASKS: "WHAT HAPPENS WHEN KING ALAN GOES?"

2001

Alas, technology has not allowed us to see into the future any more clearly than we could previously.[1]

—*Alan Greenspan, January 11, 2002*

January 2001 was a banner month for stocks. The Nasdaq Composite gained 21 percent. Yet, business and financial news was uniformly awful. Technology-production capacity grew at a 49 percent annual rate in December, but sales were scarce. In Janaury, Cisco Systems announced the value of its inventory rose from $1.2 billion to $2.0 billion in the previous quarter.[2] Companies announced plans (or hopes) to reduce inventories by the end of 2002. This unwinding across the whole economy would take years to complete—unless some artificial paper printing inflated prices

---

[1] Alan Greenspan, "The Economy," speech at the Bay Area Council Conference, San Francisco, January 11, 2002.

[2] Fred Hickey, The High Tech Strategist, February 2, 2001, pp. 3–5. Production capacity growth had compounded at a 35 percent to 45 percent annual rate since 1995. The profit collapse among technology companies should not have been a surprise.

even more and tricked Americans into another (and worse) imaginary sense of prosperity.

The only good news was not news at all, but a premise: the Fed will always bail us out. And it did. January 2, the first trading day of the year extended the spirit of the old. The Nasdaq Composite lost 7.2 percent. The FOMC cut the funds rate cut from 6.5 percent to 6.0 percent on January 3.

Greenspan's rescue effort pumped the index by 14 percent by the closing bell. This was the greatest one-day gain in the Nasdaq's history.[3]

The Greenspan legend preyed on poor memories. Toward the end of Greenspan's chairmanship, celebrated figures sang his praises. Lawrence Lindsey wrote a *Wall Street Journal* guest editorial in December, 2004. In "Life After Greenspan," Lindsey reviewed the January 3, 2001, fed funds rate cut: "Mr. Greenspan combined his access to, and understanding of, anecdotal information with his accumulated knowledge of market signals to make what, in Washington at least, was a very contrarian decision. The country was fortunate that Mr. Greenspan's experience as a trader and business consultant trained him to combine instinct, experience, reason and facts to operate in the real-time manner required for making successful judgments."[4]

THE PANIC–RATE-CUT CONFERENCE CALL

The Nasdaq Composite had lost more than half its value from its 2000 high. Greenspan's "accumulated knowledge of market signals" had proved no more a guide in this situation than to the day traders selling the fractional remnants of Cisco Systems, which had fallen from $82 to $43 a share.

Greenspan had not expressed much concern at the December 19, 2000, FOMC meeting. "Recession" was mentioned 25 times at that meeting before Greenspan decanted what would be the official opinion: the FOMC could not know if the current growth rate was sustainable.[5]

---

[3] William A. Fleckenstein with Frederick Sheehan, *Greenspan's Bubbles: The Age of Ignorance at the Federal Reserve* (New York: McGraw-Hill, 2008), p. 114.

[4] Lawrence B. Lindsey, Editorial, "Life After Greenspan," *Wall Street Journal*, December 6, 2004.

[5] FOMC meeting transcript, December 19, 2000, p. 69.

The chairman changed tactics during a January 3, 2001, FOMC conference call. Greenspan had a new twist on stock analysts. He noted: "[A]nalysts' estimates for both the fourth quarter and the current first quarter are negative versus a year ago."[6] When analysts had been in vogue, he quoted their five-year forecasts, but on this day, their next-quarter forecasts came in handy. Maybe Greenspan decided he needed a rationale for cutting the funds rate, given his ostrich act at the December FOMC meeting only two weeks before. Nothing much had changed in the economy over the previous two weeks: prospects had looked as bleak on December 20, 2000, as they did on January 3, 2001. Not many economic reports are released between Christmas and the New Year. It was the stock market that shattered the chairman's *sangfroid*.

Lawrence Lindsey should have been praising his own aptitude. On January 4, 2001, the day after the conference call, Martin Feldstein, chairman of the Council of Economic Advisers under President Reagan, was quoted in the *New York Times*: "Larry [Lindsey], to his credit, has been saying for some time that there are some real weaknesses in this economy. It sure looks that way now."[7]

It is a safe bet that, if Lindsey had still been at the Fed in 2000 or 2001, his opinion would have made no difference. Greenspan's hold on the FOMC was tighter than ever. The FOMC met on January 30–31, 2001. The decision was made to cut the funds rate again, from 6.0 percent to 5.5 percent. Toward the end of the meeting Greenspan mentioned "the preliminary draft of our press statement that I'll read to you."[8] It appears the chairman had brought this to the meeting. There was some talk; then Greenspan moved to adjourn. The transcript next shows:

> MR. KOHN. Do you want to vote first? You haven't taken the vote yet.
> CHAIRMAN GREENSPAN. We didn't? [Laughter][9] After a temporary recess, the vote was unanimous.

---

[6] FOMC conference call transcript, January 3, 2001, p. 3.

[7] Joseph Kahn, "Contrarian of Boom Decade Put in Bush Inner Circle," *New York Times*, January 4, 2001, p. C8.

[8] FOMC meeting transcript, January 30–31, 2001, p. 182.

[9] Ibid., p. 188.

FLASHBACK—1997: THE FOMC WARNED GREENSPAN OF "IRRATIONAL EXUBERANCE"

Lindsey had resigned from his post as Federal Reserve Governor on February 5, 1997. The FOMC had met on December 17, 1996. This was shortly after Greenspan's "irrational exuberance" speech. Lindsey opened his comments by thanking Mr. Greenspan for his best efforts, then predicted, "1997 is going to be a very good year for irrational exuberance."[10] Lindsey discussed good news forming on the fiscal, credit, and international fronts. "But," Lindsey continued, "in each case it is going to be creating bigger problems for us to solve down the road. So, 1998 looks like the year in which irrational exuberance will meet its match."[11] The chairman responded:

CHAIRMAN GREENSPAN. I will make another speech [Laughter]
MR. LINDSEY. Don't wait a whole year.
CHAIRMAN GREENSPAN. Governor Yellen.[12]

Governor Janet Yellen followed. (Immediately—the chairman made no reply to Lindsey.) Her assessment of the economy and markets paralleled Lindsey's:

GOVERNOR YELLEN. Like Governor Lindsey and some of the rest of you, I consider the stock market a significant continuing risk.... Maybe your speech also served to heighten just a little the appreciation by the market that there do remain real risks around what is admittedly a very rosy scenario.
CHAIRMAN GREENSPAN. Thank you all. We can go to coffee now.
[Coffee break][13]

Coffee breaks were as much an ally as faulty models, another means to ignore problems.

---

[10] FOMC meeting transcript, December 17, 1996, p. 28.
[11] Ibid., p. 30.
[12] Ibid.
[13] Ibid., pp. 31–32.

FLASH FORWARD: JANUARY 30–31, 2001

At the January 30 and 31 FOMC meeting, Greenspan made a surprising claim: "[A]fter experiencing this huge bubble of speculative activity and looking at price-earnings ratios, which are not by any means depressed, we can't be sure that this expansion will just slow down, then pop up, and continue the way it was."[14]

It's a shame he did not gather the fortitude to address a recession at the time he finally discussed a bubble, maybe the stock market bubble, possibly the inventory bubble, but, the admission of a bubble looks like a momentary whim. He did not use the word *bubble* in the other 2001 FOMC meetings or in public.

Greenspan believed "there is little evidence of which I'm aware that long-term profit expectations have deteriorated to any significant extent." He lectured on the wonders of "Internet and electronic interface systems," on the demand for "a broad range of products in the high-tech area," on "the continuing leap in structural productivity," on the "emergence of extraordinary improvements in the cost structure on business-to-business applications,"[15] and on and on. This being true (in Greenspan's mind), he missed how this compression of time was putting many of the high-flyers in liquidation faster than before. His point seemed to be that technology was so great that the future could not be compromised by stock market losses or by bankruptcies. His pleadings are either face-saving or evangelical. The man who was not sure if he existed in his late twenties may have discovered a spiritual home with technology in his late seventies. This would complement large segments of the public that found a spiritual home with Alan Greenspan.

Yet—and this is the mark of a zealot—the Federal Reserve could not forecast a recession because of the limited technology of models—all models: "There is no way to forecast when [a recession will] happen except by luck.... There are those who look back and say 'I forecasted the recession,' and I'm saying it was good luck because that's what it was."[16] The late January 2001 meeting was chock-full of confessions. He

---

[14] FOMC meeting transcript, January 30–31, 2001, p. 181.

[15] Ibid., pp. 174–181.

[16] Ibid., p. 124.

finally admitted that he believed in the new era: a description he had
deliberately avoided: "I think part of the answer is the new economy.
We can't explain it all [recessions] in terms of the new economy because
the model reflects the history of all previous periods."[17] "All previous
periods" is all a model can reflect.

On February 13, 2001, in testimony before the Senate Banking Committee, Greenspan was upbeat about "strength in capital accumulation and sustained elevated growth of structural productivity over the
longer term."[18] An article in the *Financial Times* reported Greenspan's
testimony under the title: "Greenspan Sees a Quick Rebound."[19] Andy
Grove, chairman of Intel Corporation, disagreed. On a March 6 conference call, Grove, paterfamilias of the semiconductor industry, admittted:
"I don't expect the end demand to snap back.... We are in this state for
some period of time."[20] He explained the recent cycle: "For a number of
years, technology had huge momentum.... We built in an overcapacity
of all physical things." To eliminate this overcapacity, demand had to rise
or investment had to fall until "the two levels cross, or the investments
of the past several years have been obsoleted [*sic*]" by new technology.
"Both of these require some time."

Grove went on to discuss the specific problem that caused such mayhem: "The viciousness of the down cycle was made more so by all the
[supply-chain management software]. It blew through the supply-chain
in a much faster ripple than previous cycles. Nothing in supply-chain
management can read minds. End demand is what end demand is."[21]

Greenspan's productivity gains, if they existed at all, including the
"Internet and electronic interface systems" that had prompted the
"viciousness of the down cycle," since they are machines programmed
by people, and the machines cannot read minds.

---

[17] Ibid., p. 123.

[18] Senate Committee on Banking, Housing, and Urban Affairs, "Federal Reserve Board's
Semiannual Monetary Policy Report to the Congress," February 13, 2001.

[19] Gerard Baker, "Greenspan Sees a Quick Rebound," *Financial Times*, February, 14, 2001.

[20] "Intel Co-Founder Sees No Quick Turnaround," "Technology Briefing: Hardware,"
New York Times, March 7, 2001.

[21] William A. Fleckenstein, *The Market Rap*, grantsinvestor.com, March 8, 2001. Grove
spoke on a conference call and Webcast hosted by Lehman Brothers and its semiconductor and PC-company analyst Dan Niles.

BELIEVING IN GREENSPAN; BETTING ON GROVE

Schizophrenia reigned. Investment outflows paid heed to Grove, but sentiment bought shares in Greenspan: "Greenspan Is the Man Who Can Do No Wrong in the Eyes of a Prosperous Citizenry" was the headline in the March 8, 2001, *Wall Street Journal*. The drawing accompanying the article is of Alan Greenspan, a halo circling his head in the motif of a Byzantine icon. We learned in the essay that in a *Wall Street Journal*/NBC News poll, 9 in 10 Americans knew the Fed chairman's name. In the late 1970s, that figure had been fewer than 1 in 10. Moreover, 55 percent of the American people thought (in 2001) that Greenspan was doing a fine job; only 8 percent were critical.[22]

Greenspan was not a lone wolf in sheep's clothes. On March 20, 2001, James Glassman and Kevin Hassett were back on the *Wall Street Journal* editorial page. Under the less-than-compelling headline "Dow 36000? It's Still a Good Bet," the authors wrote: "[W]e checked the facts. Stocks are still a good buy. Our position hasn't changed."[23] A few days later, Cisco announced it was writing off $2.5 billion of inventory. This was new equipment, hot off the assembly line, that could not be sold.[24]

"SHOOT ALL THE ANALYSTS"

At the late June 2001 FOMC meeting Greenspan second-guesses analysts' double-digit, third-quarter rise in profit forecasts. Greenspan wondered if "the SEC's financial disclosure requirement … may have had a major inhibiting effect on the ability of corporate executives to communicate to security analysts."[25]

This was the least of the analysts' limitations. The March 20, 2001, *Financial Times* had published an article with the title "Shoot All the Analysts." In May 2001, *Barron's* illustrated its cover with a drawing of Mary Meeker accompanied by the title: "How to Fix Wall Street's

---

[22] Elizabeth Crowley, "Greenspan Is the Man Who Can Do No Wrong in the Eyes of a Prosperous Citizenry," "American Opinion (A Special Report)," *Wall Street Journal*, March 8, 2001.

[23] James K. Glassman and Kevin A. Hassett, "Dow 36,000? It's Still a Good Bet," *Wall Street Journal*, March 20, 2001.

[24] Fred Hickey, *High-Tech Strategist*, May 4, 2001, p. 6.

[25] FOMC meeting transcript, June 26–27, 2001, p. 140.

Research Problem."[26] The March 8, 2001, *Wall Street Journal* reported that Morgan Stanley had received $479.6 million of investment banking fees for underwriting IPOs and follow-on offerings in 1998–2000. Meeker told the *Journal* that "she wasn't seduced by the fat fees she and her firm stood to earn on the deals she helped push."[27] Salomon Smith Barney technology analyst Jack Grubman did not seem to tire of degrading his profession, or at least himself, with such commendably honest comments as: "Let's call a spade a spade. Nobody on the sell side puts negative ratings on stocks."[28]

Also at the June 26–27 FOMC meeting, Greenspan enlightened the committee with an observation that only he could think was original: "These are not security analysts in the old sense of the term who really looked at the company and made their own judgments."[29]

One week before the FOMC met, Congress, usually the last institution to grasp a trend, had interrogated several analysts about their "buy" recommendations. They were accused of being "pawns" who produced "biased and unreliable advice." The politicians had their own axe to grind: "According to congressional financial disclosure forms issued [on June 14, 2001], several senators engaged in hectic trading of high-tech stocks as the market began its precipitous slide."[30] Yet Greenspan still did not seem to know there had been a stock market bubble.

The Federal Reserve chairman appeared before the politicians in July. The subterfuges, such as coffee breaks, that Greenspan employed during FOMC meetings were unavailable during these sessions. Texas Senator Phil Gramm asked the chairman: "[I]f this is the bust, the boom was sure as hell worth it. You agree with that, right?" "Yes, Senator," responded the

---

[26] *Barron's*, May 28, 2001.

[27] Randall Smith and Mylene Mangalindan, "A Year After the Peak: For E-Business Booster Meeker, Fame Is E-Phemeral," *Wall Street Journal*, March 8, 2001.

[28] Randall Smith, Deborah Solomon, and Suzanne McGee, "Grubman's Missed Call on AT&T Could Affect Influential Analyst's Stature," *Wall Street Journal*, October 4, 2000, p. C1.

[29] FOMC meeting transcript, June 26–27, 2001, p. 140.

[30] Richard Wolffe and Julia Levy, "Senators Quick to Buy and Sell in Market Turmoil," *Financial Times*, June 15, 2001.

under caffeinated Federal Reserve chairman.[31] It appeared this was the popular opinion, as an August 2 *Wall Street Journal* headline queried: "What Happens When King Allen Goes?"

The Fed's rate cuts were gunning a credit expansion, but the lending was not directed toward business, nor toward the stock market. Paul McCulley, a bond manager at PIMCO, the largest bond mutual fund institution, was ahead of his contemporaries when he wrote to his clients in July 2001: "There is room for the Fed to create a bubble in housing prices, if necessary, to sustain American hedonism. And I think the Fed has the **will** to do so, even though political correctness would demand that Mr. Greenspan would deny any such thing."[32]

Real estate looked more attractive all the time. The Fed aroused housing speculation by cutting the funds rate halfway to zero by the middle of 2001. Longer-term treasury yields, to which fixed-rate mortgage rates are tied, were also falling. The comparative virtues of the housing market were obvious to the speculating, debt-bound head of the house: at midyear, national housing market prices were rising at an 8 percent rate.

A Crisis Solved: "Alan Greenspan Has Been Everywhere"

In the aftermath of the September 11 attacks on the World Trade Center and the Pentagon, the Federal Reserve chairman received heaps of praise. According to the *New York Times*: "Alan Greenspan has been everywhere in guiding economic policy in the wake of the terrorist attacks, slashing interest rates, helping to get Wall Street running again, shaping the tax cuts being developed by Congress and evaluating which airlines

---

[31] Senate Committee on Banking, Housing, and Urban Affairs, "First Session on Oversight of the Monetary Policy Report to Congress Pursuant to the Full Employment and Balanced Growth Act of 1978," July 24, 2001, p. 16. This was not the only memorable tête-à-tête with Senator Gramm. Gramm called Alan Greenspan a "national phenomenon" and an oracle (Richard W. Stevenson, "Suddenly, Critics Are Taking Aim at Greenspan," *New York Times*, April 2, 2001). Gramm would call Greenspan "the greatest central banker of the century," presumably the twentieth century (Ian A. Gordon, *The Long Wave Analyst*, vol. 5, no. 1, January 2003, p. 5, www.thelongwaveanalyst.ca).

[32] Paul McCulley, "Show a Little Passion, Baby," *PIMCO Fed Focus*, July 2001, www.pimco. com/LeftNav/Featured+Market+Commentary/FF/1999-2001/FF_07_2001.htm.

should receive government loan guarantees."[33] The description was apt but possibly embellished. Evidence of Greenspan's airline intervention is lacking, but that was emblematic of the man's grip on America's pulse.

In a less flamboyant summary, the Federal Reserve printed a lot of money. The Fed had already chosen this path in August, when the monetary base rose 12.5 percent (on an annualized basis). The Fed cut the funds rate from 3.75 percent to 3.50 percent on August 21. In September the monetary base rose 55 percent (annualized). The Fed cut the funds rate from 3.50 percent to 1.75 percent between September 17 and December 11, 2001.

The Fed's expansion in August may have been prodded by ominous warnings, signals that accumulated into the week before the terrorist attack. On September 5, auto sales for August were announced: GM's sales fell 7 percent; Ford's were off 7.5 percent; and Chrysler's had fallen 24 percent from August 2000.[34] Financial markets from around the globe indicated a synchronized, worldwide slump. On September 10, Japan's Nikkei 225 average dropped 3%, to the lowest level since 1984.[35] Also on September 10, the FTSE 100 (a broad-based index of Britain's stocks) fell to its lowest level since 1998.[36] The Nasdaq Composite had fallen from 1,843 on August 29 to 1,695 at the close on September 10, an 8 percent drop.

On September 20, Greenspan spoke to the Senate. He reported an economy that had been improving: "[C]onsumer spending moved higher in August and appeared to be reasonably well maintained in the first part of September. Industry analysts suggest that motor vehicle sales were running close to August levels...."[37]

If motor vehicle sales were running close to August levels, the stock markets around the world were correct—we were entering a severe

[33] Richard W. Stevenson, "Expansive Role for Greenspan Brings Out Critics of Fed's Chief," New York Times, October 11, 2001.

[34] Danny Hakim, "Detroit's Big Three May Shuffle as Chrysler Struggles," New York Times, September 5, 2001, p. C4

[35] "What's News," Wall Street Journal, September 11, 2001, Front page.

[36] Alan Cowell, "California Energy Crisis Hits Scottish Power," New York Times, September 11, 2001, p. W1.

[37] Senate Committee on Banking, Housing, and Urban Affairs, "The Condition of the Financial Markets," September 20, 2001.

recession. But a legend grew that a strengthening economy had entered a death spiral after the terrorist attacks and it was Greenspan's policies that prevented an economic catastrophe.

Meanwhile, patriotism was taking a bizarre form. William McDonough, president of the New York Federal Reserve, made a most unbankerly proposal: "What we dearly want is for Americans to behave like Americans—to do the patriotic thing and go out and spend."[38] President Bush told Americans to "get down to Disneyworld."[39] Alan Greenspan explained the faltering economy to the Senate: "During the past week, of course, the level of activity has declined. The shock is most evident in consumer markets where many potential purchasers stayed riveted to their televisions and away from shopping malls. Both motor vehicle sales and sales at major chain stores ... have fallen off noticeably."[40] Earlier in the year, Dallas Federal Reserve Governor Bob McTeer urged all Americans to "join hands and go buy a new SUV... preferably a Navigator."[41]

In the history of the human race, no society had ever before urged its members to spend when anticipating war (and in this case, it was being called the "forever" war). The government did not even take advantage of the average citizen's desire to pitch in—the Treasury could have issued zero-coupon war bonds from the Broadway TKTS tickets booth in New York. To those who still doubted that the American economy would collapse if the pace of around-the-clock shopping ever slowed, here was the government's plea for perpetual, accelerating consumption.

On November 8, Enron Corporation, a power-generation company in Texas that generated little power but a wealth of off-balance-sheet derivative gimmicks, announced that it had overstated profits by about $600 million over the past five years. This was not a particularly conspicuous

---

[38] Ian A. Gordon, *The Long Wave Analyst*, vol. 4, no. 1, January 2002, p. 15, www.thelongwaveanalyst.ca.

[39] http://www.time.com/time/specials/packages/article/0,28804,1872229_1872230_1872236,00.html.

[40] Senate Committee on Banking, Housing, and Urban Affairs, "The Condition of the Financial Markets," September 20, 2001.

[41] Bob McTeer, Remarks Before the Richardson Chamber of Commerce, Richardson, Texas, February 2, 2001; http://www.dallasfed.org/htm/dallas/speeches/2001/020201.html.

event in the scheme of things. Cisco Systems's third-quarter sales fell
32 percent from the year before, and Intel's dropped 25 percent.[42] Cisco's
stock price had recently fallen to $11.24 a share (down 86 percent from its
2000 high) and Intel's to $18.96 (a 75 percent loss). Shareholders in the
two companies had lost over $800 billion.[43] And these were among the
best in show: they would survive.

Within a few days of its announcement, it was clear that Enron's activities were either juvenile or diabolical. As it turned out, they were both.
Foresight was lacking, as is true in every boom. While expansion endures,
there is no end to the accounting and financial tricks that companies
employ. The list of transgressors was soon better known than the top
Nasdaq performers: Global Crossing, Tyco International, WorldCom,
Adelphi Communications, Arthur Andersen.

THE ENRON PRIZE

On November 13, 2001, Alan Greenspan accepted the Enron Prize for
Distinguished Public Service in Dallas. This was a few days after Enron
announced that it had filed five years of fictional financial reports.[44] Tact
and political acumen being Greenspan's specialties, he talked about oil,
not integrity.

The day after Greenspan's oil forecast, Henry Blodget resigned from
his distinguished seat in Internet hokum. Greg Smith had resigned from
Prudential Securities a week before, where he had been equity strategist for nearly two decades. Smith, interviewed by *Barron's*, captured
the essence of success in the new era—both Greenspan's and Blodget's:
"'During the 1990s, the stock market became a media phenomenon.'
Television … all too predictably, decided to 'personalize what was happening in the market.… [T]elevison created the idea that people moved
markets, and it covered Abby Joseph Cohen as though her outlook was
a news event.'" Smith lamented the securities firms that unleashed their

---

[42] Chris Gaither, "Market Place," *New York Times*, November 6, 2001, p. C6; Fred Hickey,
   High-Tech Strategist, November 2, 2001.

[43] Losses are not adjusted for share repurchases, share dilution, and so on.

[44] Richard A. Oppel Jr. and Andrew Ross Sorkin, "Enron Admits to Overstating Profits by
   About $600 Million," *New York Times*, November 9, 2001, p. C1.

"marketing dogs, who turned strategists' projections into promotional fare.... 'This was always meant to be a cottage industry, not part of a multi-billion-dollar enterprise.' "[45] The analyst TV stars and Greenspan (also a TV star) owed their reputations to the fascination with celebrities. They were failures, but few noticed.

Greenspan came to the December 11, 2001, FOMC meeting full of news: "It may be ... not an overvaluation but possibly a new way of looking at the market.... [I]t may be that the markets stay overvalued or undervalued for protracted periods of time."[46] It might also be a superabundance of cheap credit that continued to speculate in the stock market. Whatever the answer, the chairman did not propose that the stock market was accurately assessing the economy.

The FOMC cut the funds rate another 0.50 percent in December 2001. The Fed had now cut rates 11 times in 2001 to 1.75 percent by the end of the year. This was a 76 percent cut from 6.5 percent at the beginning of 2001.[47] Short-term rates were lower than the inflation rate. The Federal Reserve Chairman was doing his best to restore the vitality of the "Greenspan put."

The FOMC was taking more interest in houses than in productivity. *Mortgage* was mentioned 40 times at the December meeting.[48] This was anticipated by the chairman on a September 13 conference call. Prior to September 11, "[t]he general level of consumer expenditures seemed to be holding up, I suspect in large part because of capital gains in homes."[49]

Technology and productivity were yesterday's obsessions. In January 2002, the Federal Reserve chairman squashed the new era when he spoke in San Francisco: "[A]las, technology has not allowed us to see into the future any more clearly than we could previously."[50]

---

[45] Alan Abelson, "Fun and Games," *Barron's*, November 12, 2001.

[46] FOMC meeting transcript, December 11, 2001, p. 83.

[47] Fleckenstein and Sheehan, *Greenspan's Bubbles*, p. 120.

[48] FOMC meeting transcript, December 11, 2001.

[49] FOMC conference call transcript, September 13, 2001, p. 1.

[50] Alan Greenspan, "The Economy," speech at the Bay Area Council Conference, San Francisco, January 11, 2002.

21

THE FED'S PRESCRIPTION FOR ECONOMIC DEPLETION

1994–2002

Why care? I think there is a long-term social cost we are going to pay from all this.... consumption has expanded more quickly than the income of the great majority of American households.[1]

—Federal Reserve Governor Lawrence Lindsey to the FOMC, 1996

It is time to part with the stock market and to address mortgages—or, more to the point, debt. The increasing burden of consumer debt had been an FOMC topic since the early 1990s. Federal Reserve Governor Larry Lindsey expressed fears about the overindebted American. His lectures occasionally animated another FOMC member (or, more often, a Fed staffer) to respond, but the Federal Reserve spent far more time talking about its "symmetrical" or "asymmetrical" communiqués.

The first half of this chapter steps back to FOMC meetings between 1994 and 1996. Larry Lindsey spoke while the committee sat. Lindsey was not ahead of his time. The danger was present. He was not only ignored but also listened as other FOMC members explained that Americans were not spending enough.

---

[1] FOMC meeting transcript, July 2–3, 1996, p. 33.

The second half of the chapter reviews FOMC meetings in 2002. Greenspan and others dedicated a good part of their time to monitoring the latest data on rising house prices, home-equity withdrawals, and how much Americans contributed to GDP growth by spending their cashouts.

Across the bridge between the earlier and later FOMC meetings, there are two trends worth remembering:

1. U.S. households borrowed $336 billion in 1996; they borrowed $1.1 trillion in 2006.
2. U.S. consumers held $5.2 trillion of debt in 1996; this had risen to $12.9 trillion in 2006.[2]

THE LINDSEY LECTURES

Between 1994 and 1996, Federal Reserve Governor Lawrence Lindsey gave several presentations to the FOMC on a single theme. The middle class was not recovering from the recession of the early 1990s, but it continued to spend. Americans were relying on more credit and gains from financial markets. Cash earnings from work were slipping. At the February 1994 FOMC meeting, Lindsey explained that among the "bottom 99 percent … what we're seeing is a big change in the functional distribution of income away from wages."[3] He compared the period from 1983 to 1988, when "56 percent of all the increase in personal income was paid in the form of wages."[4] In 1992 and 1993 that fell to 47 percent, and "during 1993 that fell to 38 percent."[5] [Lindsey's second reference to 1993 seems to mean the fourth quarter—author's note.]

In Lindsey's conclusion, "the non-rich, non-old live paycheck to paycheck, quite literally. That's where all their income comes from. Remember, virtually none of the capital income or business income goes to them. They have to live on their wages and that wage share is also declining.… [T]he middle-class, middle-aged people who are

---

[2] Federal Reserve Flow-of-Funds Accounts, Z-1
[3] FOMC meeting transcript, February 3–4, 1994; "the bottom 99 percent," p. 20; rest of quote, p. 21.
[4] Ibid., p. 22.
[5] Ibid.

borrowing are really getting their income squeezed."[6] At another point in the meeting, Fed staffer Michael Prell noted a developing trend: "[W]e've already gotten to a period of high-level housing activity."[7]

At the May 1995 FOMC meeting, Lindsey again pestered the committee, warning, "[T]here has been a lot of easing of credit terms. At some point this is going to stop."[8] Lindsey made one of his few errors in prophecy: "This is certainly not the kind of environment that is sustainable."[9] Lindsey warned that the Fed's own forecasts for 1996 assumed a decline in the saving rate from 1995.

To an economist, a declining savings rate is a good thing; a rising savings rate is bad. Janet Yellen, an academic economist by training, expressed the standard interpretation taught in college classrooms. Her worry was the opposite of Lindsey's: she was "concerned about the possibility" of the savings rate remaining too high. It had averaged 4.1 percent in 1993 and 1994 and had risen to "5.1 or 5.2 percent" in the first quarter of 1995.[10]

1994: INSTALLMENT DEBT FINANCED PERSONAL CONSUMPTION

Lindsey took the opposing view: that 44 percent of the growth in personal consumption expenditures (PCE) during 1994 "was financed through installment debt, and this can't go on forever."[11] Yellen feared that if the Fed's prediction of a 4.4 percent or 4.5 percent savings rate in 1996 was correct, this could have "significant repercussions for the forecast,"[12] meaning that GDP growth would slow down significantly. If individuals saved too much (even though 4 percent or 5 percent was a very low rate by historical standards), a recession might follow.

Lindsey predicted that the high percentage of personal consumption expenditure financed from installment debt would slow because banks

---

[6] Ibid. Lindsey explains each step of his study on p. 21. Lindsey also discusses what he discovered within each income group in much greater detail than can be covered in this book.

[7] Ibid., p. 13.

[8] FOMC meeting transcript, May 23, 1995, p. 25.

[9] Ibid.

[10] Ibid., p. 27.

[11] Ibid., p. 25.

[12] Ibid., p. 27.

were lending recklessly.[13] He might have added—although there was no reason to do so, since even the FOMC presumably understood—that the longer it went on, the worse the carnage would be. Since it went on for another 12 years, the bankruptcy of both parties—the lenders and the borrowers—was complete.

Greenspan also talked about installment debt. Of Governor Lindsey's concern, "I would only respond by suggesting that part of the problem with this big increase in installment credit, which really is outsized," is a product of the mortgage market. "[L]arge realized capital gains ... have been financed in the mortgage market. [Gains from selling houses at a profit.] Those funds are going disproportionately into the financing of consumer durables."[14]

1995—GREENSPAN'S CONCERN: MORTGAGE MARKET SLOWING DOWN

Greenspan seemed concerned the mortgage market was slowing. Consumers had switched to credit cards and the like to continue spending at a fast clip, since home equity was apparently receding. It might not be a coincidence that at the FOMC meetings in July 1995, December 1995, and January 1996, the Fed cut the funds rate from 6.00 percent to 5.25 percent. Greenspan wanted to be reappointed Federal Reserve chairman in 1996. Lower mortgage rates would aid his cause.

At the July 1995 meeting, Greenspan expanded on how important mortgages were to the economy: "The home builders data clearly indicate that things are moving. This is important not only because of the importance of the residential construction sector, but also because history suggests that motor vehicle sales and some parts of the residential building industry move together. If there is firmness in the home building area it has to exert, if history is any guide, some upward movement in the motor vehicle area, which would be very useful."[15] It would be especially useful to a civil servant whose popularity is measured by GDP growth.

---

[13] Another possibility: "all these backward-looking assumptions our examiners make about the quality of the balance sheet begin to go in reverse."

[14] FOMC meeting transcript, May 23, 1995, p. 32.

[15] FOMC meeting transcript, July 5–6, 1995, p. 57.

Lindsey continued his lecture series, whether it interested the FOMC or not. If one can judge by formality of composition, Lindsey was less interested in Federal Reserve decorum than his compatriots were. For instance, after warning about "asset re-diversification" in 1993, he raised the Boston Chicken IPO as a sign of speculation, then suggested the Fed cook up its own fast-food IPO, asking: "What do you think, Al?"[16] Nobody at the FOMC ever called Greenspan "Al" and very rarely "Alan." He was "Mr. Chairman."

In January 1996, Lindsey was "more pessimistic than the staff about the state of the household sector."[17] He thought the debate of rich versus poor was the wrong question. The normal separation of income brackets missed a larger problem. He was not concerned so much with income distribution as he was with the indebtedness of American households, rich, poor, and in-between. All of the income brackets—from rich to poor—received interest income, but it was "highly skewed." In the $50,000–$100,000 income bracket, the top 8.4 percent of taxpayers received 70 percent of all interest income in that class.[18] Lindsey calculated that more than half of the "well-to-do" range had more *non*-mortgage debt than financial assets.[19] "In other words, far more than half of upper income households, not to mention lower income households, do not now have financial assets that exceed their debt."[20] This was in 1996, when Americans were relatively unburdened with debt (in comparison to the present).

LINDSEY'S WARNINGS

In July 1996, Lindsey grasped the problem of indifferent lenders: "[T]he new computerized underwriting procedures continue to extend ever more credit even as debt levels grow. The traditional warning flags simply are not present for the great majority of people who are taking on new debt."[21]

---

[16] FOMC meeting transcript, December 21, 1993, p. 27.

[17] FOMC meeting transcript, January 30–31, 1996, p. 10.

[18] Ibid., p. 11. Lindsey also discusses the $20,000–$30,000 income class: "[T]he top 4.7 percent got 60 percent and the top 13 percent got 79 percent of the interest income received by that class."

[19] Ibid. Lindsey had "thrown out the very poor and the very rich income classes because there are problems in interpreting both of those."

[20] Ibid.

[21] FOMC meeting transcript, July 2–3, 1996, p. 31.

Lindsey went on to teach a lesson that made little impression on the Federal Reserve chairman. "[F]rom my experience at Neighborhood Reinvestment[22] and from the studies done here at the Board, it is clear that high LTV [loan-to-value] loans are a big risk for future delinquency....[W]hen economic distress occurs, *individuals with no equity in their homes have less incentive to stay* than those who have such equity. Our experience shows these high LTV loans can be successfully and profitably made, but they require enormous amounts of handholding and follow-through with the borrower....*Why care? I think there is a long-term social cost we are going to pay from all this....* Consumption has expanded more quickly than the income of the great majority of American households"[23] [author's italics]. His recollection of Neighborhood Reinvestment illuminates the nonsense of mass, subprime, and HUD 3 percent down payment lending. It cannot be done.

Lindsey wasn't through. He again admitted that he had been wrong about the endurance of the borrowing madness, then warned: "*[T]he price we are paying is the increasing fragility of the underlying financial structure of the household sector*"[24] [author's italics].

MR. LINDSEY AND MR. COFFEE

Lindsey was nearing the end of his Federal Reserve governorship at the September 1996 FOMC meeting:

> MR. LINDSEY. [O]ur luck is about to run out in the financial markets because of what I would consider a gambler's curse: We have won this long, let us keep the money on the table.... But the long-term costs of a bubble to the economy and society are potentially great. They include a reduction in the long-term saving rate, a seemingly random redistribution of wealth, and the diversion of scarce financial human capital into the acquisition

---

[22] In 1978, Congress established the Neighborhood Reinvestment Corporation. The act defined Neighborhood Reinvestment's mission as "revitalizing older urban neighborhoods by mobilizing public, private and community resources at the neighborhood level."

[23] FOMC meeting transcript, July 2–3, 1996, p. 33.

[24] Ibid.

of wealth.... I think it is far better that we [burst the stock market bubble] while the bubble still resembles surface froth and before the bubble carries the economy to stratospheric heights. Whenever we do it, it is going to be painful however.... [I]f the optimists are wrong, then indeed not only our luck but that of the markets and of the economy has run out. Thank you.[25]

CHAIRMAN GREENSPAN. On that note, we all can go for coffee.

Mr. Coffee escaped once again.[26]

Lindsey had summed up our future. His only error was timing. He did not—but who did?—predict that the stock market bubble would grow for 3½ more years. The stock market bubble forestalled a reckoning. That bubble concealed much that was wrong with a misaligned economy—specifically, the amount of borrowing required to boost the GDP.

The gambler's curse did not strike for another 10 years. First, the stock market cured all that plagued the "real" economy. After that failed, Greenspan seeded a national housing carry trade.

"[T]he non-rich, non-old liv[ing] paycheck to paycheck"[27] would live off the profits and collateral as the Dow rose from 5,000 to 11,000. This collateral, whether physical, conceptual, or psychological, "carried the economy to stratospheric heights."[28] When the stock market ceased to deliver, houses collateralized spending. In 2009, "not only our luck but that of the markets and of the economy has run out."[29]

INTERLUDE—1999: GREENSPAN DISSEMBLES

Federal Reserve Chairman Alan Greenspan, before the Committee on Ways and Means, U.S. House of Representatives, January 20, 1999, "State of the Economy":

---

[25] FOMC meeting transcript, September 24, 1996, pp. 24–25.

[26] One could interpolate Greenspan's statement later in the meeting, "I recognize there is a stock market bubble at this point" (p. 29), as being inspired by Lindsey, but Greenspan's train of thought in FOMC meetings was rarely methodical.

[27] Lawrence Lindsey, FOMC meeting transcript, February 3–4 1996, p. 21.

[28] Lawrence Lindsey, FOMC meeting transcript, September 24, 1996, p. 25.

[29] Ibid.

[D]iscussions of consumer spending often continue to emphasize current income from labor and capital as the prime sources
of funds, during the 1990s, capital gains, which reflect the valuation of expected *future incomes*, have taken on a more prominent role in driving our economy. The steep uptrend in asset
values of recent years has had important effects on virtually all
areas of our economy, but perhaps most significantly on household behavior. It can be seen most clearly in the measured personal saving rate, which has declined from almost six percent
in 1992 to effectively zero today. ... In fact, the net worth of the
average household has increased by nearly 50 percent since the
end of 1992.... Households have been accumulating resources
for retirement or for a rainy day, despite very low measured saving rates. The resolution of this seeming dilemma illustrates
the growing role of rising asset values in supporting personal
consumption expenditures in recent years. It also illustrates the
importance when interpreting our official statistics of taking
account of how they deal with changes in asset values.

The Federal Reserve chairman spent the nineties reinterpreting—
really reinventing—productivity. Now he was off to the races redefining
household wealth.

2002: THE FEDERAL IMPOVERISHMENT COMMITTEE

The FOMC was preoccupieal with the Stock Market through 2001. In
2002, houses drew greater interest, when members were of two minds.[30]
Some committee members worried that the funds rate was too low.
They thought current policy was inflationary and speculative. (The Fed
had cut the funds rate 11 times in 2001, from 6.5 percent to 1.75 percent.) Some worried that the economy was too weak—current policy
was not stimulative. Under Greenspan, such a tussle would always favor
the stimulators. In the end, the former group was routed: the funds rate
would be cut from 1.75 percent to 1.25 percent in November.

---

[30] FOMC Transcripts are released five years after the meetings. This book addresses transcripts through December 2002. The 2003 transcripts were recently released.

Even on the day the FOMC cut the funds rate, Anthony Santomero, president of the Fed's Philadelphia branch, warned about increased borrowing and leveraging: "Real estate lending has continued to rise, and some banks indicate that the pace of refinancings has accelerated."[31] At the next meeting, a Federal Reserve staffer noted: "[T]his productivity growth really reflects higher productivity in the mortgage banking business.... that's real productivity."[32] The economy was operating upside down. It was the speed of financing—of which Lindsey had warned in the previous decade—that operated at a post-human rate and caused a confederacy of mischief.

The case for a higher funds rate was frequently voiced by FOMC members, especially early in the year. They argued that zero or negative real interest rates—when borrowing rates are below the rate of inflation—encourage senseless borrowing. Greenspan recognized their concern. At the March 2002 meeting, he thought "one could argue in retrospect that we may have moved too fast on the downside."[33] In other words, the fed funds cut from 6.5 percent to 1.75 percent during 2001 was too much, too fast. Nevertheless, Greenspan had a greater concern: "[I]f the mortgage rate goes up, we will get some restraining effects on personal consumption expenditures because a goodly part of PCE [the personal consumption rate] has been financed by equity extraction from the appreciation in housing values."[34]

Greenspan's reasoning follows: if the Fed were to reintroduce a positive real rate of interest—when borrowing rates are above the inflation rate—consumers might not borrow as much against the equity they had accrued on their houses. He had long believed that consumers needed to spend their equity extraction to buoy the economy.

This had colored Greenspan's view at the mid-1990s FOMC meetings and his 1999 Ways and Means testimony. To a central planner, the urgency was greater by 2002, since very little else was expanding. At the November 6 meeting, Edward Gramlich's opinion catalogued the

---

[31] FOMC meeting transcript, November 6, 2002, p. 43.
[32] FOMC meeting transcript, December 10, 2002, p. 16.
[33] FOMC meeting transcript, March 19, 2002, p. 88.
[34] Ibid., p. 89.

FOMC's struggle to identify the source of recovery: "What is going to drive the economy? In the late 1990s it was investment; more recently it has been consumption and housing. What's next? I can't find much."[35] Other FOMC members were also at a loss. That was the meeting at which the committee cut the funds rate from 1.75 percent to 1.25 percent. Mortgage finance carried the economy for the next four years.

Greenspan's speeches and testimony extolled America's rising "wealth." This was a charade. House prices were the major portion of household wealth. (This is a number released on the quarterly Federal Reserve flow-of-funds statement.) As house prices rose, dwellers could borrow more against this imaginary wealth. This home-equity extraction kept the GDP growing. This rising tide was an illusion, since what it did not change was the debt owed.

Greenspan was living for the moment: "I believe that equity extractions from homes will continue to be a source of positive growth in personal consumption expenditures."[36] Greenspan then extolled some Fed model (Greenspan ignored them, blamed them, cited them, or cited and then dismissed models as opportunities to salvage a hypothesis as his reputation arose) that calculated 20 percent of personal consumption came from consumers cashing out their "wealth." Rising house prices were essential to America's continuous shopping spree.

Through the summer and fall meetings, some members of the FOMC worried about low interest rates. This was often expressed as a concern about house prices. Federal Reserve Governor Edward Gramlich described his growing fears. At the August 13 meeting, he was "uncomfortable that the refinancing of housing should be the source of so much of the support for our recovery."[37] Greenspan was having none of that: "You sound like a true conservative."[38]

House-flipping stories grew more bizarre. They left the FOMC in gales of laughter. Al Broaddus, president of the Federal Reserve Bank of Richmond, in September: " 'I spoke to the CEO of one of the larger

---

[35] FOMC meeting transcript, November 6, 2002, pp. 67–69.
[36] FOMC meeting transcript, June 25–26, 2002, p. 120.
[37] FOMC meeting transcript, August 13, 2002, p. 82.
[38] Ibid.

North Carolina furniture companies, and his theory is that younger families are stretching so hard to pay the elevated prices for new homes that once they move in they have to sleep on the floor!' [Laughter]"[39] Jack Guynn, president of the Atlanta branch, in November: "'The south Florida housing market would have to be characterized as red hot. One director reported that when a moderately priced development on the west coast of Florida opened, demand was so great that sales had to be limited to three homes per customer. That's a semi-true story.' [Laughter]"[40]

The chairman accentuated the positive. In September, he reported record spending: "We know, for example, that the level of existing home turnover is quite brisk and that the average extraction of equity per sale of an existing home is well over $50,000. A substantial part of the equity extraction related to home sales, which is running at an annual rate close to $200 billion, is expended on personal consumption and home modernization, two components, of course, of the GDP."[41]

Greenspan had eliminated the negative at an earlier meeting: "There clearly is concern at this stage about a housing value bubble that is going to burst."[42] He dismissed it: "It's the notion that there is an equivalency between equity bubbles and housing bubbles that I think is an illusion."[43] This is the first time he had addressed the recent stock market bubble (although, strictly speaking, Greenspan is making a general comment and does not admit to his personally autographed Nasdaq bubble here). He told the FOMC that housing bubbles were different. "[W]ith transaction costs as high as they are ... and the necessity to move if the house is sold, the incentive to sell a house is nowhere near what it is to sell a stock to take advantage of a capital gain."[44] Granted, Americans never did sell two billion houses a day. Transaction and brokerage costs are high, but it was the next meeting he told the FOMC that the average equity extraction

---

[39] FOMC meeting transcript, September 24, 2002, p. 48.
[40] FOMC meeting transcript, November 6, 2002, p. 56.
[41] FOMC meeting transcript, September 24, 2002, p. 78.
[42] FOMC meeting transcript, August 13, 2002, p. 74.
[43] Ibid.
[44] Ibid.

was $50,000.[45] That (minus fees) was adequate compensation for many, even with the headache of moving.

Greenspan was starting to warm up to another theme at the August meeting: that the *decline* of interest rates plays an important role in trading, extracting, and spending: "That decline [in the 10-year Treasury yield] ... has had a major impact on thirty-year fixed mortgage rates.... [W]e are seeing very significant churning in the mortgage markets.... What we are observing at this point is a very high rate of house turnover. Existing home sales are very high."[46]

Churning was important. Not only was this true psychologically (the momentum and day-trading swagger), but greater volume contributed funds to the economy. A faster rate of house trading, multiplied by profits from house sales, prompted greater cash-out consumer spending. Also, construction workers, Realtors, mortgage companies, title insurers, and new strip-mall employees (in the new towns that blotted the landscape) had more money to spend.

The Fed can usually nudge longer-term interest rates lower by cutting the funds rate. Greenspan might have wanted to wait until spending slowed, and that, in fact, had already happened by the November meeting: "The important issue here is that we're seeing some erosion in the props that support demand in the consumer area."[47] Greenspan thought that "it's hard to escape the conclusion that at some point our extraordinary housing boom and its carryover into *very large extractions of equity, financed by very large increases in mortgage debt*, cannot continue indefinitely into the future"[48] [author's italics].

Prefacing his suggestion to cut the funds rate, Greenspan leaned on consumer spending more than ever: "In sum, it strikes me that we are looking at an economy that potentially has significant upside momentum if it can get through the current soft spot.... [M]y suggestion would

---

[45] Extraction—equity extraction—is the amount of the equity in a house that is borrowed (extracted). It is not the same as a capital gain but it gives an idea of the amount of additional money a house owner could acquire from a sale. Also of note: unlike stock or bond capital gains taxes when a house is sold there is often no capital gains tax.

[46] FOMC meeting transcript, August 13, 2002, p. 71.

[47] FOMC meeting transcript, November 6, 2002, p. 81.

[48] Ibid.

be to lower the funds rate 50 basis points—it is possible that such a move may be a mistake. But it's a mistake that does not have very significant consequences."[49]

Once again, Greenspan was wrong.

ALL HAIL THE PROFESSOR

Greenspan received help from another source, the newest Federal Reserve governor, Ben Bernanke. Joining the board in August, he seemed at peace with the world: "[P]olicy stances, both monetary and fiscal, remain expansionary."[50] At the September meeting, the former chairman of Princeton University's economics department rolled out his academic thesis: "I think inflation as low as projected is potentially a serious risk for the economy. ... [T]his seems to me to be a prima facie case for easing policy at this point."[51] By November, he could barely control himself: "The FOMC has been quite patient. We've kept the funds rate unchanged for almost a year. So I think it is time to consider taking some action."[52]

Bernanke believed that if inflation were too low, deflation would be a risk. Deflation (to Bernanke) is always ruinous. This view is rooted in his papers, most of which analyze the Great Depression of the 1930s. That particular depression was both deflationary and ruinous. There have been many deflations that were not ruinous, but the professor preferred the simplicity of his model.

Although we have not incorporated FOMC transcripts beyond 2002, Bernanke's thesis would overwhelm any dissenters. The chairman might be light on theory, but his future speeches invoked Bernanke's jargon. Greenspan needed to keep inflating the housing market, and the ivy-covered professor would awe most audiences with his blinkered knowledge.

---

[49] Ibid., pp. 82–83.
[50] FOMC meeting transcript, August 13, 2002, p. 55.
[51] FOMC meeting transcript, September 24, 2002, pp. 73–74.
[52] FOMC meeting transcript, November 6, 2002, p. 74.

22

THE MORTGAGE MACHINE

1989–2007

Groups of women were crushing each other ..., a real mob, more
brutal for covetousness.... [T]he furnace-like heat with which the
shop was ablaze came above all from the selling, from the bustle at the
counters.... There was the continuous roar of the machine at work,
of customers crowding into the departments, dazzled by the merchan-
dise and then propelled towards the cash-desk. And it was all regulated
and organized with the remorselessness of a machine: the vast horde
of women were as if caught in the wheels of an inevitable force.

—*Émile Zola:* The Ladies' Paradise *(1883)*

To give the same kick to the economy as the stock market bubble, the
volume of growth in the mortgage market needed to grow year-in and
year-out. Household net worth had risen $2.8 billion from stock gains
in 1995, $2.5 billion in 1996, $3.8 billion in 1997, $3.3 billion in 1998,
and $4.75 billion in 1999.[1] This does not count stock-option cash outs
or the contribution of house sales and home equity.

In the 1990s, total mortgage debt (commercial, residential, and farm)
rose an average of $268 billion a year.[2] In 1995, total mortgage debt
increased $233 billion, and home mortgage debt increased $153 billion.[3]

---

[1] *Gloom, Boom & Doom Report,* September 2000.
[2] Doug Noland, "Credit Bubble Bulletin," Prudent Bear Web site, March 9, 2007, p. 12.
[3] Federal Reserve Flow-of-Funds Accounts, Z-1.

That was when Larry Lindsey told the FOMC, "[T]here has been a lot of easing of credit terms. At some point that is going to stop." As it turned out, easy credit was not enough. The stock market bubble was needed as a supplement. In 2000, home mortgage debt rose $380 billion.[4] Stock market collateral could, in part, explain how households were able to buy more and higher-priced houses. By 2001, though, the mirage of Internet wealth was collapsing. Median household incomes were falling (after having risen between 1994 and 2000),[5] and layoffs were rising. Yet, Americans acquired $506 billion of new mortgage debt. By most standards, 2002 was an even worse year for Americans (stock prices and incomes continued to fall), but they added an additional $708 billion of mortgage debt.

GREENSPAN'S ATTEMPT TO BLOCK FANNIE AND FREDDIE

The backbones of the government effort to stoke credit were Fannie Mae and Freddie Mac. These government-sponsored entities (GSEs) played the central role in the mortgage balloon. If Fannie and Freddie had not grown to such mammoth proportions, it is doubtful that the rest of the machinery could have achieved such destructive capacity.

Alan Greenspan spoke out against Fannie Mae's and Freddie Mac's promiscuity, to no avail. The interests supporting the federal agencies were too great to be swayed by even the most influential public figure in the United States.

The Federal Reserve chairman gave a speech in May 2005 titled "Government-Sponsored Enterprises." This speech was a primer on the original purpose of the GSEs. He explained how they had restructured their mode of operation to serve themselves rather than the country. Greenspan cited statements by Freddie Mac in 1989 and 1990. When Freddie implied it was important to remain small. The Fed chairman quoted from Freddie's 1990 annual report: Its function was to buy "mortgages from lenders, pooling and packaging them into securities, and selling these securities to investors."[6]

---

[4] Federal Reserve, Flow-of-Funds Accounts, Z-1

[5] U.S. Census Bureau, "Historical Tables—Household," Table H-6; www.census.gov.

[6] Alan Greenspan, "Government-Sponsored Enterprises," speech at the Conference of the Federal Reserve Bank of Atlanta, May 19, 2005.

Greenspan explained that a portfolio of mortgages would compromise its function. That would encumber its ability to maintain "a presence in the secondary mortgage market each and every day—regardless of economic conditions."[7] To meet its stated objective, in Greenspan's opinion, its portfolio should hold Treasury bills or cash and not mortgage-backed securities: "To sell mortgaged-backed securities to purchase other mortgage-backed securities clearly adds no net support to the mortgage markets."[8] At the end of 1990, Fannie and Freddie's portfolios held 5.6 percent of the single-family home-mortgage market. Their combined portfolios were worth $132 billion.[9] (A clarification of the distinction: In 1990, Fannie and Freddie bought mortgages that banks and S&Ls had made to homeowners; it packaged them together and sold the package as a security. Its balance sheet was not a warehouse for mortgages. It held only very liquid securities such as Treasury bills. By 2005, Fannie's Mae's "mortgage purchases" were bought, and many remained on its balance sheet, which grew by leaps and bounds.)

Freddie caught the growth bug. Greenspan explained why: "When Freddie Mac became owned by private shareholders and began to realize the potential for exploiting the risk-adjusted profit-making of a larger portfolio, the message changed."[10] Greenspan explained how, quoting from its 1993 annual report: "[T]o achieve our earnings objective, we are striving to [grow] faster than residential mortgage debt growth ... [and] generate earnings growth in excess of revenue growth."[11] By 2003, Greenspan noted, the two agencies' portfolio's held 23 percent of the U.S. home mortgage market.[12]

Yet Greenspan had reason to thank the supersizing agencies. When, in 1994, the bond market went into a tailspin (described in Chapter 10), the GSEs held a commanding presence in the secondary market. They increased liquidity when injections were badly needed. In the five years before 1994, they added between $132 billion and $173 billion of agency- and GSE-backed securities; in 1994, $292 billion of these securities were

---

[7] Ibid.
[8] Ibid.
[9] Ibid.
[10] Ibid,
[11] Ibid.
[12] Ibid.

sold to the market.[13] Fannie and Freddie performed the same service when Long-Term Capital Management sent banks scurrying for their bunkers in 1998 (described in Chapter 15). Volume had dropped to a range of $205 billion to $229 billion between 1995 and 1997; in 1998, volume rose to $473 billion.[14]

These efforts may not have involved Greenspan. More important, the Federal Reserve chairman did not turn the government agencies into shareholder-friendly companies. Fannie and Freddie were way stations of political patronage. The bigger they were, the more favors and money could be distributed.

Fannie projected (in mid-2003) mortgage originations of $3.7 trillion for the year—in an economy with a GDP of $10 trillion.[15] The volume of total mortgage borrowings (not just by the GSEs, but also by banks, credit unions, and so on) in the first six years of the 1990s was $1 trillion.[16] In this context, Fannie's April 2003 mortgage purchases of $139 billion would have gobbled up nearly a single year's mortgage volume during the earlier period.[17]

By 2003, the GSEs had attracted scrutiny. Congress would not hear of it: "These two entities—Fannie Mae and Freddie Mac—are not facing any kind of financial crisis," claimed Congressman Barney Frank of Massachusetts, the ranking Democrat on the Financial Services Committee.[18] Whatever Frank's qualifications for his post, reading a balance sheet was not one of them. In fact, reading Fannie's balance sheet was impossible. When a government report criticizing Fannie Mae was later delivered, it "[offered] little in the way of quantifiable analyses."[19] This was because Fannie Mae had ignored requests by its regulating agency to release

---

[13] Federal Reserve Flow of Funds Accounts, Z-1

[14] Federal Reserve Flow of Funds Accounts, Z-1

[15] David W. Berson, Fannie Mae chief economist, statement on June 2, 2003, quoted in Doug Noland, "Credit Bubble Bulletin," June 6, 2003, p. 6. The $3.7 trillion included $1.1 trillion of mortgage originations and $2.6 trillion of refinancings.

[16] Noland, "Credit Bubble Bulletin," June 6, 2003, p. 7.

[17] Noland, "Credit Bubble Bulletin," May 16, 2003, p. 4.

[18] Stephen Labaton, "New Agency Proposed to Oversee Freddie Mac and Fannie Mae," New York Times, September 11, 2003; http://tinyurl.com/ovv3zt.

[19] Timothy O'Brien, "Mortgage Giant Agrees to Alter Business Ways," New York Times, September 28, 2004.

financial information for the past five years.[20] [Despite their pretense of being publicly traded companies, Fannie and Freddie did not file financial statements with the SEC, but only with an underfunded government agency: the Office of Federal Housing Enterprise Oversight (OFHEO).]

Chairman Greenspan's first warning to Congress was on February 24, 2004. This was late in the day, but that he threw his body in front of the GSEs is commendable. Very few did. The date of Greenspan's first broadside is interesting—one day after his ode to adjustable-rate mortgages. (This will be discussed in the next chapter.) An obvious interpretation is a Greenspan attempt to take business from the GSEs and move it to the banks. This might have been true earlier, but by 2004, the largest banks and brokerage houses needed the higher mortgage volume that flowed through the agencies to create more complicated and profitable securities, such as collateralized debt obligations (see "The Washington-New York Symbiosis" which follows).[21]

Testifying before the Senate Banking Committee, Alan Greenspan took up the cudgels and warned that "GSEs need to be limited in the issuance of GSE debt and in the purchase of assets, both mortgages and non-mortgages, that they hold."[22] Later the same year, the Office of Federal Housing Enterprise Oversight cited "numerous examples of accounting irregularities and managerial conflicts that OFHEO examiners contended were used to doctor Fannie's earnings and inflate executive compensation."[23]

Fannie Mae's chairman, Franklin Raines, who had been Bill Clinton's budget director, declared his innocence even as he was escorted out the door. Raines was paid over $90 million between 1998 and 2003; of that, more than $52 million was directly tied to achieving earnings per share targets.[24]

---

[20] Timothy O'Brien and Jennifer S. Lee, "A Seismic Shift under the House of Fannie Mae," *New York Times*, October 3, 2004.

[21] It has also been suggested that the timing was Greenspan's effort to move variable-rate mortgage risk from the GSEs to the banking system, where the interest-rate risk would presumably be better managed.

[22] Alan Greenspan, "Government-Sponsored Enterprises," before the Committee on Banking, Housing and Urban Affairs, U.S. Senate, February 24, 2004.

[23] O'Brien and Lee, "A Seismic Shift."

[24] James B. Lockhart III, acting director, Office of Federal Housing Enterprise Oversight, "OFHEO's Special Report of the Special Examination of Fannie Mae," before the Committee on Banking, Housing and Urban Affairs, U.S. Senate, June 15, 2006.

The models purchased by Fannie Mae to achieve earning targets were corrupt. Given how models are worshipped, it's a wonder that the models weren't thrown in jail. A 2004 OFHEO report cited a "March 1999 memorandum from an employee in the Controller's Department [that] described the benefits of a particular brand of software for modeling amortization, noting the software allowed a user to 'manipulate factors to produce an array of recognition streams,' which 'strengthens the earnings management that is necessary when dealing with a volatile book of business.'"[25]

In 2006 testimony before the Senate, acting OFHEO Director James Lockhart reported: "Fannie Mae's management directed employees to manipulate accounting and earnings to trigger maximum bonuses for senior executives from 1998 to 2004. The image of Fannie Mae as one of the lowest-risk and 'best in class' institutions was a façade."[26]

The software that Fannie Mae bought was designed by another company to disguise the truth about quarterly earnings.[27] Raines received a higher bonus. Multiply this software design a thousandfold. Multiply the bonus chasers across financial organizations a thousandfold. That goes along way to explaining why Wall Street needed a bailout.

The "quants" or "geeks" or "nerds" wrote computer programs to bundle hundreds of mortgages into a single security. This was another wonder of technology. The math and physics Ph.D.s built their models; the models were simply a product of the quants' assumptions. Their models showed that a bundle of subprime loans, when combined and overcollateralized, were among the most creditworthy securities: AAA. It was important for a security to be awarded a very high rating, since, among other reasons, a big chunk of mortgage securities are sold to large institutions that will buy (and hold) only securities above a certain grade.

The bank must acquire a rating for the securities from an independent party. The credit-rating agencies—S&P, Moody's, and Fitch—were paid by the banks to rate the securities created from bundling the mortgages. Often the quants, geeks, and nerds at the agencies found themselves

---

[25] Office of Federal Housing Enterprise Oversight, Office of Compliance, "Report of Findings to Date: Special Examination of Fannie Mae," September 17, 2004, p. iii.

[26] Lockhart, "OFHEO's Special Report of the Special Examination of Fannie Mae," p. 2.

[27] Office of Federal Housing Enterprise Oversight, Office of Compliance, "Report of Findings to Date: Special Examination of Fannie Mae," p. iii.

in agreement with the banks' model makers. Many of these AAA-rated bonds are in default, a consequence of bond holders not receiving interest payment from the subprime borrowers (e.g., for a house, a car, a student loan) The credit-rating agencies, banks, and Fannie Mae created or bought models that distorted reality. The math worked when house prices rose. When prices fell, overcollateralized securities defaulted.

CONGRESS AND FANNIE MAE

Congress made loud noises. It held hearings. Reform legislation was passed in committees. There, it died.[28] Three years of winks and mirrors followed before the government officially took Fannie and Freddie under its wing in September 2008. Between 2004 and 2008, politicians, commercial banks, rating agencies, and investment banks suspended their disbelief and pretended that all was fine. Wall Street and Greenwich hedge funds finance many congressional reelection campaigns.

The credit agencies belatedly lowered their AAA ratings. In May 2007, 16 of 27 brokerage houses still had a "buy" recommendation for Fannie Mae, even though Fannie had not yet produced a financial statement for 2006.[29] The investment banking side of brokerage cherished their relationships with the GSEs. A firm that was unable to package Fannie mortgages into a more complicated (and profitable) derivative would lose a substantial amount of revenue. The securitized loan market produced the most profits and the largest bonuses.

Consumers also relied on this whirlwind of finance. From 2001 through 2005, 54 percent of U.S. borrowing had been consumer debt, more than was borrowed by corporations, the federal government, and municipalities combined.[30] Much of the debt was bundled into credit-card receivables or bonds backed by mortgages. America could not buy this volume of securities since it was borrowing to spend. A solution evolved: more of the debt was sold overseas. Senior executives

---

[28] William Poole, president, Federal Reserve Bank of St. Louis, "The GSEs: Where Do We Stand?" January 17, 2007: "Congressional hearings were held, and GSE reform legislation was passed in oversight committees of both houses of Congress in 2004 and 2005, although no final legislation has been enacted as of this time."

[29] Karen De Coster and Eric Englund ,"Fannie Mae: Another New Deal Monstrosity," July 2, 2000, www.mises.org.

[30] Federal Reserve Flow-of-Fund accounts, Z-1

from Fannie and Freddie were making regular trips to Asia by 2006. A Bloomberg story from February of that year quotes Tim Bitsberger, Freddie's newly hired treasurer. Quoted from Tokyo, he said Asia was "very important." The treasurer went on: "Our goal is to fund at the lowest cost over a broad investor base."[31] Bloomberg reported foreigners had bought 53 percent more agency debt in 2005 than in 2004.[32]

Just how important foreign buying had become to the U.S. housing market was evident in July 2007, when foreigners were slowing down purchases of Fannie and Freddie debt. Department of Housing and Urban Development Secretary Alphonso Jackson made an emergency trip to meet with officials from China's central bank: "It's not a matter whether they're going to do more business in mortgage-backed securities, it's who they're going to do business with."[33] When the Chinese government stopped buying U.S. mortgage securities in July 2008, U.S. Treasury Secretary Hank Paulson asked Congress for a bazooka: an unlimited line of credit to support Fannie and Freddie.[34]

BROKERAGE LEVERAGE

It may be a coincidence, or it may not be, that the Securities and Exchange Commission removed the 12:1 leverage limit on broker-dealers in 2004.[35] When Wall Street collapsed in 2008, Goldman Sachs, Merrill Lynch, Bear Stearns, Morgan Stanley, and Lehman Brothers were leveraged at 30:1 or 40:1. This allowed broker-dealers to expand their balance sheets. They absorbed much of the rising issuance of mortgage securities, which they might sell or lend to hedge funds.

The government used other agencies, such as the Federal Housing Authority (FHA), to produce the American Nightmare. The FHA was

---

[31] Chris Cooper, "Freddie Mac's Bitsberger Says Asia Funding Important," Bloomberg, February 8, 2006.

[32] Ibid.

[33] Josephine Lau, "U.S. Urges China to Buy Mortgage-Backed Securities," Bloomberg, July 13, 2007.

[34] "Paulson: 'This Is Not Chrysler,'" *Wall Street Journal*, WSJ.com, July 15, 2008.

[35] The SEC's "Alternative Net Requirements for Broker-Dealers That Are Part of Consolidated Supervised Entities." Effective August 20, 2004, 17 CFR Parts 200 and 240; RIN 3235-AI96. The 12:1 ratio is a rough figure. See, for instance, Lee A. Pickard, "Viewpoint: SEC's Old Capital Approach Was Tried—and True," *American Banker*, August 8, 2008, p. 10.

an unusually innovative bureaucracy. Its loans—often to down-and-out, first-time buyers—usually require a down payment of 3 percent to 4 percent. The FHA had taken an additional step, allowing charities to pay the down payment.

Nehemiah was a large charity in California. As a charity, Nehemiah Corporation of America received donations. One contributor was Countrywide Financial. Nehemiah Ministries is the economic development arm of the African Methodist Episcopal (AME) Fifth District Church. A Nehemiah representative spoke from Long Beach, California: "Homes for these young families are not just a place to lay their heads down at night. These are little prosperity factories.[36] Not all Nehemiah parishioners would agree. A 2001 survey estimated that 19.39 percent of the Nehemiah-aided mortgages were in default.[37]

THE WASHINGTON–NEW YORK SYMBIOSIS: THE FALL OF WALL STREET

Wall Street did not participate much in real estate until the 1990s. The collapse of Texas real estate in the 1980s did wonders for the commercial mortgage-backed security (CMBS) market. The carcasses of malls and office buildings were swept into derivative mortgage securities by Wall Street firms. Awakened to this money-making market, Wall Street looked for other opportunities it might exploit.

The Community Reinvestment Act was revised in 1995.[38] Banks now had an "affirmative obligation" to meet the housing needs of the poor. By 2000, U.S. banks had committed $1 trillion for inner-city and low-income mortgages.[39]

---

[36] Martha Irvine, "Sold! Low Interest Rates Affording Savvy 20somethings Their Piece of the American Dream," Associated Press, January 17, 2003.

[37] Gloria Irwin, "Nonprofit Group Helps Disadvantaged Home Buyers Get Federal Loans," *Acron Beacon Journal*, August 24, 2003; survey conducted by U.S. Department of Housing and Urban Development. The 19.39 percent default rate hurdled the 9.7 percent default rate of non-Nehemiah FHA loans in the same cities. Source: Office of Inspector General, Department of Housing and Urban Development, "Follow Up of Down Payment Assistance Programs Operated by Private Non Profit Entities," 2002–SF-0001, September 25, 2002, p. iii.

[38] 12 U.S.C. § 2901(a)(3).

[39] Howard Husack, "The Trillion-Dollar Bank Shakedown Bodes Ill for Cities," *City Journal*, Winter 2000.

Wall Street was pleased to package and sell loans that the banks did not want. Between 1989 and 2000, Wall Street securitized and sold $316 billion of subprime loans.[40] But Wall Street was impatient with the bank mortgage flows. To sell faster, the large banks and brokerage houses financed subprime lenders such as First Alliance of Irvine, California, home to Lincoln Savings and Loan. Lehman Brothers' due diligence of First Alliance included a field trip by a Lehman vice president, who reported that First Alliance was a "sweat shop" specializing in "high pressure sales for people who are in a weak state."[41] The vice president noted that First Alliance employees leave their "ethics at the door."[42] So enlightened, Lehman lent the mortgage company $500 million and sold $700 million in loans backed by First Alliance customers' loans.[43] Lehman did not know when to stop. CEO Dick Fuld bought BNC Mortgage in 2004 and Aurora Loan Services, both in Irvine.[44] Lehman was the eleventh-largest subprime lender in the country in 2005.[45]

Dick Fuld does not deserve all the credit. The *Wall Street Journal* reported: "[T]he big banks have been snapping up subprime lenders and bolstering their own internal subprime lending units.... Citicorp purchased Associates First Capital, a big Dallas subprime lender.... Meanwhile, No.2 bank J.P. Morgan Chase ... purchased the subprime-mortgage operations of Advanta.... Bank of America.... "[46] The list continued. This was in 2001, when the underwriting fees from the Internet and telecom boom had shriveled. The *Journal* mentioned the obvious attraction: "[S]ubprime ... can be as much as three times as profitable as their equivalent 'prime' products."[47]

---

[40] Diana B. Hendriques, "Profiting from Fine Print with Wall Street's Help," *New York Times*, March 15, 2000.

[41] Michael Hudson, "How Wall Street Stoked the Mortgage Meltdown," *Wall Street Journal*," June 27, 2007.

[42] Ibid.

[43] Ibid.

[44] Peter Robison and Yaiman Onaran, "Fuld's Bets Fueled Profits, Undermined Lehman," *Bloomberg*, September 15, 2008.

[45] Hudson, "How Wall Street Stoked the Mortgage Meltdown."

[46] Paul Beckett and John Hechinger, "'Subprime' Could Be Bad News for Banks—Riskier Loans, Now Prevalent in Industry, Show Problems," *Wall Street Journal*, August 9, 2001.

[47] Ibid.

Even with this buying spree, Wall Street still could not create enough volume for the country to live off cash-out equity. The brokerage houses needed Fannie Mae, Freddie Mac, and the mortgage lenders. These parties worked well together. Jim Johnson, CEO of Fannie Mae in the early and mid-1990s, courted Angelo Mozilo at Countrywide Credit Industries. Fannie Mae "needed volume and Mozilo was the man who could deliver it."[48] Mozilo offered Johnson loan originations, and Fannie Mae reduced the fee it charged Countrywide.[49] Countrywide was not a bank. (It would buy a bank later.) It had no deposits, so it relied on warehouse lines of credit to finance its mortgage business. Bear Stearns and Lehman Brothers were among the first Wall Street firms to offer warehouse lines.[50] In turn, the nonbank mortgage lenders promised the firms a percentage of their loans, which the brokerage houses bundled into securities and sold to the public.[51]

Was Alan Greenspan aware of the whirlwind? Whatever the case, he made his contribution to the Gramm-Leach-Bliley Act of 1999, which revoked the last vestiges of the Glass-Steagall Act of 1934. This was the legislation that had separated investment banking (dealing in securities) from commercial banking (lending). The distinction had blurred over the years. Greenspan's Fed had stimulated the new era when it permitted J.P. Morgan to underwrite debt and equity issues early in his term.[52] There were still encumbrances to unfettered financial dealings by banks, a specific case being Citicorp's merger with Travelers. The latter had a large insurance business.[53] Without the repeal of Glass-Steagall, Citicorp

---

[48] Paul Muolo and Matthew Padilla, *Chain of Blame: How Wall Street Caused the Mortgage and Credit Crisis*, (Hoboken, N.J.; John Wiley & Sons, 2008), p. 112.

[49] Ibid., p. 112–113. Fannie Mae charged a guarantee fee to lenders from whom it bought mortgages.

[50] Ibid., p. 42–43

[51] Ibid. In November 2006, Salomon Brothers funded a start-up subprime lender, New Century, by allowing it to borrow $105 for every $100 New Century accounted for on its balance sheet as its loan balance. The extra $5 was to pay for New Century's operating costs. In return, Salomon "got first peek at 70% of the lender's first $500 million in loans for sale." Muolo and Padilla, *Chain of Blame*, p. 155

[52] "History of J.P. Morgan Chase, 1799 to the Present"; www.jpmorganchase.com.

[53] Travelers had bought Salomon Brothers and Smith Barney, both combinations of investment banking and trading firms. "The Long Demise of Glass-Steagall," *Frontline*, May 8, 2003; www.pbs.org/wgbh/pages/frontline/shows/wallstreet.

would have been required to divest Travelers insurance functions.[54] Alan Greenspan's efforts at chipping away Glass-Steagall's restrictions were echoed by other governmental voices after he became Fed chairman.[55] Robert Rubin, cochairman of Goldman Sachs in the early 1990s, held a senior post at Citigroup after government service. He urged Congress to repeal the act from the time he was named treasury secretary in 1995.[56]

The Gramm-Leach-Bliley Act (its formal name: The Financial Services Modernization Act) became law on November 12, 1999.[57] Rubin had left his treasury post to join Citicorp.[58] Larry Summers, treasury secretary when the act passed, claimed: "This historic legislation will better enable American companies to compete in the new economy."[59]

Greenspan, Rubin, and Summers played a major role ensuring that the wildest derivatives remained unregulated. To thrive, the mortgage machine needed such developments as collateralized debt obligations (CDO) and credit default swaps (CDS). The trio led the offense against regulation of over-the-counter derivatives. Deputy Treasury Secretary

---

[54] With possibilities of extensions by the Fed. "The Long Demise of Glass-Steagall."

[55] See, for instance, Alan Greenspan, "Need for Financial Modernization," Before the Committee on Banking, Housing, and Urban Affairs, U.S. Senate, February 23, 1999.

[56] http://www.govtrack.us/congress/bill.xpd?bill=s106-900#votes. Joseph Kahn, "Former Treasury Secretary Joins Leadership Triangle at Citigroup," *New York Times*, October 27, 1999. From the article: "Mr. Rubin acknowledged that even while he [was] negotiating his own job with Citigroup, he had helped broker the compromise agreement repealing Glass-Steagall." Also "Rubin Calls for Modernization through Reform of Glass-Steagall Act," *Journal of Accountancy*, May 1, 1995: "Robert E. Rubin, secretary of the Treasury, recommended that Congress pass legislation to reform or repeal the Glass-Steagall Act of 1933 to modernize the country's financial system. In testimony before the House Committee on Banking and Financial Services, Rubin said Clinton administration proposals would permit affiliations between banks and other financial services companies, such as securities firms and insurance companies."

[57] "The Long Demise of Glass-Steagall." The bill was signed into law by President Clinton on November 12, 1999: "President Clinton Signed into Law Today a Sweeping Overhaul of Depression-Era Banking Laws," Reuters, November 12, 1999.

[58] He had announced his decision to leave his treasury post in May 1999. Editorial, "Mr. Rubin Leaves the Treasury," *New York York Times*, May 13, 1999.

[59] From Stephen Labaton, "Congress Passes Wide-Ranging Bill Easing Bank Laws," *New York Times*, November 5, 1999; and "Depression-Era Rules Undone," *New York Times*, November 13, 1999: "'With this bill,' Treasury Secretary Lawrence H. Summers said, 'the American financial system takes a major step forward toward the 21st Century— one that will benefit American consumers, business and the national economy.'"

Larry Summers told Congress that any oversight would cast "a shadow of regulatory uncertainty over an otherwise thriving market."[60] Without the contributions of Greenspan, Rubin, and Summers, the credit bubble might have been a muted affair. Timothy Geithner, secretary of the treasury in 2009, served under both Robert Rubin and Larry Summers as undersecretary of the treasury for international affairs. He was president of the Federal Reserve Bank of New York from 2003 to 2009. The New York president is traditionally the eyes and ears for the Fed on Wall Street. It was during his term that the leverage and derivative operations of the major banks passed the point of no return.

A flurry of large bank mergers were consummated after the Gramm-Leach-Bliley Act was passed. Government approval often hinged on the degree to which banks had met their "affirmative obligation" under the Community Reinvestment Act revision of 1995.[61] (Secretary Rubin "had a hand in urging Congress and the White House to preserve the Community Reinvestment Act" before the Gramm-Leach-Bliley Act was passed.[62])

CONGRESS THROWS FAT INTO THE FIRE

Congress could not resist throwing money at the mortgage market. In 2003, Representative Robert Ney, chairman of the House Financial Services Housing Subcommittee, proposed a bill in which first-time U.S. home buyers would be permitted to buy a house without making a down payment. Under the "zero down payment" bill, people who sought Federal Housing Administration–insured loans would be able to add the down payment and closing costs into their loan amount. Ney decried the fractured American dream: "Many people who can afford monthly payments in a home save for years to come up with the down payment."

[60] Anthony Faiola, Ellen Nakashima, and Jill Drew, "What Went Wrong," *Washington Post*, October 15, 2008. Also see "Joint Statement by Treasury Secretary Robert E. Rubin, Federal Reserve Chairman Alan Greenspan and Securities and Exchange Commissioner Arthur Levitt," dated May 7, 1998. Also see Treasury Deputy Secretary Lawrence H. Summers, Testimony Before the Senate Committee on Agriculture, Nutrition, and Forestry on the CFTC Concept, Release, July 30, 1998.
[61] Husack, "Trillion-Dollar Bank Shakedown Bodes Ill for Cities."
[62] Kahn, "Former Treasury Secretary Joins Leadership Triangle at Citigroup."

Ney wanted Americans to buy overpriced houses "ten years earlier." He
added, "It's good for their families and good for their communities."[63]
(In 2007, Congressman Ney would be sentenced to a 30-month jail term
for, among other offenses, a "long-term pattern of defrauding the public
of his unbiased, honest services as an elected official."[64] Convincing the
public it deserved to own houses it could not afford would have fit the
description, but was not what the court had in mind.)

Home ownership was integrated into President Bush's public appeal
for a second term. He decided that 70 percent of Americans should
own a house. (The ratio of owners to renters had been 60 to 65 percent
over the past few decades.) In a July 14, 2004, reelection pep rally, he
told his Waukesha, Wisconsin, audience: "Homeownership rate [sic] is
at an all-time high. That's a fantastic statistic, isn't it? We want more
people owning their own home. When you own something you have a
vital stake in the future of the United States of America."[65] He made it
sound like a ball game with the whole nation rooting for a .700 batting
average.

PRODUCTIVITY OF THE MORTGAGE BANKERS

> [T]his productivity growth really reflects higher productivity in
> the mortgage banking industry, … that's real productivity.[66]
>
> —FOMC staffer at the December 2002
> FOMC meeting

Greenspan's "months weeks, days" refrain not only proved true but was
necessary to accelerate the volume of mortgage trading. Edward N. Jones,
a former NASA engineer for the Apollo and Skylab missions, was interviewed by the *New York Times*: "[T]he old way of processing mortgages

---

[63] Susan Schmidt and James V. Grimaldi, "Ney Sentenced to 30 Months in Prison for
Abramoff Deals," *Washington Post*, January 20, 2007.

[64] Ney was sentenced for accepting benefits from lobbyists. "Statement of Assistant Attorney
General Alice S. Fisher of the Criminal Division Regarding Congressman Robert W. Ney,"
September 15, 2006; www.usdoj.gov. *United States of America v. Robert W. Ney*. United
States District Court for the District of Columbia, September 15, 2006.

[65] "In His Own Words," *New York Times*, July 15, 2004.

[66] FOMC meeting transcript, December 10, 2002, p. 16.

involved a loan officer or broker collecting reams of income statements and ordering credit histories, typically over several weeks. But by retrieving real-time credit reports online, then using algorithms to gauge the risks of default, Mr. Jones's software allowed subprime lenders ... to grow at warp speed."[67] The *Times* reported that "speed became something of an arms race, as software makers and subprime lenders boasted of how fast they could process and generate a loan. New Century Financial [of Irvine, California,] ... promised mortgage brokers on its Web site that with its FastQual automated underwriting system, 'We'll give you loan answers in just 12 seconds!'" In 2001, New Century originated $6.2 billion of mortgages. This rose to $42.2 billion in 2004.[68]

The efficiency gains were comparable to Henry Ford's assembly line: "With small staffs, the companies typically sell their software to home lenders with vast networks of call centers employing hundreds of thousands of loan officers. Some big Wall Street banks and housing lenders bought the software, then developed their own systems."[69] The *Times* quoted Scott Berry, executive vice president, artificial intelligence (that was his actual title) at Countrywide: "Without the technology, there is no way we would have been able to do the amount of business that we did and continue to do."[70]

The stripping of the standards reduced the frictional costs of trading houses: a report from the West Coast in 2002 stated: "At California-based Countrywide Credit, owners with existing 30-year loans at around 7% have been able to refinance at 6% without paying a dime in closing costs—'nirvana for homeowners,' [said] Countrywide chief executive Angelo Mozilo. Countrywide is on pace to originate $170 billion in loans this year. 'And it's accelerating,' said Mozilo[.]"[71]

As much as Americans take pride in the private sector's efficiency, it was the government Brunhildes that set world records: "[T]he mortgage

---

[67] Lynnley Browning, "The Subprime Loan Machine," *New York Times*, March 23, 2007.

[68] "Bearish on New Century," *Grant's Interest Rate Observer*, June 17, 2005, p. 2.

[69] Browning, "The Subprime Loan Machine."

[70] Ibid.

[71] Sean Corrigan, *Daily Reckoning*, August 22, 2002; www.dailyreckonong.com. Corrigan is quoting an interview of Mozilo from the *Charleston Daily Mail*.

business has been transformed into a largely high-volume national market. Instead of holding on to mortgages, lenders tend to sell them in big bundles, often through government-sponsored financial firms Fannie Mae and Freddie Mac. In turn, Fannie and Freddie in the 1990s developed automated underwriting systems that allow quick approval of mortgages. Often, customers are asked for little more than a credit report, a pay stub, a bank statement and a few tax forms. These changes turned selling mortgages into a commodity business[.]"[72] This was written in 2003. The request for a credit report, a pay stub, a bank statement, and a few tax forms would soon look antiquated.

The Daily Crime Report

The daily papers were full of crime reports. Appraisal fraud was pushing the sales prices of some houses up by 30 percent: The *Washington Post* reported that "[n]early 75 percent of licensed appraisers interviewed as part of the ongoing National Appraisal Survey said they had felt pressure from a mortgage broker in the past year 'to hit a certain value.'" And 59 percent reported similar pressure from a loan officer working for a lending institution or mortgage company.[73] From the *Wall Street Journal* in 2001: "Appraisers are frequently encouraged to fudge the numbers."[74] In 2002: "Rising House Prices Cast Appraisers in a Harsh Light: Inflated Valuations Figure in More Mortgage Fraud; Buyers, Banks are Victims."[75]

Greenspan's testimony was regularly used to sell houses. David Seiders, chief economist of the National Association of Home Builders, relayed the chairman's forecast: "The time has come to put this

---

[72] John Hechinger, "The Refinancing Boom Spells Big Money for Mortgage Brokers; Huge Fees Draw the Scrutiny of Regulators and Spawn Lucrative Small Companies; From Machinist to Millionaire," *Wall Street Journal*, February 24, 2003.

[73] Kenneth R. Harney, "Many Appraisers Pressed to 'Hit the Number,'" *Washington Post*, September 13, 2003.

[74] Patrick Barta, "Is Appraisal Process Skewing Home Values? Appraisers Are Frequently Encouraged to Fudge the Numbers," *Wall Street Journal*, August 13, 2001.

[75] John Hechinger, "Shaky Foundation: Rising Home Prices Cast Appraisers in a Harsh Light:Inflated Valuations Figure in More Mortgage Fraud; Buyers, Banks Are Victims," *Wall Street Journal*, December 13, 2002.

issue to rest. The nation's home builders have said it ... and now Alan Greenspan has said it once again, in no uncertain terms: there is no such thing as a current or impending house price bubble."[76]

Home mortgage debt increased by $800 billion in 2003, and by $1.1 trillion in 2005.[77] There was no turning back. House prices had to keep rising to unburden those of houses they could not afford. Rising prices were the incentive to draw traders into the market. The mortgage machine needed to increase its production, or it would collapse.

[76] "Housing Groups Refute Housing 'Bubble,' Laud Greenspan Testimony," *Business Wire*, July 22, 2002.

[77] Federal Reserve Flow-of-Funds Accounts, Z-1, Historical Data Tables.

23

GREENSPAN'S VICTORY LAP: HIS LAST YEARS AT THE FED

2002–2006

That the economists ... can explain neither prices nor the rate of interest nor even agree what money is, reminds us that we deal here with belief not science.

—*James Buchan, author of* Frozen Desire *(1997)*[1]

On February 27, 2002, the Senate Banking Committee attended a forecasting session conducted by Chairman Greenspan. He declared himself "guardedly optimistic" of economic growth. The politicians and the press furrowed their brows. On March 7, Greenspan's optimism was back on track. To quote the headline from the *New York Times*: "What a Difference a Week Makes: After Recent 'Maybe,' Greenspan Now Says Recovery Is On."[2] It required the top of the crop to interpret for the *Times*: "A close parsing of Mr. Greenspan's words shows a slight but nonetheless significant change in his discussion of the labor market, said Jan Hatzius, senior economist at Goldman Sachs. Last week, Mr. Greenspan said performance of the labor market 'is' expected to lag. This week he said this performance 'was' expected to lag. 'In discussing the labor market's deterioration, he

---

[1] James Buchan, *Frozen Desire: The Meaning of Money* (London, Picador, 1997), p. 180.
[2] Gretchen Morgenstern, "What a Difference a Week Makes," *New York Times*, March 8, 2002.

presented the view that he was talking in the past tense,' Mr. Hatzius said."
These arcane distinctions could melt down markets, though Greenspan
had not yet addressed the Nasdaq bubble.

INFAMOUS SPEECHES: NUMBER ONE

In March 2002, Greenspan gave a speech in which he again discussed
Wall Street analysts—he scolded them: "The sharp decline in stock and
bond prices following Enron's collapse has chastened many of the uncritical practitioners of questionable accounting."[3] This was spoken by the
most uncritical practioner of all, and he did not sound a bit chastened.
(Nor did he mention the Enron Prize for Distinguished Service.) As for
this "sharp decline in stock and bond prices following Enron's collapse,"
prices had gone *up*. From the previous October, the Nasdaq had risen
about 5 percent. This may have been a furtive attempt to blame the stock
market's problems on Enron.

Then he really let the analysts have it: "[L]ong-term earnings forecasts
of brokerage-based securities analysts, on average, have been persistently
overly optimistic. Three- to five-year earnings forecasts for each of the S&P
500 corporations ... averaged almost 12 percent per year between 1985 and
2001. Actual earnings growth over that period averaged about 7 percent."

Almost anyone with experience knew that this was true before
Greenspan started serenading analysts' forecasts in the previous
decade. Given the 1985 starting date, Greenspan's productivity charade was build on estimates that had already produced 13 years of
incompetence (1985 to 1998) by the time he insisted that they proved
his hypothesis. The chairman continued to lash out: "[T]he persis-
tence of the bias year after year suggests that it more likely results ...
from the proclivity of firms that sell securities to retain and promote
analysts with an optimistic inclination. Moreover, the bias apparently
has been especially large when the brokerage firm issuing the forecast
also serves as an underwriter for the company's securities."

Greenspan was by no means the only celebrity without regrets. On
August 1, Glassman and Hassett asserted their credentials: "When our

---

[3] Alan Greenspan, "Corporate Governance," speech at the Stern School of Business,
New York University, New York, March 26, 2002.

book, 'Dow 36,000,' was published in September, 1999, the Dow Jones Industrial Average stood at 10,318. The Dow closed yesterday at 8,736. What went wrong? Actually, nothing."[4]

SPEECH NUMBER TWO

Each year, the Kansas City branch of the Federal Reserve System holds a late-summer symposium in Jackson Hole, Wyoming. The discussions are meant to be more reflective than immediate. Chairman Greenspan's 2002 contribution is still cause for reflection. It deserves an entire chapter. It was the most lamentable speech of his career.

He claimed that the "struggle to understand developments in the economy and financial markets since the mid-1990s has been particularly challenging for monetary policymakers. We were confronted with forces that none of us had personally experienced. Aside from the recent experience of Japan, only history books and musty archives gave us clues to the appropriate stance for the policy."[5]

The man who preened about his 50 years of market experience now admitted that his accumulated knowledge was useless. Since he, the FOMC, thousands of Federal Reserve studies, and the Federal Reserve models were useless, why were economists on the payroll?

The chairman continued. The Fed "considered a number of issues related to asset bubbles—that is, surges in prices of assets to unsustainable levels. As events evolved, we recognized that, despite our suspicions, it was very difficult to definitively identify a bubble until after the fact— that is, when its bursting confirmed its existence."

There is little point in discussing this. He knew exactly how to prick a bubble in 1994, 1995, and 1996, but then hid in the tall grass. His memory lapse also applies to the following Jackson Hole assertion:

"The notion that a well-timed incremental tightening could have been calibrated to prevent the late 1990s bubble is almost surely an illusion."[6]

---

[4] James K. Glassman and Kevin A. Hassett, "Dow 36000 Revisited," *Wall Street Journal*, August 1, 2002.

[5] Federal Reserve Bank of Kansas City's Annual Economic Symposium, "Economic Volatility," Jackson Hole, Wyoming, August 30, 2002.

[6] Ibid., p. 3.

Again, his mid-1990s actions and statements show that he held the opposite view.

Greenspan continued to rewrite history, his own history: "Some have asserted that the Federal Reserve can deflate a stock-price bubble— rather painlessly—by boosting margin requirements. The evidence suggests otherwise." He clung to this "rather painlessly" qualification again and again. This had been the biggest stock market bubble in the history of the world. Nobody in his right mind would make such a statement.

The *Economist* commented: "[T]he correct test is not whether a bubble can be deflated without some loss of output. Rather, it is whether the early pricking of a bubble causes less pain than letting it grow only to burst later. The longer a bubble is allowed to inflate, the more it encourages the build-up of other imbalances, such as too much borrowing and investment, which have the power to turn a mild downturn into something nastier."[7]

Greenspan's speech met some resistance, but was generally accepted as gospel. Still, he may have found the Jackson Hole speech was not quite the success he had expected. He launched a two-pronged attack from the podium for the rest of the year. First, an embellishment of his "can't see a bubble" line. Second, a new emphasis on "price stability."

Speaking to the Economic Club of New York on December 19, 2002, the chairman rationalized his inaction from a different angle: "The evidence of recent years, as well as the events of the late 1920s, casts doubt on the proposition that bubbles can be defused gradually."[8]

This contradicted the chairman's "Gold and Economic Freedom" essay of 1966. It is reasonable to suppose he may have changed his mind. But that is not so. Congressman Ron Paul handed Greenspan a copy of his essay and asked if he would like to add a disclaimer. Greenspan replied with uncharacteristic candor: "No. I reread this article recently—and I wouldn't change a single word."[9]

---

[7] "To Burst or Not to Burst," *Economist*, September 7, 2002.

[8] Alan Greenspan, speech to the Economic Club of New York, New York, December 19, 2002.

[9] William Bonner and Addison Wiggen, *Financial Reckoning Day: Surviving the Soft Depression of the 21st Century* (Hoboken, N.J.: Wiley, 2003), p. 159.

TERRORIZING THE AMERICAN PEOPLE—
GREAT DEPRESSION II

On June 25, 2003, the FOMC cut the funds rate to 1.00 percent. This was as low as it would go until December 18, 2008. Three-month Treasury bills traded at 0.90 percent, the lowest yield in nearly half a century.[10] It is said that Americans know very little history, but of one sequence, three-quarters of a century back, Americans come mentally equipped: the 1929 stock market crash was followed by the Great Depression. Ergo, a deflation and a depression go hand in hand.

The Fed was more interested in pumping up the housing market, but it tactfully developed its depression thesis. New theses were never hard work. Whatever the Fed said, was. It controlled the debate, talked it up, then down. Greenspan may not have made the front cover of *People* magazine—then again, maybe he has—but he defined what economists and Wall Street debated.

Greenspan's emphasis on price stability is a case in point. It was by no means true that central banks had, in the past, targeted only the prices of goods and services (a glance through William McChesney Martin's speeches is a case in point), but now, if one were to hear a Fed official, economist, or the media, this sole focus was writ in stone.

Speeches by Federal Reserve governors linked deflations with depressions. We *needed* inflation. This was new to the FOMC's table of woes, but now the man who wrote the book (at least part of it) was sitting at the table: *Inflation Targeting: Lessons from the International Experience* (Princeton University Press, 1999).[11] According to Professor Bernanke the economy needed positive price inflation to prevent deflation. Now was the time to test his thesis on a laboratory of 300 million Americans.

Besides writing, Bernanke talked. On November 21, 2002, Federal Reserve Vice Chairman Ben Bernanke stood at the Washington National Economists Club's podium and delivered a fearful message: "Deflation: Making Sure 'It' Doesn't Happen Here."

---

[10] Sidney Homer and Richard Sylla, *History of Interest Rates*, 4th ed. (Hoboken, N.J.: Wiley, 2005); the previous yield below 0.90 percent was 0.88 percent in 1958.

[11] There were four authors: Ben S. Bernanke, Thomas Laubach, Frederic S. Mishkin, and Adam S. Posen.

Bernanke offered several strategies to choke this gorgon, including a most frightful prospect: "Like gold, U.S. dollars have value only to the extent that they are strictly limited in supply. But the U.S. government has technology, called a printing press (or, today, its electronic equivalent), that allows it to produce as many U.S. dollars as it wishes at essentially no cost. By increasing the number of U.S. dollars in circulation ... the U.S. government can also reduce the value of a dollar in terms of goods and services, which is equivalent to raising the prices in dollars of those goods and services. We conclude that, under a paper-money system, a determined government can always generate higher spending and hence positive inflation."[12]

The branch banks spread the word. In May 2003, the Dallas Federal Reserve Bank published a research paper. The authors declared the "Fed could even implement what is essentially the classic textbook policy of dropping freshly printed money from a helicopter." The authors also proposed a tax on savings. To make sure Americans kept spending, the currency would be stamped periodically, and savers would pay a tax "in order to retain its status of legal tender." They seemed to favor 1 percent a month, or 12 percent a year.[13]

The whole Fed team marketed "price stability" as its sole function. In 2005, St. Louis Federal Reserve Bank President William Poole responded to the question of whether the institution should identify and manage asset price bubbles: "I'm really a hardliner on this.... I think it is incompatible with a market economy to have a government agency setting asset prices that are meant to allocate capital."[14] Milton Friedman also lectured from the audience: "The role of the Fed is to preserve price stability. Period.... It should not be concerned with the asset markets as such, only as they affect indirectly—somehow—the price stability as a

---

[12] Ben Bernanke, "Deflation: Making Sure 'It' Doesn't Happen Here," speech at the National Economists Club, Washington, D.C., November 21, 2002.

[13] William A. Fleckenstein with Frederick Sheehan, *Greenspan's Bubbles: The Age of Ignorance at the Federal Reserve* (New York: McGraw-Hill, 2008), p. 147; Evan F. Koenig and Jim Dolmas, "Monetary Policy in a Zero-Interest Rate Economy," May 2003. This was a presentation made to the Federal Reserve Bank of Dallas.

[14] Doug Noland, "Credit Bubble Bulletin," Prudent Bear Web site, July 8, 2005, p. 11. Noland writes that the Poole and Friedman quotes are "from a recording of Wednesday's [that is, July 6, 2005] Western Economic Association's panel in San Francisco."

whole."[15] The professor's argument turns on itself. Asset bubbles desta-bilize an economy. The larger question is how Poole (and such "free-market" advocates as Friedman and Greenspan) could ignore the central bank's influence on capital allocation from its monopoly of short-term interest rates.

These certified economists were the most detached bureaucrats since mandarins from the Zhou Dynasty. Between the fall of 1997 and the fall of 2002, the average house price in the United States rose 42 percent. In New York City, prices had risen 67 percent; in Jersey City, 75 percent; in Boston, 69 percent, and in San Francisco, 88 percent.[16] The median price for an existing, single-family house in California rose from $237,060 in April 2000 to $262,420 in April 2001 to $319,590 in May 2002 to $369,290 a year later.[17] An application of the Fed's pro-inflation policy appeared in a November 2002 *Time* magazine article with some timely advice: "Cash Out Now! It Only Sounds Crazy. Here's Why You Should Borrow against Your House and Buy Stocks."[18]

Americans could not escape the bombardment of consumer finance. From a radio ad in St. Louis: "If you own a home and have a pulse you can get a home equity loan."[19] There were more choices than at a used car lot. The FLEX-ARM mortgage was designed to drive the homeowner to drink. Each month the lender sent the borrower a payment coupon that calculated four payment options: negative amortization, interest only, 30-year fixed and 20-year fixed terms.[20]

SPEECH NUMBER THREE AND CONGRESSIONAL TESTIMONY—2003

On March 4, 2003, Greenspan addressed the Independent Community Bankers of America. He congratulated the bankers and encouraged them to keep up the good work. Greenspan told his audience that as

[15] Ibid.

[16] Noland, "Credit Bubble Bulletin," February 21, 2003, p. 6.

[17] California Association of Realtors.

[18] Daniel Kadlec, "Cash Out Now! It Only Sounds Crazy. Here's Why You Should Borrow against Your House and Buy Stocks," *Time*, November 22, 2002.

[19] Chuck Butler, *Daily Pfennig*, September 19, 2005; Everbank.com Web site.

[20] Stacey L. Bradford, "Mortgages Get More Exotic," *Wall Street Journal.com*, July 25, 2004.

"part of 2002's process of refinancing, households 'cashed out' almost $200 billion of accumulated home equity" and "perhaps ... half was used to finance home modernization and personal consumption expenditures." This was clearly a good thing in the chairman's mind. He loved any new technology, and here was an advance that cleaned out homeowners' equity efficiently: "Even as recently as the late 1980s, a family that wanted to use housing *wealth* [author's italics] to finance consumption would have faced an expensive and time-consuming process.... [O]nly in the last decade or so has secured borrowing against home equity become such a cost-effective source of credit."[21]

There were the naysayers. That spending one's equity was driving Americans to the poorhouse. That rising home prices and spending the equity cushion reduced the margin of safety. Greenspan was having none of that. He told America that its financial footing was growing stronger every day. Testifying before Congress on July 15, 2003, Greenspan opined that this transfer of wealth—from homeowners to the automobile salesmen—was key to economic recovery: "The prospects for a resumption of strong economic growth have been enhanced by steps taken in the private sector over the past couple of years to restructure and strengthen balance sheets.... Nowhere has this process of balance sheet adjustment been more evident than in the household sector."[22]

The household sector dove head first into cheap borrowing rates and bid up asset prices to unsustainable levels. Greenspan acknowledged this, in his euphemistic manner: "On the asset side of the balance sheet, the decline in longer-term interest rates and diminished perceptions of credit risk in recent months have provided a substantial lift to the market value of nearly all major categories of household assets."[23] House prices traded up; mortgagees spent their equity back down. The people's representatives did not find this disclosure alarming.

---

[21] Alan Greenspan, speech to the annual convention of the Independent Community Bankers of America (via satellite), March 4, 2003 "Home Mortgage Market".

[22] Alan Greenspan, "Federal Reserve Board's Semiannual Monetary Policy Report to the Congress," Before the Committee on Financial Services, U.S. House of Representatives, July 15, 2003.

[23] Ibid.

Greenspan very rarely used the word *debt*. He did before Congress, and he found it a virtue: "On the liability side of the balance sheet, despite the significant increase in debt encouraged by higher asset values, lower interest rates have facilitated a restructuring of existing debt."[24] Restructuring applied to the terms of loans (lower rates and longer maturities), but the only restructuring that reduces the level of debt owed is a write-off.

The economy had officially exited recession, but one of the glaring deficiencies of the recovery was the atrophy of industry. The chairman told the House Committee on Financial Services not to worry: "Is it important for an economy to have manufacturing?" No, was Greenspan's answer. A thriving economy depended upon the value created, and this could be accomplished by "fabricating ... something consumers want ... or by various services consumers want." He claimed that both goods and services produce the same standard of living. In either case, "the capability to purchase goods is there." National defense considerations aside, "[I]t does not really matter whether or not you produce goods."[25]

Pandering to the interests discussed in the previous chapter, he dismissed concerns about production at a time when production was collapsing. Manufacturing jobs decreased by 3.1 million between 1998 and 2003: a fall of 18.3 percent. This was the largest percentage drop since the Great Depression.[26] Between January 2001 (the recent recession officially started in March 2001) through the end of 2003, consumer spending accounted for 101.6 percent of "real" GDP growth.[27]

What was America making? The man from Nehemiah said that houses were "little prosperity factories." Whoever was right or wrong about production, we learned in November 2003 that, over the past two years, 750,000 high-tech jobs had been lost and 125,000 Americans had

---

[24] Ibid.

[25] Noland, "Credit Bubble Bulletin," July 25, 2003, p. 8, quoting Greenspan, "Federal Reserve Board's semiannual monetary policy report to the Congress."

[26] *The Richebächer Letter*, January 2004, p. 4.

[27] *The Richebächer Letter*, February 2004, p. 4.

become real estate agents.[28] By 2006, at least 600,000 people sold mortgage loans in California.[29]

SPEECH NUMBER FOUR, A DATE TO REMEMBER: FEBRUARY 23, 2004

On January 4, 2004, Ben Bernanke predicted that "2003 will be remembered as the year when this recovery turned the corner."[30] He celebrated the "diversified and resilient U.S. economy," ignoring or unaware that over 100 percent of the so-called recovery was produced by consumer spending. Bernanke was another who ignored debt, but his influence was (and is) more dangerous than Greenspan's. His was the voice of the academic and Washington policymaking establishments a consortium whose models needed to hush up the influence of debt balances to rationalize such an unbalanced economy.

If the economy had turned the corner, it is difficult to understand the motivation behind the chairman's speech of February 23, 2004. He addressed the Credit Union National Association in Washington. In a startling performance, Greenspan tried his best to convince Americans their best interests would be served by grasping for the highest-priced houses by means of the riskiest loans.

He opened his pitch by noting, "American homeowners clearly like the certainty of fixed mortgage payments." He advised insulated Americans to look overseas, "where adjustable-rate mortgages are far more common.... Fixed rate mortgages seem unduly expensive to households in other countries." He informed his constituents that the "traditional fixed-rate mortgage may be an expensive method of financing a home."[31]

---

[28] "750,000 High-Tech Jobs Lost in Two Years," *Financial Times*, November 19, 2003. Ron Peebles, Prudent Bear Web site, November 18, 2003; number of real estate agents from National Association of Realtors.

[29] Seth Lubove and Daniel Taub, "Subprime Fiasco Exposes Manipulation by Mortgage Brokers," Bloomberg, May 30, 2007.

[30] Ben S. Bernanke, "Monetary Policy and the Economic Outlook: 2004," speech at the American Economic Association, San Diego, California, January 4, 2004.

[31] Alan Greenspan, "Understanding Household Debt Obligations," speech at the Credit Union National Association 2004 Governmental Affairs Conference, Washington, D.C., February 23, 2004.

The most famous civil servant since Caligula's horse continued: "[M]any homeowners might have saved tens of thousands of dollars had they held adjustable-rate mortgages rather than fixed-rate mortgages over the past decade." He went on to acknowledge that "this would not have been the case, of course, had interest rates trended sharply upward." This was his only acknowledgment that his infomercial only worked in one direction.[32]

It cannot have been a coincidence that Greenspan was addressing the Credit Union National Association in Washington. The Federal Reserve chairman pushed risky mortgages in the same week that the California Association of Realtors announced that house price sales in the state had risen 20.7 percent from a year before and those in Los Angeles County had increased 27.4 percent.[33] By June 2005, the median California residential house price cost $542,720.[34]

The next week, speaking before the Economic Club of New York, Greenspan inferred that interest rates would rise.[35] Three months later (on June 30, 2004), the Federal Reserve raised the federal funds rate.

Few people read speeches by Federal Reserve governors. However, almost everyone wanted to know what Greenspan had to say, on whatever topic, on whatever day—in 30 seconds or less. The February 24 *Wall Street Journal* exclaimed: "In a rare evaluation of the interest-rate options that households face, Federal Reserve Chairman Alan Greenspan questioned whether homeowners are well-served by popular fixed-rate long-term mortgages."[36] The title of the article said it all: "Fed Chief Questions Loan Choices."

Whether this was the launching pad or not, mortgage mania was reaching a feverish pitch. Manhattan apartment prices rose 23 percent between January and March 2005 (from an average price of $987,257 to $1.21 million).[37] Over 20 percent of Californians who bought houses

---

[32] Ibid.

[33] "Median Price of a Home in California Increases 20.7 Percent in January, Sales Up 5.3 Percent, C.A.R. Reports," PR Newswire, February 25, 2004.

[34] Noland, "Credit Bubble Bulletin," August 5, 2005, p. 8.

[35] Alan Greenspan, "Current Account," speech at the Economic Club of New York, New York, March 2, 2004.

[36] Greg Ip, "Fed Chief Questions Loan Choices," *Wall Street Journal*, February 24, 2004.

[37] Noland, "Credit Bubble Bulletin," April 1, 2005.

over the previous two years devoted more than one-half of their earnings to mortgage payments.[38] In Colorado, banks lured illegal aliens into loans that were insured by the federal government. "They didn't even have to come up with any money. ... They just moved in," and some immediately went into default, moaned the local district attorney.[39]

Across the country, house prices rose 13.6 percent between the second quarter of 2004 and 2005, the fastest pace since 1979, an earlier period of runaway inflation. In July, the National Association of Realtors was worried: "The most notable problem in the housing market is the shortage of homes available."[40] In August, the *New York Times* reported: "[N]ew homes are going up faster now than they have in more than 30 years.... Large tracts of Queens, once home to factories and power plants, are being readied for apartment complexes[.]"[41]

Earlier in the summer, the *Times* alerted its readers: "For two months now, federal banking regulators have signaled their discomfort about the explosive rise in risky mortgage loans.... Then they expressed worry about the surge in no-money-down mortgages, interest only [mortgages] and 'liar's loans' that require no proof of a borrower's income. The impact so far? Almost nil." [42]

Why? Steve Fritts, associate director for risk management policy at the Federal Deposit Insurance Corporation (FDIC) explained: "We don't want to stifle financial innovation. We have the most vibrant housing and housing-finance market in the world, and there is a lot of innovation."[43] That the Federal Reserve and alphabet soup bureaucracies encouraged, rather than warned, was unpardonable. That current proposed legislation would give such organizations more power is a disgrace.

---

[38] Jim Christie, "California Home Buyers Stretch to Afford Homes," Reuters, August 18, 2005.

[39] Ross Wehrner, "Colorado Authorities Indict Real Estate Agent Loan Officer for Forgery," *Denver Post*, July 14, 2005.

[40] Noland, "Credit Bubble Bulletin," July 15, 2005, p. 8.

[41] Jennifer Steinhauer, "Housing Boom Echoes in All Corners of the City," *New York Times*, August 4, 2005.

[42] Edmund L. Andrews, "Loose Reins on Galloping Loans," *New York Times*, July 15, 2005, p. C1.

[43] Ibid.

In October 2004, Greenspan had told the America's Community Bankers Annual Convention "the surge in cash-out mortgage refinancings likely improved rather than worsened the financial condition of the average homeowner."[44] Possibly, the Federal Reserve chairman allayed lenders' doubts about their borrowers creditworthiness, since, by July 2005, 42 percent of first-time home buyers were putting no money down.[45]

Playboy's May 2005 Playmate, Jamie Westenhiser, decided to really make some money when she joined the world's hottest profession. Her goal: "a successful career in real estate."[46] She had company. California's Department of Real Estate doubled the number of test centers for such career moves.[47]

On it went: in Sunny Isles Beach, Florida, Carlos and Betti Lidsky had bought and sold two condominiums and bought and sold two houses within six months. None of the homes had been built. The couple made a half-million-dollar profit. "It is much better than the stock market," according to Mr. Lipsky.[48] Heavenly skyscraper ambitions have always been indicators of tops. This time would not be the exception—but with a twist. Now the skyscrapers were for living, not working. In May 2005, two 110-story hotel and apartment buildings were proposed in Miami.[49] A 2,000-foot, 115-story condominium was planned in Chicago.[50]

Greenspan entered the late autumn of his chairmanship. He had plenty to say, and everyone wanted his opinion. Caroline Baum at Bloomberg cut to the heart of the matter. "Congress considers him an expert on almost all subjects, and Greenspan is generally willing to offer

---

[44] Alan Greenspan, "The Mortgage Market and Consumer Debt," speech at America's Community Bankers Annual Convention, Washington, D.C., October 19, 2004.

[45] *Grant's Interest Rate Observer*, July 29, 2005, p. 4, quoting David Rosenberg, economist at Merrill Lynch.

[46] Daniela Deane, "Everybody's an Investor Now," *Washington Post*, May 21, 2005.

[47] "Frenzied Froth," *Economist*, May 28, 2005.

[48] Motoko Rich, "Speculators Seeing Gold in Boom in Prices for Homes," *New York Times*, March 1, 2005.

[49] Matthew Haggman, "Developer Leon Cohen Considering Twin 100-story Towers," *Miami Herald*, May 5, 2005.

[50] Alex Frangos, "Could Chicago Tower Pop the Real Estate Market?" *Wall Street Journal*, July 26, 2005.

his counsel on everything from education to energy markets."[51] Between 2001 and the end of his service as Federal Reserve chairman, Greenspan gave eight speeches on education, six on energy, two on community development, two on the U.S. currency, two on labor skills, one on rural economic issues, and one on property rights. Since everything he said was broadcast on page one, the casual reader might have thought that he was running the Departments of Housing and Urban Development, Education, Energy, Treasury, Labor, Interior, Justice, and Defense. (In early February 2003, Greenspan handicapped the "U.S. ability to take out Saddam Hussein reasonably quickly" as a 95 percent probability.[52])

SPEECH NUMBER FIVE—APRIL 2005

In April 2005, he made a speech appropriate for a man who never got it right:

> With these advances in technology, lenders have taken advantage of credit-scoring models and other techniques for efficiently extending credit to a broader spectrum of consumers.... These improvements have led to rapid growth in subprime mortgage lending; indeed, today subprime mortgages account for roughly 10 percent of the number of all mortgages outstanding, up from just 1 or 2 percent in the early 1990s.
>
> [W]e must conclude that innovation and structural change ... [has] been critical in providing expanded access to credit for the vast majority of consumers, including those of limited means. Without these forces, it would have been impossible for lower-income consumers to have the degree of access to credit markets that they now have."[53]

It was a speech his worst enemy could not write.

There was a significant structural change in the composition of buyers. The National Association of Realtors would find that

---

[51] Caroline Baum, Bloomberg, February 16, 2005, p. 32.

[52] Alan Murray, "Resolving War Issue May Be President's Best Economic Plan," *Wall Street Journal*, January 28, 2003, p. A4.

[53] Alan Greenspan, "Consumer Finance," speech at the Federal Reserve System's Fourth Annual Community Affairs Research Conference, Washington, D.C. April 8, 2005.

nearly 40 percent of the houses bought in 2005 were second homes. Two-thirds of these houses were bought for investment—also called trading and flipping.[54]

Alan Greenspan, Knight Commander of the British Empire, awarded the *Ordre national de la Légion d'honneur* (France), the Presidential Medal of Freedom (U.S), the (U.S.) Department of Defense Medal for Distinguished Public Service, and the Enron Prize for Distinguished Service, entered the Olympic stadium for his final lap, the torch held aloft, the crowd on its feet, cheering, weeping, and swooning. In July, a 24-year-old painter in New York opened a gallery show of 20 paintings and sketches of the highly decorated economist. CNBC aired the spectacle across the nation. The gallery owner was overwhelmed. "I've never seen anything like it. I had money managers calling from Nevada, Dallas, California."[55]

Greenspan attended a Washington Nationals baseball game in August. "Security guards urged the Federal Reserve chairman to sit in an air-conditioned executive suite but Mr. Greenspan ... chose a seat in the stands[.]" He loved to be liked. "The 79-year-old central banker was ... cheered as he arrived. People nearby asked him to autograph their tickets. From further back, there were shouts of 'Go, Alan!' and 'Yeah, Alan, keep' em low.'"[56]

SPEECHES SIX AND SEVEN—JACKSON HOLE AND LOOSE ENDS

Greenspan attended his final active-duty séance at Jackson Hole in August. His former vice chairman, Alan Blinder, spoke. He claimed that Greenspan might be the "greatest central banker who ever lived."[57] The departing chairman spoke of a potential flaw in the storied price "stability." Investors are likely to project stability "over an ever more

---

[54] *Grant's Interest Rate Observer*, April 21, 2006, p. 2.

[55] Ben White, "Greenspan, Her Art-Throb," *Washington Post*, August 11, 2005.

[56] Andrew Balls, "Greenspan's Record," *Financial Times*, August 22, 2005.

[57] From paper "Understanding the Greenspan Standard," presented by Alan S. Blinder and Ricardo Reis of Princeton University at a symposium sponsored by the Federal Reserve Bank of Kansas City (Jackson Hole, Wyoming, August 25, 2005: "The Greenspan Era Lessons for the Future.") The authors contended, "when the score is toted up, we think he has a legitimate claim to being the greatest central banker who ever lived."

extended time horizon." If they do so, higher values "can readily disappear."[58] This is another way of saying they could be wiped out.

Greenspan admitted that central banks should at least consider acting beforehand. The Fed's "forecasts and hence policy are becoming increasingly driven by asset price changes."[59] Permitted the closing remarks to the conference, the chairman sounded like an escapee from a POW camp when he declared: "Debates on the relative merits of asset targeting also will continue and possibly intensify in years ahead."[60] This should have sparked a debate of the Greenspan doctrine, but apparently, his audience was content.[61]

Greenspan tied another loose end before the American Bankers Association in September. The value of houses had risen from $8 trillion at the end of 1995 to $18 trillion in 2005. "[W]e can have little doubt that the exceptionally low level of home mortgage interest rates has been a major driver of the recent surge of home building and home turnover and the steep climb in home prices."[62]

Greenspan thought the decline of interest rates implied that the "increase over the past decade in consumption expenditure [was] financed by home equity extraction, rather than by income and other assets. [This] would account for much of the decline in the personal saving rate since 1995."[63] It took Greenspan an extra decade to conclude what Larry Lindsey told him in 1995.

The chairman discussed "a long list of novel mortgage products," such as 40-year loans, option ARMs, piggyback mortgages, and HELOCs ("home equity lines of credit") used as piggyback loans. If house prices cooled, "these borrowers, and the institutions that service them, could be exposed to significant losses."[64]

---

[58] Alan Greenspan, "Reflections on Central Banking," speech at Jackson Hole, Wyoming, August 26, 2005, p. 4.

[59] Ibid.

[60] Alan Greenspan, "Closing Remarks," August 27, 2005.

[61] A headline from the *Financial Times*, three years later: "Greenspan Doctrine on Assets Questioned," article by Krishna Guha, March 28, 2008. There have been a few noises since Guha wrote the article, a year ago, but the doctrine is still cited.

[62] Alan Greenspan, "Mortgage Banking," speech to the American Bankers Association Annual Convention, Palm Desert, California (via satellite), September 26, 2005.

[63] Ibid.

[64] Ibid.

The hosannas flowed. In the *Wall Street Journal*, Milton Friedman wrote that Alan Greenspan was right and he (Friedman) was wrong: rather than "strict rules to control the amount of money created," Greenspan had told Friedman that discretion was preferable. "Greenspan's great achievement is to have demonstrated that it is possible to maintain stable prices" without strict rules. Friedman wrote that price stability under Greenspan "supported a high level of productivity."[65] Friedman opposed any Fed action that would consider asset prices (bubbles) a menace. By admiring Greenspan's term as a "great achievement," Friedman tacitly absolved the Fed from any responsibility for the stock bubble and the mortgage bubble. He never mentioned "credit" or "debt," the expansion and acceleration of which was the reason the economy grew.

The *Economist* was less deferential. It stated that Greenspan was "leaving behind the biggest economic imbalances in American history."[66] The magazine was not impressed with productivity: "[T]he main reason why America's growth has remained strong in recent years has been a massive monetary stimulus." It threw a fit about rising debt: "By borrowing against capital gains on their houses, households have been able to consume more than they earn." The rising GDP was "at the cost of a negative personal savings rate, a growing burden of household debt, and a huge current-account deficit." The *Economist* did not expect much from Chairman Bernanke: "He is likely to continue the current asymmetric policy of never raising interest rates to curb rising asset prices, but always cutting rates after prices fall."[67]

FAREWELL

Greenspan retired on January 31, 2006.

"It was a farewell dinner at the White House that only Alan Greenspan could have engineered."[68] The *New York Times* continued with this breathless party review: "[S]everal dozen of Mr. Greenspan's closest friends" were

---

[65] Milton Friedman, "He Has Set a Standard," *Wall Street Journal*, January 31, 2006.

[66] "Danger Time for America," "Leaders" section, *Economist*, January 14, 2006.

[67] Ibid.

[68] Edmund L. Andrews, "Greenspan, Another Monument in Washington, Prepares to Leave," *New York Times*, January 30, 2006.

hosted by President Bush in the Blue Room. "But it was the list of guests ... that highlighted his stature as both an icon and an iconoclast."[69] It could be argued that William McChesney Martin Jr. was more of an iconoclast when he addressed the gathered at his White House farewell: "I wish I could turn the bank over to Arthur Burns as I would have liked. But we are in deep trouble. We are in the wildest inflation since the Civil War."[70]

The collection of guests is almost "unheard-of in today's bitterly divided capital."[71] Robert Rubin and Vice President Dick Cheney attended. Greenspan "made few enemies in his 18-year tenure." The *Times* went on: "Mr. Greenspan is almost an institution in Washington—ubiquitous on the party circuit and a constant dispenser of economic advice to top lawmakers and presidents."[72] A few years earlier, the social editor of the *Washington Times* considered Greenspan's social rank "up into the stratosphere." The Federal Reserve chairman was "definitely A-list."[73]

It was a half-century back when Ayn Rand asked Nathaniel Branden: "Do you think Alan might basically be a social climber?"[74]

---

[69] Ibid.

[70] Robert P. Bremner, *Chairman of the Fed: William McChesney Martin and the Creation of the Modern American Financial System* (New Haven, Conn.: Yale University Press, 2004), p. 276.

[71] Andrews, "Greenspan, Another Monument in Washington, Prepares to Leave."

[72] Ibid.

[73] Justin Martin, *Greenspan, The Man Behind the Money,* (Cambridge, MA: Perseus, 2000), p. 228.

[74] Nathaniel Branden, *My Years with Ayn Rand* (San Francisco: Jossey-Bass, 1999), p. 212; original from the University of California.

Introduction to Part 3
The Consequences of Power

2006–2009

[I]t is most astonishing that huge private fortunes and imposing concentrations of capital were amassed [in Germany] in the years 1919–1923: years which were not, on the whole, a time of general economic prosperity. The fact is certainly surprising, although the surprise is lessened if we consider that even in the past times of economic regressions, of social dissolution, and of profound political disturbances have often been characterized by a concentration of property. "In those periods the strong recovered their primitive habits as beasts of prey."[1]

—Constantino Bresciani-Turroni, The Economics of Inflation, *1937*

Alan Greenspan retired from the Federal Reserve on January 31, 2006. A week later, he appeared as a "holographic image in Tokyo" and told investors the high price of gold did not reflect fears of inflation. Rather, he explained there were people who believed that a nuclear weapon could be detonated within five years.[2] In February, he reportedly received $250,000 to speak at a dinner that Lehman Brothers hosted for hedge-fund managers.[3] He could not stop talking. A year later, he responded to

---

[1] Constantino Bresciani-Turroni, *The Economics of Inflation: A Study of Currency Depreciation in Post-War Gernmany, 1914–1923*, p. 289, George Allen & Unwin Ltd., London, Third Impression, 1968. The book was originally published in Italian in 1931.

[2] "Terror Threat Responsible for High Gold Price—Greenspan," *The Times*, February 8, 2007.

[3] Roddy Boyd and Niles Lathem, "Want Alan Greenspan to Come to Dinner? That'll Be $250,000..."*New York Post,* February 9, 2006.

criticism: "I was beginning to feel quite comfortable that I was fully back to the anonymity I was seeking."[4] He was also well paid for his private advice. Deutsche Bank, Pimco, the worlds largest bond manager, and John Paulson, a hedge fund manager who profited magnificently from the real estate crash, all hired Greenspan as an advisor.

THE PEAK

All asset classes were inflating. This worldwide credit bubble developed after the stock market crash in 2000. Now, stock markets around the world, and also bonds, commodities, and art (of all periods), were rising.[5] As markets rose and credit spreads shrank, there seemed to be one explanation: liquidity. This is a word with several meanings. Probably most timely was that practically anything was tradeable. Houses and dining-room sets were securitized, as were trees and art. Of course, there had to be a willing buyer and there was no shortage of purchasers for the most dubious of assets. (Home-equity loans was bundled and sold. They were backed by rising house prices. Thus, the word *liquidity:* assets flowed like a river after a monsoon.

In 2005, U.S. house prices stalled. In 2006, prices fell. "Illiquidity" followed. Many of the other asset classes (if not all the others) were supported by the higher level of collateral and credit that spilled back from elevating house prices. When house prices peaked, so did the collateral. But credit kept rising.

Banks and brokerages borrowed to lend. By 2007, brokerage firms were leveraged at 30:1 and 40:1. (At 40:1 leverage, the firm becomes insolvent if the prices of its assets fall more than 2.5 percent.) Investment banks and brokerages lent to those who were already highly leveraged: hedge funds, funds of funds, and buyout funds. Leveraged structures were compounded on top of other leveraged structures. The global derivative market rose above $500 trillion: some now calculate that it is over a quadrillion dollars, but what was the point of counting? To both institutional investors and mortgage recipients, there was no limit to what they could borrow.

---

[4] James M. O'Neill, "Greenspan's Long Shadow Needs to Shrink, Management Gurus Say," Bloomberg.com, March 7, 2007, http://www.bloomberg.com/apps/news?pid=2067 0001&refer=home&sid=aXFdEFhGhKrl.

[5] The general observation was made in Marc Faber's *Gloom, Boom & Doom Report*, March 1, 2007, p. 8.; Zimbabwe's currency was an exception to the rise.

Alan Greenspan reportedly received $8.5 million for a book contract. The *Age of Turbulence* was published September 2007.[6] This was shortly after public awareness of financial problems arose. Greenspan was talking to everyone. He was full of insights. Greenspan claimed that "the abrupt upheaval in markets due to the sub-prime crisis 'was an accident waiting to happen.'"[7] This was true, but it was Greenspan, in 2005, who extolled "techniques for efficiently extending credit to a broader spectrum of consumers [which has] led to rapid growth in sub-prime mortgage lending."[8]

Greenspan would accept no blame for the rapidly deteriorating American landscape. Greenspan's prophecies no longer moved markets. He received withering criticism from some well-known economists. Greenspan then complained about the economists who complained about Greenspan.

The former chairman was called before the Committee of Oversight and Reform on October 23, 2008. Greenspan looked withered. Congressmen filleted and roasted the man who once was God. The attacks on Greenspan were well deserved, but the prosecuting politicians were most intent on saving their own hides.

Greenspan opened his testimony by stating, "[W]e are in the midst of a once-in-a-century credit tsunami."[9] The real once-in-a-history-of-the-universe stimulant was Greenspan.[10]

Greenspan admitted to a "flaw" in his model that impugned "40 years or more of considerable evidence." Until this latest model problem, he thought that financial institutions were the best regulators.[11] Did he

---

[6] A non-definitive number proposed by *Publisher's Weekly*: http://www.publishersweekly. com/article/CA6469524.html?q="age+of+turbulence".

[7] Reuters, "Highlights—Speeches from UK's Brown and Darling; Greenspan," October 1, 2007, http://www.reuters.com/article/companyNewsAndPR/idUSBROWN20071001?sp=true.

[8] Alan Greenspan, *Consumer Finance* At the Federal Reserve System's Fourth Annual Community Affairs Research Conference, Washington, D.C. April 8, 2005.

[9] Testimony of Dr. Alan Greenspan, Committee of Oversight and Reform, October 23, 2008, p.1.

[10] Caroline Baum at Bloomberg listed Greenspan's once-in-a-century proclamations. Greenspan had told us a few years back that we were in the midst of a "once-in-a-life-time" technological boom. In July 2002, he announced a "once-in-a-generation frenzy of speculation" was over. In the summer of 2008, he ordained the solvency crisis a "once-in-a-century phenomenon." Caroline Baum, "No Limit to Greenspan's Once-In-A-Century Events," Bloomberg, August 18, 2008.

[11] Scott Lanman and Steve Mathews, "Greenspan Concedes to 'Flaw' in Market Ideology," Bloomberg, October 23, 2008.

really believe this? He saw that bank risk departments did not monitor counterparty holdings with Long-Term Capital Management.

Greenspan blamed his model. It had miscalculated his input that the "self-interest of lending institutions" protected shareholder interests. He may have believed this, but a moment's reflection would have reminded him the "bank holding companies that control an increasing proportion of all the commercial banking in our country"—as Senator Proxmire had lectured Greenspan 21 years earlier—acted exactly as the senator had warned. They used their bulk to indulge their own desires and left their institutions (and the United States) on the precipice of collapse.

HIS CONTRIBUTION

It was not just Alan Greenspan's model that failed. There were many parties at fault. The erosion started long before Greenspan's chairmanship. He ignited a keg of dynamite under a financial system that was already wobbling. When the economy faltered, Greenspan drove the Fed funds rate below the rate of inflation. Annual borrowing, by all parties in the United States, rose from $1 trillion in 1988 to $4.1 trillion in 2006.[12] During Greenspan's time at the Fed, the nation's debt rose from $10.8 trillion to $41.0 trillion.[13] He was the Federal Reserve chairman who increased the money supply from $233 billion to $792 billion.[14]

Greenspan was not wholly at fault. Banks did not have to lend the money. Debtors did not have to borrow. Bankers and brokerage houses are to blame for reckless lending and reckless leveraging.

He took orders as well as issued them. Congress bullied Greenspan, but that had been true of all Federal Reserve chairmen. New during Greenspan's chairmanship was the path of former politicians to hedge funds, private-equity funds, and banks. Greenspan spurred the financial economy, and those who interrogated him took advantage of it.

---

[12] Federal Reserve, Flow-of-Funds Accounts, Z-1.

[13] Figures from year end of years he entered and left office. "Beginning of office" is December 31, 1987: "End of office" is December 31, 2005; From Federal Reserve, Flow of Funds Accounts, Z-1

[14] Federal Reserve Publication, *Aggregate Reserves of Depository Institutions and Monetary Base,* Table 1.

The United States has been devaluing its currency for the past century. What one could buy with $1 in 1913 (the year the Federal Reserve Act was passed) costs about $20 today. William McChesney Martin's battles against Congress and influential economists, chronicled in the early chapters, were losing efforts. Congress was not entirely at fault for pestering the Fed. The American people lived inflationary lives. They bargained for wages and benefits that could not be paid in constant dollars. They worked fewer hours. Americans were buying more from abroad than they were selling. The government was spending more than its revenues by the 1960s.

The economists kept revising their theories to rationalize these practices. The theories were new and beguiling. The imbalances were as old as civilization. These contradictions have always ended in tears.

By the 1970s, the gold standard had to go. Economists offered new theories. The influential academics bolted to the head of the class. Barely mentioned was the immense liberation of a paper-currency world. Imbalances no longer had to be settled in gold. Governments found deficit financing to be an opium to the masses. Government programs abounded. The masses grew accustomed to inflation and borrowing in currencies that tended toward depreciation. Thus, debtors paid back less real money than they had borrowed. Bankers could lend more after the link to gold was severed, since no final settlement of claims existed. This was also a platform to launch speculative derivative products.

Other central banks decided to degrade their currencies in coordination with dollar devaluations. The bonfire of the paper currencies is a matter of time. Then, the institution of central banking will wear no clothes. Nobody contributed more to the denouement than Alan Greenspan.

His Successor

Ben S. Bernanke succeeded Alan Greenspan as Federal Reserve chairman. When Bernanke is evaluated, the wreckage he inherited should be a consideration. If Bernanke had followed Paul Volcker, his Fed would still have possessed a substantial degree of influence over the nation's credit system and over the large financial institutions.

Nevertheless, his influence in the economy and markets has amplified the United States' problems. The "Greenspan put" has become the "Bernanke put." Its consequences are far more pervasive than Greenspan's. (It might be argued that Greenspan would have done much of the same, but such a debate is unfruitful It is acts that count.)

Bernanke did not just cut interest rates to ward off a recession. He lent money to brokers, bought the largest insurance company in the world (AIG), allowed over-leveraged investment banks to convert themselves into commercial banks, thus permitting them to snuggle underneath the Fed's too-big-to-fail umbrella.

When the commercial paper market floundered, the Federal Reserve decided it would lend to corporations. (Commercial paper is used by large corporations to fund short term obligations.) Thus, General Electric, General Motors Acceptance Corporation, and American Express were among the companies fortunate enough to sell their paper to the Fed.

Bernanke opened more borrowing facilities (at last count there were 16). Even when the credit markets heal, the precedent has been established, just as Continental Illinois was the precursor, in 1984, to too-big-to-fail-banks.

General Electric Chairman Jeffrey Immelt wrote in his company's 2009 annual report: "The interaction between government and business will change forever… [T]he government will be an industrial policy champion, a financier, a key partner."[15]

The Mortgage Machine (see Chapter 22) showed what can happen when government plays a role similar to what Immelt envisioned. The other troubling aspect is what happens to companies that are not one of the government's champions? In a very different context, President George W. Bush said: "You are either with us or against us."

Consequences of the "Bernanke put" will be interesting to watch.

---

[15] General Electric, 2008 Annual Report, Letters to Shareowners; released early March 2009.

24

THE GREAT DISTORTION

—————

2006

—————

[I]ncreases in home values, together with a stock-market recovery
that began in 2003, have [aided] … [t]he expansion of U.S. housing
wealth, much of it easily accessible to households through cash-out
refinancing and home-equity lines of credit[.][1]

—*Federal Reserve Governor Ben S. Bernanke, 2005*

What did Alan Greenspan bequeath to his successor?

Foremost was a recovery that distorted the American economy more
than ever. Americans borrowed from abroad and spent at home. In 2000,
the U.S. imported about $400 billion more than it exported. By 2004, this
had risen above $600 billion, and was close to $800 billion by 2006.[2]

Personal consumption drove the economy. Between 2001 and 2006,
Asha Bangalore, economist at Northern Trust, estimated that 40 percent
of new jobs were related to housing.[3] This was not sustainable.

The manufacturing economy kept shrinking. From the end of 2000
to 2004, manufacturing wages and salaries fell from $819 billion to

---

[1] Ben S. Bernanke, "The Global Savings Glut and the U.S. Current Account Deficit,"
Sandridge Lecture, Virginia Association of Economics, Richmond, Virginia, March 10,
2005.

[2] OECD.StatExtracts. Dataset: balance of payments, United States. Annual data. Actual
numbers: $417 billion in 2000, $624 billion in 2004, and $788 billion in 2006.

[3] William A. Fleckenstein with Frederick Sheehan, *Greenspan's Bubbles: The Age of Ignorance at the Federal Reserve* (New York: McGraw-Hill, 2008), pp. 193–194; information
from *Grant's Interest Rate Observer*, April 21, 2006.

$683 billion.[4] Manufacturing profits fell from $144 billion in 2000 to $96 billion in 2003.[5] The attenuation of manufacturing was a reason that Americans were falling behind. In 2008, goods-producing jobs (manufacturing, mining, and construction) paid an average of $21.54 an hour while service workers earned $11.22 an hour.[6]

From March 2001, the official starting date of the recession, through the end of 2004, employment fell by about 500,000. There were 1.2 million jobs lost in the private economy. (The government had gone on a hiring splurge; 700,000 additional public servants contributed to the deceivingly low half-million job losses.[7])

Official voices implored Americans to buy: "I encourage you to all go shopping more," was President Bush's advice five days before Christmas in 2006.[8]

In sum, the U.S. economy was spending (consuming) much more than it earned. This was financed by foreigners purchasing American securities and by the appreciation of U.S. assets. Foreign buying supported the dollar. The appreciation of U.S. house prices provided the cash to spend, through refinancing and home-equity loans. Financial services never had it so good.

How this arrangement worked as an economic system is a story in itself.

THE SEVENTIES, AGAIN

The process over this past decade is similar to that in the 1970s, when Volkswagen shipped the dollars it had received (from sales in the United States) to the Bundesbank. (The Chinese central bank has received the most excess dollars in the current decade, but the process is the same, so the original example is continued.)

Volkswagen sold a car in the United States. It received dollars from the buyer. The German central bank issued deutschmarks to Volkswagen in return for the dollars. In the post-2000 decade, the Bundesbank made the

---

[4] From the month of December 2000 to the month of September 2004; *Richebächer Letter*, December 2004, p. 2.

[5] *Richebächer Letter*, July 2004, p. 11; NIPA data.

[6] Bureau of Labor Statistics, "Employer Costs for Employee Compensation–December 2008," Table 1, released March 12, 2009.

[7] *Richebächer Letter*, December 2004, p. 2.

[8] "Should Bush Tell America to Go Shopping Again?" *WSJ.com*, October 7, 2008.

decision that its excess dollars would be allocated to investment in U.S. Treasury securities. Thus, by buying the U.S. debt, the German central bank funded American shoppers. When the Bundesbank bought U.S. securities, the German central bank also controlled the slide of the U.S. dollar in relation to the deutschmark.

A central bank may be influenced by its government. The German government had a motivation to prop up the dollar. If the dollar fell too far, Volkswagens would be unaffordable to Americans.

This same pattern of currency circulation anchored the world trade and financing system when Bernanke became Fed chairman. China was most often cited, but there were many countries exporting more goods to the United States than they received in return. Americans were buying from foreign industries, but foreigners did not buy as much from American manufacturers and service providers. This shortfall meant that American companies did not participate in these international flows. As a result, U.S. companies sold fewer goods. Domestic companies had fewer revenues, since workers were not spending their money on U.S. goods. Lower revenues of U.S. companies reduced profits and salaries. American corporations were forced to restructure in order to compete with foreign competition. Layoffs followed, and companies outsourced jobs overseas. This had been true since the 1970s.

The dollars that bought toys from the Chinese were sent by the toy manufacturer to the Chinese central bank. The toy manufacturer received Chinese currency (the yuan) from the central bank. The yuan entered the Chinese economy: the "real" economy as opposed to the financial economy.

The Chinese central bank then shipped the Chinese toy manufacturer's dollars back to the United States. Earlier in this decade, foreign central banks recycled dollars into U.S. Treasury securities. As the current account deficit rose further, they bought agency securities (from Fannie Mae and Freddie Mac), believing the U.S. government would back these bonds should the underlying assets in the securities default (mortgage payments in San Diego, for instance). Between 2002 and 2007, almost 40 percent of the increase in Fannie Mae, Freddie Mac and other U.S. government agency securities were bought by foreign central banks.[9]

---

[9] Russell Napier, "Nationalizing America," *CLSA Asia-Pacific Markets*, March 2008, p. 12.

When the Chinese central banks sent dollars back to the United States, investment banks and brokerage houses were on the receiving end. The banks and brokerages manufactured the securities. The dollars did not return to the "real" economy but to the financial economy. Goldman Sachs or Lehman Brothers received the dollars; the Chinese paid for securities produced by Goldman Sachs. Financial company revenues and profits rose. Securities firms hired more workers. This overseas bond trade shifted significant amounts of corporate profits in the United States toward financial institutions.

These distortions caused malignancies in the U.S. economy. From 1950 to 1980, about $1.40 or $1.45 of debt was required to produce each dollar of GDP. From 2001 through 2005, the ratio was $4.30 of debt to every dollar of nominal growth.[10] Finance, rather than capital investment, generated growth.

BERNANKE'S WORLD

Ben Bernanke seemed to think that all was well. He was not concerned about the trade and finance imbalances. He was a leading missionary of a hot phrase: the "global savings glut." He chided foreigners for saving too much. In Bernanke's world, Americans were consuming as they should. His statement at the head of the chapter is from a "global savings glut" speech delivered in March 2005. In April, with time to revise his insight, he showed no better grasp of home economics: "[T]he recent capital inflow into the developed world has shown up in higher rates of home construction and in higher home prices. Higher home prices in turn have encouraged households to increase their consumption. Of course, increased rates of homeownership and household consumption are both good things."[11] Even today, Bernanke's economics remain uncluttered with the possibility of too much debt. He is still a gung-ho apostle of renewing economic growth through consumer borrowing and spending.

---

[10] *Richebächer Letter*, March 2006, p. 10.

[11] Ben S. Bernanke, "Global Savings Glut and the U.S. Current Account Deficit," Homer Jones Lecture, St. Louis, Missouri, April 14, 2005.

Before his chairmanship, he gave a speech entitled "The Great Moderation." In that 2004 address, Bernanke offered interpretations of the "remarkable decline in the variability of both output and inflation" over the past two decades. He permitted the possibility that structural changes to the economy and luck may have played their role, but left no doubt that *"improved performance of macroeconomic policies,* particularly monetary policy" should receive the Nobel Prize.[12] [Bernanke's italics].

Bernanke's "great moderation" has since exploded, leaving this speech as a testament to the accumulated wisdom of central bankers. He was blind to the financial mayhem that accompanied his economic moderation. In 2008, researchers at the International Monetary Fund (IMF) identified 124 international banking crises since 1970. Four were in the 1970s, 39 were in the 1980s, 74 were in the 1990s, and 7 were after the millennium.[13] The current worldwide banking crisis is not included. It would be premature to quantify it.

The Great Moderation was, in fact, the Great Distortion.

THE PEAK

We now know that the housing bubble peaked sometime in 2005 or early 2006. Ben S. Bernanke was sworn in as Federal Reserve chairman on February 1, 2006. The brightest guys in the room thought that the excesses were about to collapse. Sam Zell, owner of Equity Office Properties, offered his opinion: "The enormous monetization of hard assets has created a massive amount of liquidity.... Together with [the rising demand for income in the developed world], these factors ... are reducing the relative expectations on equity."[14]

Another who saw the sun setting was Stephen Schwartzman, head of Blackstone Group, perhaps the premier buyout firm over the past two decades. He told an audience: "We have low [interest] rates, tons of

---

[12] Ben Bernanke, "The Great Moderation," speech at the meetings of the Eastern Economic Association, Washington, D.C., February 20, 2004.

[13] Luc Laeven and Fabian Valencia, "Systemic Banking Crises: A New Database," IMF, October 2008, p. 56.

[14] From Sam Zell's 2005 electronic Christmas card, "The Theory of Relativity," www.yieldsz.com; quoted in Ted Pincus, "Zell Remains Relaxed about Economy as Others Fret," *Chicago Sun-Times,* September 12, 2006.

money in both the private equity and debt markets.... But when it ends,
it always ends badly. One of those signs is when the dummies can get
money and that's where we are now."[15]

However, Zell and Schwartzman misestimated. Even though the
housing splurge was over, the financial economy's credit machinery was
speeding up. The nominal value of derivative contracts held by U.S. *commercial* banks (those over which the Fed has direct regulatory authority)
leapt from $33 trillion at the end of 1998 to $101 trillion at the end of
2005, about the time Greenspan left office. This was roughly a 17 percent annual increase. By the second quarter of 2007, 18 months later, the
nominal value had risen by 50 percent—to $153 trillion in derivatives.[16]
Did the credit creators take advantage of the novice? Whatever the case,
Bernanke seemed unaware of the ruckus.

Finance was called upon to prevent the direst threat to Washington: a
recession. Funds were directed at the most egregious commercial propositions. Wall Street funded the builders. Finding bodies to occupy the
new developments would be the greatest challenge, but not now. The
investment banks financed developers to increase the flow of mortgage
securitization. The banks wound up owning half-finished developments
in the desert, abandoned by bankrupt builders.

Likewise, banks were not, as was generally believed, selling all the
mortgages they wrote. In early 2007, they held $3.4 trillion worth of direct
mortgages, land development, and construction loans on their books.
This was about 33 percent of commercial bank assets. Adding mortgage
securities increased real estate exposure to 43 percent of assets.[17]

The United States was not the only economy that was vulnerable to
financial excesses. In 2005, McKinsey Global Institute calculated that the
ratio of global financial assets to annual world output had risen from
109 percent in 1980 to 316 percent in 2005.[18]

Financing fed on itself. Increasing leverage was important. The brokers and dealers had doubled their trading assets since 2000. This growth

---

[15] Doug Noland, *Credit Bubble Bulletin*, February 25, 2006, p. 10.

[16] From Office of the Controller of the Currency Quarterly Reports on Bank Derivative
Activities.

[17] Federal Deposit and Insurance Commission, Statistics on Depository Institutions,
March 31, 2007.

was not to help companies finance new inventions, but to leverage their balance sheets. Broker/dealers expanded their assets by $282 billion in 2005 (the largest increase in a single year), then added $615 billion in 2006.[19] The carry trade was estimated in trillions of dollars.

The Federal Reserve creates money but does not control where it flows. The banks distribute funding through the economy where they believe it will be most profitable to them. Funding brokerage operations was very profitable. It might also have been seen as necessary, since hedge funds were buying a large proportion of derivative securities, underwritten by the banks.

Mortgage securities had grown more complex. The asset-backed or mortgage-backed bonds of the late 1990s were gathered into collateralized debt obligations (CDOs). The volume of CDOs rose from $157 billion in 2004 to $557 billion in 2006. This does not include synthetic CDOs, which rose from $225 billion in 2005 to $450 billion in 2006.[20] (Synthetic CDOs are derivatives of CDOs, so they are not backed by any mortgage payments, subprime or not.)

These numbers address only a portion of the rising risk in the financial institutions and hedge funds. The leverage employed at different levels of ownership was at least as important as the poor quality of the mortgages. Gillian Tett of the *Financial Times* quoted from an e-mail sent by a banker. The banker had worked "in the leveraged credit and distressed debt sector for 20 years." His career had never been more exciting: "I don't think there has ever been a time in history when such a large proportion of the riskiest credit assets have been owned by such financially weak institutions ... with very limited capacity to withstand adverse credit events and market downturns." The leveraged-credit specialist described the case of a typical hedge fund, two times leveraged. That hedge fund is supported by a fund of funds, which is three times leveraged. The fund of funds invested in "deeply subordinated tranches

---

[18] *Financial Times*, June 19, 2007. Also from McKinsey: "The global stock of financial assets had reached $140 trillion."

[19] Doug Noland, "Credit Bubble Bulletin," Prudent Bear Web site, March 9, 2007, p. 11.

[20] Noland, "Credit Bubble Bulletin," February 16, 2007, p. 8; Noland is quoting from Paul J. Davies, "Sales of Risky 'Synthetic' CDOS Boom," *Financial Times*, February 12, 2007.

of collateralized debt obligations, which are nine times leveraged." The result: "Thus every $1 million of CDO bonds is supported by $20,000 of end user's capital—a 2% decline in the CDO paper wipes out the capital supporting it."[21]

A CDO is a theoretical financial institution. In James Grant's phrase, it is a "paper bank, lacking walls and depositors but possessing assets and liabilities and equity."[22] It collects various debt obligations—bonds, bank loans, car loans, and mortgages, for instance—and sells pieces of the package to different investors. The pieces of the package carry different investment grades, from AAA on down.

This complexity is beyond the resources of buyers. They rely on the credit rating agencies—Standard & Poor's, Moody's, and Fitch—which rate each tranche. The AAA ratings were taken as given by buyers, despite their undoubted poor understanding of what they were buying.

The complexity of the AAA-rated "ACE Securities, Series 2005-HE5 CDO" was not uncommon. It included 7,212 first- and second-lien mortgages when it was issued.[23] Some of these CDOs owned pieces of millions of mortgages, sometimes owning the same mortgage three or four times, since one layer of a CDO might be owned by another layer and so on.

One other growing class of derivatives deserves mention, especially since Alan Greenspan sang its praises into 2008: credit default swaps (CDS). These were originally designed to hedge against losses should a company enter bankruptcy. The purchaser pays a premium for bankruptcy protection. Credit default swaps would appeal to General Motors bondholders who wanted to hedge—hold an "insurance" policy— against General Motors declaring bankruptcy.

The original intention expanded. Credit default swaps were written for other derivatives, such as CDOs. The complications of credit default swaps written on CDOs that combined several CDOs (CDOs squared) were recreational mathematics played with other people's money.

---

[21] Gillian Tett, "The Unease Bubbling in Today's Brave New Financial World," *Financial Times* (London edition), January 19, 2007, p. 36. Tett wrote that she did not know the banker, but the numbers put into writing what we were hearing at the time.

[22] *Grant's Interest Rate Observer*, April 6, 2007, p. 2.

[23] *Grant's Interest Rate Observer*, March 7, 2008, p. 10.

25

FAST MONEY ON THE CRACK-UP

2006

> I'm going to be a rich man when this war is over, Scarlett.... I told
> you once before that there were two times for making big money, one
> in the upbuilding of a country and the other in its destruction. Slow
> money on the upbuilding, fast money in the crack-up. Remember my
> words.[1]
>
> —*Rhett Butler, in* Gone with the Wind *(1936)*

On February 12, 2006, two weeks after chairman Greenspan retired, he
reportedly received $250,000 to speak at a dinner that Lehman Broth-
ers hosted for hedge-fund managers.[2] It was a surprise to many that he
spoke at all. That he spoke publicly, and for money, was undignified.
This reflected solely on Greenspan. Worse, he was interfering with the
Bernanke Fed. On the lecture circuit, he would talk about interest rates,
inflation, and the dollar. His predictions overshadowed his successor's
attempts to establish credibility.

He told the Bond Market Association that "credit default swaps are
becoming the most important instrument I've seen in decades.... For

---

[1] Margaret Mitchell, *Gone with the Wind* (New York: Scribner, 1936), pp. 241–242.
[2] Roddy Boyd and Niles Lathem, "Want Alan Greenspan to Come to Dinner? That'll Be
$250,000 ..." *New York Post*, February 9, 2006.

decades we used to have monetary crises because banks" could "freeze up." Credit default swaps "lay off all these loans."[3] Greenspan could not have been more wrong if he tried, but he was speaking to the bond industry, so his listeners enjoyed the quotable endorsement. The failure of Lehman Brothers in 2008 would show the degree to which financial institutions froze up from exposure to credit default swaps. The Bond Market Association announced that it was creating the annual "Alan Greenspan Award for Market Leadership."[4]

In October, speaking in Canada, Greenspan claimed that the housing boom was due to global integration, but the system "ran out of steam because no one could afford houses anymore."[5] Two weeks later, Greenspan claimed: "Most of the negatives in housing are probably behind us. It's taking less out of the economy."[6] Exactly one week after Greenspan predicted a housing recovery, his opinion was expertly choreographed into a National Association of Realtors $40 million advertising campaign. The full-page newspaper ads spread good news: "It's a Great Time to Buy or Sell a House." Greenspan's contribution to the layout (which filled the upper right-hand quadrant) fell under the heading of "Positive Outlook" He assured us that the fourth quarter of 2006 will "certainly be better than the third quarter."[7]

In October, Greenspan also noted it was fashionable to short the dollar: "Central banks around the world and private investors are beginning to shift holdings from the dollar to the euro." He contended that "the trade and budget deficits aren't a problem."[8] They weren't *a* problem, they were *the* problem. Some countries made no effort to disguise their

[3] Caroline Salas, "Derivatives, Not Bonds, Show What Pimco, TIAA-CREF Really Think," Bloomberg, May 31, 2006.

[4] Press release, "Association Announces Creation of the Alan Greenspan Award for Market Leadership," May 18, 2006.

[5] Krishna Guha, "Housing Boom Due to Global Integration," *Financial Times*, October 9, 2006.

[6] Jessica Holzer, "Greenspan Sees a Soft Landing," *Forbes*, October 26, 2006.

[7] PDF of ad, from National Association of Realtors Web site: http://tinyurl.com/yz33ym. Under "Positive Outlook": "Former Federal Reserve Chairman Alan Greenspan recently said that housing prospects are looking up. 'Most of the negatives in housing are probably behind us. The fourth quarter should be reasonably good, certainly better then the third quarter.'"

[8] Chuck Butler, "Greenspan Is Still Crazy," *Daily Reckoning*, October 27, 2006.

antagonisms towards the United States, but it is doubtful that they would have threatened to leave the dollar orbit if the United States had paid its bills and ran an honest monetary policy.[9] In December, he was once again down on the dollar because, with such a large current account deficit, it was "imprudent" to hold a single currency."[10]

Greenspan was as confused in retirement as he had been when he was at the Fed: nobody could afford a house; housing had bottomed. The current account deficit did not matter; the current account deficit was all that mattered.

LEVERAGED BUYOUTS, AGAIN

By the middle of 2006, new dimensions were appearing too fast to comprehend. Private-equity firms elbowed hedge funds from the center ring. "Private equity" was this cycle's euphemism.[11] *Conglomerateur* was passé; *entrepreneur* was worn out; and the most accurate description, *LBO firm*, was not good for public relations. In July 2006, Kohlberg Kravis Roberts set a new LBO record with a $33 billion buyout of Hospital Corporation of America (HCA).[12] Henry Kravis was elated: he had never seen a market with so much liquidity.[13] A few months later, Kravis would crow: "The private equity world is in its golden era right now."[14]

---

[9] Several countries had recently threatened to conduct trade in other currencies.

[10] Chuck Butler, "Big Al Coming Over to Our Side," *Daily Reckoning*, December '12, 2006.

[11] It was also confusing. "Equity" means the ownership in a company. But as the private equity boom proceeded, the private equity firms borrowed more to finance the deals—they became more leveraged. The confusing terminology (thus, understanding) can be seen in the following: "[Blackstone Group] took on about $80 bn in debt over the past three years. Blackstone ... has deployed a total of $98 bn in financing over the three years, including equity from its private equity funds. Sources close to the company confirmed that about 80% of this was in debt financing." Source: James Mawson and David Rothnie, "Private equity group to use partnership structure," *Financial News*, March 22, 2007.

[12] "Hospital Move Presents Buy-Out Groups with New Risks," *Financial Times*, July 25, 2006.

[13] James Taylor, "KKR Fund Splashes $200m on Mystery Investment," *Financial News Online*, August 18, 2006.

[14] Richard Teitelbaum, "KKR Outspends Blackstone, Instills Profit-First Creed," Bloomberg, June 29, 2007. Kravis had spoken at a dinner in April 2007.

Stephen Schwarzman's Blackstone Group had raised $30 billion over the previous 12 months. This was only $2 billion short of the total it had raised in its previous 19 years of operation.[15] On July 24, Reuters ran a headline that contradicted the central banking establishment, a confused flock that made speech after speech congratulating itself for stabilizing prices: "Bubbles Caused by Cheap Cash Menace World Economy."[16] Late in the summer, Ed Keon from Prudential Securities was more emphatic: "Clearly I'm exaggerating here, but what's the difference between a $30 billion and a $300 billion deal? It's just a few more phone calls."[17] If history was to repeat itself, asset levitation was peaking. Conglomerations of the early 1970s and LBOs of the late 1980s were the last word in excess.

As the bankruptcies of U.S. corporations pile up, private equity's role should not be exaggerated. Corporate managements had gladly added debt to their balance sheets for decades. Financial theory (the efficient market hypothesis and its siblings) led corporations to borrow more to increase earnings. Theory took a practical form by suggesting that stock options for senior executives would prod them to work harder. This went under the banner of "maximizing shareholder value." Stock options grew in stature, and LBO firms spread the gospel. In 1976, the average CEO was paid 36 times the average worker's salary. In 1993, the multiple was 131. In 2006, it was 369 times average pay.[18] Equity was often replaced with debt. Nonfinancial companies were paying out more than 100 percent of their profits in dividends and buybacks.[19]

Competition to lend to private equity firms was fierce. There was practically no spread between the borrowing and lending rates. Yet, bank loans to finance leveraged syndicated deals grew from $220 billion in 2005 to

---

[15] Peter Smith, "Blackstone Quickens Pace with $15.6bn Fund," *Financial Times*, July 12, 2006.

[16] Stella Dawson, "Bubbles Caused by Cheap Cash Menace World Economy," Reuters, July 24, 2006.

[17] "The LBO Gang Storms the Valley," *BusinessWeek*, September 11, 2006.

[18] *Wall Street Journal*, "Behind Executive Pay, Decades of Failed Restraints," October 12, 2006.

[19] Andrew Smithers, "Why Balance Sheets Are Not in Good Shape," *Financial Times*, August 30, 2007. Since 1984, stock buybacks and dividend payouts have exceeded profit retention. Equity of U.S. corporations has fallen more than 3 percent annually. A 3-percent-per-year decrease over 20 years is significant.

$360 billion in 2006, and to $570 billion in the *first half* of 2007.[20] Recipients of funds warned the banks. Steven Rattner, managing principal of Quadrangle Group LLC, a successful private-equity fund, was quoted by Reuters in April 2007: "Of all the bubbles, the bubble in the credit market today is one of the greatest—it is beyond any rational measure. Frankly, we are feasting on the imprudence of our lenders. They are subsidizing our transactions and are allowing us to make deals that wouldn't have made sense."[21]

Why would banks take such risks? Lloyd Greif, an investment banker in Los Angeles, was quoted in the July 7, 2006, edition of *American Banker*: "The greed factor has kicked in as lenders see they can collect fees not just once or twice, but sometimes several times from refinancing leveraged buyout deals over and over again."[22]

No one stopped the money machinery. The Fed cannot direct banks where to lend, but, as regulator, it has the authority to halt dangerous excesses. The Federal Reserve restricted bank credit used for acquisitions in 1980.[23] It would have been worth the trouble to do so again. Bank loans to finance irrational deals started defaulting at a worrisome pace after Greenspan retired, but the latest LBO craze was destroying wealth while he was still at the Fed. Greenspan, unlike Bernanke, had had a front-row seat during the conglomerate and junk-bond climaxes. The aftermath of both left companies and industries in ruin. It was happening again.

Despite Bernanke's inexperience, he should have known. In March 2007, reporters at the *Wall Street Journal* told readers: "Hedge-fund managers, buyout artists, and bankers get paid for short-term performance.... People inside the big banks ... don't want to get caught missing the next big deal. Their banks, and their own bonuses, might suffer."[24]

---

[20] Profits and Balance Sheet Developments at U.S. Commercial Banks in 2007, *Federal Reserve Bulletin*, Volume 94, 2008.

[21] Mark McSherry, "LBO Players Say Debt Boom Won't Go On Forever," Reuters, April 11, 2007.

[22] Lloyd Greif, "Lenders Absorbing More Risk in LBOs These Days," *American Banker*, July 7, 2006.

[23] Barrie A. Wigmore, *Securities Markets in the 1980s*, vol. 1 (New York: Oxford University Press, 1997), p. 354.

[24] "Sketchy Loans Abound," *Wall Street Journal*, March 28, 2007.

HOLLOWING OUT AMERICA

The allotment of bank loans to private equity firms was the reason that a $300 billion deal was worth imagining. Chapter 3 quoted John Brooks's assessment of how the conglomerate craze hollowed out the soul of America: "The result was the repeated reduction of mid-American cities' established industries from the independent ventures to subsidiaries of conglomerate spiderwebs based in New York or Los Angeles."[25]

In 2005, David Urban, chief operating officer of Firebird Management LLC, New York, wrote about the decline of Wilkes-Barre, Pennsylvania, where he had grown up: "The manufacturing base had been hollowed out decades before.... In the mid to late 1980's, banks from Pittsburgh and Philadelphia moved into the area pursuing their growth strategy by attempting to offer branch banking services on a statewide basis. All of the major banks were bought up and in the ensuing consolidations the back office and service jobs were cut in the area. The downtown fell into disrepair while corrupt politicians argued and pointed fingers over who was to blame while fattening the pockets of their supporters. The young people, as I was one, left the area to pursue better opportunities after high school since we did not see any value in staying behind. There were no growth industries and the jobs remaining were mainly family businesses or chain restaurants."[26]

In 2009, the zany infatuation with "GDP growth," no matter what the source, continues. Over 40 years ago, Robert Kennedy said that the gross national product "measures everything ... except that which makes life worthwhile."[27]

PROXMIRE'S FEAR: THE LEVERAGED TOO-BIG-TO-FAIL MEGABANK

The end was near. Stephen Schwatzman's Blackstone Group paid $39 billion for Sam Zell's Equity Office Properties. Zell had cashed out. Schwartzman started selling the properties immediately. Others were playing Russian roulette, borrowing as much as they could as fast as they could.

---

[25] John Brooks, *The Go-Go Years* (New York: Weybright and Talley, 1973), p. 177.

[26] *Gloom, Boom & Doom Report*, December 9, 2005.

[27] Robert F. Kennedy, Remarks at the University of Kansas, March 18, 1968.

Senator William Proxmire foresaw the conflict of interests when he interrogated Alan Greenspan in 1987, though the senator probably did not imagine the "massive amount of liquidity" that now poured into buying and trading some of the largest corporations in the world. During the first quarter of 2007 (December 2006 through February 2007), the balance sheet assets of Goldman Sachs, Lehman Brothers, Morgan Stanley, and Bear Stearns rose by $237 billion, a $1 trillion annual rate and a 34 percent annualized growth rate.[28] Goldman Sachs had a bigger balance sheet than the Fed's.[29] These were brokerage firms, not commercial banks.

Commercial and investment banks opened hedge funds; the largest hedge fund in the world was at Goldman Sachs.[30] Private-equity firms launched hedge funds. Banks opened private-equity funds. All were buying and selling property—housing developments, ports, power grids, hotel chains, airports, railroads, and highways. All were paying one another: hedge funds borrowing from brokers; investment banks buying mortgages from commercial banks; LBO firms borrowing from commercial banks; LBO firms paying investment banks for underwriting services. Kohlberg Kravis Roberts, Henry Kravis's firm, paid investment banks $837 million for advice during the first 11 months of 2006.[31] The U.S. securities industry paid itself $455 billion between 2003 and 2007.[32] This was a much more concentrated form of asset inflation than housing. The casing of the cocoon had to remain solid. The level of credit and profits rose inside the casing.

Stephen Schwartzman collected billions of dollars from Blackstone's IPO.[33] This was a big media story, although it's not clear why, since he had been collecting billions for quite a while.[34] *Time* called him

---

[28] Doug Noland, "Credit Bubble Bulletin," Prudent Bear Web site, April 20, 2007, p. 10.

[29] Goldman Sachs Group Inc. and Subsidiaries, condensed Consolidated Statements of Financial Condition (Unaudited), released April 3 or 4, 2007, for quarter ending February 28, 2007: total assets, $912 billion. Federal Reserve's total assets on February 28, 2007: $853 billion: Federal Reserve Statistical Release H.4.1, March 1, 2007.

[30] Alistair Barr, "Goldman Is Now World's Largest Hedge Fund Manager," *MarketWatch*, June 21, 2006.

[31] Edward Evans, "KKR to Pay Most in Fees in Record Year for Buyouts," Bloomberg, January 4, 2007.

[32] Christopher Wood, "Greed & Fear," *CLSA Asia-Pacific Markets*, August 22, 2008.

[33] Justin Fox, "Blackstone: Too Rich for Congress," *Time*, June 28, 2007.

[34] Barbara Kiviat, "The Time 100: Steven Schwarzman," *Time*, April 30, 2007.

one of the "100 most influential people." His sixtieth birthday party in February 2007 was the place to be. Guests included CNBC's Maria Bartiromo, perhaps the most familiar face in trading rooms during the boom years other than Alan Greenspan. She was accompanied by her husband, Jonathan Steinberg, son of Saul Steinberg.[35]

Saul's is a cautionary tale. His insurance company, Reliance Holdings, was forced into bankruptcy; his Old Masters collection was auctioned. He sold his 36-room duplex at 740 Park Avenue—first owned by John D. Rockefeller—to Stephen Schwarzman in 2000.

By the time of Schwarzman's party, private equity—a term that was as unfamiliar to the public as IPO was before 1995—attracted wide attention, as well it might, since no company was too big to buy and then dismiss the employees. The *Financial Times* produced a Special Report with the title: "Barbarians or Emperors?"[36] *CFO* magazine described Goldman Sachs's $20 billion private equity fund as "Gargantuans at the Gate."[37]

Politicians were foaming and ranting about private equity. This is the moment, as we've seen before, when politicians take charge and shut the casino—Saul Steinberg's attempt to buy Chemical Bank; Kohlberg Kravis Roberts's gathering of 400 dealmakers to celebrate to celebrate the RJR takeover—the script is clear.

But it didn't happen.

The elected representatives came to their senses. The members of House of Representatives could no longer represent; they were beholden to Fannie Mae, hedge funds, and private equity. It was not only contributions but their own futures that were at stake. The ex-pols used to cross the street and join lobbying firms. Now they hitched onto a hedge fund, private-equity firm, or both (these were growing more difficult to tell apart). Or they joined banks. Phil Gramm, former Republican senator from Texas, was vice chairman of UBS (United Bank of Switzerland); Robert Rubin, secretary of the treasury under President Clinton, served as a director at Citicorp. Leading politicians from the

---

[35] Dan Ackman, "Forbes Face: Saul Steinberg," *Forbes.com, June 18, 2001.*

[36] *Financial Times,* Special Report "Private Equity: Barbarians or Emperors?" April 24, 2007.

[37] Stephen Taub, "Gargantuans at the Gate," *CFO.com,* April 23, 2007.

Clinton and two Bush presidencies had joined hedge funds or private-equity firms. A roll call in mid-2007: Lawrence Summers (secretary of the treasury, Clinton administration, and former voting member of the Harvard Corporation's then-$29 billion endowment) joined D.E. Shaw, a $25 billion hedge fund,[38] President George H. W. Bush, James Baker (secretary of the treasury and state, Reagan administration; secretary of state, Bush I), and former British Prime Minister John Major, all served the Carlyle Group in different capacities; Former President Bill Clinton marketed a retail hedge fund in his spare time.[39] Former Vice President Al Gore[40] and Madeline Albright (secretary of state, Clinton)[41] launched their own hedge funds as well.

THE PINNACLE

The tendency for politicians to join hedge funds or LBO firms rather than Wall Street banks was for a good reason: they paid better. Average weekly pay for investment bankers in New York was $16,849 a week. In Fairfield County, Connecticut, where hedge funds are more concentrated, average weekly pay was $23,846 a week.[42] In 2006, the top 100 hedge fund managers in the world each earned an average of $241 million.[43]

The hedge fund capital is Greenwich, Connecticut, a 40-minute train ride from Manhattan. For decades, it has been home to corporate CEOs, stockbrokers, and investment bankers who boarded the 8:01 to Grand Central Station. The commute was reversing. In 2006, approximately

---

[38] Marcella Bombardieri, "Ex-Harvard Chief Joins Hedge Fund Company," *Boston Globe,* October 20, 2006.

[39] William Hutchings, "Bill Clinton Endorses Quadriga's Retail U.S. Hedge Funds," *efinancialnews.com,* which is: Dow Jones financial news online, March 10, 2005. "Bill Clinton, the former U.S. president, is set to open a New York retail outlet for the products of Quadriga, the Viennese hedge fund manager that was last year stopped from selling its products in Germany by the local regulator because it had no banking licence.[sic]"

[40] www.generationim.com.

[41] Otis Bilodeau, "Madeleine Albright Raises $329 Million for New Fund," Bloomberg, January 18, 2007.

[42] David Cay Johnston, "Pay at Investment Banks Eclipses All Private Jobs," *New York Times,* September 1, 2007. This was calculated by the Bureau of Labor Statistics for the first quarter of 2006.

[43] "Richest Hedge Fund Managers Get Richer," *CNNMoney,* April 9, 2007.

10 percent of the world's hedge-fund money was managed from offices in Greenwich. Analysts and traders caught the 5:09 (a.m.) from Grand Central to Greenwich. These offices commanded rents nearly 30 percent higher than prime office space in New York.

Hedge-fund managers, generally quick to trade, buy, and dispose, demonstrated the same relish in bulldozing houses built in the 1920s for Rockefellers, Havemayers, and Greenways. The teardown, knock-up construction turned North Street into a traffic jam of road graders, dump trucks, and wrecking balls. Tudor mansions with 6,000 square feet fell; 15,000-square-foot trophy homes scampered up. (That is the size of an industrial warehouse.) When the 15,000-square-foot pile was deemed inadequate, 20,000-, 25,000-, and 30,000-square-foot havens from humanity rose both east and west. Paul Tudor Jones II built a testament described as "a cross between Tara and a national monument." Steve Cohen's house resembled Windsor Castle from the air, and was littered with Gaughins, Van Goghs, Hirsts, and Warhols. Standard features in Greenwich included indoor basketball and squash courts, dishwashers from Asko, windows from Zeluck, basements with wine cellars, waterfalls, hockey rinks, panic rooms, and patios and polo fields surrounded by English country gardens.

The staffing never stopped—chauffeurs, butlers, maids, Scottish nannies, sommeliers, decorators, lighting-control specialists, stonemasons, carpenters, marble cutters, personal trainers, Zen masters, and fashion assistants. Seven-figure gardening bills require estate superintendents, irrigation specialists, and hedge trimmers.

The trickle-down effect runs to the busloads of housekeepers, busboys, gardeners, pool boys, masseurs, hairdressers, and manicurists who made the reverse commute from New York.[44]

THE BOTTOM

At the other end of the Great Distortion, house prices were out of reach, so terms had been relaxed. The "2 and 28" mortgage—a two-year

---

[44] Nina Munk, "Greenwich's Outrageous Fortunes," *Vanity Fair,* July 2006; Tom Wolfe, "The Pirate Pose," *Portfolio.com,* May 2007; Philip Shishkin, "Out with the Old: Storied Mansions Fall in Greenwich," *Wall Street Journal,* April 12, 2008; *Greenwich Time* newspaper.

"teaser" rate that adjusted ("reset") for the next 28 years—was booming. Since the 2/28 was fairly new to the market, the consequences were not well understood in 2006. (Better put: there were few who let on that they anticipated the inevitable.) The resets would hit hard in 2007.

Sam Zell's observation in 2005 that the "enormous monetization of hard assets has created a massive amount of liquidity" put food on the table, but for how long? More Americans were liquefying their equity and monetizing the proceeds. Since 2001, the GDP had grown by $2.5 trillion; over $800 billion of home equity had been withdrawn in 2005. This was equal to 9 percent of Americans disposable income, in a country where wages were basely rising. ACNielson published a report that described Americans as "among the world's most cash-strapped people."[45] With 22 percent of Americans having no money left after they paid for essential living expenses, the U.S. ranked number one among 42 countries for "saving futility."[46]

The new Federal Reserve chairman gave a speech in June 2006. He proclaimed: "U.S. households have been managing their personal finances well."[47] It seemed as though Greenspan had never left.

---

[45] Les Christie, "Americans: World's Worst Savers," *CNNMoney.com*, January 25, 2006.

[46] Ibid.

[47] Ben S. Bernanke, "Increasing Economic Opportunity: Challenges and Strategies," speech at the Fifth Regional Issues Conference of the Fifteenth Congressional District of Texas, Washington, D.C., June 13, 2006.

26

CHEAP TALK: GREENSPAN AND THE BERNANKE FED

2007

New York Times: [T]here are at least 15,000 professional economists in this country, and you're saying only two or three of them foresaw the mortgage crisis?

James K. Galbraith: Ten or 12 would be closer than two or three.... It's an enormous blot on the reputation of the profession. There are thousands of economists. Most of them teach. And most of them teach a theoretical framework that has been shown to be fundamentally useless.

—New York Times Sunday Magazine, *November 2, 2008*

In 2007, Greenspan came out talking. Speaking to a Hong Kong audience in late February, he warned of a possible recession in the United States. The Shanghai Stock Exchange fell 9 percent that day, and U.S. stock markets suffered their worst day of trading since they reopened after the September 11, 2001 respite.[1] The oracle later clarified his prediction. He thought a 2007 recession was "possible" but not "probable."[2] Still, he was at odds with the Federal Reserve's position.

There is no reason that he should have agreed, but given his influence on markets, a better man would have discussed the weather. He could not

---

[1] Rachel Beck, "Greenspan Rocks Markets," Associated Press, February 27, 2007.
[2] Krishna Guha, "Greenspan Again at Odds with Fed over Recession Risk," *Financial Times*, March 6, 2007.

restrain himself. The March 2 headline of the *Independent* (London) said it all: "Greenspan Uses 'R' Word Again; Someone Shut Him Up before He Does Serious Damage."[3] But there was no stopping the man. A *Financial Times* headline on March 6 cited the freelance economist: "Greenspan Again at Odds with Fed over Recession Risk."[4] (He now thought there was a one-third chance of a U.S. recession in 2007.[5]) Greenspan had more to say that day: "We are in the sixth year of a recovery, imbalances can emerge as a result."[6] This was already the most imbalanced economy since the Emerald City of Oz.

Greenspan responded to his detractors: "I was beginning to feel quite comfortable that I was fully back to the anonymity I was seeking." He added: "I try as much as I can to avoid comments relevant to what the Fed is doing. But I have a profession and I'm a private citizen.... I adhere to the law."[7] His face was straight as ever, but he sounded like a stand-up comedian.

By the end of 2006, the Implode-O-Meter Web site listed nine defunct mortgage lenders.[8] By the end of March 2007, the list had grown to 49, including some of the largest vacuums that sucked in borrowers: HSBC Mortgage Services, Ameriquest, ACC Wholesale, New Century, and Wachovia Mortgage. Underwriting standards had collapsed and defaults were rising fast. It seems condescending to mention that this combination meant house prices had risen above an affordable level, but that comment was central to a Greenspan speech on March 15 as reported by MSNBC: "Greenspan said ... subprime woes ... seemed to result primarily from buyers coming into lofty housing markets late after big price run-ups that had left them vulnerable to hikes in adjustable mortgage rates."[9] This was announced by newswires around the world.

---

[3] Jeremy Warner, "Greenspan Uses 'R' Word Again; Someone Shut Him Up before He Does Serious Damage," *Independent* (London), March 2, 2007.

[4] Guha, "Greenspan Again at Odds with Fed."

[5] Craig Torres, "Greenspan Sees One-Third Chance of Recession in 2007," Bloomberg, March 6, 2007.

[6] Ibid.

[7] "Greenspan: Not Trying to Cause Trouble for Ben," Reuters, March 8, 2007.

[8] Implode-O-Meter. These were not necessarily bankrupt, but they had abandoned at least a major segment of their lending activities.

[9] "Housing Advocates Warn of Default 'Tsunami,'" MSNBC.com, March 15, 2007.

Greenspan was speaking in Boca Raton, Florida, where he was named the American Hero of 2007.[10] Greenspan might have made the same observation in 2004; instead, he recommended that Americans take advantage of adjustable-rate mortgages. He might have made the same comment in October 2006, at the time of the National Association of Realtors ad campaign. He made some other elementary observations at Boca Raton. The law-abiding American Hero told his audience that if house prices "would go up 10 percent, the subprime problem would disappear."[11] And if pigs could fly. Greenspan also predicted that subprime mortgage problems would not spread their troubles.[12]

Greenspan's cachet was more ambiguous by now. *USA Today*, referring to the speech, quoted Hugh Johnson, chairman of Johnson Illington Advisors, an investment advisory firm in Albany, New York: "I wish he'd just go away."[13] This was less likely than house prices rising 10 percent. Greenspan had been talking from the moment he retired. It might be added that the chairman's retirement party was on a par with Schwartzman's splurge, the difference being that Greenspan's farewell was in the Blue Room.

Subprime Lending

"Subprime" was soon to join "IPO" and "private equity" as an insider's financial term that enters the national discussion.[14] It was no surprise

---

[10] "Greenspan Revels in New Freedom of Speech," *Palm Beach Post*, March 15, 2007. Also from the *Palm Beach Post*: "*Stocks, Futures and Options* magazine hosted the Boca Raton lunch and gave the 500 attendees money clips and coin-shaped paperweights emblazoned with the market maestro's image."

[11] "Greenspan: Subprime Spillover Unlikely," Associated Press, March 15, 2007; http://tinyurl.com/p8c9mo.

[12] "Subprime Spillover Unlikely," Associated Press, March 15, 2007.

[13] "When Alan Greenspan Talks, People Listen," *USA Today*, March 21, 2007.

[14] One definition of subprime: "'Prime' lending was based on the idea that all three C–questions had to get at least a minimally correct answer before proceeding.... If you had, say, two of the three, you might qualify for a near prime (like FHA) or subprime loan...." The 3 Cs are: 1—Credit: "Does the borrower's history establish creditworthiness, or the willingness to repay debt?" 2—Capacity: "Does the borrower's current income and expense situation (and likely future prospects) establish the capacity or ability to repay debt?" 3—Collateral: "Does the house itself, the collateral for the loan, have sufficient value and marketability to protect the lender in the event the debt is not repaid?" From "What Is 'Subprime'?" Calculated Risk blog, November 25, 2007; calculatedrisk.blogspot.com.

that defaults were rising. Default rates remained near zero percent as long as houses could be sold at higher prices.

New Century, one of the largest subprime lenders, depended on house prices to appreciate 4 percent a year. When house prices stopped appreciating in 2005, home buyers defaulted without making a single mortgage payment.[15] Separately, the Mortgage Asset Research Institute had already published a study of what were known as "liar's loans": those in which the borrower's stated income is not verified by the lender. The institute found that 60 percent of those who received such mortgages had overstated their income by at least 50 percent.[16]

Having run out of solvent home buyers, the percentage of high-risk loans came to dominate the marketplace. During the first nine months of 2006, 22 percent were subprime mortgages.[17] By February 2007, 6 percent of mortgages packaged into a security during 2006 were already delinquent.[18]

Bernanke had used practically the same data in a November 2006 speech: "In 1994, fewer than 5 percent of mortgage originations were in the subprime market, but by 2005 about 20 percent of new mortgage loans were subprime." In the same speech, Bernanke went on to discuss other data that should have caused a stir: "[T]he expansion of subprime lending has contributed importantly to the substantial increase in the overall use of mortgage credit. From 1995 to 2004, the share of households with mortgage debt increased 17 percent, and in the lowest income quintile, the share of households with mortgage debt rose 53 percent." Reading the transcript, it appears Bernanke considered this to be good news. He did advise "greater financial literacy" for "borrowers with lower incomes and education levels."[19] The

---

[15] Paul Muolo and Matthew Padilla, *Chain of Blame, How Wall Street Caused the Mortgage and Credit Crisis* (Hoboken, N.J.: Wiley, 2008), pp. 170–171. In 2006, New Century made $60 billion in mortgage loans. Total mortgage loans in the U.S. had been $153 billion in 1995 (see chapter 22). New Century's existence, and contribution to America's GDP, was mostly a product of warehouse lines of credit from investment banks.

[16] *Gloom, Boom & Doom Report*, September 2006, p. 7.

[17] *Grant's Interest Rate Observer*, March 9, 2007, p. 1.

[18] Ibid., March, 2007, p. 1.

former South Carolina seventh-grade spelling bee champion often urged self-improvement.

On May 17, 2007, Bernanke spoke for the Federal Reserve: "[W]e believe the effect of the troubles in the subprime sector on the broader housing market will likely be limited, and we do not expect significant spillovers from the subprime market to the rest of the economy or to the financial system."[20] Bernanke had trouble seeing past the infield, but he should have known two thing: (1) his banking system was dangerously exposed to real estate, and (2) his banking system had never been this leveraged.

The mortgage mills were shutting down, yet Bernanke and Greenspan said problems were contained. In May 2007, house sales in Southern California dropped 35 percent from a year before.[21] Builders could not sell their inventory; first-time owners, many of whom bought with the intention of selling into a rising valuation were, in business terms, "cash-flow negative."

SPRINGTIME FOR GREENSPAN

In June, Greenspan spread the word that the great liquidity boom was near an end and offered fin-de-siècle advice: "Enjoy it while it lasts." He claimed that the liquidity boom started with the end of the cold war.[22] That was about the time Greenspan took up residence in the Eccles Building.

Central bankers dropped their gloves. Mervyn King, governor of the Bank of England (and former colleague of Ben Bernanke when they were both graduate student at MIT), announced: "I'm very grateful to Eddie George that he hasn't been in the newspapers and on the radio all

---

[19] Ben S. Bernanke, "Community Development Financial Institutions: Promoting Economic Growth and Opportunity,"speech at the Opportunity Finance Network's Annual Conference, Washington, D.C., November 1, 2006.

[20] Ben S. Bernanke, speech at the Federal Reserve Bank of Chicago's 43rd Annual Conference on Bank Structure and Competition, Chicago, May 17, 2007.

[21] doctorhousingbubble.com June 14, 2007, citing data released the day before-so these were figures for May.

[22] Pedro Nicolaci da Costa, "Greenspan Not Worried Chinese Will Dump Treasuries," Reuters, June 12, 2007.

the time commenting on what the Monetary Policy Committee is doing. In due course I will do the same."[23] European Central Bank President Jean-Claude Trichet told an audience in Frankfurt: "I do not consider Alan to still be a member of the Fed.... I trust the Fed."[24]

In February 2007, an event of monumental importance went largely unnoticed: a new index of securities based on subprime mortgages was introduced. The securities in this index were each composed of bundles of mortgages that had been originated in the second half of 2006. The BBB-rated portion of the ABX.HE 07-01 dropped like a rock on the first day it was traded. The bonds in the index were still valued at par on bank balance sheets, mostly because CDOs were very rarely traded. *Grant's Interest Rate Observer* thought the "rating agencies seem curiously detached" from the discrepancy between market prices and book values.[25]

The cocoon ruptured in the early summer of 2007. Bear Stearns slowly revealed that two of its aggressively managed hedge funds were worth very little. This was during June and July 2007. On June 15, 2007, Merrill Lynch, which had lent money to Bear Stearns (so that Bear Stearns could leverage its hedge funds), announced that it was seizing $400 million in collateral from the fund.[26] After Merrill demanded its money back, some of the investors in Bear Stearns's funds wanted to take their money out.[27] What should they be paid? Since the value was calculated from a model and not from transactions, Bear Stearns did not know.[28]

The *Financial Times* reported: "These elaborately constructed securities ... are designed to yield juicy returns while also carrying high credit ratings.... Indeed, a distinct irony of the 21st-century financial world is that, while many bankers hail them as the epitome of modern

---

[23] Scheherazade Daneshkhu, "King Takes Greenspan to Task," *Financial Times*, May 16, 2007.

[24] Jean-Claude Trichet, ECB press conference, Frankfurt am Main, Germany, March 8, 2007; http://tinyurl.com/pkpxn7.

[25] *Grant's Interest Rate Observer*, February 26, 2007, p. 7.

[26] Serena Ng and Kate Kelly, "Ills Deepen in Subprime-Bond Arena," *Wall Street Journal*, June 18, 2007.

[27] Paul Muolo and Matthew Padilla, *Chain of Blame: How Wall Street Caused the Mortgage and Credit Crisis*, (Hoboken, N.J.: Wiley, 2008), p. 244.

[28] Ibid., p. 242.

capitalism, many of these new-fangled instruments have never been priced through market trading."[29]

It was ironic, but also necessary. Half of these houses could never have been sold (and would not have been built) without some form of illusory pricing along the conveyor belt. AAA ratings on CCC borrowers had accelerated the mortgage machine. The practice of holding derivatives at par value when there were no prices at all was essential.

AMERICA'S BEST: A TOWER OF BABBLE

At the time Bear Stearns's problems came to light, Bernanke saw clear skies: "[W]e have not seen major spillovers from housing onto other sectors of the economy."[30] Worthy establishment figures demonstrated no understanding of conditions. Bank of America President Ken Lewis said that the worst of the housing slump was just about over: "We're seeing the worst of it."[31] Stanley O'Neal, CEO of Merrill Lynch, earned his bonus the following day, stating that subprime defaults were "reasonably well contained."[32]

It would be unfair to blame the Federal Reserve chairman for the institution's somnolence. From public comments at the time, all of the governors seemed as unenlightened as Bernanke. In January 2007, Frederic Mishkin, former (and future) professor of economics at Columbia University andan author, with Ben S. Bernanke, of *Inflation Targeting: Lessons from the International Experience* (the two were considered the intellectual heavyweights at the Fed); stated: "To begin with, the bursting of asset price bubbles often does not lead to financial instability.... There are even stronger reasons to believe that a bursting of a bubble in house prices

---

[29] Saskia Scholtes and Gillian Tett, "Worries Grow about the True Value of Repackaged Debt," *Financial Times*, June 28, 2007.

[30] Ben S. Bernanke, "The Housing Market and Subprime Lending," speech to the 2007 International Monetary Conference, Cape Town, South Africa (via satellite), June 5, 2007.

[31] Will Edwards, "Bank of America's Lewis Says U.S. Housing Slump Is Almost Over," Bloomberg, June 20, 2007.

[32] Bob Ivry, "Bernanke Was Wrong: Subprime Contagion Is Spreading," Bloomberg, August 10, 2007.

is unlikely to produce financial instability.... [D]eclines in home prices generally have not led to financial instability."[33]

In July 2007, Federal Reserve Board Governor Kevin Warsh announced: "[F]rom the perspective of the institutions we oversee, [the commercial banks], we don't see any immediate systemic risk issues."[34] Warsh added: "[T]he most important providers of market discipline are the large, global commercial and investment banks that are [the hedge funds'] principal creditors and counterparties."[35]

In September, Federal Reserve Governor Randall Kroszner, a former professor of economics at the Booth School of Business at the University of Chicago, relieved fears: "[O]ne of the major lessons to be learned from past banking crises is the importance of a healthy banking system.... Effective banking supervision has helped foster a banking system in the United States that today is safe, sound, and well-capitalized.... Fortunately, this recent period of turbulence in financial markets has occurred at a time when U.S. commercial banks are strongly capitalized, reflecting years of robust profits."[36]

Bernanke seemed incapable of learning from his own experience. In August, Countrywide Bank, a part of Angelo Mozilo's empire, suffered a bank run when depositors fought their way into Countrywide branches. By that time, the Implode-O-Meter Web site listed 126 imploded mortgage companies, including 10 that closed up shop the same week.[37] Yet, Bernanke told a group of central bankers and

---

[33] Frederic S. Mishkin, "Enterprise Risk Management and Mortgage Lending," speech at the Forecaster's Club of New York, New York, January 17, 2007; in addition to Mishkin and Bernanke, there were two other authors of *Inflation Targeting* (Princeton, NJ.: Princeton University Press, 2001): Thomas Laubach and Adam S. Posen.

[34] Kevin Warsh, "Hedge Funds and Systemic Risk: Perspectives on the President's Working Group on Financial Markets," Hearing of the House Financial Services Committee, July 11, 2007.

[35] Ibid.

[36] Randall S. Kroszner, "Analyzing and Assessing Banking Crises," speech at the Federal Reserve Bank of San Francisco Conference on the Asian Financial Crisis Revisited, San Francisco (via videoconference), September 6, 2007.

[37] The Fed followed with a surprising announcement. It would "continue to accept a broad range of collateral for discount window loans, including home mortgages and related assets." This was an extraordinary change on the part of the Fed.

economists in October that he had no way of knowing if there had been a housing bubble.[38]

Elsewhere in Washington, Secretary of the Treasury Hank Paulson told *Fortune* in July 2007: "This is far and away the strongest global economy I've seen in my business lifetime."[39] In August 2007, Paulson said that the subprime mortgage fallout remained "largely contained."[40] (By February 2008, Paulson admitted: "In terms of subprime and the resets, the worst isn't over, the worst is just beginning. We all know that."[41])

In October 2007, Chairman Bernanke abandoned his professorial demeanor at the Economic Club of New York when asked about CDOs: "I'd like to know what those damn things are worth."[42]

---

[38] John Cassidy, "Anatomy of a Meltdown," *New Yorker*, December 1, 2008, p. 9 of 15, from *New Yorker* Web site www.newyorker.com.

[39] Rik Kirkland, "The Greatest Economic Boom Ever," *Fortune*, July 12 2007.

[40] Transcript of Secretary Paulson's Press Roundtable, Beijing, China, August 1, 2007.

[41] http://www.youtube.com/watch?v=ETQj3a221EQ.

[42] Ben Bernanke, in response to a question after his speech at the Economic Club of New York, New York, October 15, 2007, quoted in Edmund L. Andrews, "Treasury Chief Moves to Stabilize Markets; Bernanke Is Troubled by Housing Trend," *New York Times*, October 16, 2007.

27

"I PLEAD NOT GUILTY!"

2007–2008

Fame could distort [reality] but it could not destroy it. It did its own destroying. In the end, we turn [the famous] into characters and put them in a show, a modern version of the passion play. The ones we respect burn like angels. The ones who ask for worship burn like witches. Fame, like happiness destroys anyone who pursues it for its own sake, and exalts only those who have proper work to do.... Achievement without fame can be a good life. Fame without achievement is no life at all.[1]

—*Clive James,* Fame in the Twentieth Century

Penguin published Greenspan's autobiography, *The Age of Turbulence,* in mid-September 2007. Penguin needed to sell a warehouse of books to earn back its advance. The heart of its publicity campaign was Greenspan. He talked everywhere. Unfortunately for him (though maybe not for Penguin), he had become a more controversial figure. The reception of the book as a whole was more favorable than not, but he may have been surprised at the sources of criticism. The day after publication, a *New York Times* editorial ("Mr. Greenspan Spins the Bubble") stated that the "issue is what the Fed did, under Mr. Greenspan's leadership to rein in [the] lending. The answer is nothing." The *Times* established, quite accurately, what to expect from him: "One thing is sure. As long as Mr. Greenspan is defining the terms

---

[1] Clive James, *Fame in the Twentieth Century* (New York: Random House, 1993), pp. 248, 252, 121.

of the debate, there will never be an illuminating discussion of what went wrong to land the economy in the place it is today."[2]

The *Wall Street Journal* kicked off the book tour with a similar editorial ("The Fed's Alibi"): "Mr. Greenspan has emerged from the six-figure speaking circuit with his memoir, 'The Age of Turbulence.'" The *Journal* castigated Greenspan—and Bernanke—for "offering alibis for how we arrived at this pass." It had little patience with a recent speech by the new chairman, in which Bernanke used the "global savings glut" as "his full-field explanation of just about everything.... The problem with this explanation is it omits the Fed's role in producing this 'savings glut.' Billions of people around the world didn't suddenly become more thrifty this decade. It was the Fed's low interest rate policy—especially a 1% fed funds ... that helped spur a global commodity price boom."[3]

The *Journal* went on to condemn the dissembling by Bernanke and Greenspan: "Contrary to the dreams of Wall Street there is no free monetary lunch.... Many on Wall Street want their bubble back and they are begging the Fed to reflate."[4] There was no need to beg; Bernanke loved to cut rates and print money. The *Journal* criticism appeared just before Bernanke slashed rates like a mad professor. He cut the funds rate from 5.25 percent on September 18, 2007, to 1.0 percent on October 29, 2008. By that time, Fed funds were trading at close to zero percent. Bernanke's market support operations were not often labeled the "Bernanke put," but he was as determined as Greenspan to support the stock market. "Millions of intelligent investors" may have appreciated the government's artificial pricing, but if they were, in fact, intelligent, they would have remembered that "the Greenspan put" had failed and led Greenspan to cut the fund's rate to 1.0 percent.

Greenspan was quick to retract any statement from his book that provoked controversy. In *The Age of Turbulence*, he was uncommonly forthright in stating, "I am saddened that it is politically inconvenient to acknowledge what everyone knows: the Iraq War is largely about oil."[5]

---

[2] "Mr. Greenspan Spins the Bubble," *New York Times*, September 18, 2007.

[3] "The Fed's Alibi," *Wall Street Journal*, September 17, 2007.

[4] Ibid.

[5] Alan Greenspan, *The Age of Turbulence: Adventures in a New World* (New York: Penguin, 2007), p. 463.

(In *The Age of Turbulence*, Greenspan is often saddened when others do not live up to his standards, particularly presidents.[6]) After publication, he told the *Washington Post*, "I was not saying that that's the administration's motive."[7] He seemed to think that American troops discovered the Iraqi oil fields after the war started.

Most reviewers and initial media commentary concentrated on his unhappiness with President Bush. Greenspan's scolded the president's fiscal incontinence. There was no disputing this. Bush spent money like a drunken sailor who then sells the ship to keep spending. He introduced a fiscal year 2009 budget with a $400 billion deficit.[8] Greenspan grew mischievous in claiming his staunch opposition to deficit spending. A fallacy laid at the heart of the media critiques. Since they cover political squabbles the way a football announcer would—two distinct teams engaged in a win-or-lose competition—the media attached great importance to this lifelong Republican casting his Republican president into the night.

Greenspan had never really been a Republican or a libertarian or however else he described himself. He has devoted his life to a modern pursuit. Greenspan's interests seemed aligned to a genus that congregated in Washington—the personal Opportunist Party. Thus, the controversy (when *Age of Turbulence* was published) of Greenspan praising Bill Clinton and chiding Bush was the same Greenspan who went along with expelling the Brandens from Ayn Rand's inner circle in the 1960s. Bush's days were coming to an end; Hillary Clinton was running for president. Ergo, Greenspan was positioning himself for something or other in a new Clinton administration.

Greenspan did find favor with the Clintons, although Hillary did not receive the Democratic nomination. One of her proposed initiatives was an "emergency group" to "deal with high-risk mortgages." Greenspan was

---

[6] Ibid. For instance: "I was saddened years later when I discovered that President Bush blamed me for his loss," p. 122; after Greenspan learned about President Clinton's affair with Monica Lewinsky, "It seemed so alien to the Bill Clinton I knew, and made me feel disappointed and sad," p. 187.

[7] Bob Woodward, "Greenspan: Ouster of Hussein Crucial for Oil Security," *Washington Post*, September 17, 2007.

[8] Michael Abramowitz and Jonathan Weisman, "Bush's Budget Projects Deficits," *Washington Post*, February 5, 2008.

one of those she'd appoint. When an opponent questioned her selection of the former Federal Reserve chairman, Clinton offered an enigmatic endorsement. He had "a calming influence.... Don't ask me why, because I never understand what he's saying."[9]

GREENSPAN IN THE AUTUMN

Greenspan found it difficult to break a smile on his *Age of Turbulence* publicity tour. He spent the first couple of weeks answering questions about his Bush-Clinton opinions. Greenspan "glumly" told the *New York Times* that he was "very disappointed" with the Republicans.[10] "They swapped principle for power."[11] This sounds like a self-evaluation.

Criticism of Greenspan's role in the subprime meltdown was growing. He was miffed: "There has been a bit of historical revisionism going on," Mr. Greenspan complained to the *New York Times*.[12] Greenspan "acknowledged the housing frenzy had been pumped up in part because of very low interest rates," but "it was a mistake to blame the Fed," since the Fed "needed to reduce interest rates in order to fend off the recession of 2001."[13] Reworded, the Fed decided to avoid a recession by igniting the housing bubble and home-equity spending splurge.

Again, the general reception of *The Age of Turbulence* was pleasant, but Greenspan insisted on defending himself when any question was posed that might impinge his reputation. By doing so, he called more attention to his past deeds. This probably damaged his reputation, although, it is difficult to separate these wounds from the arrows that would have been directed at Greenspan in any case, given that the financial system was both degenerating and beyond the capacity of any human to understand. On the television program *60 Minutes*, he insisted that while he knew subprime "practices were going on, I had

---

[9] Nick Timiras, "Clinton Looks to Greenspan," *Wall Street Journal*, March 26, 2008.

[10] Keach Hagey, "Greenspan Backtracks on Iraq War Oil Claim," *CBS News.com*, September 17, 2007. Hagey quotes various reports from newspapers.

[11] Edmund L. Andrews and David E. Singer, "Former Fed Chief Attacks Bush on Fiscal Role," *New York Times*, September 15, 2007.

[12] Edmund L. Andrews, "A 'Disappointed' Greenspan Lashes Out at Bush's Economic Policies," *New York Times*, September 17, 2007.

[13] Ibid.

no notion of how significant they had become until very late. I didn't really get it until very late in 2005 and 2006."[14] This did not persuade many viewers, since, presumably, most viewers knew, long before that, of sleazy practices and deadbeats who received home loans. He then defended the Fed's lack of initiative by claiming that it was not his job. He claimed that central banks and market regulators lacked the resources to address criminal or illegal acts. "We are not skilled enough in these areas and we shouldn't be expected to." He offered advice: "It should be with the states' attorney general and, frankly, it should be beefed up a considerable amount from where it is at this stage."[15] The question was about regulation, not crime: nobody proposed that the Federal Reserve should open a prosecution office. If Greenspan had given half as many speeches admonishing irresponsible bankers as he did on energy, Citicorp's CDO team would have been disbanded. Greenspan instinctively scolded the attorneys general and rejected responsibility for his own failure.

Greenspan's Grand Tour

Greenspan showed great stamina for a man in his eighties. After selling *The Age of Turbulence* on the domestic press circuit, he headed to Europe. In Paris, Greenspan told *Le Figaro* that Dominique Strauss-Kahn (France's candidate to head the IMF) should be the next managing director, but the "IMF has to rethink its mission."[16] Greenspan was never at a loss to identify others' faults.

Safely across the border, he told a Bundesbank fiftieth-anniversary gathering that the newly elected president of France, Nicolas Sarkozy, should not be lobbying the European Central Bank to lower rates. After he hemmed, he hawed: Greenspan said that Sarkozy was doing a good job. In London, he told the *Daily Telegraph* that "Britain is more exposed than we are [to mortgage defaults]—in the sense that you have a good deal more adjustable-rate mortgages."[17] That would seem to contradict

---

[14] Interview with Leslie Stahl, *60 Minutes*, September 16, 2007.

[15] Jane Wardell, "Greenspan Defends Subprime," Associated Press, October 2, 2007.

[16] "World Markets Still Affected by Fear: Greenspan," *Le Figaro*, September 23, 2007.

[17] "UK More Vulnerable than America to the Credit Crunch, Greenspan says," *Daily Telegraph* (London), September 18, 2007.

his variable-rate advice in February 2004, when he advised Americans to look overseas, "where adjustable-rate mortgages are far more common."[18] His statement to the *Telegraph* was on September 17, in the midst of a bank run on Northern Rock, a British bank. He may not have heightened the hysteria sweeping Britain, but he could have kept his mouth shut.

After Britain, he was seen in Vienna, where he said, "[T]here is no doubt about the fact that low interest rates for long-term government bonds have caused the real estate bubble in the US" and "[real estate] prices are going to fall much lower yet."[19] In Amsterdam, Greenspan fueled a cabinet crisis (about unemployment) when he told the press and ING Bank's guests that the unemployment numbers are so low in the United States because it's easy to fire an employee and it's also easy to find a job.[20]

The author grew more defensive. The same day the *New York Times* had upbraided him in September, Greenspan told CNBC: "I'm fully aware of the fact that everyone thinks that the Federal Reserve, back when I was chairman, inflated the economy. Well, we didn't."[21] "Everyone" went too far, but celebrity economists were about to speak out. Nobel Prize winner Joseph Stiglitz claimed: "Alan Greenspan really made a mess of all this."[22] Patrick Artus, economic advisor to the French government and "one of France's most listened to 'pundits'" told Bloomberg that "Greenspan was an arsonist and fireman combined.... He absolutely failed to see where the malfunctions in the U.S. economy were."[23]

"I Didn't Do It!" was the December 12, 2007, headline of a *Salon.com* story that described recent Greenspan excuses.[24] This sort of headline

---

[18] Alan Greenspan, "Understanding Household Debt Obligations," speech at the Credit Union National Association 2004 Governmental Affairs Conference, Washington, D.C., February 23, 2004.

[19] "House Prices to Drop Much Lower: Greenspan," Reuters, September 21, 2007.

[20] *De Telegraaf*, September 29, 2007, translated by Hans Merkelbach.

[21] Alister Bull, "Critics Charge Greenspan but Maestro Legacy Endures," Reuters, September 18, 2007.

[22] Reed V. Landberg and Paul George, "Greenspan 'Mess' Risks U.S Recession, Stiglitz Says," Bloomberg, November 16, 2007.

[23] Farah Nayeri, "Greenspan Was 'Very Bad' Fed Chairman, Says Artus of Natixis," Bloomberg, November 30, 2007.

[24] Andrew Leonard, "Alan Greenspan on the Mortgage Crisis: 'I Didn't Do It!'" *Salon. com*, December 12, 2007.

had become a sport: "Not My Fault" was *New York* magazine's synthesis;[25] The *Sunday Times* (of London): "Don't Blame Me!";[26] *Palm Beach Post*: "Will Alan Greenspan just shut up and let someone else try to clean up the damage he allowed to happen?"[27]

Greenspan did not agree. The problem was in not explaining himself, the chairman told Steve Inskeep on NPR radio.[28] This was a puzzling self-critique, since he was doing little else. Greenspan rejected criticism that the Fed had fueled the housing bubble by lowering interest rates. That argument "doesn't coincide with the facts. … [W]e've had housing bubbles in two dozen or more countries around the world." Greenspan had grown astonishingly adept at identifying bubbles—at least 24 this time.[29] He did not mention what many critics now argued: there was no one more responsible for the two dozen real estate bubbles than Alan Greenspan. He printed the dollars the rest of the world absorbed. This led to the worldwide asset inflation.

Greenspan addressed derivative problems as if he were a rookie financial reporter recently transferred from the Arts & Leisure section. Greenspan told Reuters the abrupt upheaval in markets as a result of the subprime crisis "was an accident waiting to happen."[30] He revealed: "It was a failure to properly price these risky assets that set off the tidal wave of risk contamination."[31] On another topic: "Markets from their earliest days have been plagued by bubbles."[32]

His most obvious claims were quoted as nuggets of wisdom: "The markets for certain complex, structured products, will surely contract."[33] A few days later, he "defended the U.S. subprime mortgage market, arguing the repackaging and sale to investors of risky home loans—not the

[25] "Not My Fault," *New York*, September 14, 2007.

[26] "Alan Greenspan: Don't Blame Me; I Couldn't Alter Asset Prices," *Sunday Times* (London), January 27, 2008.

[27] "The Greenspan Bubble," *Palm Beach Post*, December 19, 2007.

[28] "Greenspan: Recession Odds 'Clearly Rising,'" NPR, December 14, 2007.

[29] Ibid.

[30] "Highlights—Speeches from UK's Brown and Darling; Greenspan," Reuters, October 1, 2007.

[31] Ibid.

[32] Ibid.

[33] Ibid.

loans themselves—was to blame for the current global credit crisis."[34] Any diversion would do.

On January 24, 2008, the itinerant author was in Vancouver, Canada. He told Sherry Cooper at BMO Financial Group that his now-infamous adjustable-rate mortgage speech in February 2004 had been misrepresented. Greenspan, in defending himself, told Cooper that he spoke to the Economic Club of New York seven days later, "where I strongly clarified my remarks," and "[s]o I plead not guilty."[35] (Greenspan had blamed several guilty parties over the past few weeks: reporters, Dick Cheney, George Bush I, George Bush II, the cold war, models, history, commercial lenders, mortgage companies, appraisers, and home buyers.) His speech to the Economic Club was about the trade deficit. He discussed the mortgage issue during the question-and-answer session. The Federal Reserve Web site posts only speeches. If Greenspan thought he had been misunderstood, he should have addressed adjustable-rate mortgages in a speech, or several speeches.

Anna Schwartz spoke to the *Daily Telegraph* from her office at the National Bureau of Economic Research, where she had worked since 1941. The coauthor with Milton Freidman of *A Monetary History of the United States* offered a new monetary interpretation. According to the *Telegraph*: "She is scornful of Greenspan's campaign to clear his name by blaming the bubble on an Asian savings glut." In Schwartz's opinion: "This attempt to exculpate himself is not convincing.... It can't be blamed on global events.... It is clear that monetary policy was too accommodative. Rates of one percent were bound to encourage all kinds of risky behavior."[36]

BIG MONEY

Greenspan was hired by John Paulson in January 2008. This was Greenspan's lucky day: a chance to really make fast money on the

---

[34] Jane Wardell, "Greenspan Defends Subprime, Sees Some Early Signs of Easing in Credit Crisis," Associated Press, October 2, 2007.

[35] Bill Fleckenstein, "Did Greenspan Push Risky Home Loans?" *Contrarian Chronicles*, February 4, 2008; moneycentral.msm.

[36] Ambrose Evans-Pritchard, "Anna Schwartz Blames Fed for Sub-Prime Crisis," *Daily Telegraph* (London), January 13, 2008.

crack-up. Paulson saw the future of housing by 2005, when he told one of his colleagues: "We've got to take as much advantage of this as we can."[37] Paulson & Co. took the short side of mortgage security credit default swaps. The strategy paid off handsomely in 2007 when two of Paulson's hedge funds rose 590 percent and 350 percent.[38] Paulson earned a personal paycheck of $3 to $4 billion.[39]

Greenspan was more responsible than any other person for the bust, which might have caused a moral dilemma before he tackled his new job, but Greenspan had a knack for rationalizations. After the Paulson hiring, the *Wall Street Journal* asked Greenspan: "All three of your clients—Pimco, Deutsche Bank, and now Paulson—were bearish early on housing and mortgages. Is there a connection?" The absent-minded Ph.D responded: "I hadn't [noticed] until you just raised the issue."[40]

Pimco had hired Greenspan as an advisor in May 2007, and Deutsche Bank had done so in August. The *Wall Street Journal* asked Deutsche Bank's CEO Joseph Ackerman why Greenspan is "uniquely qualified to help his clients." Ackerman said that he admired Greenspan's ability to "explain very complicated subjects and situations in simple terms."[41]

"Don't Blame the Crisis on Me"

Greenspan defended himself on the editorial pages. "We Will Never Have a Perfect Model of Risk" was both the title and the theme of a March 16, 2008, *Financial Times* op-ed: "[M]athematically elegant economic forecasting models ... once again have been unable to anticipate a financial crisis or the onset of a recession."[42] It was unseemly. Richard Russell, the renowned author of the oldest financial news-

---

[37] Gregory Zuckerman, "Trader Made Billions on Subprime," *Wall Street Journal*, January 15, 2008.

[38] Ibid.

[39] Ibid.

[40] "Greenspan: Subprime Sales May Be Near Bottom," *Wall Street Journal*, January 15, 2008.

[41] Greg Ip, "Fed Ex-Chief Greenspan to Advise Deutsche Bank," *Wall Street Journal*, August 13, 2007.

[42] Alan Greenspan, "We Will Never Have a Perfect Model of Risk," *Financial Times*, March 16, 2007.

letter in the country (*Richard Russell's Dow Theory Letters*), wrote to his clients: "Greenspan with his proclivity to creating bubbles is largely responsible for the sub-prime mess. But this publicity-seeking ego-maniac continues to act like the great oracle. Is there any way of getting Greenspan off the public scene? The man has absolutely no shame."[43]

Greenspan was consumed with his own legacy. He did not have the decency to retreat when the Wall Street collapse commenced. On March 16 the Fed announced an "overnight loan facility" that would provide "funding to primary dealers."[44] In a flash, the Fed had increased its mandate to fund brokers and dealers, not just banks. Bernanke's Fed opened this facility when Bear Stearns could not borrow. Investment banks needed constant government borrowing support just to exist. The Fed arranged a wedding between JP Morgan Chase and Bear Stearns to save the latter. It was now obvious the derivatives that Greenspan still extolled (credit derivative swaps) had concentrated risk in financial institutions rather than spreading risk among parties. His record for wrongheadedness remained intact.

Paul Volcker was distraught. He spoke at the Economic Club of New York on April 8, 2008. Earlier in the year, Volcker told the *New York Times* that "[t]oo many bubbles have been going on for too long. The Fed is not really in control of the situation."[45] This day, he shredded the Bernanke Fed. Volcker was asked if he predicted a dollar crisis in future years. "You don't have to predict it, we're in it."[46] The former Federal Reserve chairman explained: "As custodian of the nation's money, the Federal Reserve has the basic responsibility to protect its value and resist chronic pressures toward inflation."[47] It was apparent that Bernanke's concerns did not include the dollar. He was busy

---

[43] Richard Russell, *Dow Theory Letter*, March 17, 2008, pp. 7–8.

[44] Federal Reserve Bank of New York, "Primary Dealer Credit Facility: Frequently Asked Questions." www.ny.frb.org

[45] Roger Lowenstein, "The Education of Ben Bernanke," *New York Times Magazine*, January 20, 2008.

[46] "Volcker's Demarche," "Review & Outlook," online.wsj.com, April 9, 2008.

[47] Paul Volcker, remarks at a luncheon of the Economic Club of New York, New York, April 8, 2008.

bailing out participants in the crony capitalism that was making the United States look like a fourth-world country. [48]

While Volcker worried about the country, Greenspan had more parochial concerns. He was back in the *Financial Times* on April 7. The newspaper seemed to be using Greenspan more than the other way around. In the weekend edition (April 5–6, 2008), there was a large advertisement for his Monday column. A solid, black background housed the topic in pink letters: "Greenspan: Don't Blame the Crisis on Me."[49] His immaculate record had become a joke.

The title of Greenspan's article said more than enough: "The Fed Is Blameless on the Property Bubble."[50] More model problems. The press was less subservient than before. Some headlines on April 8: *New York Post*: "Greenspan Blames Investors for Crisis"[51]; Reuters (Singapore): "Greenspan Says Unfairly Blamed, Has No Regrets"; *Sydney Morning Herald*, Australia: "Greenspan Rejects Interest Rates Criticism"; *Gulf Times* (Qatar): "Investors to Blame for Crisis, not Fed, Says Greenspan"[52]; *Los Angeles Times*: "Memo to Greenspan: Enough Already." (The first sentence from L.A. Land, the newspaper's blog: "The unseemly, globe-trotting, money-grabbing, legacy-spinning, responsibility-denying tour of Alan Greenspan continues, as relentless as a bad toothache."[53])

On the same day, April 8, the *Wall Street Journal* published a long self-defense in an interview with Greenspan. The bull market icon who used to be God told the *Journal* that he didn't regret a single

---

[48] Bernanke was just warming up. Within a few months, all the investment banks had either failed, been absorbed, or been allowed to hide under a commercial banking umbrella. The big five had been Bear Stearns, Goldman Sachs, Morgan Stanley, Merrill Lynch, and Lehman Brothers. Aside from the various Federal Reserve windows (soon there were more than in the cathedral at Chartres), the government (through the Treasury Department) was pouring billions of dollars into Citicorp, Fannie Mae, Freddie Mac, and Bank of America (the government had absorbed Mozilo's Countrywide Credit), and the Fed was running the biggest insurance company in the world: AIG.

[49] *Financial Times*, April 5–6, 2008, p. 9.

[50] Alan Greenspan, "The Fed Is Blameless on the Property Bubble," *Financial Times*, April 7, 2008.

[51] The headline was in the *New York Post*; the accompanying article is from Reuters.

[52] The headline was in *Gulf Times* (Qatar); the accompanying article is from Reuters.

[53] Peter Viles, "Memo to Greenspan: Enough Already," *Los Angeles Times*, blog called "L.A. Land," April 8, 2008.

decision.[54] Greenspan was particularly upset with criticisms "by friends and former colleagues, many of them respected economists who backed his policies at the time but now say, in hindsight, that the calls were wrong."[55] This was a fair point. It does seem that professional economists waited until the housing meltdown before tossing the former chairman overboard. Among possible explanations, those who now spoke may have believed what they now said all along, but there was no one in the media interested in quoting them; they may have waited until it was safe to talk; they may have been as inept as Greenspan at looking ahead; they may have grown sick and tired of his whining or they may have, in concert, derided Greenspan, using him as a sacrificial offering, since the fallacy of economics as taught over the past half century was unraveling.

After reading the *Journal* article, Senator Jim Bunning commented, "He protests too loudly of the criticism that is justly due him. I've never seen someone who doesn't think he needs defending himself so much."[56]

Comparisons the next day were inevitable. Caroline Baum wrote: "Volcker is a man of few words; Greenspan won't shut up." Baum quoted another apostate to the Greenspan legend, former Federal Reserve Governor Alice Rivlin: "[T]he culprit was not imperfect models. It was a failure to ask common sense questions, such as, 'will housing prices keep going up forever?'"[57] The title of Baum's article captured a general mood: "Volcker Stands Tall, Greenspan Keeps Shrinking."[58]

---

[54] Greg Ip, "His Legacy Tarnished, Greenspan Goes on Defensive," *Wall Street Journal*, April 8, 2008, p. 1.

[55] Ibid.

[56] "Greenspan's Senate Antagonist Attacks His Defense," Blogs.wsj.com, April 9, 2008.

[57] Caroline Baum, "Volcker Stands Tall, Greenspan Keeps Shrinking," Bloomberg, April 9, 2008.

[58] Ibid.

28

GREENSPAN'S HOMETOWN

2008

[O]ver-confidence finds exuberant expression in a bull stock market.... Once stock prices reach the point at which it is hard to value them by any logical methodology, [Greenspan] warns, stocks will be bought, as they were in the late-1920's—not for investment but to be unloaded at a still higher price. The ensuing break could be disastrous. Panic psychology, Greenspan believes, cannot be summarily altered or reversed by easy money policies or any built in stabilizers.[1]

—Fortune *magazine, March 1959*

What Alan Greenspan really believed is beyond the scope of this book. We know what he said in public. Quoting him again, from earlier chapters, offers a synopsis of where we have traveled during his lifetime.

There are two categories in which his statements on investment can be channeled. The first is bubbles. The second is the need for long-term investment in a sustainable economy.

Of the first, bubbles, he stated what everyone at the local Rotary Club luncheon knows: "I think the downside risks are basically coming from the possibility of significant increases in stock and bond prices.... Ironically, the real danger is that things may get too good. When things get too good, human beings behave awfully."[2] At a different time:

---

[1] Gilbert Burck, *Fortune,* "A New Kind of Stock Market," March 1959, p. 201.
[2] FOMC Meeting transcript, March 28, 1995, p. 42.

"Mr. Greenspan declared that a rising stock market tended to put strong upward pressure on stockholder inclination to spend. If market values rise, and do not quickly fade again, he said, the gain gets built into the individual stockholder's permanent assets and his standard of living ideas change, with consumption rising accordingly."[3]

At the intersection of bubbles and investment, Greenspan explained "that a break in stock market trends was not just a harbinger of boom or recession, as is commonly held, but a crucial factor in causing a boom or a recession."[4] The larger the boom the larger the bust: these are not the words of Alan Greenspan, but at the time the New Economics (circa 1960) toyed with the idea that it had discovered how to cure the business cycle (there would be no more recessions), Greenspan "questioned the theory that the enlargement of the Government's role in the national economy had brought a 'new era' in which an old-fashioned financial contraction was impossible."[5]

This merges with the second category of Greenspan's statements on investment, more important than the first. The first—bubbles—come about because the second operates poorly. Greenspan explained that long-term investment "is needed each year just to replace this depreciated capital stock, and more investment yet is needed to increase the nation's net capital stock." He stated the consequence of only investing for the short-term: "What happens if you have inadequate capital investment, is you wind up with lower standards of living than you otherwise would."[6]

That is, lower standards of living for the majority. An earlier Federal Reserve chairman, William McChesney Martin, had explained to the Senate in 1957 the importance of asset inflation—monitoring the inflation of goods and services was not enough. He told the legislators that "if further inflation is expected, speculative commitments are encouraged and the

---

[3] *New York Times*, "Economists Sift Jobs and Stocks," December 28, 1959, p. 39.

[4] Ibid.

[5] Ibid.

[6] Steven Greenhouse, *New York Times*, "Pitfalls in the Capital Spending Boom," June 3, 1984.

[7] William McChesney Martin, Statement before the Committee on Finance, U.S. Senate, August 13, 1957, p. 14.

pattern of investment and other spending—the decisions on what kinds of things to buy—will change in a way that threatens balanced growth."[7] Alan Greenspan expanded on this explanation in 1959 when he spoke to *Fortune* reporter Gilbert Bruck. In Bruck's words, Greenspan explained that before the Federal Reserve was established "prices could not get too far out of line with real values because the supply of credit was automatically constricted by a limited money supply." Since 1914, "[w]ith one eye necessarily cocked on politics, the Fed has always maintained a more than adequate money supply even when speculative booms threaten."[8] (This was really what Martin was telling the senators in 1957: stop putting pressure on the Fed to inflate.)

It was about that time when James Joseph Ling was forming his conglomerate (see Chapter 3). His was a speculative venture of spectacular proportions. Federal Reserve or no Federal Reserve, there always were and always will be speculative manias. But it was the size of the conglomerate craze in the 1960s (when Saul Steinberg's Leasco stock appreciated 5,410 percent) that acted as a destructive force on the economy.[9] Such destruction was allied to excessive money printing by the Fed. This was also true when LBOs battered companies in the late 1980s and of private equity most recently.

In the same 1957 speech to the Senate, Martin worried that the heaviest burden would be borne by those who could not protect the value of their income or savings.[10] That is the "little man." Martin predicted those with "savings in their old age would tend to be the slick and clever rather than the hard-working and thrifty."[11]

The lower standards of living for the majority today are partly attributable to the lack of long-term investment, the need for which Alan Greenspan explained above. Instead, we have tended more and more to the opposite: short-term investment by financiers with (what seems)

---

[8] Gilbert Burck, *Fortune*, "A New kind of Stock Market," March 1959, p. 201. Greenspan continued, again, in the words of Gilbert Burck: "The Fed, furthermore, has recently been boxed in by a huge and partially monetized federal debt, which tends to produce an addition to the money supply, whose size is unrelated to the needs of private business."

[9] John Brooks, *The Go-Go Years* (New York: Weybright and Talley, 1973), p 238.

[10] Martin, Statement Before the Committee on Finance, p. 15-16.

[11] Ibid, p. 23.

limitless access to borrowed money that is loaded onto company balance sheets. (Alan Greenspan worried about this in the 1980s: "We are increasing debt at levels which should make us all uncomfortable. It certainly makes me uncomfortable."[12]

Wealth has risen to the top as most Americans work under the weight of unsound business structures: downsizing and all the rest of the burdens borne by those who are toiling in a haze of uncertainty.

GREENSPAN'S HISTORY LESSON

In his 1966 essay "Gold and Economic Freedom," Greenspan dramatized (maybe overdramatized) an earlier period when the Federal Reserve paid little attention to asset prices: "When business in the United States underwent a mild contraction in 1927, the Federal Reserve created [excessive] paper reserves.... The excess credit which the Fed pumped into the economy spilled over into the stock market—triggering a fantastic speculative boom.... As a result, the American economy collapsed.... The world economies plunged into the Great Depression of the 1930's."

Money pouring into speculation in the 1920s went not only into the stock market, it also went into an asset class that probably received more speculative funds than the stock market: real estate. Speculative real estate lending then bore a sickening resemblance to the present. But by the late 1920s, New York banks lent to commercial builders long after they should have stopped. The city's office space rose 92 percent in the last half of the 1920s and by another 56 percent after the stock market crash.[13]

One notable growth story was the Bank of United States. Its asset base grew from $46 million in 1923 to $315 million in 1929.[14] It failed in 1930. Among other problems, it had caught the skyscraper bug. It financed two monuments designed by the esteemed architect Emory Roth: the

---

[12] Senate Committee on Banking, Housing and Urban Affairs transcript, July 21, 1987, pp. 36–37.

[13] Robert A. Stern, Gregory Gilmartin, and Thomas Mellins, *New York 1930: Architecture and Urbanism between the Two World Wars* (New York: Rizzoli, 1994).

[14] James Grant, *Money of the Mind: Borrowing and Lending in America from the Civil War to Michael Milken* (New York: Farrar Straus Giroux, 1992), p. 203.

San Remo and Beresford apartment houses. The builders were soon in bankruptcy. The San Remo and Beresford became instantly fashionable, yet they sold at a deep discount in 1940.[15] To this day, they are two of the most distinguished silhouettes on Central Park West. Vikram Pandit, the current CEO of Citigroup, paid $18 million for a 10-room apartment in the Beresford.[16] The San Remo is home to Steven Spielberg, Steve Martin, and Bono.[17]

A critique of the 1932 skyline published in the *New Republic* indicates the destructive capacity of an unstable banking system: "[W]inter evenings were cruelly revealing, for when the sun set before the close of daily business it was all too apparent how many of these towers stood 'black and untenanted against the stars.... With some few exceptions, the newest New York may be described as a sixty-story city unoccupied above the twentieth floor.'"[18]

ALAN GREENSPAN'S HOMETOWN

New York is at the pinnacle of America's financial economy. When Alan Greenspan entered New York University, New York was an industrial center. When he joined William Townsend, it was a headquarters town, the center for marketing and selling. In 1960, developer William Zeckendorf understood how New York had changed: "Precisely because New York is a national headquarters, it is also a middle-income as well as high-income town."[19] To Zeckendorf, New York was "an unparalleled consumer's market."[20]

---

[15] "Two Block Fronts Sold on West Side," *New York Times*, July 14, 1940. The original investment for land and building was $16,500,000. The sale price is ambiguous in this article; it looks as if it was between $7.4 million and $9.8 million.

[16] Sharon L. Crenson, "Pandit Buys Tony Randall's Co-op for $17.9 Million," Bloomberg, September 26, 2007.

[17] Allen Salkin, "Among the Rich and Famous ...," *New York Times*, May 15, 2007.

[18] Elmer Davis, *New Republic*, 1932, quoted in Stern, Gilmartin, and Mellins, *New York 1930*, p. 603.

[19] Robert A. M. Stern, Thomas Mellins, and David Fishman, *New York 1960: Architecture and Urbanism between the Second World War and the Bicentennial* (New York: Monacelli Press, 1995), p. 29.

[20] Ibid.

The United States was consuming more than it was making. This imbalance needed to be financed. Alan Greenspan worked in the city that produced the finance. Greenspan profited. By the late 1960s, he was a millionaire and lived in a fashionable New York apartment house.

Alan Greenspan was born for the times. The excesses required a spokesman who could talk nonsense with a straight face. He could tell Americans that they were rich when they were really poor. Americans believed him and kept spending. Greenspan was awarded a doctrine after he adopted Friedman's and Bernanke's interpretation of the Great Depression. Americans revered Greenspan, to a large degree because their lives had gone haywire from distortions that only economists could explain, and Alan Greenspan was the world's most famous economist.

He was a celebrity. In today's culture, that meant he could say anything. Finance kept borrowing and leveraging, believing (or pretending to believe) that its fortunes would continually compound. Fifty years, or maybe a hundred years, of accumulating imbalances—of finances and beliefs—have reached their logical conclusion in New York City. We are unlikely to see its kind for a long while.

You're the Top!

A walk around town is a testament to the man who turned the country into a leveraged carry trade (see Chapter 10). Many people on Wall Street cashed in, even if the banks they ran were struggling for survival. Robert Rubin collected $150 million from Citicorp in the decade after he left the Treasury Department.[21] Yet, until the bubble burst he had "no familirity at all with CDOs"[22] Citicorp had received $45 billion from the federal government when Rubin left. Goldman Sachs's CEO Lloyd Blankfein received a $68 million bonus in 2007, before his firm needed the protection of the Federal Reserve in 2008.[23] Between 2000 and when

---

[21] Josh Fineman, "Rubin's Career at Citigroup Ends after $20 Billion of Losses," Bloomberg, January 10, 2009.

[22] Grant's Interest Rate Observer, February 22, 2008, p. 1, quoting article in Fortune magazine.

[23] Miles Weiss, "Goldman Change to Bonuses Helped Cut Compensation Costs in 2008," Bloomberg, March 13, 2009.

it failed in 2008, Lehman Brothers' CEO Richard Fuld received $484 million in salary, bonuses, and stock options.[24]

William Zeckendorf's prediction has come true, except for one mis-estimation: it is no longer a middle-income town. In Manhattan, 51 percent of neighborhoods are identified as high income and 40 percent as low income.[25] In 2006, New York investment bankers were paid a weekly wage of $16,849 a week; the average weekly pay for all private-sector jobs was $841 (not necessarily in New York).[26]

Inflation has priced out the middle class. By 2005, 57 percent of Manhattan residents over the age of 25 were college graduates; 25 percent held graduate degrees.[27] The majority of adults in Brooklyn, Bronx, and Queens did not speak English as their first language.[28]

"Forty is the new thirty," noted Richard Coraine, of the rising price of entrees, including the 1¾-ounce lunchtime lobster appetizer ($42) at the Modern, his restaurant in New York.[29] Shopping in New York City was beyond the reach of more Americans. Stores started to accept euros and other foreign currency as payment for merchandise.[30]

Manhattan is structured for the rich. Whole Foods opened a 71,000-square-foot supermarket at Columbus Circle, on the upper West Side.[31] Yet, there are one-third fewer supermarkets in the five boroughs than there were six years ago.[32] Retail space rose to $500 a square foot on the Upper East Side; restaurants and groceries abandoned the space amidst

[24] Brian Ross and Alice Gomstyn, "Lehman Brothers Boss Defends $484 Million in Salary, Bonus," *ABC News*, October 6, 2008.

[25] Sam Roberts, "Study Shows a Dwindling Middle Class," *New York Times*, June 26, 2006.

[26] David Cay Johnston, "Pay at Investment Banks Eclipse All Private Jobs," *New York Times*, September 1, 2007.

[27] Patrick McGeehan, "New York Area Is a Magnet for Graduates," *New York Times*, August 16, 2006.

[28] www.city-data.com/top2/his.html.

[29] Jodi Kantor, "Entrees Reach $40, and, Sorry, the Sides Are Extra," *New York Times*, October 21, 2006.

[30] Angela Moore and Bill Berkrot, "'Euros Accepted' Signs Pop Up in New York City," Reuters, February 6, 2008.

[31] Robin Shulman, "Groceries Grow Elusive for Many in New York City," *Washington Post*, February 19, 2008.

[32] Ibid.

"the Big Bank-Leasing Madness." According to the *New York Post*, "[o]nce lively shopping stretches.... now resemble banking malls."[33]

Noteworthy apartment buildings continued to rise in 2008. They were built on CDOs. New York is more dependent than ever on the financial industry. Between 2000 and 2007, tax revenue rose 41 percent.[34] In 2006, the top 1 percent of taxpayers paid nearly 48 percent of the city's personal income tax, compared to 34 percent two decades ago.[35] Finance occupied an ever-growing percentage of Manhattan office space, and Fifth Avenue shops paid the most expensive retail rents in the world, double the cost of five years before.[36]

Apartment prices were still rising in 2008. Gregory Heym, from Terra Holdings LLC, explained: "At the high end of the market, you are dealing with wealth and not income. People buy apartments with cash."[37]

William Zeckendorf III (the visionary's grandson) has built the finest apartment house since the early 1930s: 15 Central Park West. Designed by esteemed architect Robert A. M. Stern, its twin 41-story towers cast silhouettes a few blocks south of the San Remo. Zeckendorf paid $400 million for the land. There was a lot of headshaking at this folly. He sold the apartments before completion. Financially, it is "the most successful apartment building in the history of New York."[38]

Lloyd Blankfein, chairman of Goldman Sachs, is a resident. Sandy Weill, former chairman of Citigroup, paid $42 million for a penthouse.

The apartments are laid out "almost exactly like classic apartments from the 20s, with semi-private elevator halls, large entry foyers, formal dining rooms and libraries." There is a waiting room for chauffeurs, 80 wine cellars, and maids' apartments, sold separately.[39]

---

[33] Steve Cuozzo, "Prime Neighborhoods Overrun by Big Bank-Leasing Madness," *New York Post*, January 2, 2007.

[34] Nicole Gelinas, "New York's Next Fiscal Crisis," *City Journal*, Summer 2008.

[35] Ibid. The 2006 figure is "even after adjusting for the temporarily higher tax rate."

[36] Cushman & Wakefield, "1Q Report Shows Manhattan Office Rents Are On the Rise," news release, April 4, 2006.

[37] Sharon L. Crenson, "Rotating Rooms, Yacht Berths Spur Dubai, Moscow Apartment Boom," Bloomberg, April 25, 2007.

[38] Paul Goldberger, "Past Perfect: Retro Opulence on Central Park West," *New Yorker*, August 27, 2007.

[39] Goldberger, "The King of Central Park West," *Varity Fair*, September 2008.

At 15 Central Park West, inflation has now hit the top. This is the history of inflation: it moves, from the bottom and doesn't stop until it consumes the top. One of the apartments, sold by the Zeckendorfs for $21.9 million, went on the market for $80 million. Another was offered for $90 million, and a third for $150 million.[40] Paper money is in abundance, CDOs are worthless, the skills honed to create and sell derivatives are sitting in Bryant Park drinking café lattes. In the estimation of architectural critic Paul Goldberger: "No one knows, of course, whether the speculative frenzy at 15 Central Park West will hold. But since the building was created to support the fantasy of living in the 20s or 30s, it's no big deal to pretend also that it's 2005, when prices were still soaring. At 15 Central Park West it's still 2005—unless, that is, it's really 1929."[41]

THE BOTTOM

Some of the rich must think it is 1930. Protestors have marched in front of 740 Park Avenue—not because Steven Schwartzman is in the penthouse, but because Henry Kravis also lives in the building.[42] In Greenwich, "For Sale" signs are illegal. If they were allowed, the New Yorker suspects that Greenwich might look like "a giant and very expensive tag sale."[43]

The lower 99 percent have made many mistakes of their own. The cry for "growth" since the 1950s has taken mutant forms. Maricopa, Arizona, is an example. A 40-mile commute from Phoenix, it had a population of 600 in the early 1990s. "[By] 2005, three new people moved to Maricopa each hour."[44] More than one-third of the mortgages were subprime. In June 2009, 1,042 houses were in foreclosure and up for auction at $172. (That is not a misprint.)[45]

Phoenix, Arizona, is a case in point. It is a city in the middle of the desert. The population has grown from 100,000 in 1950 to nearly

---

[40] Ibid.

[41] Ibid.

[42] Andrew Ross Sorkin, "Henry Kravis in Focus as Buyout Backlash Spreads," New York Times, December 6, 2007.

[43] Nick Paumgarten, "A Greenwich of the Mind," New Yorker, August 25, 2008.

[44] Sanartha M. Shapiro, "The Boontown Mirage," New York Times, April 6, 2008.

[45] At least, according to foreclosures.roost.com. on June 23, 2009: "There are 1042 homes that are up for auction at an average auction price of $172."

3,000,000 today. The temperature in Phoenix at night is now 12 degrees hotter than in surrounding rural areas.[46] There are days when Phoenix uses more energy than New York City.[47]

David Rosenberg, then Merrill Lynch's chief North American economist, observed, "[T]he bottom line is that all those McMansions [the 4,000 or 5,000-square-foot houses] that were bought during this housing boom are going to go the way of the 1973 Lincoln Continental." Rosenberg went on to say the "housing bubble was the most over-owned, overleveraged and oversupplied real-estate market ever and its unwinding will take years."[48]

The McMansions are and will continue to draw energy like a 1973 Lincoln Continental. The average new house had grown from 1,500 square feet in 1970 to nearly 2,400 square feet in 2004; 90 percent of new houses in 2004 were equipped with central air conditioning.[49] The houses were getting bigger, but they were not big enough. Rentable self-storage space has risen by 740 percent since 1985, with over 20 square feet of storage space per U.S. household.[50] To carry all the stuff, cars grew: the average weight of a passenger vehicle increased from 3,236 pounds in 1996 to 4,021 pounds in 2003.[51] It was not only stuff that needed more room, Americans grew. In 2006, the obesity rate of 16-year-old boys in the United States was the highest in the world; American girls had to settle for second place, behind overweight Cypriots.[52]

THE GREAT IMPOVERISHMENT

Many Americans need to diet, but many others are being starved, thanks to the Federal Reserve. This failed institution deserves blame for

---

[46] Patricia Gober, *Metropolitan Phoenix: Place Making and Community Building in the Desert* (Philadelphia: University of Pennsylvania Press, 2005), pp. 50–51.

[47] Dan Roberts, "Phoenix Gives Its Newcomers the American Dream They Can Afford," *Financial Times*, September 28, 2005.

[48] James Quinn, "Green Ashes and Black Swans—The Alan Greenspan Legacy, Part II," *The Cutting Edge*, September 29, 2008.

[49] U.S. Census Bureau, C-25 and Characteristics of New Housing.

[50] Self Storage Association Fact Sheet; www.selfstorage.org.

[51] Joshua T. Johnson, Motor Vehicles, Appendix N, Table 3, Weight of material in a typical family vehicle, 1978 to 1996.

[52] *Economist Handbook of Facts and Numbers, 2009.* Profile Books Ltd., 2008.

"the Great Impoverishment." Monetary policy has operated like a jackhammer opening a pickle jar. Over the past two decades, the Fed funds rate was cut from 9 percent to 3 percent, raised from 3 percent to 6.5 percent, cut from 6.5 percent to 1 percent, raised from 1 percent to 5.25 percent, and (most recently) cut from 5.25 percent to zero. This was Federal Reserve Chairman Ben S. Bernanke's "Great Moderation." *A History of Interest Rates,* which catalogs interest rates since Mesopotamian times, shows no such precedent except in times of hyperinflation, total war, and social disintegration.[53]

Our age of turbulence has shackled Americans to financial markets to a degree that was—literally—unthinkable a generation ago. A large proportion of Americans knew nothing about the stock market or the concept of a bond or the structure of a mutual fund. They were perfectly content to save and watch their dollars accumulate. Such proposals as "stocks for the long run" were directed at a small segment of the population. The Federal Reserve—or, rather, central banking as a whole—is not the sole cause of disturbances, but neither is it what it pretends to be.

Alan Greenspan condemned asset inflation during the 1950s and 1960s; by the 1990s, he claimed that it didn't exist, and even if it did, there was nothing that the Federal Reserve could do, since it could not recognize a bubble. The oldest generation was not up to running these personal hedge funds; it earned 1 percent on money market funds and ate cat food.

Ben Bernanke has driven short-term interest rates below zero (after subtracting price inflation) to refloat the financial system that the Fed has overindulged and mismanaged at every turn. Now, suffering another asset deflation—following another asset bubble—the Federal Reserve is driving the young and old to cat food.

Only Congress can dissolve the Federal Reserve. It is time to do so.

---

[53] Sidney Homer and Richard Eugene Sylla, *A Profile of Interest Rates,* 4th ed. (Hoboken, N.J.: Wiley, 2005).

29

LIFE AFTER GREENSPAN

———
2009—
———

Alan Greenspan is an old friend. He has devoted unfailing and broadly successful attention to his own career—he's wonderfully avoided any action that might seem to make him responsible for a slump, but that does not rule out the possibility.[1]

—*John Kenneth Galbraith (1999)*

Alan Greenspan was the forerunner of a type, a type that has come to dominate public life in the United States. Economists are running national policy, proposing to solve a crisis that was anticipated by some Americans from all walks of life, but apparently not by any of the celebrity bankers and economists. Ben Bernanke is Federal Reserve chairman. Larry Summers (see Chapters 11 and 22) is the director of President Obama's National Economic Counsel. Timothy Geithner (see Chapter 22) is secretary of the treasury (and not an economist). *People* magazine recently named Geithner to its annual list of the "50 most beautiful people."[2] These are the most highly regarded minds in an administration that spent over $1 trillion more than it collected during fiscal year 2009.[3] Alexis de Tocqueville foresaw that a democratic

---

[1] William Keegan, "Sitting Out the Party with Galbraith," *Guardian Unlimited,* July 4, 1999.

[2] "Barack's Beauties," *People,* May 11, 2009, p. 89.

[3] Martin Crustinger, "Budget Deficit Tops $1 Trillion for First Time," *SFGate.com,* July 13, 2009.

age could elevate a dwarf who appears on top of a huge wave, and gives the impression he is riding and governing it.[4]

Too much money produced by the Federal Reserve at subsidized interest rates will not solve the problem of too much money produced by the Federal Reserve at subsidized interest rates. Extending more loans to those who could not meet their monthly mortgage payments will not solve the problem of extending too much money to those who could not meet their mortgage payments. Not understanding the problem that has accumulated since they were children, our leaders are compounding the costs that must be paid. The solution must lie in reducing the debt and eliminating the institutions that, through either ignorance or arrogance, ignored their responsibilities.

No matter who holds those positions today, it is doubtful that the decisions made would differ. Other top candidates are products of the same institutions, and, as we could see during the subprime meltdown, they could not see what was happening even after they were run over by a hearse. They are apparatchiks for our time, a decay of aptitude and spirit matched by a parallel decay in Federal Reserve chairmen—from William McChesney Martin to Alan Greenspan.

Another parallel is to capitalism itself. From its earliest days it has developed in conformity to current tendencies of democracies and their governments. What might we expect from here?

Capitalism as practiced in the late nineteenth century was a rigid affair. It was inseparable from the international gold standard. Both were inseparable from personal discipline. When Alan Greenspan wrote his gold-standard diatribe in 1966, he was not referring to the then-current Bretton Woods arrangement.[5] He was discussing the pre-1914 international gold standard. Whether one lived in Hungary or California, the

---

[4] John Lukacs, *A New Republic: A History of the United States in the Twentieth Century* (New Haven, Conn.: Yale University Press, 2004), p. 425.

[5] There are calls today for a return to a Bretton Woods gold standard. This is posed as an agreement that worked for nearly 30 years (1944–1971). However, it was already failing in the 1950s. It was failing because the United States did not live within the limits imposed on the reserve currency. It was *able* to fail because, as with the CDO trade, there were no market prices. Only governments could redeem currency for gold. This led to subterfuges, which were hidden from the people when it was thought better to do so.

national currency could be redeemed for a fixed amount of gold. The people could decide for themselves if they trusted their government. They also had to live with strict limits on credit: it was a world with little sympathy (or, at least, little money) for those who were down on their luck. And it was not a world for mad financial conquest.

In 1934, Simone Weil, a young French philosopher, expressed how capitalism had changed. She wrote, in *Sketch of Contemporary Social Life*: "[C]apital increase brought about by actual production ... counts for less and less as compared with the constant supply of fresh capital."[6] She made this observation without the advantage of having participated in a leveraged buyout. Here, Weil hints at how the word *liquidity* has evolved.

In 1950, an American household's liquidity was its bank account, not its credit line. The bank's liquidity was its cash and certain deposits, not its (assumed perpetual) access to credit. The bank's profits were slow (interest earned minus interest paid) and built up over time. (An analogue exists to the industrial company.) More recently, profits were instant. Because of bank-deposit insurance, a depositor does not consider whether a bank holds gold or confederate dollars in reserve. That being so, banks do not make such distinctions either. Money—inseparable from credit in the mind—will always be as accessible as the air we breathe.

Weil described the more material world of the late nineteenth century: "To increase the size of an undertaking faster than its competitors, and that by means of its own resources—such was, broadly speaking, the aim and object of economic activity. Saving was the rule of economic life; consumption was restricted as much as possible, not only that of the workers, but also that of the capitalists themselves."[7]

Partly, the limits on consumption were attached to the monetary standard of the day. Debts were ultimately settled in reference to the fixed price of gold. Today, accounts are settled in dollars, and more dollars are printed every minute. There is no ultimate settling of accounts. When we are not required to settle our accounts, the size and price of houses have no limits.

---

[6] Simone Weil, *The Simone Weil Reader*, ed. George A. Panichas (New York: David McKay Company, 1977), p. 34.

[7] Ibid., p. 33.

Capital is no longer fixed; balance sheets are now flows. This is true for the producer and the consumer. The producer depends upon the consumer's free-flowing balance sheet. The parties must think alike. If a house were still a home, home-equity withdrawal would not exist. (Quoting again the August 25, 1957, edition of the *New York Times*: "Times have changed. Owning a house is no longer so important as being able to use it while paying for it."[8]) The moorings were loose on each side of the transaction.

Weil described how "saving is replaced by the maddest form of expenditure. The term property has almost ceased to have any meaning; the ambitious man no longer thinks of being owner of a business and running it at a profit, but of causing the widest possible sector of economic activity to pass under his control."[9] Weil concluded that this struggle for economic power was far less about building up than conquering.[10] In 2009, the consequences of this conquest destruction are the abandoned housing developments that line I-5 from San Diego, through Bakersfield, Stockton, and on to Sacramento.

Capitalists no longer save; profits are not needed to raise capital; the term *property* has lost its former meaning; workers labor for a new owner each year. How will this end? Quoting Weil: "[T]he state tends more and more, and with an extraordinary rapidity, to become the center of economic and social life."[11] In 2009, Alan Greenspan proposed that the state nationalize U.S. banks.[12] In 2009, Jeffrey Immelt, chairman of General Electric, wrote: "The interaction between government and business will change forever.... [T]he government will be ... an industry policy champion; a financier; and a key partner."[13] Now, General Electric is using government guarantees to sell bonds. This cooperation is not new. General Electric President Gerard Swope helped construct the

---

[8] John Lukacs, *Outgrowing Democracy: A History of the United States in the Twentieth Century* (Garden City, N.Y.: Doubleday, 1984), p. 115.

[9] Weil, *The Simone Weil Reader*, p. 34.

[10] Ibid.

[11] Weil, *The Simone Weil Reader*, p. 34.

[12] Krishna Guha and Edward Luce, "Greenspan Backs State Control for Banks," *Financial Times*, February 18, 2009.

[13] General Electric, 2008 Annual Report, Letter to Shareowners; released early March 2009.

National Recovery Act at the time Simone Weil wrote *Sketch of Contemporary Social Life*.[14] She was 25 years old. Weil was a philosophy teacher at the time.

THE GREENSPAN LEGACY

Alan Greenspan adapted his talents to a period of flux, flow, and weakness in the moral fiber of the nation. He could say anything because there were no fixed parameters. Greenspan's creation of endless credit—for any and all, in good times and bad, for the rich and the bankrupt—is building to a culmination.

Alan Greenspan was caretaker during a transient period, a time when democracies could inflate and buy the middle class with uncollateralized credit, not backed by goods and services. During the twentieth century (roughly speaking), impossible promises by governments were accepted by the people, between a period of hard money that ended in 1914 and a future and protracted period of bumbling and experiment. Greenspan was attuned to the illusion that he orchestrated. In 1996, Federal Reserve Governor Larry Lindsey bemoaned a problem related to inflation. Chairman Greenspan told Lindsey that he had a solution: "We just have to make our dollar bills smaller and smaller to reflect the loss of purchasing power. The total amount of paper would be the same."[15]

Given today's credit collapse, the virtues of Greenspan's endowment—monetary inflation and endless credit—must be rethought, but not yet. This is a world with no intentions of paying its bills or paying for its mistakes. Vague and vanishing currencies serve many interests. The inflation of the past century will explode in the new century.

---

[14] William E. Leuchtenburg, *The Perils of Prosperity, 1914–1932* (Chicago: University of Chicago Press, 1958), pp. 41–42.

[15] FOMC meeting transcript, July 2–3, 1996, p. 55.

APPENDIX

The Federal Reserve System

The Federal Reserve Act was passed in 1913; the body first met in August 1914. Literalists insist that the Federal Reserve is not a central bank; scholars insist that the Federal Reserve is a federal agency independent of political control. These distinctions blur actual practices.

The Federal Reserve is the only authorized issuer of currency in the United States. The president nominates all Federal Reserve governors. Many tussles between politicians and the Federal Reserve are discussed in this book. Except during the early Volcker years, the politicians won.

The Federal Open Market Committee (FOMC) decides the Federal Reserve's monetary policy. It consists of seven governors (in Washington) and five regional presidents. There are 12 geographic regions in the Federal Reserve System. The presidents rotate terms on the FOMC. FOMC meetings sent Americans into apoplexy during Greenspan's tenure: "Is he going to tighten or loosen? How much?" This referred to the federal funds rate, also known as the fed funds rate or the funds rate. What is it? An explanation starts with the banks and runs back to the Fed.

Banks must hold "bank reserves." This is money that banks draw upon to meet withdrawal requests and that acts as a safety net when bad loans accumulate.

Bank reserves are held with the Federal Reserve. Each day, let us say, all banks look at their reserve position. Some find that they are now holding more reserves than they need, some have fallen below their minimum threshold.

This is where the "Fed funds" market develops. The banks trade reserves among themselves to reach an optimal level. The Federal Reserve coordinates these trades.

When the FOMC decides to lower rates (synonymous with "easing" or "loosening" money), the Federal Reserve transfers additional money into the Fed funds market. (The banks sell Treasury bills to the Fed and receive dollars. The banks then have more money to lend.) If the current rate is 5.0 percent, and the FOMC decides to cut the rate to 4.5 percent, the Fed adds money into the market until it rebalances supply and demand at 4.5 percent. This is not a stationary rate. When the "Fed funds rate is 4.5 percent," the banks trade funds at approximately that rate. The Federal Reserve continually adds or subtracts funds to hold the rate at around 4.5 percent.

When the FOMC decides to raise rates (synonymous with tightening money), the Federal Reserve sells Treasury bills to the banks and receives dollars in return. The banks then have less money to lend. If the current rate was 4.5 percent, and the FOMC decided to raise the rate to 5.0 percent, the Fed will keep selling Treasury bills into the market until it rebalances supply and demand at 5.0 percent.

When the Fed discusses whether it will or will not "move," this refers to whether or not it will change the fed funds rate, either up or down.

ACKNOWLEDGMENTS

I am thankful to Jim Grant, John Lukacs, and Maggie Mahar for their advice and for reading the early drafts.

I thank my father and John Lukacs for their encouragement when nobody wanted to publish a book about Alan Greenspan. I know this, since my attempts to raise interest in the publishing world were met with glazed eyes and "there are enough books about him already." The observation is correct, but all the others were written before Greenspan's fall.

McGraw-Hill was the only publisher with the foresight to anticipate Greenspan's demise. Its farsightedness led to *Greenspan's Bubbles*, published in 2008. Jim Grant suggested that McGraw-Hill contact me, since I had already done much of the research. Bill Fleckenstein wrote *Greenspan's Bubbles* while I fed him the evidence. Leah Spiro, my editor at McGraw-Hill for *Panderer to Power*, was even more farsighted. She thought there was a lot more to the Alan Greenspan story than could be discussed in *Greenspan's Bubbles*.

A number of people have offered advice. Most important were conversations with Bill Fleckenstein. Since *Greenspan's Bubbles* was a short book, the discussion needed to be compressed. For instance, my excavations sometimes unearthed compelling evidence of Greenspan's misjudgments but these misjudgments were, at the same time, difficult to interpret. Our protagonist made statements that compromised his previous arguments. I'd ask Bill, "Why did he say that?" During one such discussion, Bill memorably replied: "I don't know what's running through his head. Our job is to record that he said it."

And so, if the reader of *Panderer to Power* wonders, "Why did Greenspan say that?" and finds little explanation from me, it is because I am no more a mind reader now than I was during the writing of *Greenspan's Bubbles*. Filling pages with possibilities and probabilities is of limited value. *What* Greenspan (and anyone else discussed) did and said is generally accessible; *why* he (and others) made these decisions is fodder for discussion.

Editors, fact checkers, and proofreaders who gave me valuable help include Leah Spiro, Ruth Mills, Anne Greenberg, Ron Martirano Scott Pilutik, Cynthia Newberry, my father, and my daughter, Anna.

Bill Fleckenstein read several chapters in this book, for which I am most grateful. Others who read chapters, often on topics that they had personally observed or added valuable insights, include Caroline Baum, Frank Castle, Seth Daniels, Marc Faber, Earl Kishida, Bob Landis, John Lukacs, Hans Merkelbach, Jeff Poppenhagen, Dana Robinson, and Don Stanton. I thank them. They offered opinions; however, I wrote the book. All the mistakes and flaws are mine.

Most of all, I am thankful to my wife, Margaret, my daughter, Anna, and my son, Frederick.

INDEX